# PRACTICAL PERPETUAL CALENDARS

Innovative, Convenient and Green

JAMES R. SALTVOLD

iUniverse

**PRACTICAL PERPETUAL CALENDARS**
**INNOVATIVE, CONVENIENT AND GREEN**



*iUniverse books may be ordered through booksellers or by contacting:*

*iUniverse*
*1663 Liberty Drive*
*Bloomington, IN 47403*
*www.iuniverse.com*
*1-800-Authors (1-800-288-4677)*



*ISBN: 978-1-5320-2135-0 (sc)*
*ISBN: 978-1-5320-2136-7 (e)*

*Library of Congress Control Number: 2017908051*

*Print information available on the last page.*

*iUniverse rev. date: 10/26/2017*

To Roberta

# CONTENTS


List of Figures .......... ix

Preface .......... xiii

Acknowledgments .......... xv

Introduction .......... xvii

Chapter 1 Four Unique Perpetual Calendars .......... 1

Chapter 2 From Concept to Mass Production .......... 9

Chapter 3 Tables for Single-Sheet Perpetual Calendars .......... 14

Chapter 4 Tables for Multisheet and Full-Year Perpetual Calendars .......... 40

Chapter 5 Single-Sheet Perpetual Calendars—Applications and Products .......... 63

Chapter 6 Multisheet Perpetual Calendars with a Year Table on Each Sheet—Applications and Products .......... 118

Chapter 7 Multisheet Perpetual Calendars with a Single Year Table—Applications and Products .......... 140

Chapter 8 Full-Year Perpetual Calendars—Applications and Products .......... 156

Chapter 9 Applications and Products Summary .......... 170

Appendix History, Patents and Manufactured Perpetual Calendars .......... 179

Further Reading .......... 207

Annotated References .......... 209

Index .......... 213

# LIST OF FIGURES

Figures 1-1a to 1-1d: Single-sheet perpetual calendars ........ 5
Figure 1-2a to 1-2d: Multisheet perpetual calendars with a year table on each sheet ........ 6
Figure 1-3a to 1-3d: Multisheet perpetual calendars with a single year table ........ 7
Figure 1-4a and 1-4b: Full-year perpetual calendar ........ 8
Figure 5-1a: Body of a single-window tent desk calendar made from cardstock ........ 87
Figures 5-1b to 5-1d: Slider and other details for a single-window tent desk calendar ........ 88
Figure 5-1e: Single-window desk calendar made from wood ........ 89
Figure 5-2a: Double-window desk calendar made from cardstock ........ 90
Figures 5-2b and 5-2c: Alternate construction of double-window desk calendar and wood model ........ 91
Figures 5-3a and 5-3b: Pocket calendars—moving-window type and moving-slider type ........ 92
Figure 5-3c: Pocket/tent calendar ........ 93
Figure 5-3d: Fold-down moving-slider pocket calendar ........ 94
Figure 5-3e: Pocket calendar with a single slider and year tables beside the window ........ 95
Figure 5-4: Bookmark calendar ........ 96
Figure 5-5: Calendar for a lamp or a pencil holder ........ 97
Figure 5-6a: Cardstock 4 × 6 inch photo holder with dual sliders—design “A” ........ 98
Figure 5-6b: Cardstock 4 × 6 inch photo holder with dual sliders—design “B” ........ 99
Figure 5-7a: Key holder with a dual-slider calendar ........ 100
Figure 5-7b: Key holder with single-slider calendar ........ 101
Figure 5-8: Clock with a dual-slider calendar ........ 102
Figure 5-9: Clock with a single-slider double-window calendar ........ 103
Figure 5-10a: Picture frame with calendar beside photo ........ 104
Figure 5-10b: Picture frame with calendar beside photo (detail) ........ 105
Figure 5-11: Picture frame with calendar below photo ........ 106
Figure 5-12: Dual-slider calendar with 5 × 7 inch picture frame above it ........ 107
Figure 5-13a: Modifications to commercial sliding-window 13-column calendar ........ 108
Figure 5-13b: Redesigned commercial sliding-window 13-column calendar ........ 109
Figures 5-14a and 5-14b: Monthly wall planner with 13 columns ........ 110
Figures 5-15a and 5-15b: Monthly wall planner with 7 strips ........ 111

Figure 5-16a: Line-style monthly wall planner ........ 112
Figure 5-16b: Vertical-slider 3-ring binder planner ........ 113
Figure 5-17a: Ornate hybrid wall calendar, sheet 1 of 3 ........ 114
Figure 5-17b: Ornate hybrid wall calendar, sheet 2 of 3 ........ 115
Figure 5-17c: Ornate hybrid wall calendar, sheet 3 of 3 ........ 116
Figure 5-18: Stand for commercial perpetual desk calendar ........ 117
Figure 6-1a: Typical month sheets for a 14-sheet flip-down-window desk calendar ........ 131
Figure 6-1b: Flip-down-window desk calendar made from cardstock ........ 132
Figure 6-2: Two holder designs for the lift-out-pad desk calendar ........ 133
Figure 6-3: Four different formats for wall calendar sheets ........ 134
Figure 6-4: Flip-down-window wall calendar ........ 135
Figure 6-5: Clip-on-window wall calendar ........ 136
Figure 6-6: Lift-out-pad wall calendar ........ 137
Figures 6-7a and 6-7b: Two patterns for a window-on-each-sheet wall calendar ........ 138
Figure 6-8: Extension of single-sheet calendar to multisheet ........ 139
Figures 7-1a to 7-1d: Multisheet calendar with a single year table ........ 148
Figure 7-2: J-style wall/desk calendar ........ 149
Figure 7-3: Reverse J-style desk calendar ........ 150
Figure 7-4: Wooden frame desk calendar ........ 151
Figure 7-5: Multisheet single-year table calendar below a 5 × 7 inch picture frame ........ 152
Figure 7-6a: Seven-column multisheet calendar with a single year table—body and slider ........ 153
Figure 7-6b: Seven-column multisheet calendar with a single year table—assembled ........ 154
Figure 7-6c: Seven-column multisheet calendar with a single year table—day-of-month sheets ........ 155
Figure 8-1a: Face of the full-year calendar with a double-sided slider ........ 163
Figure 8-1b: Common year side of the double-sided slider for the full-year calendar ........ 164
Figure 8-1c: Leap year side of the double-sided slider for the full-year calendar ........ 165
Figure 8-2a: Slider for the single-sided slider full-year calendar ........ 166
Figure 8-2b: Face of the full-year calendar with a single-sided slider ........ 167
Figure 8-3: Vertical full-year perpetual calendar ........ 168
Figure 8-4a: Single day-of-month table full-year calendar with a horizontal slider ........ 169
Figure 8-4b: Single day-of-month table full-year calendar with a vertical slider ........ 169
Figure A-1: An early attempt at lookup tables ........ 196
Figure A-2: An early version of the single-sheet perpetual calendar with dual-slider configuration ........ 197
Figure A-3: State of the dual-slider design in October 2012 ........ 198

Figure A-4: Moving-window tent calendar ........ 199
Figure A-5: A variation of a multisheet perpetual calendar with a single year table........ 200
Figure A-6: Slider-type perpetual calendar, United States Patent 1,949,328, February 27, 1934 ........ 201
Figures A-7a to A-7c: Magnetic-type, slider-type and triple-cylinder-type perpetual calendars ........ 202
Figures A-8a to A-8e: Common rotary one-month calendar compared to my single-window desk calendar ........ 203
Figures A-9a to A-9d: Four types of commercial perpetual calendars........ 204
Figure A-10: Conceptual drawing of the face of a full-year calendar with 24 windows for the months........ 205

# PREFACE

*Practical Perpetual Calendars—Innovative, Convenient and Green* describes development work that I have done to make stand-alone perpetual calendars viable replacements for all conventional calendars that are not written on. When doing this work, I applied the skills that I acquired during a long career as a design engineer to create and refine concepts that have the potential to make perpetual calendars a common home and office item.

Although various types of perpetual calendars have been around for a long time, none have replaced conventional calendars for everyday use. The ones available either require reference to a conventional calendar to set them or are difficult to read. And whereas some patents describe ideas that are close to what is needed to make a practical perpetual calendar, there has been, to the best of my knowledge, nothing manufactured or patented that is quite like my calendars.

The purpose of *Practical Perpetual Calendars* is to make print shops, manufacturers, small craft shops, and hobbyists aware of my novel and unique practical concepts for making stand-alone perpetual calendars. Calendars made from cardstock that incorporate these concepts have a useful life of 10 years or more, compared to just one year for conventional calendars. Calendars made from more durable materials could have a useful life of a century! My designs, which look almost the same as conventional calendars, save resources and eliminate the inconvenience of annual replacement.

*Practical Perpetual Calendars* includes designs for desk calendars, wall calendars, pocket calendars, photo holders and other applications. It also describes how the tables for the calendars are developed. I hope that readers will see the value of these calendars and take steps to put my concepts into both mass-produced and one-of-a-kind products.

# ACKNOWLEDGMENTS

Thank you to my wife, Roberta, for your support and encouragement over the many years I was developing perpetual calendar concepts. Your comments on prototypes were invaluable in refining concepts to make the calendars practical. Thank you also, Roberta, for reviewing and editing *Practical Perpetual Calendars.*

Thanks to my publisher, iUniverse, for encouraging me during the writing process, for taking a manuscript and making it into a book and for guiding me through the publishing process.

Thanks in advance to the readers who accept the risks associated with manufacturing and marketing a new product in both large and small quantities. Your work is essential to convert my concepts into useful products.

# INTRODUCTION

## About This Book

*Practical Perpetual Calendars* shows how to make practical perpetual calendars for a wide variety of applications using unique concepts that I have developed.

## What Is a Perpetual Calendar?

The term *perpetual calendar* does not seem to have a universal meaning. Three definitions are as follows:

- "A chart or mechanical device that indicates the day of the week corresponding to any given date over a period of many years" (*American Heritage Dictionary of the English Language*)[1]
- "A calendar in which the day, the month, and the date are adjusted independently to show any combination of the three" (*English Oxford Living Dictionaries*)[2]
- "A table for finding the day of the week for any one of a wide range of dates" (*Merriam-Webster Dictionary*)[3]

Perpetual calendars that meet the definitions provided by the *American Heritage Dictionary* or the *Merriam-Webster Dictionary* can be considered stand-alone in that reference to a conventional calendar is not required to set them. Calendars that meet the *Oxford Dictionaries* definition are not stand-alone, as reference to another calendar is required to set them or to find the day of the week for a particular date. When a Bing or Google search is done to locate images of perpetual calendars, most of the images found meet one of the three definitions. The ones meeting the *American Heritage* definition are mechanical devices that have a part that is rotated (or moved in some other way) to line up the year and the month to obtain a display for a particular month, or where two or more parts are rotated (or moved in some other way) to indicate the day of the week for a particular date. An example of this type of device is the date display on watches.

[1] *American Heritage Dictionary of the English Language*, 5th ed., 2016, s.v. "perpetual calendar," *The Free Dictionary*, http://www.thefreedictionary.com/perpetual+calendar, accessed November 12, 2016.

[2] *English Oxford Living Dictionaries*, s.v. "perpetual calendar," https://en.oxforddictionaries.com/definition/perpetual_calendar, accessed November 12, 2016.

[3] *Merriam-Webster Dictionary*, s.v. "perpetual calendar," http://www.merriam-webster.com/dictionary/perpetual%20calendar, accessed November 12, 2016.

Many rotary devices display a month in an arc of a circle, which is not as pleasing to read as the rectangular grid of a conventional calendar. I have found some stand-alone perpetual calendars in patents that have sliding mechanisms and a rectangular grid display; however, these have the complication of requiring a table lookup, or they have some other characteristic that makes them, along with rotary calendars, unsuitable replacements for conventional calendars in most applications.

The calendars in many of the images found online meet the *Oxford Dictionaries* definition. These include

- blocks that are arranged to indicate month, day of the month and day of the week;
- markers that are moved along a numbered line; and
- tiles that are arranged to display the current month.

Some of these devices, such as a tile calendar, look like a conventional calendar after they are set up, but they are not stand-alone. And there are charts and tables that meet the *Merriam-Webster* definition.

In *Practical Perpetual Calendars*, the term *stand-alone perpetual calendar* means a calendar that, without reference to anything other than itself, can be easily set to display the day of the week for every day of the month when the year and the month are known. The year must be within the design range of the calendar, which typically is a period of 50 to 100 years.

## Overview of Contents

Chapter 1 briefly describes the four types or categories that all of my calendars fit into. Chapter 2 discusses in general terms how to bring the prototypes in Chapter 1 into mass production. Chapters 3 and 4 explain how to develop the tables that are used. Chapters 5 to 8 describe products that can be made from the four types of perpetual calendars. Chapter 9 describes which products might be attractive to various markets and manufacturers. The Appendix gives a brief history of the work I did to develop the concepts, discusses some perpetual calendar patents and describes some typical manufactured perpetual calendars. The Further Reading section indicates where to search for more information on calendars, and the Annotated References section provides references with comments.

I hope that some readers will read *Practical Perpetual Calendars* from cover to cover and find value in my detailed descriptions. I suggest that everyone read the descriptions of the four basic types of perpetual calendars described in Chapter 1. After that, look at what is interesting to you. A scan of the List of Figures may reveal something. Alternatively, you can thumb through the figures at the end of the chapters, or read the descriptions in the chapters to find figures that spark your interest. The figures are more conceptual than detailed. However, enough detail is given so that useful products can be made from them with a small amount of effort.

In keeping with this book's title, *Practical Perpetual Calendars*, I present design ideas and concepts for calendars that are easy to build and use. The ideas cover desk, wall, pocket and full-year calendars. There are also suggestions for how to add a perpetual calendar to picture frames, key holders, pencil holders, lamps, clocks and planners.

## Use of the Concepts and Designs to Manufacture Products for Sale

I have developed the concepts and tables in *Practical Perpetual Calendars* without referring to anyone else's work, and to the best of my knowledge, my arrangements and combinations of tables are not used in any commercial perpetual calendars that are presently available. While researching for the section on the patents that appear in the Appendix, I found that some of my concepts had been previously discovered, but I did not find any inventor who had put together perpetual calendars quite like mine. I believe that my book and the perpetual calendars it describes are truly unique in the following ways:

- I use concepts and tables to make calendars that are very similar in appearance to conventional calendars, but mine have the feature of being stand-alone perpetual calendars.
- I describe four different types of perpetual calendars.
- I provide a complete range of calendar sizes for various uses, and many suggestions for how my designs can be incorporated into other products so as to add a perpetual calendar to those items.

Although *Practical Perpetual Calendars* is protected by copyright, my understanding is that a copyright does not cover concepts, so anyone who uses ideas they discover within these pages has no obligation to me. From my review of a number of patents for perpetual calendars, I have concluded that some of the ideas in this book would have been patentable if I had chosen to disclose them by way of patents rather than by way of a book. Therefore, readers who use the new ideas presented in *Practical Perpetual Calendars* to manufacture calendars are effectively gaining access to patents without being required to pay royalties. Since this could be a benefit of far greater value than the cost of the book, I encourage manufacturers to send me a very modest gratuity of CAN$0.02 per calendar for the first 100,000 produced between now and December 31, 2027, in lieu of a royalty. The following table provides more details of the suggested gratuity.

| **Total number of calendars manufactured (may be all of one type or of mixed types)** | **Suggested gratuity** |
|---|---|
| 100 or fewer | Covered by purchasing *Practical Perpetual Calendars* |
| More than 100, but fewer than 1,000 | CAN$20 |
| 1,000 or more, but fewer than 100,000 | CAN$0.02 per calendar |
| 100,000 or more | CAN$2,000 |

The suggested gratuity of CAN$0.02 per calendar is based on calendars that sell for $1 or more each. When the price is less, the gratuity can be proportionally less, but the minimum payment should be $10. The gratuity can be paid to my PayPal account. Go to www.paypal.com and click on "Send." In the box "Their e-mail or phone number," enter "greencalendars@gmail.com." Next, enter the amount you would like to send, click "Continue" and click on "Goods or services."

# CHAPTER 1

# FOUR UNIQUE PERPETUAL CALENDARS

## Four Basic Types of Perpetual Calendars

All of my calendars are based on variations of the four arbitrarily defined basic types described in this chapter. They are as follows:

- Single-Sheet Perpetual Calendars
  These calendars display one month at a time and use the same sheet for all of the months.

- Multisheet Perpetual Calendars with a Year Table on Each Sheet
  These calendars also display one month at a time, but they use more than one sheet for the months. Each sheet has a year table on it.

- Multisheet Perpetual Calendars with a Single Year Table
  These calendars also display one month at a time, but they use more than one sheet for the months. There is a single year table that is used by all of the sheets.

- Full-Year Perpetual Calendars
  These are calendars that display all of the months of the year on one sheet.

In all of the above definitions, the term *sheet* can be thought of as a piece of paper or other material that has printing on one side. When a piece of paper has printing on both sides, it is two calendar sheets.

This chapter introduces the four basic types by comparing them to conventional calendars. All of the calendars in this chapter are made from cardstock. Some construction details for these calendars, along with variations and calendars made from other materials, are described in later chapters. Except for the full-year calendar, all of the calendars in this chapter are desk models. This is the largest potential market, as millions of desk calendars are discarded at the end of each year without any markings on them.

## Single-Sheet Perpetual Calendars

The single-sheet perpetual calendar can be made in a single-slider or a dual-slider configuration. Figure 1-1a shows a simple low-cost single-sheet perpetual tent calendar with a single slider, and Figure 1-1b shows a basic tent calendar that it can replace. A quantity of 150 has been produced in colour at a cost of about $1.25 each. The calendar face is 4 inches high by 6.5 inches wide, and covers the entire 21$^{st}$ century. The back of the tent can display a picture, a table of standard holidays or other information. In contrast, there is no discretionary space on the calendar in Figure 1-1b, as it has six months on each side. When one wishes to set the calendar, one moves the slider to line up the month with the year. A smaller pocket version, 2.0 inches high by 3.5 inches wide, has been made for an estimated cost of 25¢ each. It covers 50 years, and is black and white. The single-sheet calendar always displays 31 days per month; the 29$^{th}$ through the 31$^{st}$ are ignored as required. See Figures 5-1a to 5-1c for more details of the calendar in Figure 1-1a.

Figure 1-1c shows a single-sheet perpetual calendar that has the dual-slider configuration, and Figure 1-1d shows a type of conventional calendar that it can replace. The calendar in Figure 1-1c is set by lifting up the picture to see the year table, moving the top slider so that the marker is under the column that has the year of interest and then moving the bottom slider so that the *1* is under the month of interest. After the top slider has been set for the year, the direction in which to move the bottom slider is more obvious than it is for the single-slider configuration. The dual-slider perpetual calendar in Figure 1-1c can hold a 4 × 6 inch photo in landscape orientation on its face, whereas the conventional calendar in Figure 1-1d can hold only a 2.5 × 3.75 inch photo if it is the same overall height. Since the conventional calendar has only six months on its face, it has to be made as a tent calendar so that the back can display the other six months. If the dual-slider calendar in Figure 1-1c is made as a tent calendar, then it will have room on the back for a second 4 × 6 inch photo in either portrait or landscape orientation or for providing other information, such as advertisements or a table of dates on which Easter Sunday falls. Alternatively, the calendar can be made with a back prop instead of as a tent. See Figure 5-6b for more details of the calendar in Figure 1-1c.

To simplify construction and keep the cost low, the sliders in the calendars in Figures 1-1a and 1-1c are made from cardstock and are mounted in slits cut in the face, rather than mounted in tracks. With this type of construction, the marker on the dual-slider calendar has to be in the month table, as shown in Figure 1-1c, or above or below the month table. Chapter 5 shows dual-slider calendars made from rigid materials with tracks for the sliders. (See Figures 5-7a, 5-8 and 5-12.) These calendars have the year table located to the left of the window that shows the days of the month. In this configuration, the marker is on the left end of the top slider and appears in a special window above the year table. See Chapter 5 for construction details for the single-sheet perpetual calendar with single or dual sliders and for suggested products that can incorporate this calendar type.

## Multisheet Perpetual Calendars with a Year Table on Each Sheet

I have developed two slightly different perpetual calendars with a year table on each sheet for desktop use. These calendars have a sheet for each month, so they always display the correct number of days per month. There is a year table and a day-of-month table on each sheet. Figure 1-2a shows the flip-down-window configuration with calendar sheets 4.5 inches high by 7 inches wide, which is a widely used standard. The calendar is set by moving the window so that the marker is under the column that has the year of interest. With the large font shown for the days of the month, there is room for a 60-year table. To change the month, the window is flipped down and the calendar is turned to the next page. The only difference in construction between the perpetual calendar in Figure 1-2a and the conventional calendar in Figure 1-2b is the moving window of the perpetual calendar, which is estimated to add less than a dollar to the cost of each unit for large quantities. As can be seen in Figure 1-2a, the perpetual calendar has 13 columns for the days of the month, rather than the 7 of a conventional calendar. This results in the perpetual calendar's having a smaller font for a given width. See Figures 6-1a and 6-1b for more details of the calendar in Figure 1-2a.

Figure 1-2c shows the lift-out-pad configuration with a face 3.5 inches high by 8.5 inches wide. Figure 1-2d shows a similar-size picture calendar that it can replace. Instead of flipping down the window when changing the month, the pad is lifted out and the page is turned. Since the pad is not attached to the holder, it can be produced by a print shop, and an ornate holder can be made by a craft shop. See Figure 6-2 for more details of the calendar in Figure 1-2c.

Working prototypes have been made of both configurations, and little effort is expected to be required to put them into production. I estimate the development costs for adding the perpetual features to be between $5,000 and $10,000. These costs can likely be recouped by adding between 50¢ and $1 to the total retail price of the first 10,000 units produced. Although this would be in addition to the estimated extra $1 cost for the moving window or pad holder, the higher cost for the perpetual calendar would not be excessive considering its extra life and greater versatility.

Keep in mind that almost every office has a multisheet desk calendar, so the potential market is very large. The designs for desktop calendars can be modified to make wall calendars, also a very large potential market. See Chapter 6 for construction details of the multisheet perpetual calendars with a year table on each sheet and for suggested products that can incorporate this calendar type.

## Multisheet Perpetual Calendars with a Single Year Table

Figure 1-3a shows a fixed-window-style multisheet perpetual calendar with a single year table, and Figure 1-3b shows a basic tear-off sheet calendar that it can replace. The difference between this calendar and the multisheet calendars in Figures 1-2a and 1-2c is that this one has a year table on the face that is shared by all the sheets, instead of a year table on each sheet. The dimensions of this perpetual calendar are 2.5 inches high by 7 inches wide, and the tear-off sheet calendar is 3 inches high by 6 inches wide. Like the single-sheet calendars in Figures 1-1a and 1-1c, this calendar covers the entire 21st century. See Figures 7-1b and 7-1c for more details of the calendar in Figure 1-3a.

To set this calendar, find the sheet for the month of interest and then line up the marker on the sheet with the column that has the year of interest. Similar to the lift-out-pad calendar shown in Figure 1-2c, the sheets are lifted out when changing the month. The cost to produce a quantity of 100 is estimated to be about $2 each.

Since the year table is beside the days of the month, the height of this calendar is less than that of the multisheet perpetual calendar with a year table on each sheet, where the year table is above. This is not an advantage for a basic desk calendar, but it is an advantage if a picture frame is built with a calendar below the picture, or a key holder is built with a calendar above the key hooks.

Figures 1-3c and 1-3d show a seven-column multisheet calendar with a single year table. A comparison of Figure 1-3a with Figures 1-3c and 1-3d shows that the concepts are quite different. However, both of these calendars are multisheet and have a single year table. For this reason, I classify them as being the same type. See Figures 7-6a to 7-6c for more details of the calendar in Figures 1-3c and 1-3d. The calendar in Figures 1-3c and 1-3d is an alternative to the calendars in Figures 1-2a and 1-2c for replacing the conventional multisheet desk calendar in Figure 1-2b. An advantage that the calendar in Figures 1-3c and 1-3d has over the other two is lower cost. See Chapter 7 for construction details of multisheet perpetual calendars with a single year table and for suggested products that can incorporate this calendar type.

## Full-Year Perpetual Calendars

Figure 1-4a shows a full-year perpetual calendar, and Figure 1-4b shows a conventional full-year calendar that has to be replaced each year. The perpetual calendar has the following windows for the months: January leap year, February leap year, January common year, February common year and March to December, which are the same for both common and leap years. There is also a window that indicates the applicable years for the setting. See Figures 8-2a and 8-2b for more details of the calendar in Figure 1-4a. The full-year calendar concept can be used to make a permanent wall calendar or a perpetual calendar for a three-ring binder. See Chapter 8 for construction details of full-year perpetual calendars and for suggested products that can incorporate this calendar type.

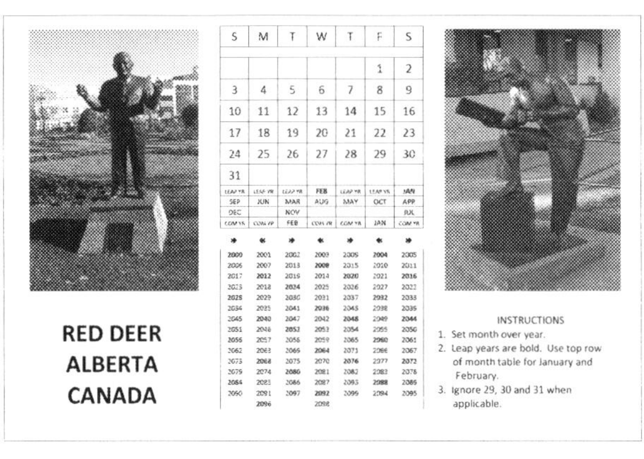
RED DEER
ALBERTA
CANADA
INSTRUCTIONS
1. Set month over year.
2. Leap years are bold. Use top row of month table for January and February.
3. Ignore 29, 30 and 31 when applicable.

a) Single-sheet perpetual tent calendar with single slider

**SAVINGS BANK OF RED DEER**

| JANUARY | | | | | | 2016 |
|---|---|---|---|---|---|---|
| S | M | T | W | T | F | S |
| | | | | | 1 | 2 |
| 3 | 4 | 5 | 6 | 7 | 8 | 9 |
| 10 | 11 | 12 | 13 | 14 | 15 | 16 |
| 17 | 18 | 19 | 20 | 21 | 22 | 23 |
| 24 | 25 | 26 | 27 | 28 | 29 | 30 |
| 31 | | | | | | |

| FEBRUARY | | | | | | 2016 |
|---|---|---|---|---|---|---|
| S | M | T | W | T | F | S |
| | 1 | 2 | 3 | 4 | 5 | 6 |
| 7 | 8 | 9 | 10 | 11 | 12 | 13 |
| 14 | 15 | 16 | 17 | 18 | 19 | 20 |
| 21 | 22 | 23 | 24 | 25 | 26 | 27 |
| 28 | 29 | | | | | |

| MARCH | | | | | | 2016 |
|---|---|---|---|---|---|---|
| S | M | T | W | T | F | S |
| | | 1 | 2 | 3 | 4 | 5 |
| 6 | 7 | 8 | 9 | 10 | 11 | 12 |
| 13 | 14 | 15 | 16 | 17 | 18 | 19 |
| 20 | 21 | 22 | 23 | 24 | 25 | 26 |
| 27 | 28 | 29 | 30 | 31 | | |

| APRIL | | | | | | 2016 |
|---|---|---|---|---|---|---|
| S | M | T | W | T | F | S |
| | | | | | 1 | 2 |
| 3 | 4 | 5 | 6 | 7 | 8 | 9 |
| 10 | 11 | 12 | 13 | 14 | 15 | 16 |
| 17 | 18 | 19 | 20 | 21 | 22 | 23 |
| 24 | 25 | 26 | 27 | 28 | 29 | 30 |

| MAY | | | | | | 2016 |
|---|---|---|---|---|---|---|
| S | M | T | W | T | F | S |
| 1 | 2 | 3 | 4 | 5 | 6 | 7 |
| 8 | 9 | 10 | 11 | 12 | 13 | 14 |
| 15 | 16 | 17 | 18 | 19 | 20 | 21 |
| 22 | 23 | 24 | 25 | 26 | 27 | 28 |
| 29 | 30 | 31 | | | | |

| JUNE | | | | | | 2016 |
|---|---|---|---|---|---|---|
| S | M | T | W | T | F | S |
| | | | 1 | 2 | 3 | 4 |
| 5 | 6 | 7 | 8 | 9 | 10 | 11 |
| 12 | 13 | 14 | 15 | 16 | 17 | 18 |
| 19 | 20 | 21 | 22 | 23 | 24 | 25 |
| 26 | 27 | 28 | 29 | 30 | | |

b) Basic tent calendar that single-slider calendar can replace

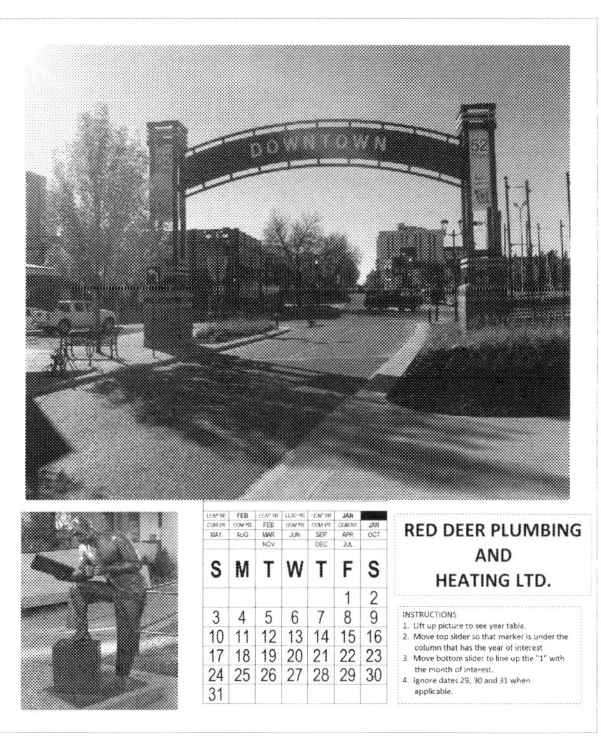
DOWNTOWN
RED DEER PLUMBING
AND
HEATING LTD.
INSTRUCTIONS
1. Lift up picture to see year table.
2. Move top slider so that marker is under the column that has the year of interest
3. Move bottom slider to line up the "1" with the month of interest.
4. Ignore dates 29, 30 and 31 when applicable.

c) Single-sheet perpetual tent calendar with dual sliders

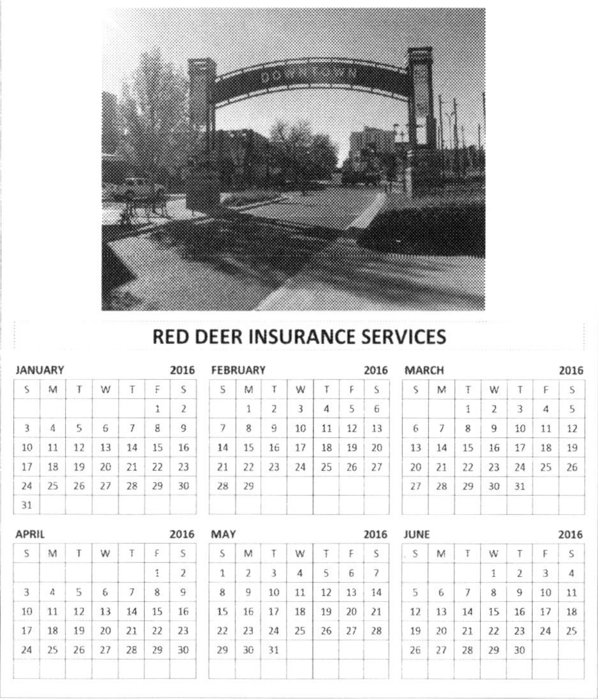
DOWNTOWN
RED DEER INSURANCE SERVICES
JANUARY 2016
FEBRUARY 2016
MARCH 2016
APRIL 2016
MAY 2016
JUNE 2016

d) Conventional tent calendar that dual-slider calendar can replace

Figures 1-1a to 1-1d: Single-sheet perpetual calendars

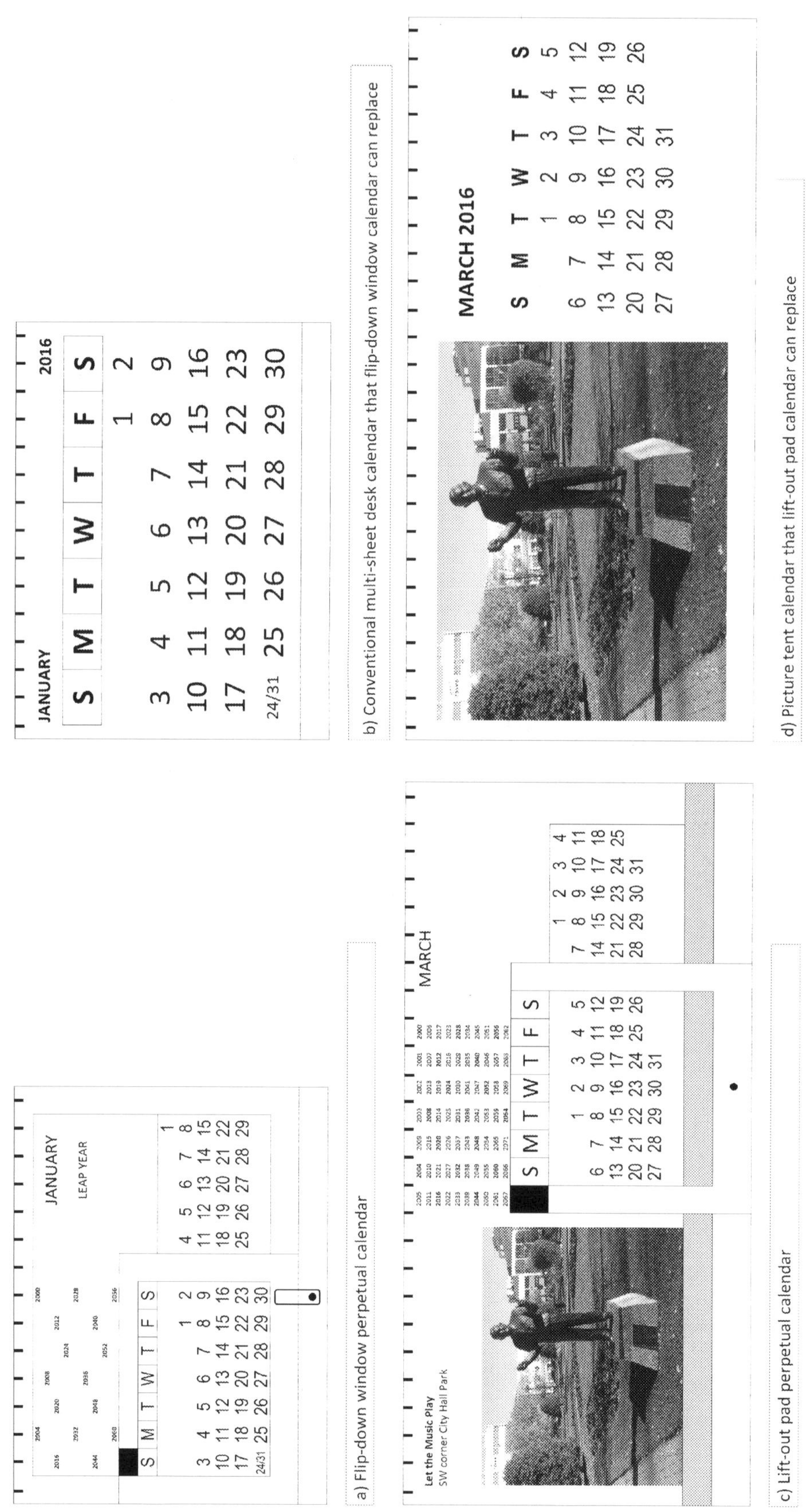
a) Flip-down window perpetual calendar
b) Conventional multi-sheet desk calendar that flip-down window calendar can replace
c) Lift-out pad perpetual calendar
d) Picture tent calendar that lift-out pad calendar can replace
JANUARY
LEAP YEAR
JANUARY 2016
MARCH
MARCH 2016
Let the Music Play
SW corner City Hall Park

Figure 1-2a to 1-2d: Multisheet perpetual calendars with a year table on each sheet

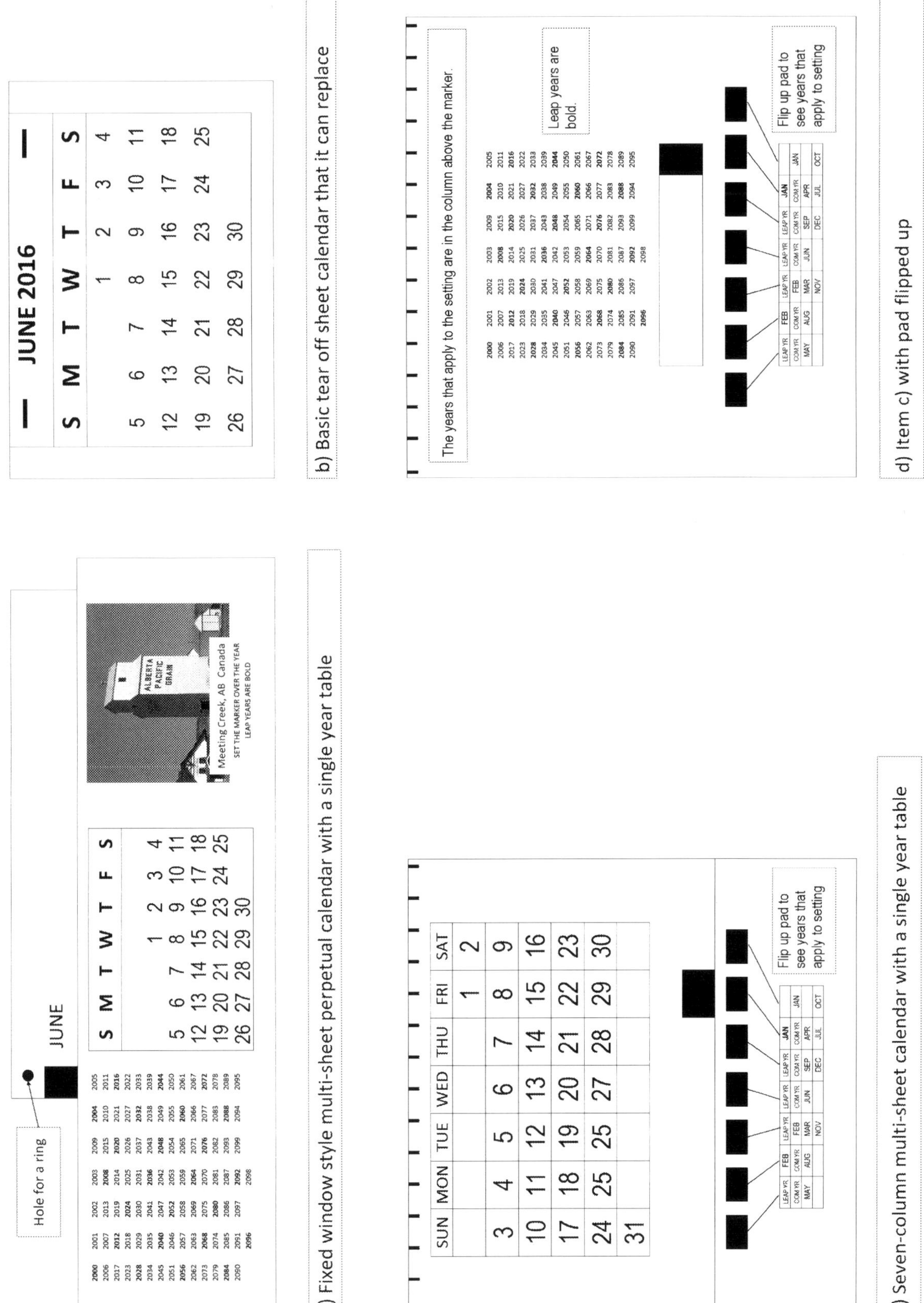
Hole for a ring
JUNE
JUNE 2016
Meeting Creek, AB Canada
SET THE MARKER OVER THE YEAR
LEAP YEARS ARE BOLD
a) Fixed window style multi-sheet perpetual calendar with a single year table
b) Basic tear off sheet calendar that it can replace
The years that apply to the setting are in the column above the marker.
Leap years are bold.
Flip up pad to see years that apply to setting
c) Seven-column multi-sheet calendar with a single year table
d) Item c) with pad flipped up

Figure 1-3a to 1-3d: Multisheet perpetual calendars with a single year table

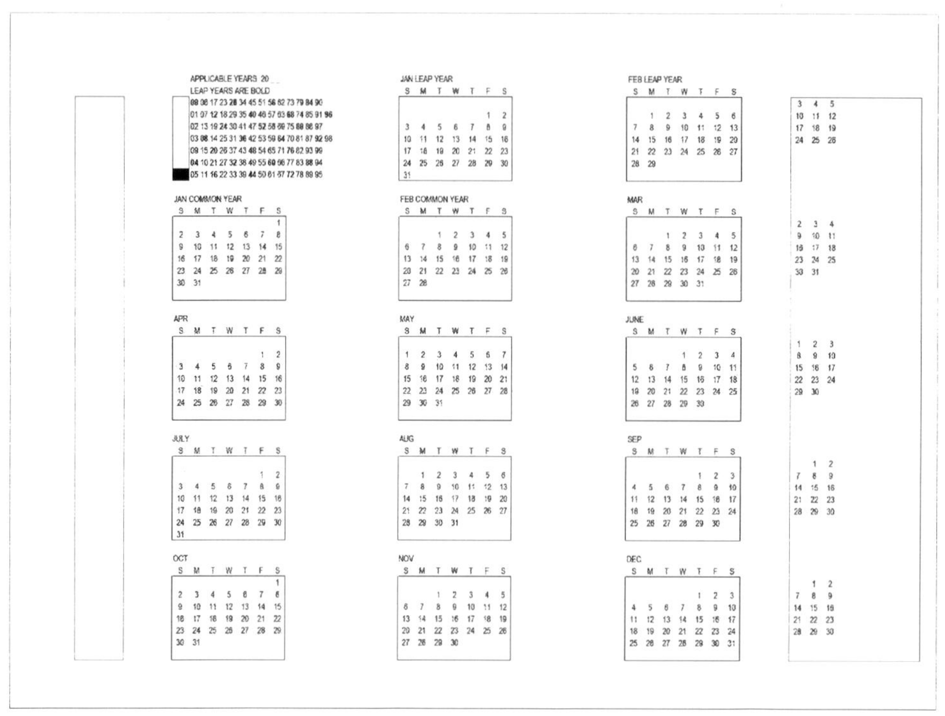
APPLICABLE YEARS 20__
LEAP YEARS ARE BOLD
JAN LEAP YEAR
FEB LEAP YEAR
JAN COMMON YEAR
FEB COMMON YEAR
MAR
APR
MAY
JUNE
JULY
AUG
SEP
OCT
NOV
DEC

a) Full year perpetual calendar

**JANUARY** 2016

| S | M | T | W | T | F | S |
|---|---|---|---|---|---|---|
| | | | | | 1 | 2 |
| 3 | 4 | 5 | 6 | 7 | 8 | 9 |
| 10 | 11 | 12 | 13 | 14 | 15 | 16 |
| 17 | 18 | 19 | 20 | 21 | 22 | 23 |
| 24 | 25 | 26 | 27 | 28 | 29 | 30 |
| 31 | | | | | | |

**FEBRUARY** 2016

| S | M | T | W | T | F | S |
|---|---|---|---|---|---|---|
| | 1 | 2 | 3 | 4 | 5 | 6 |
| 7 | 8 | 9 | 10 | 11 | 12 | 13 |
| 14 | 15 | 16 | 17 | 18 | 19 | 20 |
| 21 | 22 | 23 | 24 | 25 | 26 | 27 |
| 28 | 29 | | | | | |

**MARCH** 2016

| S | M | T | W | T | F | S |
|---|---|---|---|---|---|---|
| | | 1 | 2 | 3 | 4 | 5 |
| 6 | 7 | 8 | 9 | 10 | 11 | 12 |
| 13 | 14 | 15 | 16 | 17 | 18 | 19 |
| 20 | 21 | 22 | 23 | 24 | 25 | 26 |
| 27 | 28 | 29 | 30 | 31 | | |

**APRIL** 2016

| S | M | T | W | T | F | S |
|---|---|---|---|---|---|---|
| | | | | | 1 | 2 |
| 3 | 4 | 5 | 6 | 7 | 8 | 9 |
| 10 | 11 | 12 | 13 | 14 | 15 | 16 |
| 17 | 18 | 19 | 20 | 21 | 22 | 23 |
| 24 | 25 | 26 | 27 | 28 | 29 | 30 |

**MAY** 2016

| S | M | T | W | T | F | S |
|---|---|---|---|---|---|---|
| 1 | 2 | 3 | 4 | 5 | 6 | 7 |
| 8 | 9 | 10 | 11 | 12 | 13 | 14 |
| 15 | 16 | 17 | 18 | 19 | 20 | 21 |
| 22 | 23 | 24 | 25 | 26 | 27 | 28 |
| 29 | 30 | 31 | | | | |

**JUNE** 2016

| S | M | T | W | T | F | S |
|---|---|---|---|---|---|---|
| | | | 1 | 2 | 3 | 4 |
| 5 | 6 | 7 | 8 | 9 | 10 | 11 |
| 12 | 13 | 14 | 15 | 16 | 17 | 18 |
| 19 | 20 | 21 | 22 | 23 | 24 | 25 |
| 26 | 27 | 28 | 29 | 30 | | |

**JULY** 2016

| S | M | T | W | T | F | S |
|---|---|---|---|---|---|---|
| | | | | | 1 | 2 |
| 3 | 4 | 5 | 6 | 7 | 8 | 9 |
| 10 | 11 | 12 | 13 | 14 | 15 | 16 |
| 17 | 18 | 19 | 20 | 21 | 22 | 23 |
| 24 | 25 | 26 | 27 | 28 | 29 | 30 |
| 31 | | | | | | |

**AUGUST** 2016

| S | M | T | W | T | F | S |
|---|---|---|---|---|---|---|
| | 1 | 2 | 3 | 4 | 5 | 6 |
| 7 | 8 | 9 | 10 | 11 | 12 | 13 |
| 14 | 15 | 16 | 17 | 18 | 19 | 20 |
| 21 | 22 | 23 | 24 | 25 | 26 | 27 |
| 28 | 29 | 30 | 31 | | | |

**SEPTEMBER** 2016

| S | M | T | W | T | F | S |
|---|---|---|---|---|---|---|
| | | | | 1 | 2 | 3 |
| 4 | 5 | 6 | 7 | 8 | 9 | 10 |
| 11 | 12 | 13 | 14 | 15 | 16 | 17 |
| 18 | 19 | 20 | 21 | 22 | 23 | 24 |
| 25 | 26 | 27 | 28 | 29 | 30 | |

**OCTOBER** 2016

| S | M | T | W | T | F | S |
|---|---|---|---|---|---|---|
| | | | | | | 1 |
| 2 | 3 | 4 | 5 | 6 | 7 | 8 |
| 9 | 10 | 11 | 12 | 13 | 14 | 15 |
| 16 | 17 | 18 | 19 | 20 | 21 | 22 |
| 23 | 24 | 25 | 26 | 27 | 28 | 29 |
| 30 | 31 | | | | | |

**NOVEMBER** 2016

| S | M | T | W | T | F | S |
|---|---|---|---|---|---|---|
| | | 1 | 2 | 3 | 4 | 5 |
| 6 | 7 | 8 | 9 | 10 | 11 | 12 |
| 13 | 14 | 15 | 16 | 17 | 18 | 19 |
| 20 | 21 | 22 | 23 | 24 | 25 | 26 |
| 27 | 28 | 29 | 30 | | | |

**DECEMBER** 2016

| S | M | T | W | T | F | S |
|---|---|---|---|---|---|---|
| | | | | 1 | 2 | 3 |
| 4 | 5 | 6 | 7 | 8 | 9 | 10 |
| 11 | 12 | 13 | 14 | 15 | 16 | 17 |
| 18 | 19 | 20 | 21 | 22 | 23 | 24 |
| 25 | 26 | 27 | 28 | 29 | 30 | 31 |

b) Conventional full year calendar

Figure 1-4a and 1-4b: Full-year perpetual calendar

# CHAPTER 2

# FROM CONCEPT TO MASS PRODUCTION

## General

My concepts can be used to make a wide variety of perpetual calendars that better meet consumer needs than existing single-year calendars. In addition to saving resources, my calendars eliminate the inconvenience of having to replace them at the end of each year, and enable looking ahead and back. The only disadvantages of my calendars are that they should not be written on and that, unless the calendar is designed to hold photos, the user does not get new pictures each year.

The focus of *Practical Perpetual Calendars* is more towards describing concepts and tables for making perpetual calendars than towards providing details for how to build particular designs. However, the designs presented herein have been refined to minimize the effort needed to put the calendars into production. The conceptual designs illustrate a wide range of potential products that can be made with standard manufacturing techniques. My hope is that manufacturers and print shops will see the value of the unique concepts and incorporate them into useful products that are made in quantities of thousands or even millions. I also hope that individuals and small shops will adapt the concepts described in *Practical Perpetual Calendars* to make calendars for their own use and for small markets.

The remainder of this chapter describes what needs to be considered to mass-produce the calendars in Chapter 1.

## Setting Up for Production

The setup cost to bring one of my prototypes into mass production is dependent on the complexity of the design, the material used and the expertise of the manufacturer. All of the designs described in Chapter 1 are made from cardstock. Specialized setup work for each of these calendars is as follows:

- The single-sheet tent calendar shown in Figure 1-1a is not much more difficult to produce than a tent calendar with six months printed on each side. An extra piece of rectangular cardstock is required to make the slider, and two slits have to be cut into the face for the slider. For production of quantities of 1,000 or fewer, the slits can be cut by hand using a utility knife. The cost of a die is justified for larger quantities. The remaining work is producing the graphics. Chapter 5 shows details and also other designs that use the single-sheet calendar.
- A single-sheet calendar with two sliders, as shown in Figure 1-1c, is only slightly more complicated than the single-sheet tent calendar.
- On both of the single-sheet calendars, the windows are made by cutting a slit on each side and threading the slider through the slits instead of cutting out a window. The slits provide a guide for the slider, thus eliminating the need for a track. This works for cardstock, but a track is required for thicker material.
- The multisheet calendar with a flip-down window, shown in Figure 1-2a, is constructed similarly to a conventional multisheet desk calendar, with a window added. Chapter 6 shows a simple window concept that uses slits for sliding. A die is required to cut out the window and the slits for it to slide in. The most complicated aspect is making a mechanism for pushing the window against the sheets. Chapter 6 describes a concept that needs some refinement and also describes other applications of the multisheet calendar.
- The multisheet calendar with lift-out pad, as shown in Figure 1-2c, uses a pad that is similar to a conventional multisheet desk calendar. However, all the sheets in the pad are made from cardstock instead of paper, so they will have less tendency to curl when sitting in the holder. If one wishes to use a holder with a fixed window, such a holder is relatively easy to make. A die is required to cut out the window and the pieces for the rest of the holder. A holder with a window that slides from side to side has a more pleasing appearance but is more complicated to produce. Chapter 6 describes holder concepts. The holder can be made from cardstock, wood, plastic or a combination of materials.
- The multisheet calendar with a single year table, as shown in Figure 1-3a, is similar in construction to the lift-out-pad calendar shown in Figure 1-2c. The main difference is the single year table on the face instead of a year table on each sheet. This calendar also has one picture on the face instead of one on each sheet. Chapter 7 shows details and also other applications for the multisheet calendar.
- The seven-column multisheet calendar with a single year table, shown in Figures 1-3c and 1-3d, has a similar construction to a conventional multisheet desk calendar. Other than different material printed on the sheets, the only difference between this calendar and the conventional one is the addition of a slider at the bottom. The slider is held in place by two slits, which means that this calendar is only slightly more expensive to produce. Chapter 7 shows details.
- A full-year calendar, as shown in Figure 1-4a, has a face with 15 windows cut in it. Otherwise, the construction is similar to the face of the tent calendar in Figure 1-1a.

However, a die is required, as cutting out 15 windows by hand would be very time-consuming. Chapter 8 provides further details.

- For single-sheet calendars made from cardstock, the use of 100 lb. cardstock for the main body and 80 lb. glossy cardstock for the slider has been found to make a durable calendar with a slider that is easy to move.

## Selling Price

Many factors influence the price that customers are willing to pay for a perpetual calendar. Some of these factors are as follows:

- The simple single-sheet tent calendar shown in Figure 1-1b typically sells for less than $1 when produced in large quantities for advertising. A perpetual calendar similar to the one in Figure 1-1a is only slightly more complicated and is estimated to cost about 25 percent more to produce. Since the perpetual calendar will last five to ten years before it wears out, and since it has a shelf life of decades, it is very attractive at a price that is 25 percent higher—and probably still attractive at double the price.
- The multisheet calendar shown in Figure 1-2b typically sells for slightly more than $1 when produced in large quantities for advertising. As mentioned in Chapter 1, the window could add a dollar to the cost. (The extra cost should be considerably lower if large quantities are produced.) Therefore, the perpetual calendar in Figure 1-2a would have to sell for slightly more than $2 to recover the cost. This price is attractive if an advertiser is satisfied that the calendar will be used for at least three years before it is discarded.
- Many greeting cards sell for $5 or more. Since consumers are willing to pay this much for cards, they should be willing to pay a similar price for an artistic perpetual calendar made from cardstock. The calendar could include photos supplied by the customer.
- There are many perpetual calendars on the market that are not stand-alone in that they require reference to a conventional calendar to set the date. These calendars sell for various prices. Some can cost $50 or more if they have pleasing, well-made designs. Calendars using my concepts are superior in that they are stand-alone and should compete well in this market.
- Customers may be willing to spend some time assembling a calendar if this saves them money.

Some readers will want to make small quantities of the calendars for their own use or to sell. To assist these readers, I provide some of the construction details for many of the designs in the following chapters. Many of the details are common to all designs.

## Using Excel for Graphics

I used Excel to make all of my prototypes. It is certainly not a powerful graphics program, but it is widely available and easy to use. The following techniques may be helpful to small-quantity producers who also want to use Excel.

- Use centimetres for the ruler dimensions.
- Set up spreadsheets to a row height of 15 and a column width of 3. This makes a grid that appears to be close to square, although the width is slightly greater than the height. The "Merge & Center" function is used to make larger cells when required. On some of my spreadsheets, the row height and column width are different from 15 and 3, respectively, to accommodate a larger font, to have some rows that are a different height than others or to make a window a fraction of a row height higher than the slider.
- In many of my prototypes, the merged cells for the month table and the year table are two cells wide by one cell high. The font is Calibri 11. The merged cells for the day-of-month table are two cells wide by two cells high. The font is Calibri 18.
- Use Excel spreadsheet cells for table data that appears in rows and columns, and use text boxes for other information such as notes, parts lists and operating instructions.
- Use Arial Narrow font when there is limited width available.
- Where possible, make horizontal and vertical lines by putting borders on cells rather than using the Excel "Insert Shapes" tool to draw lines.
- Excel is not set up to make lines of an exact length. (Or if it is, I have not learned the technique.) However, by using trial and error to set the number of rows and columns, and by scaling to a reduced size when printing, I have been able to produce figures close to the desired size. In making a calendar, proportions and fitting on a page are usually more important than making an exact size. If there are some paper or cardstock parts and some wooden parts, being able to set a dimension to a desired number of inches or millimetres would make cutting the wood easier than when it has to be cut to the size of a rectangle that is printed on a piece of paper.
- When printing to fit everything on a page, reduce the default margins and print to a scale less than 100 percent if necessary. Many of my prototypes were printed to a scale of 40 percent or 50 percent.
- To paste a picture that is in JPEG (or JPG) format into Excel, first paste the picture into Word and then copy and paste from Word to Excel.
- To save an Excel drawing as a JPEG file, first copy the area of the drawing you want to save. Then paste into Paint and save as a JPEG file. If you do not want to see the gridlines in the JPEG file, go to the "View" tab in Excel and uncheck "Gridlines" before copying.
- Excel does not show leading zeros of numbers (i.e. 00 is shown as 0, and 01 is shown as 1). The leading zeros can be shown by putting an apostrophe (') in front of the number. When this is done, Excel puts a small green triangle in the upper left corner of the cell. If the cursor is rolled over the triangle, the following message appears: "The number in this cell is formatted as text or preceded by an apostrophe." The triangle is not printed when

printing from Excel and does not appear if the Excel file is saved as a PDF file. However, the triangle is seen if the standard "Copy" command is used when copying and pasting into Paint. The way to eliminate the triangle in Paint is as follows:

a) Highlight the area in the Excel spreadsheet that you want to paste into Paint.
b) Copy this area using Copy → Copy as picture → Appearance → As shown when printed. (In some versions of Excel, the procedure is Paste → As picture → Copy as picture → Appearance → As shown when printed.)
c) Paste into Paint.

The only things required to make many of the calendars described in the following pages are access to Excel or an equivalent spreadsheet program, a printer (or a nearby small-quantity print shop), a utility knife, cardstock and glue or double-sided tape. Some of the calendars require wood and basic woodworking tools.

The following chapters describe the unique tables used to make these calendars and many potential applications.

# CHAPTER 3

# TABLES FOR SINGLE-SHEET PERPETUAL CALENDARS

## Introduction

This chapter shows how the unique tables for the single-sheet perpetual calendar are developed. Readers who are not interested in the theory behind my calendars can skip this chapter and the next and turn to Chapter 5 to see applications.

In this chapter and in the following chapters, some deviations from standard writing style are employed to keep all the columns in a table the same width, or to enhance clarity. Some of these deviations are as follows:

- The abbreviations for months of the year and days of the week may be written in all capital letters without a period at the end, e.g. "JAN" instead of "Jan." and "SUN" instead of "Sun."
- "LEAP YR" and "COM YR" are written instead of "Leap year" and "Common year." In tables where there is limited column width, the abbreviations are shortened to "L Yr" and "C Yr."
- Information in tables that applies to leap years is in boldface to distinguish it from information for common years, e.g. **2012** and **JAN**.
- "SMTWTFS" means "Sunday, Monday, Tuesday, Wednesday, Thursday, Friday, Saturday."

Table 3-1 shows the basic building block for the single-sheet perpetual calendar and the other calendar types. It is a 13-column day-of-month table with six rows. Row 1 has the first six cells blank and the numbers 1 to 7 in the next seven cells. Row 2 has the numbers 2 to 14; row 3, the numbers 9 to 21; row 4, the numbers 16 to 28; row 5, the numbers 23 to 31 in the first nine cells, with the last four cells blank; and row 6, the numbers 30 and 31 in the first two cells and the remaining cells blank. Imagine a seven-column window with each column's heading being a different day of the week, in order from Sunday to Saturday. Assume that the window is placed over this building block so that the *1* in the first row is in the *Sunday* column. The window then displays the days of the month when the first of the month is on a Sunday. If the window remains stationary and the day-of-month table is moved so that the *1* in the first row is under *Monday*, then the window displays the days of the month when the first of the month is on a Monday. Thus, by moving the table, the window can display the days of the month for the first of the month falling on any day of the week. The calendar always displays 31 days per month, and 29, 30 and 31 are ignored when applicable. There are commercially available perpetual calendars based on the building block in Table 3-1 and a window. Either the 13-column table moves or the window moves. None of the calendars that I am aware of can be set without knowing on what day of the week the first of the month falls.

### Table 3-1
### 13-Column Day-of-Month Table

| | | | | | | | | | | | | |
|---|---|---|---|---|---|---|---|---|---|---|---|---|
| | | | | | | 1 | 2 | 3 | 4 | 5 | 6 | 7 |
| 2 | 3 | 4 | 5 | 6 | 7 | 8 | 9 | 10 | 11 | 12 | 13 | 14 |
| 9 | 10 | 11 | 12 | 13 | 14 | 15 | 16 | 17 | 18 | 19 | 20 | 21 |
| 16 | 17 | 18 | 19 | 20 | 21 | 22 | 23 | 24 | 25 | 26 | 27 | 28 |
| 23 | 24 | 25 | 26 | 27 | 28 | 29 | 30 | 31 | | | | |
| 30 | 31 | | | | | | | | | | | |

My perpetual calendars are truly stand-alone in that reference to a conventional calendar is not required to set them. I make possible the calendar's stand-alone nature by having a month table and a year table, as well as a day-of-month table. The month table indicates the day of the week the first of each month falls on relative to January, and the year table indicates the day of the week that January 1 falls on for the years listed. As noted in Chapter 1, the single-sheet perpetual calendar can be made in a single- or dual-slider configuration. In this chapter, the dual-slider type is described first because the single-slider type evolves from it.

## Developing Month and Year Tables for a Dual-Slider Calendar

The dual-slider calendar has Table 3-1 on a day-of-month slider, and a 13-column month table with a marker on a second slider. Table 3-2 shows the face of a desk calendar that is approximately 7 inches wide by 4 inches high. The face has three windows, a year table and a blank space for a picture or operating instructions. The sliders are behind the face, and the three windows display parts of these sliders. Window no. 1 displays the marker that is on the lower left corner of the month table slider. The marker points to the applicable column in the year table. Window no. 2 displays seven columns of the month table, and window no. 3 displays seven columns of the day-of-month table, which is Table 3-1. Conventional perpetual calendars based on Table 3-1 have one slider and window no. 3 only.

The year table is approximately 2.0 inches wide by 1.8 inches high, and has 7 columns and 15 rows. This is enough space for a whole century. The year table is not on a slider. With the month table on a slider, the calendar can be set without any complicated table lookups. An alternative arrangement to that shown in Table 3-2 is to have the year table above window no. 2 instead of beside window no. 3. In this arrangement, windows no. 1 and 2 are combined, as the marker is in the middle of the month table slider rather than in its lower left corner. Since the year table is referred to infrequently, it can be behind a picture that is easily lifted up. Figures 1-1c and 5-6b illustrate this arrangement.

The steps to set the single-sheet perpetual calendar with dual-slider configuration are as follows:

1. Move the month table slider so that the marker on it lines up with the column in the year table that has the year of interest. Window no. 2 then displays the day of the week that the first of each month falls on.
2. Move the day-of-month slider to put the first day of the month (i.e. the *1* on the slider) under the month of interest.

**Table 3-2**
**Face of Single-Sheet Perpetual Calendar with Dual-Slider Configuration**

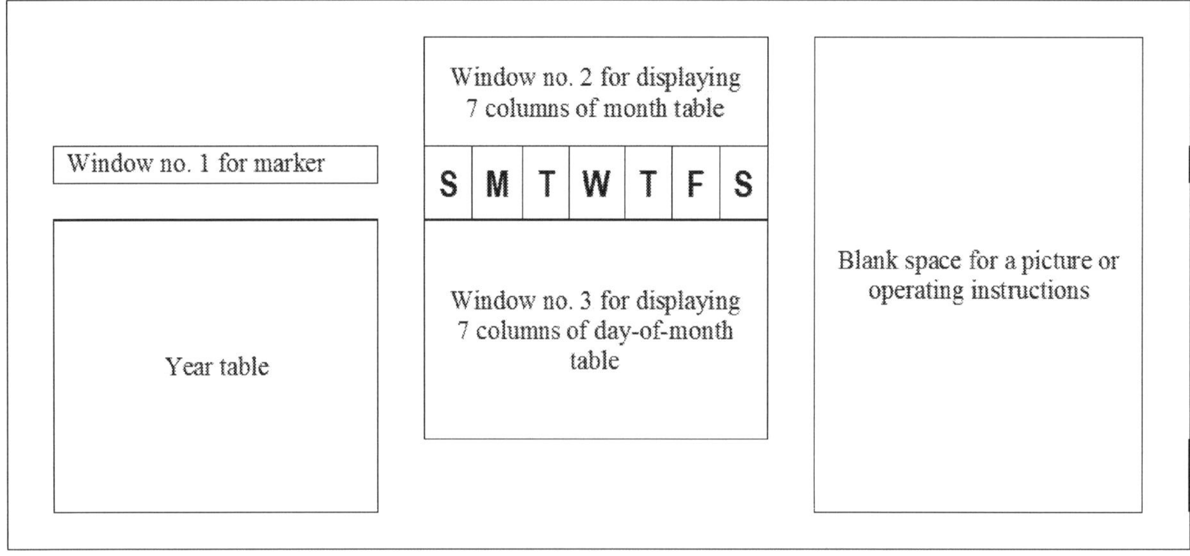
Window no. 1 for marker
Year table
Window no. 2 for displaying 7 columns of month table
S M T W T F S
Window no. 3 for displaying 7 columns of day-of-month table
Blank space for a picture or operating instructions

The month table is developed by using the data in Table 3-3, which shows the day of the week on which the first of each month falls for both leap years and common years when January 1 is on a Sunday.

**Table 3-3**
**Day of the Week That the First of Each Month Falls on when January 1 is on a Sunday**

| Year Type | Sun. | Mon. | Tue. | Wed. | Thur. | Fri. | Sat. |
|---|---|---|---|---|---|---|---|
| Leap | Jan.<br>April<br>July | Oct. | May | Feb.<br>Aug. | March<br>Nov. | June | Sept.<br>Dec. |
| Common | Jan.<br>Oct. | May | August | Feb.<br>March<br>Nov. | June | Sept.<br>Dec. | April<br>July |

The entries in the 13-column month table are developed as follows. Table 3-4 shows window no. 2 blank and what is in window no. 3 when the day-of-month slider is in its far-left position. This is the position for the first of the month falling on a Sunday. Thus, the seven rightmost columns of the 13-column day-of-month table are visible in window no. 3.

**Table 3-4**
**Developing the Month Table**

| | | | | | | |
|---|---|---|---|---|---|---|
| **S** | **M** | **T** | **W** | **T** | **F** | **S** |
| 1 | 2 | 3 | 4 | 5 | 6 | 7 |
| 8 | 9 | 10 | 11 | 12 | 13 | 14 |
| 15 | 16 | 17 | 18 | 19 | 20 | 21 |
| 22 | 23 | 24 | 25 | 26 | 27 | 28 |
| 29 | 30 | 31 | | | | |
| | | | | | | |

Assume that the month slider is also in its far-left position, and that January 1 of a common year is on a Sunday. Write *January* in the blank cell of the month slider above the left-hand *S* (*Sunday*). Since October 1 in a common year is on the same day of the week as January 1, also write *October* above the left-hand *S*. According to Table 3-3, when January 1 is on a Sunday for a common year, February 1, March 1 and November 1 are all on a Wednesday. Therefore, write *February*, *March* and *November* in the cell above *W*. Similarly, write *April* and *July* above the far-right *S* (*Saturday*). The same procedure is followed for leap years. Table 3-5a shows the completed right-hand part of the month slider for both common and leap years. This is the part of the month table that is seen when January 1 is on a Sunday. (The month slider is in its far-left position.) In Table 3-5a, the months for leap years are in boldface. Note that the part of the month table that is in Table 3-5a is identical to Table 3-3. When the month table is set as shown in Table 3-5a, any month can be displayed by moving the 13-column day-of-month table so that *1* is under the month of interest. For example, to set February, March or November of a common year, move the 13-column day-of-month table so that *1* is under *W* (*Wednesday*).

When January 1 is on a Saturday, the month table is moved to its far-right position so that *January* appears above the *Saturday* column. January is set by moving the day-of-month table so that *1* is under *Saturday.* Table 3-5b shows this, with the month table blank above the *Sunday* to *Friday* columns. Table 3-3 shows that in a common year, the day of the week that April 1 and July 1 fall on is one day before the day of the week that January 1 falls on. When January 1 is on a Saturday, April 1 and July 1 are on a Friday. Therefore, write *April* and *July* in the cell in the common year row above *Friday.* Similarly, write *September* and *December* in the cell in the leap year row above *Friday.*

**Table 3-5a**
**The part of the month table that is seen when January 1 is on a Sunday**

| **Jan. Apr. Jul.** | **Oct.** | **May** | **Feb. Aug.** | **Mar. Nov.** | **Jun.** | **Sep. Dec.** |
|---|---|---|---|---|---|---|
| Jan. Oct. | May | Aug. | Feb. Mar. Nov. | Jun. | Sep. Dec. | Apr. Jul. |
| **S** | **M** | **T** | **W** | **T** | **F** | **S** |
| 1 | 2 | 3 | 4 | 5 | 6 | 7 |
| 8 | 9 | 10 | 11 | 12 | 13 | 14 |
| 15 | 16 | 17 | 18 | 19 | 20 | 21 |
| 22 | 23 | 24 | 25 | 26 | 27 | 28 |
| 29 | 30 | 31 | | | | |
| | | | | | | |

**Table 3-5b**
**The part of the month table that is seen when January 1 is on a Saturday**

| | | | | | | **Jan. Apr. Jul.** |
|---|---|---|---|---|---|---|
| | | | | | | Jan. Oct. |
| **S** | **M** | **T** | **W** | **T** | **F** | **S** |
| | | | | | | 1 |
| 2 | 3 | 4 | 5 | 6 | 7 | 8 |
| 9 | 10 | 11 | 12 | 13 | 14 | 15 |
| 16 | 17 | 18 | 19 | 20 | 21 | 22 |
| 23 | 24 | 25 | 26 | 27 | 28 | 29 |
| 30 | 31 | | | | | |

Note: The top row, in boldface, is for leap years. The row below that is for common years.

The same reasoning is used to determine the contents of the remaining cells in the month table. Table 3-6a shows the complete month table with a marker on the bottom left. Table 3-6b shows the completed month table on a slider, along with the day-of-month table on a second slider. It also shows a year table with a limited number of entries. To understand Table 3-6b, refer back to Table 3-2 and note the following:

- The black marker on the month slider appears in window no. 1. In Table 3-6b, it is above the second-from-the-left column of the year table and points to 2001, 2007, 2018 and **2024**. These are years when January 1 is on a Monday.

- The month table is on a slider that has three sections. The top section has three rows for leap year months; the middle section has three rows for common year months; and the bottom section has one row for the marker.
- Window no. 2, which is above SMTWTFS, displays seven columns of the month table. As noted above, the month slider is set for years when January 1 is on a Monday. The six columns not displayed are shaded.
- Window no. 3, which is below SMTWTFS, displays seven columns of the day-of-month table. In Table 3-6b, the day-of-month slider is set for months where the first is on a Tuesday, which is May of a common year or October of a leap year. The six columns not displayed are shaded. (The months in the column above the *1* on the day-of-month slider are the applicable months.)
- The year table is in the lower left-hand corner of Table 3-6b. On an actual calendar, the year table is in the location shown in Table 3-2. The years in the far-left column of the year table are years when the first of January is on a Sunday; the years in the next column are years when the first of January is on a Monday; etc.
- Table 3-6b does not show the far-right part of the face, as nothing is hidden there for the settings shown.

### Table 3-6a
### Completed Month Table When Leap Years and Common Years Are Separate

| **Leap Yrs.** | | **Oct.** | **May** | **Feb.**<br>**Aug.** | **Mar.**<br>**Nov.** | **Jun.** | **Sep.**<br>**Dec.** | **Jan.**<br>**Apr.**<br>**Jul.** | **Oct.** | **May** | **Feb.**<br>**Aug.** | **Mar.**<br>**Nov.** | **Jun.** | **Sep.**<br>**Dec.** |
|---|---|---|---|---|---|---|---|---|---|---|---|---|---|---|
| **Com. Yrs.** | | May | Aug. | Feb.<br>Mar.<br>Nov. | Jun. | Sep.<br>Dec. | Apr.<br>Jul. | Jan.<br>Oct. | May | Aug. | Feb.<br>Mar.<br>Nov. | Jun. | Sep.<br>Dec. | Apr.<br>Jul. |
| ■ | | | | | | | | | | | | | | |

## Table 3-6b
## Completed Month-Table Slider Set to 2001, 2007, 2018 or 2024, and Day-of-Month Slider Set to May (Common Year) or October (Leap Year)

| | Leap Yr | | Oct | May | Feb Aug | Mar Nov | Jun | Sep Dec | Jan Apr Jul | Oct | May | Feb Aug | Mar Nov | Jun | Sep Dec | |
|---|---|---|---|---|---|---|---|---|---|---|---|---|---|---|---|---|
| | Com Yr | | May | Aug | Feb Mar Nov | Jun | Sep Dec | Apr Jul | Jan Oct | May | Aug | Feb Mar Nov | Jun | Sep Dec | Apr Jul | |
| | | | | | | | | S | M | T | W | T | F | S | | |
| | | | | | | | | | | 1 | 2 | 3 | 4 | 5 | 6 | 7 |
| | | | | 2 | 3 | 4 | 5 | 6 | 7 | 8 | 9 | 10 | 11 | 12 | 13 | 14 |
| | | | | 9 | 10 | 11 | 12 | 13 | 14 | 15 | 16 | 17 | 18 | 19 | 20 | 21 |
| | | | | 16 | 17 | 18 | 19 | 20 | 21 | 22 | 23 | 24 | 25 | 26 | 27 | 28 |
| | | | | 23 | 24 | 25 | 26 | 27 | 28 | 29 | 30 | 31 | | | | |
| | | | | 30 | 31 | | | | | | | | | | | |

| | | | | | | |
|---|---|---|---|---|---|---|
| | | | | | | **2000** |
| | 2001 | 2002 | 2003 | **2004** | | 2005 |
| 2006 | 2007 | **2008** | | 2009 | 2010 | 2011 |
| **2012** | | 2013 | 2014 | 2015 | **2016** | |
| 2017 | 2018 | 2019 | **2020** | | 2021 | 2022 |
| 2023 | **2024** | | 2025 | 2026 | 2027 | **2028** |

Note: Leap years are in boldface. See Table 3-7 for a year table that covers the entire 21st century.

Table 3-7 shows a full-century year table for use with the month-table sliders in Tables 3-6a and 3-6b. There are blank cells in the partial-year table (Table 3-6b) so that the years are consecutive from left to right and top to bottom. To make the table more compact, the blanks are eliminated in Table 3-7. This results in some years being in a row above or below where they are expected. Consequently, a year is harder to find. However, this is a minor inconvenience, as the year table is most often consulted to verify that the marker is set to the correct year rather than to find where to set the marker.

**Table 3-7**
**Full-Century Year Table for Use with the Month-Table Sliders in Tables 3-6a and 3-6b**

| | | | | | | |
|---|---|---|---|---|---|---|
| 2006 | 2001 | 2002 | 2003 | **2004** | 2010 | **2000** |
| **2012** | 2007 | **2008** | 2014 | 2009 | **2016** | 2005 |
| 2017 | 2018 | 2013 | **2020** | 2015 | 2021 | 2011 |
| 2023 | **2024** | 2019 | 2025 | 2026 | 2027 | 2022 |
| 2034 | 2029 | 2030 | 2031 | **2032** | 2038 | **2028** |
| **2040** | 2035 | **2036** | 2042 | 2037 | **2044** | 2033 |
| 2045 | 2046 | 2041 | **2048** | 2043 | 2049 | 2039 |
| 2051 | **2052** | 2047 | 2053 | 2054 | 2055 | 2050 |
| 2062 | 2057 | 2058 | 2059 | **2060** | 2066 | **2056** |
| **2068** | 2063 | **2064** | 2070 | 2065 | **2072** | 2061 |
| 2073 | 2074 | 2069 | **2076** | 2071 | 2077 | 2067 |
| 2079 | **2080** | 2075 | 2081 | 2082 | 2083 | 2078 |
| 2090 | 2085 | 2086 | 2087 | **2088** | 2094 | **2084** |
| **2096** | 2091 | **2092** | 2098 | 2093 | | 2089 |
| | | 2097 | | 2099 | | 2095 |

Note: Leap years are in boldface.

The following procedure is used to add years not shown to Table 3-7:

1. Imagine that the columns in the table are labeled *Sunday* to *Saturday* from left to right.
2. For both common years and leap years, enter the year under the day of the week that January 1 falls on.

## Making March through December the Same for Common and Leap Years

In Tables 3-6a and 3-6b, the lower part of the month-table slider is for common years and the upper part for leap years. January and February for leap years are in the same columns as January and February for common years. March to December are in different columns, but they could be in the same columns if a change were made to the year table. The first of March in a leap year is two days later in the week than the first of March in the previous year. Therefore, to make March through December the same, leap years in the year table must appear two days later in the year table than in the previous common year. *This is one day later in the week than the actual day of the week for January 1.* Tables 3-9a, 3-9b and 3-9c are three different formats for the revised year table. These tables are discussed in detail after Table 3-8.

When the year table is revised so that the months March to December are in the same columns in the month table for both common years and leap years, January and February for leap years cannot be in the same columns as January and February for common years. The correct columns for January and February for leap years can be determined by recognizing that the year in the year table is now one column ahead. Therefore, January and February must each be shifted one column back. Alternatively, the following procedure can be used:

1. Set the marker on the month-table slider above a leap year in the revised table.
2. Set the day-of-month slider so the month is correct for January of that leap year.
3. Enter *January* in boldface in an empty cell above the *1* on the day-of-month slider. (Use boldface so it will look different from the January of a common year.)
4. Move the month-table slider so that the marker is above a different leap year and the *January* entered in step 3 is not visible.
5. Repeat steps 2 and 3.
6. Repeat steps 1 to 5 for February.

Table 3-8 shows the month table that these steps produce. The advantage to having March through December in the same columns for common and leap years is that setting these months is simpler and less prone to error. January and February are in different columns for common and leap years; care is required to ensure that the correct columns are used. However, only two months, not ten, require extra care.

All of the examples of the single-sheet perpetual calendars with dual sliders in Chapter 5 use Table 3-8 as the month table and Table 3-9a, 3-9b or 3-9c as the year table. I prefer this combination. Others may prefer the combination Table 3-6a as the month table and Table 3-7 as the year table.

## Table 3-8
## Month Table When March to December Are the Same for Common and Leap Years

| | | L. Yr. | **Feb.** | L. Yr. | L. Yr. | L. Yr. | **Jan.** | L. Yr. | L. Yr. | **Feb.** | L. Yr. | L. Yr. | L. Yr. | **Jan.** |
|---|---|---|---|---|---|---|---|---|---|---|---|---|---|---|
| | | May | Aug. | Mar. | Jun. | Sep. | Apr. | Oct. | May | Aug. | Mar. | Jun. | Sep. | Apr. |
| | | | | Nov. | | Dec. | Jul. | | | | Nov. | | Dec. | Jul. |
| | | C. Yr. | C. Yr. | Feb. | C. Yr. | C. Yr. | C. Yr. | Jan. | C. Yr. | C. Yr. | Feb. | C. Yr. | C. Yr. | C. Yr. |
| | | | | | | | | | | | | | | |

Notes:

1. Use Table 3-9a, 3-9b or 3-9c for the year table.
2. In many of the designs in Chapter 5, the row for January and February in common years is next to the top, instead of where it is shown in Table 3-8.

Tables 3-9a, 3-9b and 3-9c are three formats for full-century year tables for use with Table 3-8. Table 3-9a has all the leap years in the upper part of the table and all the common years in the lower part. Table 3-9b has leap years and common years together to reduce the number of rows required. Table 3-9c also has leap years and common years together, but it has blank cells so that all the years are in the correct sequence reading from left to right. When leap years and common years are together, different fonts should be used for the two types to alert the user of which rows to use in the month table for January and February. One way of doing this is to use boldface for leap years and normal font for common years, as is done in Tables 3-9b and 3-9c. Table 3-9a also has leap years in boldface, but this is not essential, as the upper part of the table is for leap years and the lower part is for common years. Table 3-9b is formed from Table 3-9c by pushing numbers up from lower rows to fill blank cells. Table 3-9a is also formed in this way. This means that some years appear in unexpected places. For example, in Table 3-9b, the year 2009 is in the top row, between 2003 and 2004, instead of in the next row down after 2008. The arrangement in Table 3-9b minimizes the number of rows required to cover the entire 21st century (15 rows, compared to 17 rows for Table 3-9a and 18 rows for Table 3-9c). There are pros and cons with each arrangement, and which to use depends on the preference of the designer. I prefer the arrangement in Table 3-9b and use it in most of the examples in *Practical Perpetual Calendars* for both the single- and dual-slider calendars.

## Table 3-9
## Full-Century Year Tables for Use with the Month-Table Slider in Table 3-8

**a. Leap years and common years separate**

| *Leap Years* (Use top row for Jan. and Feb.) | | | | | | |
|---|---|---|---|---|---|---|
| **2000** | **2012** | **2024** | **2008** | **2020** | **2004** | **2016** |
| **2028** | **2040** | **2052** | **2036** | **2048** | **2032** | **2044** |
| **2056** | **2068** | **2080** | **2064** | **2076** | **2060** | **2072** |
| **2084** | **2096** | | **2092** | | **2088** | |
| *Common Years* (Use bottom row for Jan. and Feb.) | | | | | | |
| 2006 | 2001 | 2002 | 2003 | 2009 | 2010 | 2005 |
| 2017 | 2007 | 2013 | 2014 | 2015 | 2021 | 2011 |
| 2023 | 2018 | 2019 | 2025 | 2026 | 2027 | 2022 |
| 2034 | 2029 | 2030 | 2031 | 2037 | 2038 | 2033 |
| 2045 | 2035 | 2041 | 2042 | 2043 | 2049 | 2039 |
| 2051 | 2046 | 2047 | 2053 | 2054 | 2055 | 2050 |
| 2062 | 2057 | 2058 | 2059 | 2065 | 2066 | 2061 |
| 2073 | 2063 | 2069 | 2070 | 2071 | 2077 | 2067 |
| 2079 | 2074 | 2075 | 2081 | 2082 | 2083 | 2078 |
| 2090 | 2085 | 2086 | 2087 | 2093 | 2094 | 2089 |
| | 2091 | 2097 | 2098 | 2099 | | 2095 |

(See next page for Table 3-9c.)

**b. Leap years and common years together**

| **2000** | 2001 | 2002 | 2003 | 2009 | **2004** | 2005 |
|---|---|---|---|---|---|---|
| 2006 | 2007 | 2013 | **2008** | 2015 | 2010 | 2011 |
| 2017 | **2012** | 2019 | 2014 | **2020** | 2021 | **2016** |
| 2023 | 2018 | **2024** | 2025 | 2026 | 2027 | 2022 |
| **2028** | 2029 | 2030 | 2031 | 2037 | **2032** | 2033 |
| 2034 | 2035 | 2041 | **2036** | 2043 | 2038 | 2039 |
| 2045 | **2040** | 2047 | 2042 | **2048** | 2049 | **2044** |
| 2051 | 2046 | **2052** | 2053 | 2054 | 2055 | 2050 |
| **2056** | 2057 | 2058 | 2059 | 2065 | **2060** | 2061 |
| 2062 | 2063 | 2069 | **2064** | 2071 | 2066 | 2067 |
| 2073 | **2068** | 2075 | 2070 | **2076** | 2077 | **2072** |
| 2079 | 2074 | **2080** | 2081 | 2082 | 2083 | 2078 |
| **2084** | 2085 | 2086 | 2087 | 2093 | **2088** | 2089 |
| 2090 | 2091 | 2097 | **2092** | 2099 | 2094 | 2095 |
| | **2096** | | 2098 | | | |
| | | | | | | |
| | | | | | | |

**Table 3-9 (continued)**

**c. Leap years and common years together and with all years in the correct sequence**

| | | | | | | |
|---|---|---|---|---|---|---|
| **2000** | 2001 | 2002 | 2003 | | **2004** | 2005 |
| 2006 | 2007 | | **2008** | 2009 | 2010 | 2011 |
| | **2012** | 2013 | 2014 | 2015 | | **2016** |
| 2017 | 2018 | 2019 | | **2020** | 2021 | 2022 |
| 2023 | | **2024** | 2025 | 2026 | 2027 | |
| **2028** | 2029 | 2030 | 2031 | | **2032** | 2033 |
| 2034 | 2035 | | **2036** | 2037 | 2038 | 2039 |
| | **2040** | 2041 | 2042 | 2043 | | **2044** |
| 2045 | 2046 | 2047 | | **2048** | 2049 | 2050 |
| 2051 | | **2052** | 2053 | 2054 | 2055 | |
| **2056** | 2057 | 2058 | 2059 | | **2060** | 2061 |
| 2062 | 2063 | | **2064** | 2065 | 2066 | 2067 |
| | **2068** | 2069 | 2070 | 2071 | | **2072** |
| 2073 | 2074 | 2075 | | **2076** | 2077 | 2078 |
| 2079 | | **2080** | 2081 | 2082 | 2083 | |
| **2084** | 2085 | 2086 | 2087 | | **2088** | 2089 |
| 2090 | 2091 | | **2092** | 2093 | 2094 | 2095 |
| | **2096** | 2097 | 2098 | 2099 | | |

Note: Leap years are in boldface in all three tables.

The following procedure is used to add years not shown to Table 3-9:

1. Imagine that the columns in the tables are labeled *Sunday* to *Saturday* from left to right.
2. If the year is a common year, enter the year under the day of the week that January 1 falls on.
3. If the year is a leap year, enter the year under the day of the week *after* the day of the week that January 1 falls on.

## Combining the Month-Table Slider and the Day-of-Month Slider

The single-sheet perpetual calendar discussed thus far has a month-table slider and a day-of-month slider. The calendar is set by moving the month-table slider so that the marker is above the column in the year table that has the year of interest and then moving the day-of-month slider so that *1* is under the month of interest. The month slider and the day-of-month slider can be combined. For the combined slider, the year table is above or below the slider rather than to the left side. The calendar is set by moving the slider so that the month of interest is in the same column as the year of interest.

One way of combining the sliders is as follows. Table 3-10 shows the arrangement when the combined slider is at its far-left position. This is the location of the slider when the first of the month is on a Sunday. The seven rightmost columns of the month table are visible in the bottom part of the window, and the seven rightmost columns of the 13-column day-of-month table are visible in the top part of the window. There are six rows in the month table, and they are blank. Months applying to common years will be entered in the bottom three rows of the month table, and months applying to leap years will be entered in the top three rows. The partial year table below the slider in Table 3-10 is from Table 3-7, which is used with Table 3-6a.

To fill in the months under *1*, *8*, *15*, *22* and *29*, note that this column is above common year *2006* and leap year *2012*. Therefore, enter all the months in these years that began on a Sunday. They are January and October for common years, and January, April and July for leap years. To fill in the months under *2*, *9*, *16*, *23* and *30*, note that this column is above common year *2001* and leap year *2024*. Therefore, enter all the months in these years that began (or will begin) on a Sunday. They are April and July for common years, and September and December for leap years. The months for columns above the other years are filled in similarly. To fill in the months in the six columns that are not shown in Table 3-10, pull the slider to the far right so that *1* in the day-of-month table is under *Saturday*. With the slider in this position, write the names of the months in the columns when the first of the month was (or will be) on a Saturday. This procedure requires checking a calendar showing a common year and another showing a leap year for each of the 13 columns, which is a considerable amount of work.

An easier way of combining the sliders is to use a calendar for the current year or any known year. Assume that a calendar for 2015 is available and that we are going to develop the table that applies to common years. Set the slider at its far-left position as above, and write the names of all the months that begin on a Sunday above *2015*. They are February, March and November. Now move the slider one position to the right, and above *2015* write the names of all the months that begin on a Monday. The only month is June. Do a similar thing for the other positions. Note that more than one year may be required to fill in all the blanks. The procedure for filling in the leap year part of the month table is similar, with a known leap year (or years) used instead of a common year.

Setting the single-slider calendar each month is slightly more difficult than setting the dual-slider calendar because it is less obvious which direction to move the slider and because you need to find which column in the year table has the year of interest. Although the single-slider calendar can be designed so that a marker can be put above the column for the current year, this feature would be of limited benefit, as a person tends to remember the column after setting the calendar once or twice.

## Table 3-10
## Developing the Table for Day of Month and Month on the Same Slider

| S | M | T | W | T | F | S |
|---|---|---|---|---|---|---|
| 1 | 2 | 3 | 4 | 5 | 6 | 7 |
| 8 | 9 | 10 | 11 | 12 | 13 | 14 |
| 15 | 16 | 17 | 18 | 19 | 20 | 21 |
| 22 | 23 | 24 | 25 | 26 | 27 | 28 |
| 29 | 30 | 31 | | | | |
| | | | | | | |
| | | | | | | |
| | | | | | | |
| | | | | | | |
| | | | | | | |
| | | | | | | |
| | | | | | | **2000** |
| | 2001 | 2002 | 2003 | **2004** | | 2005 |
| 2006 | 2007 | **2008** | | 2009 | 2010 | 2011 |
| **2012** | | 2013 | 2014 | 2015 | **2016** | |
| 2017 | 2018 | 2019 | **2020** | | 2021 | 2022 |
| 2023 | **2024** | | 2025 | 2026 | 2027 | **2028** |

Enter months for leap years in the first three empty rows.

Enter months for common years in the next three empty rows.

Notes:

1. Leap years are in boldface.
2. The slider is in its leftmost position, and only the columns in the window are shown.

Table 3-11 shows the completed combined slider and corresponding year table for the calendar design when the common year and leap year months are separate from each other. By employing similar reasoning as was used to derive Tables 3-8 and 3-9 from Tables 3-6a and 3-7, a table can be made from Table 3-11 where March through December are shared by common years and leap years. The result is Table 3-12. For the reasons previously noted, I prefer the design in Table 3-12 to that in Table 3-11. Note that the months in Tables 3-6a and 3-11 are in reverse order from each other. There is a similar difference between the months in Tables 3-8 and 3-12. This is to account for the difference in the direction of movement of the month table in the dual- and single-slider calendars.

If in Table 3-11 we consider that the year columns are labeled *Sunday* to *Saturday* from left to right, the years are under the day of the week that January 1 falls on. This is also the case for common years in Table 3-12. However, in keeping with the discussion preceding Table 3-8, leap years in Table 3-12 are under the day of the week *after* the day that January 1 falls on.

**Table 3-11**
**Single-Slider Calendar with Months of Common Years and Months of Leap Years Separate**

| S | M | T | W | T | F | S |
|---|---|---|---|---|---|---|

| | | | | | | 1 | 2 | 3 | 4 | 5 | 6 | 7 |
|---|---|---|---|---|---|---|---|---|---|---|---|---|
| 2 | 3 | 4 | 5 | 6 | 7 | 8 | 9 | 10 | 11 | 12 | 13 | 14 |
| 9 | 10 | 11 | 12 | 13 | 14 | 15 | 16 | 17 | 18 | 19 | 20 | 21 |
| 16 | 17 | 18 | 19 | 20 | 21 | 22 | 23 | 24 | 25 | 26 | 27 | 28 |
| 23 | 24 | 25 | 26 | 27 | 28 | 29 | 30 | 31 | | | | |
| 30 | 31 | | | | | | | | | | | |
| Sep. | June | Mar. | Feb. | May | Oct. | Jan. | Sep. | June | Mar. | Feb. | May | Oct. |
| Dec. | | Nov. | Aug. | | | Apr. | Dec. | | Nov. | Aug. | | |
| Leap yr | Leap yr | Leap yr | Leap yr | Leap yr | Leap yr | July | Leap yr | Leap yr | Leap yr | Leap yr | Leap yr | Leap yr |
| Apr. | Sep. | June | Feb. | Aug. | May | Jan. | Apr. | Sep. | June | Feb. | Aug. | May |
| July | Dec. | | Mar. | | | Oct. | July | Dec. | | Mar. | | |
| Com yr | Com yr | Com yr | Nov. | Com yr | Com yr | Com yr | Com yr | Com yr | Com yr | Nov. | Com yr | Com yr |

| 2006 | 2001 | 2002 | 2003 | **2004** | 2010 | **2000** |
|---|---|---|---|---|---|---|
| **2012** | 2007 | **2008** | 2014 | 2009 | **2016** | 2005 |
| 2017 | 2018 | 2013 | **2020** | 2015 | 2021 | 2011 |
| 2023 | **2024** | 2019 | 2025 | 2026 | 2027 | 2022 |
| 2034 | 2029 | 2030 | 2031 | **2032** | 2038 | **2028** |
| **2040** | 2035 | **2036** | 2042 | 2037 | **2044** | 2033 |
| 2045 | 2046 | 2041 | **2048** | 2043 | 2049 | 2039 |
| 2051 | **2052** | 2047 | 2053 | 2054 | 2055 | 2050 |
| 2062 | 2057 | 2058 | 2059 | **2060** | 2066 | **2056** |
| **2068** | 2063 | **2064** | 2070 | 2065 | **2072** | 2061 |
| 2073 | 2074 | 2069 | **2076** | 2071 | 2077 | 2067 |
| 2079 | **2080** | 2075 | 2081 | 2082 | 2083 | 2078 |
| 2090 | 2085 | 2086 | 2087 | **2088** | 2094 | **2084** |
| **2096** | 2091 | **2092** | 2098 | 2093 | | 2089 |
| | | 2097 | | 2099 | | 2095 |

Notes:

1. Leap years are in boldface.
2. The slider is in its rightmost position, and all columns are shown. The bold outline is the window.

The operation of Table 3-11 is explained following Table 3-12. The procedure used to add years not shown to Table 3-11 is as follows:

1. Imagine that the columns in the year table are labeled *Sunday* to *Saturday* from left to right.
2. For both common years and leap years, enter the year under the day of the week that January 1 falls on.

## Table 3-12
## Single-Slider Calendar with March through December Shared by Common Years and Leap Years

| S | M | T | W | T | F | S | | | | | | |
|---|---|---|---|---|---|---|---|---|---|---|---|---|
| | | | | | | 1 | 2 | 3 | 4 | 5 | 6 | 7 |
| 2 | 3 | 4 | 5 | 6 | 7 | 8 | 9 | 10 | 11 | 12 | 13 | 14 |
| 9 | 10 | 11 | 12 | 13 | 14 | 15 | 16 | 17 | 18 | 19 | 20 | 21 |
| 16 | 17 | 18 | 19 | 20 | 21 | 22 | 23 | 24 | 25 | 26 | 27 | 28 |
| 23 | 24 | 25 | 26 | 27 | 28 | 29 | 30 | 31 | | | | |
| 30 | 31 | | | | | | | | | | | |
| **Jan.** | Leap yr | Leap yr | Leap yr | **Feb.** | Leap yr | Leap yr | **Jan.** | Leap yr | Leap yr | Leap yr | **Feb.** | Leap yr |
| Apr. | Sep. | June | Mar. | Aug. | May | Oct. | Apr. | Sep. | June | Mar. | Aug. | May |
| July | Dec. | | Nov. | | | | July | Dec. | | Nov. | | |
| Com yr | Com yr | Com yr | Feb. | Com yr | Com yr | Jan. | Com yr | Com yr | Com yr | Feb. | Com yr | Com yr |

| | | | | | | |
|---|---|---|---|---|---|---|
| **2000** | 2001 | 2002 | 2003 | 2009 | **2004** | 2005 |
| 2006 | 2007 | 2013 | **2008** | 2015 | 2010 | 2011 |
| 2017 | **2012** | 2019 | 2014 | **2020** | 2021 | **2016** |
| 2023 | 2018 | **2024** | 2025 | 2026 | 2027 | 2022 |
| **2028** | 2029 | 2030 | 2031 | 2037 | **2032** | 2033 |
| 2034 | 2035 | 2041 | **2036** | 2043 | 2038 | 2039 |
| 2045 | **2040** | 2047 | 2042 | **2048** | 2049 | **2044** |
| 2051 | 2046 | **2052** | 2053 | 2054 | 2055 | 2050 |
| **2056** | 2057 | 2058 | 2059 | 2065 | **2060** | 2061 |
| 2062 | 2063 | 2069 | **2064** | 2071 | 2066 | 2067 |
| 2073 | **2068** | 2075 | 2070 | **2076** | 2077 | **2072** |
| 2079 | 2074 | **2080** | 2081 | 2082 | 2083 | 2078 |
| **2084** | 2085 | 2086 | 2087 | 2093 | **2088** | 2089 |
| 2090 | 2091 | 2097 | **2092** | 2099 | 2094 | 2095 |
| | **2096** | | 2098 | | | |

Notes:

1. The top row of the month table part of the slider is for January and February in leap years. *Jan.* and *Feb.* are in boldface to indicate that they apply to leap years.
2. The bottom row of the month table part of the slider is for January and February in common years.
3. Leap years are in boldface in the year table.
4. The slider is in its rightmost position, and all columns are shown. The bold outline is the window.

In Tables 3-11 and 3-12, the top row with SMTWTFS is fixed with respect to the year table at the bottom. The day-of-month and the month tables are on a slider in the middle. The calendar is set by moving the slider to line up the month of interest with the year of interest. As in Table 3-2, there is a window below the SMTWTFS row so that only the columns of interest on the slider are visible. In Tables 3-11 and 3-12, the sliders are in their far-right positions, and the columns in the window are in the bold outline. The width of the face is 19 columns plus borders so that the columns that are not of interest are always hidden. This is to accommodate the slider's ability to extend six columns past the seven-column year table on each end. The width of the face can be reduced to 13 columns plus borders by having the SMTWTFS row and the year table move instead of the day-of-month and month tables. In this arrangement, some columns of the day-of-month and month tables that are not of interest are visible. For an example, see Figure 5-3a.

The following procedure is used to add years not shown to Table 3-12:

1. Imagine that the columns in the year table are labeled *Sunday* to *Saturday* from left to right.
2. If the year is a common year, enter it under the day of the week that January 1 falls on.
3. If the year is a leap year, enter it under the day of the week *after* the day of the week that January 1 falls on.

In both Tables 3-11 and 3-12, the moving slider is shown in its far-right position with respect to the fixed year table. Both show the month table below the day-of-month table, and the year table below the month table. In this arrangement, the month table and the day-of-month table are in the same window. An alternate arrangement is to put the month table above the day-of-month table, and the year table above the month table. In this arrangement, the line with the days of the week (SMTWTFS) is between the month table and the day-of-month table. Thus, two windows are required, which complicates construction. However, the appearance of the alternate arrangement may be preferred for some applications. See Figures 5-2a, 5-2b and 5-2c for calendars that have the alternate arrangement.

## Single Slider with the Year Table beside the Window

Table 3-12 applies to the single-slider design where the year table is above or below the window for the day-of-month table. The year table can also be beside it, as in the dual-slider design. The steps to develop the slider and face for converting Table 3-12 to the side arrangement are as follows. The first step is to make Table 3-13, which shows the view when the slider is at the extreme left of its travel. The next step is to make Tables 3-14a and 3-14b, which show outlines of two possible face arrangements with their associated sliders below them.

## Table 3-13
## Single-Slider View When the Month Table Is below the Day-of-Month Table and the Slider Is at the Extreme Left of Its Travel

| | | | | | | | S | M | T | W | T | F | S | |
|---|---|---|---|---|---|---|---|---|---|---|---|---|---|---|
| | | | | | | | 1 | 2 | 3 | 4 | 5 | 6 | 7 | |
| | 2 | 3 | 4 | 5 | 6 | 7 | 8 | 9 | 10 | 11 | 12 | 13 | 14 | |
| | 9 | 10 | 11 | 12 | 13 | 14 | 15 | 16 | 17 | 18 | 19 | 20 | 21 | |
| | 16 | 17 | 18 | 19 | 20 | 21 | 22 | 23 | 24 | 25 | 26 | 27 | 28 | |
| | 23 | 24 | 25 | 26 | 27 | 28 | 29 | 30 | 31 | | | | | |
| | 30 | 31 | | | | | | | | | | | | |
| | **Jan.** | L yr | L yr | L yr | **Feb.** | L yr | L yr | **Jan.** | L yr | L yr | L yr | **Feb.** | L yr | |
| | Apr. | Sep. | June | Mar. | Aug. | May | Oct. | Apr. | Sep. | June | Mar. | Aug. | May | |
| | July | Dec. | | Nov. | | | | July | Dec. | | Nov. | | | |
| | C yr | C yr | C yr | Feb. | C yr | C yr | Jan. | C yr | C yr | C yr | Feb. | C yr | C yr | |

| | | | | | | |
|---|---|---|---|---|---|---|
| **2000** | 2001 | 2002 | 2003 | 2009 | **2004** | 2005 |
| 2006 | 2007 | 2013 | **2008** | 2015 | 2010 | 2011 |
| 2017 | **2012** | 2019 | 2014 | **2020** | 2021 | **2016** |

Notes:

1. The top row of the month table part of the slider is for January and February in leap years. *Jan.* and *Feb.* are in boldface to indicate that they apply to leap years.
2. The bottom row of the month table part of the slider is for January and February in common years.
3. Leap years are in boldface in the year table.
4. Only the top three rows of the year table are shown.

## Table 3-14a
## Outline of Wide Face Arrangement with Slider Shown below the Face

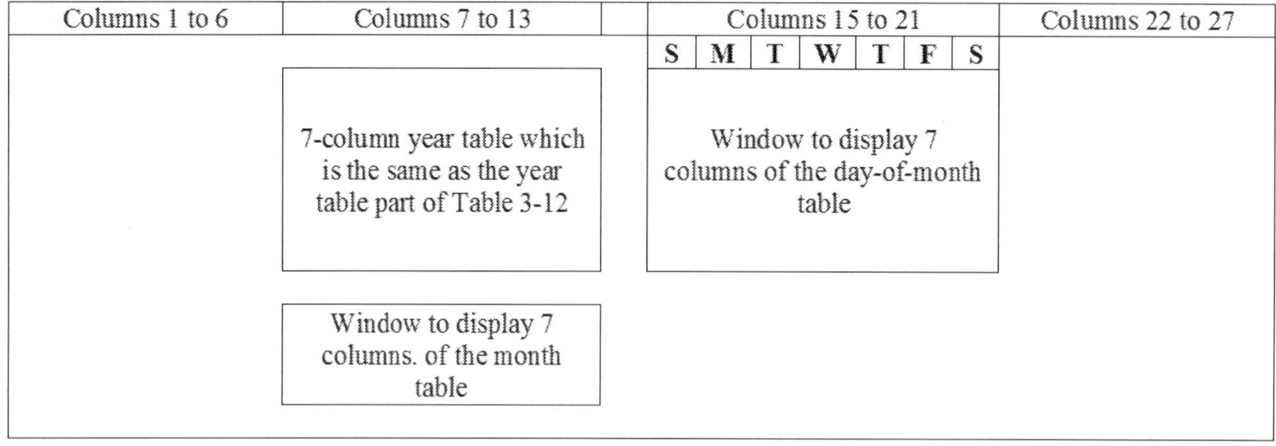
Columns 1 to 6
Columns 7 to 13
Columns 15 to 21
Columns 22 to 27
S M T W T F S
7-column year table which is the same as the year table part of Table 3-12
Window to display 7 columns of the day-of-month table
Window to display 7 columns. of the month table

13-column day-of-month table, which is the same as the day-of-month table part of Table 3-12 (also, the same as Table 3-1)

13-column month table, which is the same as the month table part of Table 3-12

Notes:

1. The slider is at the extreme left of its travel.
2. When the slider is at the extreme right of its travel, the right-hand edge of the slider is at the right-hand edge of column 27.
3. The face has 27 columns and the slider has 21.
4. The width of the face can be increased to 29 columns to provide space for a border on each end.
5. This calendar is set by putting the month under the column that has the year of interest.

## Table 3-14b
## Outline of Narrow Face Arrangement with a Blank Slider Shown below the Face

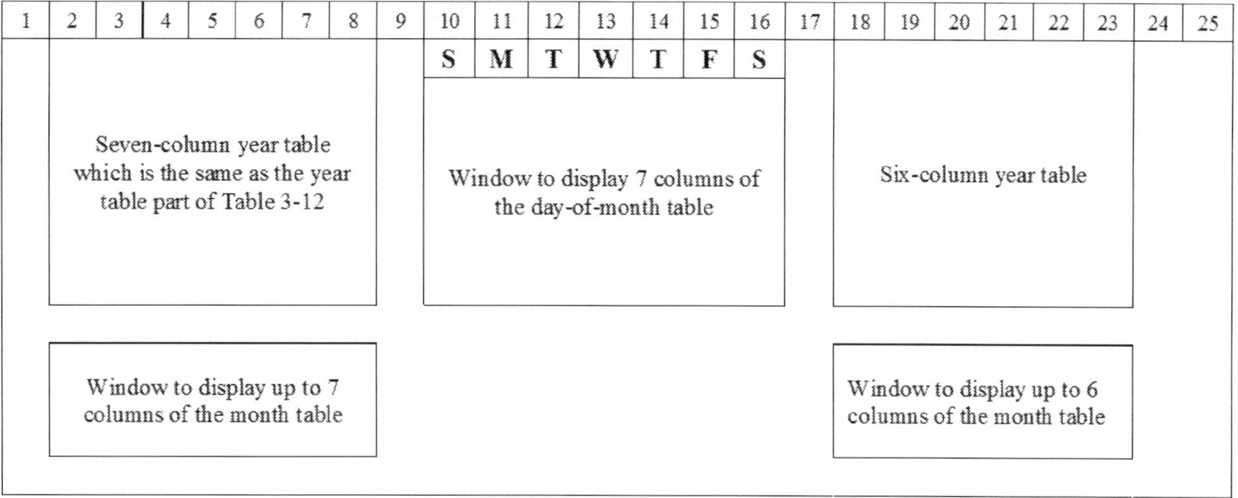
1
2
3
4
5
6
7
8
9
10
11
12
13
14
15
16
17
18
19
20
21
22
23
24
25
S
M
T
W
T
F
S
Seven-column year table which is the same as the year table part of Table 3-12
Window to display 7 columns of the day-of-month table
Six-column year table
Window to display up to 7 columns of the month table
Window to display up to 6 columns of the month table

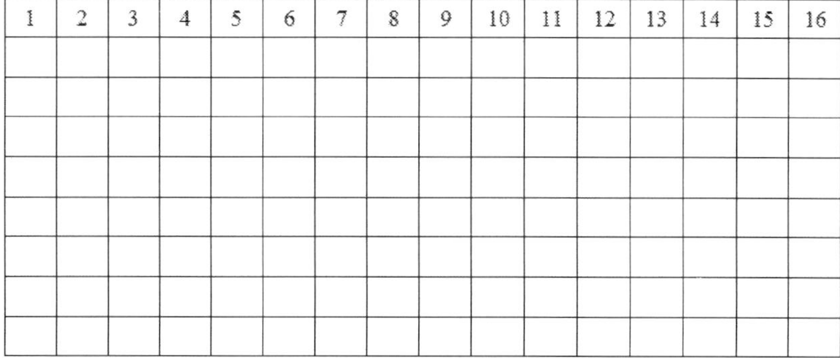
1
2
3
4
5
6
7
8
9
10
11
12
13
14
15
16

Notes:

1. The slider is at the extreme left of its travel.
2. When the slider is at the extreme right of its travel, the right-hand edge of the slider is at the right-hand edge of column 23.
3. The face has 25 columns and the slider has 16.
4. The face has one more column on the right than is needed so that the window is at the centre of the face.

The wide face in Table 3-14a is a simple rearrangement of Table 3-12. The year table is placed to the left of the day-of-month window instead of below it, and the month table is offset eight columns to the left from the day-of-month table. The window for the day-of-month table is not centred. For an application such as below an 8 × 10 inch picture frame, the wide face and off-centre day-of-month window may be acceptable and even desirable. However, for other applications, such as below a 5 × 7 inch picture frame, a narrower face would be preferred.

In Table 3-14b, the face is divided into columns that have the following functions. Column 1 is the left border; columns 2–8 are for a 7-column year table and a window below the year table; column 9 is a space; columns 10–16 are for the window that shows the applicable columns of the day-of-month table; column 17 is a space; columns 18–23 are for a second year table and a window below the year table; and columns 24–25 are the right border. The second year table is needed because there are seven columns of the month table below the left-hand year table only when the slider is at the extreme left of its travel.

In Table 3-14b with the slider in its far-left position, the part of the day-of-month table that shows is columns 9–15. This part has to have the same information as is in the window in Table 3-13. Therefore, the day-of-month table can be copied to the partially filled-in slider in Table 3-15. The same part of the month table that is visible above the years in Table 3-13 has to be visible below the years in Table 3-14b. Therefore, this part of the month table (which is the seven right-hand columns in Table 3-13) can be copied to columns 1–7 of the partially filled-in slider in Table 3-15.

**Table 3-15**
**Partially Filled-in Slider for Narrow Face Arrangement**

| 1 | 2 | 3 | 4 | 5 | 6 | 7 | 8 | 9 | 10 | 11 | 12 | 13 | 14 | 15 | 16 |
|---|---|---|---|---|---|---|---|---|---|---|---|---|---|---|---|
| | | | | | | | | 1 | 2 | 3 | 4 | 5 | 6 | 7 | |
| | | 2 | 3 | 4 | 5 | 6 | 7 | 8 | 9 | 10 | 11 | 12 | 13 | 14 | |
| | | 9 | 10 | 11 | 12 | 13 | 14 | 15 | 16 | 17 | 18 | 19 | 20 | 21 | |
| | | 16 | 17 | 18 | 19 | 20 | 21 | 22 | 23 | 24 | 25 | 26 | 27 | 28 | |
| | | 23 | 24 | 25 | 26 | 27 | 28 | 29 | 30 | 31 | | | | | |
| | | 30 | 31 | | | | | | | | | | | | |
| L yr | **Jan.** | L yr | L yr | L yr | **Feb.** | L yr | | | | | | | | | |
| Oct. | Apr. | Sep. | June | Mar. | Aug. | May | | | | | | | | | |
| | July | Dec. | | Nov. | | | | | | | | | | | |
| Jan. | C yr | C yr | C yr | Feb. | C yr | C yr | | | | | | | | | |

Note: *Jan.* and *Feb.* are in boldface in the top row of the month part of the table to indicate that they are associated with leap years.

To fill in the rest of the slider, move it one column to the right. Column 1 of the slider is now under column 3 of the face, and column 16 of the slider is under column 18 of the face. The month table is blank under the years in column 2 of the face. At all positions of the slider, there must be months associated with the years in every column. Since there are no months associated with the years in column 2 of the face, make a second year table to the right of the day-of-month window, and put a second month table window below this year table. In column 18 of the face, write the same years as are in column 2. To fill in the months in column 16 of the slider, refer back to Table 3-13 and imagine that the slider is moved one column to the right.

In this position, the month of *May* is over the years that are in columns 2 and 18 on the face. Write *May* in column 16 on the bottom part of the slider, and note that *May* is also in column 7 of the slider. Move the slider one more column to the right and repeat the above process, this time filling in column 19 on the face and column 15 on the bottom part of the slider. In this case, the years in column 3 of the face are written in column 19 of the face, and the months in column 6 of the slider are written in column 15 of the slider. Doing this process a total of six times yields the slider in Table 3-16 and the year table in Table 3-17b. When a slider is made for a calendar, the top row in Table 3-16, which indicates the column numbers, is usually not included so as to minimize the height. See Figures 5-3e, 5-7b and 5-18 for calendars that use Tables 3-16 and 3-17.

### Table 3-16
### Completed Slider for Narrow-Face Single-Slider Calendar with Side Year Tables

| 1 | 2 | 3 | 4 | 5 | 6 | 7 | 8 | 9 | 10 | 11 | 12 | 13 | 14 | 15 | 16 |
|---|---|---|---|---|---|---|---|---|---|---|---|---|---|---|---|
| | | | | | | | | 1 | 2 | 3 | 4 | 5 | 6 | 7 | |
| | | 2 | 3 | 4 | 5 | 6 | 7 | 8 | 9 | 10 | 11 | 12 | 13 | 14 | |
| | | 9 | 10 | 11 | 12 | 13 | 14 | 15 | 16 | 17 | 18 | 19 | 20 | 21 | |
| | | 16 | 17 | 18 | 19 | 20 | 21 | 22 | 23 | 24 | 25 | 26 | 27 | 28 | |
| | | 23 | 24 | 25 | 26 | 27 | 28 | 29 | 30 | 31 | | | | | |
| | | 30 | 31 | | | | | | | | | | | | |
| L yr | **Jan.** | L yr | L yr | L yr | **Feb.** | L yr | | | | **Jan.** | L yr | L yr | L yr | **Feb.** | L yr |
| Oct. | Apr. | Sep. | June | Mar. | Aug. | May | | | | Apr. | Sep. | June | Mar. | Aug. | May |
| | July | Dec. | | Nov. | | | | | | July | Dec. | | Nov. | | |
| Jan. | C yr | C yr | C yr | Feb. | C yr | C yr | | | | C yr | C yr | C yr | Feb. | C yr | C yr |

Note: *Jan.* and *Feb.* are in boldface in the top row of the month part of the table to indicate that they are associated with leap years.

**Table 3-17**
**Year Tables for Narrow-Face Single-Slider Calendar with Side Year Tables When March through December Are Shared between Common Years and Leap Years**

**a. Year table on left side of window**

| | | | | | | |
|---|---|---|---|---|---|---|
| **2000** | 2001 | 2002 | 2003 | 2009 | **2004** | 2005 |
| 2006 | 2007 | 2013 | **2008** | 2015 | 2010 | 2011 |
| 2017 | **2012** | 2019 | 2014 | **2020** | 2021 | **2016** |
| 2023 | 2018 | **2024** | 2025 | 2026 | 2027 | 2022 |
| **2028** | 2029 | 2030 | 2031 | 2037 | **2032** | 2033 |
| 2034 | 2035 | 2041 | **2036** | 2043 | 2038 | 2039 |
| 2045 | **2040** | 2047 | 2042 | **2048** | 2049 | **2044** |
| 2051 | 2046 | **2052** | 2053 | 2054 | 2055 | 2050 |
| **2056** | 2057 | 2058 | 2059 | 2065 | **2060** | 2061 |
| 2062 | 2063 | 2069 | **2064** | 2071 | 2066 | 2067 |
| 2073 | **2068** | 2075 | 2070 | **2076** | 2077 | **2072** |
| 2079 | 2074 | **2080** | 2081 | 2082 | 2083 | 2078 |
| **2084** | 2085 | 2086 | 2087 | 2093 | **2088** | 2089 |
| 2090 | 2091 | 2097 | **2092** | 2099 | 2094 | 2095 |
| | **2096** | | 2098 | | | |

**b. Year table on right side of window**

| | | | | | |
|---|---|---|---|---|---|
| **2000** | 2001 | 2002 | 2003 | 2009 | **2004** |
| 2006 | 2007 | 2013 | **2008** | 2015 | 2010 |
| 2017 | **2012** | 2019 | 2014 | **2020** | 2021 |
| 2023 | 2018 | **2024** | 2025 | 2026 | 2027 |
| **2028** | 2029 | 2030 | 2031 | 2037 | **2032** |
| 2034 | 2035 | 2041 | **2036** | 2043 | 2038 |
| 2045 | **2040** | 2047 | 2042 | **2048** | 2049 |
| 2051 | 2046 | **2052** | 2053 | 2054 | 2055 |
| **2056** | 2057 | 2058 | 2059 | 2065 | **2060** |
| 2062 | 2063 | 2069 | **2064** | 2071 | 2066 |
| 2073 | **2068** | 2075 | 2070 | **2076** | 2077 |
| 2079 | 2074 | **2080** | 2081 | 2082 | 2083 |
| **2084** | 2085 | 2086 | 2087 | 2093 | **2088** |
| 2090 | 2091 | 2097 | **2092** | 2099 | 2094 |
| | **2096** | | 2098 | | |

Note: Leap years are in boldface.

The following procedure is used to add years not shown to Tables 3-17a and 3-17b:

1. Imagine that the columns in Table 3-17a are labeled *Sunday* to *Saturday* from left to right and the columns in Table 3-17b are labeled *Sunday* to *Friday*.
2. If the year is a common year, enter it in Table 3-17a under the day of the week that January 1 falls on. If January 1 falls on Sunday to Friday, also enter the year in Table 3-17b.
3. If the year is a leap year, enter it in Table 3-17a under the day of the week *after* the day of the week that January 1 falls on. If the day of the week *after* the day of the week that January 1 falls on is Sunday to Friday, also enter the year in Table 3-17b.

## Single-Slider Vertical Calendar

Table 3-18 shows a single-sheet perpetual calendar with one slider in a vertical arrangement. The slider is between a year table and lines numbered 1 to 31. The slider moves up and down, and has the days of the week (Sun. to Sat.) repeated as many times as required. The slider also has a month table on it. The calendar is set at the beginning of each month by simply moving the slider to line up the month with the applicable year in the year table. The basic principle of this vertical calendar is the same as the one for Table 3-12.

The following indicate how the calendar in Table 3-18 is different from the one in Table 3-12:

1. The slider moves vertically instead of horizontally.
2. The day-of-month table is a single column with the numbers 1 to 31 (instead of a 13-column, 6-row table).
3. The day-of-the-week table is a column with *Sun.* to *Sat.* repeated five times, plus *Sun.* and *Mon.* at the end, whereas in Table 3-12 this table is a row, with *SMTWTFS* entered only once. The day-of-the-week table has 37 entries, which is an entry for every day of a 31-day month, plus 6 entries to allow for the slider to be in its starting position and in 6 additional positions.
4. The month table has 4 columns and 13 rows (instead of 13 columns and 4 rows).
5. The year table presents the years in 7 rows instead of in 7 columns. (Table 3-18 shows only 30 years, compared to 100 in Table 3-12. Columns can be added to Table 3-18 to show more years.)
6. The day-of-the-week table and the month table move relative to the day-of-the-month table and the year table. (In Table 3-12, the day-of-the-month table and the month table move relative to the day-of-the-week table and the year table.)

The first five differences accommodate the change from horizontal orientation to vertical orientation. The last difference is a deviation from Table 3-12 in that different tables are paired. This is arbitrary. The year table could be on the slider instead of the month table and then the pairing would be the same. If this were done, then the slider would be wider, as the year table is wider than the month table. However, the overall width would be the same. See Figures 5-16a and 5-16b for calendars based on Table 3-18.

**Table 3-18**
**Single-Slider Vertical Calendar**

| Applicable years, 20__ | | | | | | | | | | |
|---|---|---|---|---|---|---|---|---|---|---|
| Leap years are in boldface | | | | | **L yr** | All years | | C yr | Sun | 1 |
| | 05 | 11 | **16** | 22 | | May | | | Mon | 2 |
| | **04** | 10 | 21 | 27 | **Feb** | Aug | | | Tue | 3 |
| | 09 | 15 | **20** | 26 | | Mar | Nov | Feb | Wed | 4 |
| 03 | **08** | 14 | 25 | 31 | | Jun | | | Thu | 5 |
| | 02 | 13 | 19 | **24** | | Sep | Dec | | Fri | 6 |
| 01 | 07 | **12** | 18 | 29 | **Jan** | Apr | Jul | | Sat | 7 |
| | **00** | 06 | 17 | 23 | | Oct | | Jan | Sun | 8 |
| | | | | | | May | | | Mon | 9 |
| | | | | | **Feb** | Aug | | | Tue | 10 |
| | | | | | | Mar | Nov | Feb | Wed | 11 |
| | | | | | | Jun | | | Thu | 12 |
| | | | | | | Sep | Dec | | Fri | 13 |
| | | | | | **Jan** | Apr | Jul | | Sat | 14 |
| | | | | | **L yr** | All years | | C yr | Sun | 15 |
| | | | | | | | | | Mon | 16 |
| | | | | | | | | | Tue | 17 |
| | | | | | | | | | Wed | 18 |
| | | | | | | | | | Thu | 19 |
| | | | | | | | | | Fri | 20 |
| | | | | | | | | | Sat | 21 |
| | | | | | | | | | Sun | 22 |
| | | | | | | | | | Mon | 23 |
| | | | | | | | | | Tue | 24 |
| | | | | | | | | | Wed | 25 |
| | | | | | | | | | Thu | 26 |
| | | | | | | | | | Fri | 27 |
| | | | | | | | | | Sat | 28 |
| | | | | | | | | | Sun | 29 |
| | | | | | | | | | Mon | 30 |
| | | | | | | | | | Tue | 31 |
| | | | | | | | | | Wed | |
| | | | | | | | | | Thu | |
| | | | | | | | | | Fri | |
| | | | | | | | | | Sat | |
| | | | | | | | | | Sun | |
| | | | | | | | | | Mon | |

INSTRUCTIONS

1. Move slider up and down to put month beside year.
2. Use left-hand side of slider for January and February in leap years and right-hand side for common years.
3. Ignore 29, 30 and 31 when applicable.

Note: The section with the thick outline is a slider that moves up and down. It is shown in its lowest position. This is the setting for January and October in 2017.

The following procedure is used to add years not shown to Table 3-18:

1. Imagine that the rows in the year table are labeled *Saturday* to *Sunday* from top to bottom.
2. If the year is a common year, then enter it beside the day of the week that January 1 falls on.
3. If the year is a leap year, then enter it beside the day of the week *after* the day of the week that January 1 falls on.

## Variations of the Single-Sheet Perpetual Calendar

The tables developed in this chapter can be used to make the following variations of the single-sheet perpetual calendar:

1. Dual-slider, which has the year table beside the day-of-month window. (Use Tables 3-1, 3-8 and 3-9.)
2. Dual-slider, which has the year table above the day-of-month window. (Use Tables 3-1, 3-8 and 3-9. Modify Table 3-8 so that the marker is in the same column as January common year.)
3. Single-slider, with the year table below the day-of-month window and the slider. (Use Table 3-12 for the month and year tables. The year table in Table 3-12 is Table 3-9b. If preferred, Table 3-9a or 3-9c can be used instead.)
4. Single-slider, with the year table above the day-of-month window and the slider. (Use Table 3-12 with the slider modified so that the month table is above the day-of-month table instead of below it.)
5. Single-slider, with year tables beside the day-of-month window. (Use Tables 3-16 and 3-17.)
6. Single-slider vertical calendar. (Use Table 3-18.)

Note that all of these variations have March through December in the month table being the same for common and leap years. Other than Table 3-1, all of the tables referred to in these variations are either Table 3-8 for the month table, or 3-9 for the year table or derivations of them. Similar calendars can be made using Table 3-6a or 3-6b as the month table and Table 3-7 as the year table, or derivations of them. When these tables are used, all the months in the month table for common years are separate from the ones for leap years.

The single-slider design with the year table below or above the slider is ideal for a simple desk calendar where height is not a concern. The dual-slider design with the year table to one side requires less height and is preferred when a picture is above the calendar or key hooks are below it. An advantage of the dual-slider design over the single-slider design is that once the month slider is set for the year of interest, the day of the week that the first of each month falls on is displayed. Where minimum height is desired, the single-slider design with year table(s) beside the day-of-month window is an alternative to the dual-slider design. The single-slider vertical calendar can be used for planners, wall calendars and lamps. See Chapter 5 for various applications of these six variations.

# CHAPTER 4

# TABLES FOR MULTISHEET AND FULL-YEAR PERPETUAL CALENDARS

## Day-of-Month Tables for Every Month

This chapter shows how the unique tables for the multisheet perpetual calendar with a year table on each sheet, the multisheet perpetual calendar with a single year table and the full-year perpetual calendar are developed. Readers who are not interested in the theory behind these calendars can skip this chapter and go on to Chapters 6, 7 and 8 to see working tables and applications.

The basic building block is the 13-column day-of-month table (Table 3-1). The table for January is the same as in Table 3-1. The tables for the other months are offset from January according to which day of the week the first of the month is on relative to January 1. For example, when January 1 is on a Sunday, February 1 is on a Wednesday. In Table 3-1, the *1* is in the centre column (column 7). For February, the *1* appears three columns further right, which is column 10. Tables 4-1 and 4-2 have the day-of-month tables for common and leap years, respectively.

**Table 4-1**
**Day-of-Month Tables for a Common Year**

January

| | | | | | | | | | | | | |
|---|---|---|---|---|---|---|---|---|---|---|---|---|
| | | | | | | 1 | 2 | 3 | 4 | 5 | 6 | 7 |
| 2 | 3 | 4 | 5 | 6 | 7 | 8 | 9 | 10 | 11 | 12 | 13 | 14 |
| 9 | 10 | 11 | 12 | 13 | 14 | 15 | 16 | 17 | 18 | 19 | 20 | 21 |
| 16 | 17 | 18 | 19 | 20 | 21 | 22 | 23 | 24 | 25 | 26 | 27 | 28 |
| 23 | 24 | 25 | 26 | 27 | 28 | 29 | 30 | 31 | | | | |
| 30 | 31 | | | | | | | | | | | |
| | | | | | | | | | | | | |

February

| | | | | | | | | | | | | |
|---|---|---|---|---|---|---|---|---|---|---|---|---|
| | | | | | | | | | 1 | 2 | 3 | 4 |
| | | 1 | 2 | 3 | 4 | 5 | 6 | 7 | 8 | 9 | 10 | 11 |
| 6 | 7 | 8 | 9 | 10 | 11 | 12 | 13 | 14 | 15 | 16 | 17 | 18 |
| 13 | 14 | 15 | 16 | 17 | 18 | 19 | 20 | 21 | 22 | 23 | 24 | 25 |
| 20 | 21 | 22 | 23 | 24 | 25 | 26 | 27 | 28 | | | | |
| 27 | 28 | | | | | | | | | | | |
| | | | | | | | | | | | | |

March

| | | | | | | | | | | | | |
|---|---|---|---|---|---|---|---|---|---|---|---|---|
| | | | | | | | | | 1 | 2 | 3 | 4 |
| | | 1 | 2 | 3 | 4 | 5 | 6 | 7 | 8 | 9 | 10 | 11 |
| 6 | 7 | 8 | 9 | 10 | 11 | 12 | 13 | 14 | 15 | 16 | 17 | 18 |
| 13 | 14 | 15 | 16 | 17 | 18 | 19 | 20 | 21 | 22 | 23 | 24 | 25 |
| 20 | 21 | 22 | 23 | 24 | 25 | 26 | 27 | 28 | 29 | 30 | 31 | |
| 27 | 28 | 29 | 30 | 31 | | | | | | | | |
| | | | | | | | | | | | | |

April

| | | | | | | | | | | | | |
|---|---|---|---|---|---|---|---|---|---|---|---|---|
| | | | | | | | | | | | | 1 |
| | | | | | 1 | 2 | 3 | 4 | 5 | 6 | 7 | 8 |
| 3 | 4 | 5 | 6 | 7 | 8 | 9 | 10 | 11 | 12 | 13 | 14 | 15 |
| 10 | 11 | 12 | 13 | 14 | 15 | 16 | 17 | 18 | 19 | 20 | 21 | 22 |
| 17 | 18 | 19 | 20 | 21 | 22 | 23 | 24 | 25 | 26 | 27 | 28 | 29 |
| 24 | 25 | 26 | 27 | 28 | 29 | 30 | | | | | | |
| | | | | | | | | | | | | |

May

| | | | | | | | | | | | | |
|---|---|---|---|---|---|---|---|---|---|---|---|---|
| | | | | | | | 1 | 2 | 3 | 4 | 5 | 6 |
| 1 | 2 | 3 | 4 | 5 | 6 | 7 | 8 | 9 | 10 | 11 | 12 | 13 |
| 8 | 9 | 10 | 11 | 12 | 13 | 14 | 15 | 16 | 17 | 18 | 19 | 20 |
| 15 | 16 | 17 | 18 | 19 | 20 | 21 | 22 | 23 | 24 | 25 | 26 | 27 |
| 22 | 23 | 24 | 25 | 26 | 27 | 28 | 29 | 30 | 31 | | | |
| 29 | 30 | 31 | | | | | | | | | | |
| | | | | | | | | | | | | |

June

| | | | | | | | | | | | | |
|---|---|---|---|---|---|---|---|---|---|---|---|---|
| | | | | | | | | | | 1 | 2 | 3 |
| | | | 1 | 2 | 3 | 4 | 5 | 6 | 7 | 8 | 9 | 10 |
| 5 | 6 | 7 | 8 | 9 | 10 | 11 | 12 | 13 | 14 | 15 | 16 | 17 |
| 12 | 13 | 14 | 15 | 16 | 17 | 18 | 19 | 20 | 21 | 22 | 23 | 24 |
| 19 | 20 | 21 | 22 | 23 | 24 | 25 | 26 | 27 | 28 | 29 | 30 | |
| 26 | 27 | 28 | 29 | 30 | | | | | | | | |
| | | | | | | | | | | | | |

July

| | | | | | | | | | | | | |
|---|---|---|---|---|---|---|---|---|---|---|---|---|
| | | | | | | | | | | | | 1 |
| | | | | | 1 | 2 | 3 | 4 | 5 | 6 | 7 | 8 |
| 3 | 4 | 5 | 6 | 7 | 8 | 9 | 10 | 11 | 12 | 13 | 14 | 15 |
| 10 | 11 | 12 | 13 | 14 | 15 | 16 | 17 | 18 | 19 | 20 | 21 | 22 |
| 17 | 18 | 19 | 20 | 21 | 22 | 23 | 24 | 25 | 26 | 27 | 28 | 29 |
| 24 | 25 | 26 | 27 | 28 | 29 | 30 | 31 | | | | | |
| 31 | | | | | | | | | | | | |

August

| | | | | | | | | | | | | |
|---|---|---|---|---|---|---|---|---|---|---|---|---|
| | | | | | | | | 1 | 2 | 3 | 4 | 5 |
| | 1 | 2 | 3 | 4 | 5 | 6 | 7 | 8 | 9 | 10 | 11 | 12 |
| 7 | 8 | 9 | 10 | 11 | 12 | 13 | 14 | 15 | 16 | 17 | 18 | 19 |
| 14 | 15 | 16 | 17 | 18 | 19 | 20 | 21 | 22 | 23 | 24 | 25 | 26 |
| 21 | 22 | 23 | 24 | 25 | 26 | 27 | 28 | 29 | 30 | 31 | | |
| 28 | 29 | 30 | 31 | | | | | | | | | |
| | | | | | | | | | | | | |

September

| | | | | | | | | | | | 1 | 2 |
|---|---|---|---|---|---|---|---|---|---|---|---|---|
| | | | | 1 | 2 | 3 | 4 | 5 | 6 | 7 | 8 | 9 |
| 4 | 5 | 6 | 7 | 8 | 9 | 10 | 11 | 12 | 13 | 14 | 15 | 16 |
| 11 | 12 | 13 | 14 | 15 | 16 | 17 | 18 | 19 | 20 | 21 | 22 | 23 |
| 18 | 19 | 20 | 21 | 22 | 23 | 24 | 25 | 26 | 27 | 28 | 29 | 30 |
| 25 | 26 | 27 | 28 | 29 | 30 | | | | | | | |
| | | | | | | | | | | | | |

October

| | | | | | | 1 | 2 | 3 | 4 | 5 | 6 | 7 |
|---|---|---|---|---|---|---|---|---|---|---|---|---|
| 2 | 3 | 4 | 5 | 6 | 7 | 8 | 9 | 10 | 11 | 12 | 13 | 14 |
| 9 | 10 | 11 | 12 | 13 | 14 | 15 | 16 | 17 | 18 | 19 | 20 | 21 |
| 16 | 17 | 18 | 19 | 20 | 21 | 22 | 23 | 24 | 25 | 26 | 27 | 28 |
| 23 | 24 | 25 | 26 | 27 | 28 | 29 | 30 | 31 | | | | |
| 30 | 31 | | | | | | | | | | | |
| | | | | | | | | | | | | |

November

| | | | | | | | | | 1 | 2 | 3 | 4 |
|---|---|---|---|---|---|---|---|---|---|---|---|---|
| | | 1 | 2 | 3 | 4 | 5 | 6 | 7 | 8 | 9 | 10 | 11 |
| 6 | 7 | 8 | 9 | 10 | 11 | 12 | 13 | 14 | 15 | 16 | 17 | 18 |
| 13 | 14 | 15 | 16 | 17 | 18 | 19 | 20 | 21 | 22 | 23 | 24 | 25 |
| 20 | 21 | 22 | 23 | 24 | 25 | 26 | 27 | 28 | 29 | 30 | | |
| 27 | 28 | 29 | 30 | | | | | | | | | |
| | | | | | | | | | | | | |

December

| | | | | | | | | | | | 1 | 2 |
|---|---|---|---|---|---|---|---|---|---|---|---|---|
| | | | | 1 | 2 | 3 | 4 | 5 | 6 | 7 | 8 | 9 |
| 4 | 5 | 6 | 7 | 8 | 9 | 10 | 11 | 12 | 13 | 14 | 15 | 16 |
| 11 | 12 | 13 | 14 | 15 | 16 | 17 | 18 | 19 | 20 | 21 | 22 | 23 |
| 18 | 19 | 20 | 21 | 22 | 23 | 24 | 25 | 26 | 27 | 28 | 29 | 30 |
| 25 | 26 | 27 | 28 | 29 | 30 | 31 | | | | | | |
| | | | | | | | | | | | | |

**Table 4-2**
**Day-of-Month Tables for a Leap Year**

January

| | | | | | | 1 | 2 | 3 | 4 | 5 | 6 | 7 |
|---|---|---|---|---|---|---|---|---|---|---|---|---|
| 2 | 3 | 4 | 5 | 6 | 7 | 8 | 9 | 10 | 11 | 12 | 13 | 14 |
| 9 | 10 | 11 | 12 | 13 | 14 | 15 | 16 | 17 | 18 | 19 | 20 | 21 |
| 16 | 17 | 18 | 19 | 20 | 21 | 22 | 23 | 24 | 25 | 26 | 27 | 28 |
| 23 | 24 | 25 | 26 | 27 | 28 | 29 | 30 | 31 | | | | |
| 30 | 31 | | | | | | | | | | | |
| | | | | | | | | | | | | |

February

| | | | | | | | | | 1 | 2 | 3 | 4 |
|---|---|---|---|---|---|---|---|---|---|---|---|---|
| | | 1 | 2 | 3 | 4 | 5 | 6 | 7 | 8 | 9 | 10 | 11 |
| 6 | 7 | 8 | 9 | 10 | 11 | 12 | 13 | 14 | 15 | 16 | 17 | 18 |
| 13 | 14 | 15 | 16 | 17 | 18 | 19 | 20 | 21 | 22 | 23 | 24 | 25 |
| 20 | 21 | 22 | 23 | 24 | 25 | 26 | 27 | 28 | 29 | | | |
| 27 | 28 | 29 | | | | | | | | | | |
| | | | | | | | | | | | | |

March

| | | | | | | | | | | 1 | 2 | 3 |
|---|---|---|---|---|---|---|---|---|---|---|---|---|
| | | | 1 | 2 | 3 | 4 | 5 | 6 | 7 | 8 | 9 | 10 |
| 5 | 6 | 7 | 8 | 9 | 10 | 11 | 12 | 13 | 14 | 15 | 16 | 17 |
| 12 | 13 | 14 | 15 | 16 | 17 | 18 | 19 | 20 | 21 | 22 | 23 | 24 |
| 19 | 20 | 21 | 22 | 23 | 24 | 25 | 26 | 27 | 28 | 29 | 30 | 31 |
| 26 | 27 | 28 | 29 | 30 | 31 | | | | | | | |
| | | | | | | | | | | | | |

April

| | | | | | | 1 | 2 | 3 | 4 | 5 | 6 | 7 |
|---|---|---|---|---|---|---|---|---|---|---|---|---|
| 2 | 3 | 4 | 5 | 6 | 7 | 8 | 9 | 10 | 11 | 12 | 13 | 14 |
| 9 | 10 | 11 | 12 | 13 | 14 | 15 | 16 | 17 | 18 | 19 | 20 | 21 |
| 16 | 17 | 18 | 19 | 20 | 21 | 22 | 23 | 24 | 25 | 26 | 27 | 28 |
| 23 | 24 | 25 | 26 | 27 | 28 | 29 | 30 | | | | | |
| 30 | | | | | | | | | | | | |
| | | | | | | | | | | | | |

May

| | | | | | | | | 1 | 2 | 3 | 4 | 5 |
|---|---|---|---|---|---|---|---|---|---|---|---|---|
| | 1 | 2 | 3 | 4 | 5 | 6 | 7 | 8 | 9 | 10 | 11 | 12 |
| 7 | 8 | 9 | 10 | 11 | 12 | 13 | 14 | 15 | 16 | 17 | 18 | 19 |
| 14 | 15 | 16 | 17 | 18 | 19 | 20 | 21 | 22 | 23 | 24 | 25 | 26 |
| 21 | 22 | 23 | 24 | 25 | 26 | 27 | 28 | 29 | 30 | 31 | | |
| 28 | 29 | 30 | 31 | | | | | | | | | |
| | | | | | | | | | | | | |

June

| | | | | | | | | | | | 1 | 2 |
|---|---|---|---|---|---|---|---|---|---|---|---|---|
| | | | | 1 | 2 | 3 | 4 | 5 | 6 | 7 | 8 | 9 |
| 4 | 5 | 6 | 7 | 8 | 9 | 10 | 11 | 12 | 13 | 14 | 15 | 16 |
| 11 | 12 | 13 | 14 | 15 | 16 | 17 | 18 | 19 | 20 | 21 | 22 | 23 |
| 18 | 19 | 20 | 21 | 22 | 23 | 24 | 25 | 26 | 27 | 28 | 29 | 30 |
| 25 | 26 | 27 | 28 | 29 | 30 | | | | | | | |
| | | | | | | | | | | | | |

July

| | | | | | | 1 | 2 | 3 | 4 | 5 | 6 | 7 |
|---|---|---|---|---|---|---|---|---|---|---|---|---|
| 2 | 3 | 4 | 5 | 6 | 7 | 8 | 9 | 10 | 11 | 12 | 13 | 14 |
| 9 | 10 | 11 | 12 | 13 | 14 | 15 | 16 | 17 | 18 | 19 | 20 | 21 |
| 16 | 17 | 18 | 19 | 20 | 21 | 22 | 23 | 24 | 25 | 26 | 27 | 28 |
| 23 | 24 | 25 | 26 | 27 | 28 | 29 | 30 | 31 | | | | |
| 30 | 31 | | | | | | | | | | | |
| | | | | | | | | | | | | |

August

| | | | | | | | | | 1 | 2 | 3 | 4 |
|---|---|---|---|---|---|---|---|---|---|---|---|---|
| | | 1 | 2 | 3 | 4 | 5 | 6 | 7 | 8 | 9 | 10 | 11 |
| 6 | 7 | 8 | 9 | 10 | 11 | 12 | 13 | 14 | 15 | 16 | 17 | 18 |
| 13 | 14 | 15 | 16 | 17 | 18 | 19 | 20 | 21 | 22 | 23 | 24 | 25 |
| 20 | 21 | 22 | 23 | 24 | 25 | 26 | 27 | 28 | 29 | 30 | 31 | |
| 27 | 28 | 29 | 30 | 31 | | | | | | | | |
| | | | | | | | | | | | | |

September

| | | | | | | | | | | | | 1 |
|---|---|---|---|---|---|---|---|---|---|---|---|---|
| | | | | | 1 | 2 | 3 | 4 | 5 | 6 | 7 | 8 |
| 3 | 4 | 5 | 6 | 7 | 8 | 9 | 10 | 11 | 12 | 13 | 14 | 15 |
| 10 | 11 | 12 | 13 | 14 | 15 | 16 | 17 | 18 | 19 | 20 | 21 | 22 |
| 17 | 18 | 19 | 20 | 21 | 22 | 23 | 24 | 25 | 26 | 27 | 28 | 29 |
| 24 | 25 | 26 | 27 | 28 | 29 | 30 | | | | | | |
| | | | | | | | | | | | | |

October

| | | | | | | | 1 | 2 | 3 | 4 | 5 | 6 |
|---|---|---|---|---|---|---|---|---|---|---|---|---|
| 1 | 2 | 3 | 4 | 5 | 6 | 7 | 8 | 9 | 10 | 11 | 12 | 13 |
| 8 | 9 | 10 | 11 | 12 | 13 | 14 | 15 | 16 | 17 | 18 | 19 | 20 |
| 15 | 16 | 17 | 18 | 19 | 20 | 21 | 22 | 23 | 24 | 25 | 26 | 27 |
| 22 | 23 | 24 | 25 | 26 | 27 | 28 | 29 | 30 | 31 | | | |
| 29 | 30 | 31 | | | | | | | | | | |
| | | | | | | | | | | | | |

November

| | | | | | | | | | | 1 | 2 | 3 |
|---|---|---|---|---|---|---|---|---|---|---|---|---|
| | | | 1 | 2 | 3 | 4 | 5 | 6 | 7 | 8 | 9 | 10 |
| 5 | 6 | 7 | 8 | 9 | 10 | 11 | 12 | 13 | 14 | 15 | 16 | 17 |
| 12 | 13 | 14 | 15 | 16 | 17 | 18 | 19 | 20 | 21 | 22 | 23 | 24 |
| 19 | 20 | 21 | 22 | 23 | 24 | 25 | 26 | 27 | 28 | 29 | 30 | |
| 26 | 27 | 28 | 29 | 30 | | | | | | | | |
| | | | | | | | | | | | | |

December

| | | | | | | | | | | | | 1 |
|---|---|---|---|---|---|---|---|---|---|---|---|---|
| | | | | | 1 | 2 | 3 | 4 | 5 | 6 | 7 | 8 |
| 3 | 4 | 5 | 6 | 7 | 8 | 9 | 10 | 11 | 12 | 13 | 14 | 15 |
| 10 | 11 | 12 | 13 | 14 | 15 | 16 | 17 | 18 | 19 | 20 | 21 | 22 |
| 17 | 18 | 19 | 20 | 21 | 22 | 23 | 24 | 25 | 26 | 27 | 28 | 29 |
| 24 | 25 | 26 | 27 | 28 | 29 | 30 | 31 | | | | | |
| 31 | | | | | | | | | | | | |

Tables 4-1 and 4-2 are used for multisheet calendars where common years and leap years do not share any sheets. This is called the 24-sheet design. By following a procedure similar to that used to develop Table 3-7, the March–December sheets can be the same for both common and leap years. This is called the 14-sheet design. Table 4-3 shows the leap year day-of-month tables for January and February for the 14-sheet design. The remaining 12 sheets are the same as for the common year shown in Table 4-1. Since the day-of-month tables for January and February in Table 4-1 apply to common years only, these tables are renamed "January Common Year" and "February Common Year" in the 14-sheet design.

**Table 4-3**
**Leap Year Day-of-Month Tables for January and February for the 14-Sheet Design**

January Leap Year

| | | | | | | | | | | | | |
|---|---|---|---|---|---|---|---|---|---|---|---|---|
| | | | | | | | | | | | | 1 |
| | | | | | 1 | 2 | 3 | 4 | 5 | 6 | 7 | 8 |
| 3 | 4 | 5 | 6 | 7 | 8 | 9 | 10 | 11 | 12 | 13 | 14 | 15 |
| 10 | 11 | 12 | 13 | 14 | 15 | 16 | 17 | 18 | 19 | 20 | 21 | 22 |
| 17 | 18 | 19 | 20 | 21 | 22 | 23 | 24 | 25 | 26 | 27 | 28 | 29 |
| 24 | 25 | 26 | 27 | 28 | 29 | 30 | 31 | | | | | |
| 31 | | | | | | | | | | | | |

February Leap Year

| | | | | | | | | | | | | |
|---|---|---|---|---|---|---|---|---|---|---|---|---|
| | | | | | | | | 1 | 2 | 3 | 4 | 5 |
| | 1 | 2 | 3 | 4 | 5 | 6 | 7 | 8 | 9 | 10 | 11 | 12 |
| 7 | 8 | 9 | 10 | 11 | 12 | 13 | 14 | 15 | 16 | 17 | 18 | 19 |
| 14 | 15 | 16 | 17 | 18 | 19 | 20 | 21 | 22 | 23 | 24 | 25 | 26 |
| 21 | 22 | 23 | 24 | 25 | 26 | 27 | 28 | 29 | | | | |
| 28 | 29 | | | | | | | | | | | |
| | | | | | | | | | | | | |

## Development of the Year Table for the 24-Sheet Design

The preceding day-of-month tables can be used to make a multisheet perpetual calendar with a year table on each sheet. A window displays 7 of the 13 columns of the day-of-month table, and a marker on the window points to the column of the year table that has the years applicable to the window location. The year table that is used depends on whether the calendar is a 24-sheet design or a 14-sheet design. Table 4-4 illustrates the development of the year table for the 24-sheet design.

**Table 4-4**
**Development of the Year Table for the 24-Sheet Design**

| | | | | | | | | | | | | |
|---|---|---|---|---|---|---|---|---|---|---|---|---|
| | | | | | | | January | | | | | |
| | | | | | | | | | | | | |
| | | | | | | | | | | | | |
| | | | | | | | | | | | | |
| | | | | | | S | M | T | W | T | F | S |
| | | | | | | 1 | 2 | 3 | 4 | 5 | 6 | 7 |
| 2 | 3 | 4 | 5 | 6 | 7 | 8 | 9 | 10 | 11 | 12 | 13 | 14 |
| 9 | 10 | 11 | 12 | 13 | 14 | 15 | 16 | 17 | 18 | 19 | 20 | 21 |
| 16 | 17 | 18 | 19 | 20 | 21 | 22 | 23 | 24 | 25 | 26 | 27 | 28 |
| 23 | 24 | 25 | 26 | 27 | 28 | 29 | 30 | 31 | | | | |
| 30 | 31 | | | | | | | | | | | |
| | | | | | | | | | | | | |

Note: In the following discussion, the calendar sheets are assumed to be fixed and the window is assumed to move. An arrangement where the calendar sheets move and the window is fixed is also possible.

In Table 4-4, the blank cells at the top left are the year table, the shaded outline is the moving window and the table with the numbers is the day-of-month table for January from Table 4-1 or Table 4-2. The window is shown in its far-right position for January 1 falling on a Sunday. The marker above the cell that has *S* for "Sunday" points to a column in the year table. When January 1 is on a Sunday, the marker points to the far-right column of the year table. Therefore, the years when January 1 falls on a Sunday are entered in this column. When the window is moved one column to the left, the window is set for January 1 falling on a Monday. In this position, the marker points to the next to the far-right column. Therefore, the years when January 1 falls on a Monday are entered in this column. Similarly, the years when January 1 falls on a Tuesday are entered in the third column from the far-right column. Since there is one set of sheets for common years (based on Table 4-1) and another set for leap years (based on Table 4-2), only common years are shown in the year tables on common year sheets and only leap years are shown in the year tables on leap year sheets. Table 4-5 is a full 21st-century year table for common years, and Table 4-6 is the same for leap years. A comparison of Tables 4-5 and 4-6 with Table 3-7 shows that Table 3-7 has the order Sunday to Saturday from left to right, whereas Tables 4-5 and 4-6 have the reverse order.

**Table 4-5**
**Year Table for Common Year Sheets for the 24-Sheet Design**

| | 2010 | | 2003 | 2002 | 2001 | 2006 |
|---|---|---|---|---|---|---|
| 2005 | | 2009 | 2014 | | 2007 | |
| 2011 | 2021 | 2015 | | 2013 | 2018 | 2017 |
| 2022 | 2027 | 2026 | 2025 | 2019 | | 2023 |
| | 2038 | | 2031 | 2030 | 2029 | 2034 |
| 2033 | | 2037 | 2042 | | 2035 | |
| 2039 | 2049 | 2043 | | 2041 | 2046 | 2045 |
| 2050 | 2055 | 2054 | 2053 | 2047 | | 2051 |
| | 2066 | | 2059 | 2058 | 2057 | 2062 |
| 2061 | | 2065 | 2070 | | 2063 | |
| 2067 | 2077 | 2071 | | 2069 | 2074 | 2073 |
| 2078 | 2083 | 2082 | 2081 | 2075 | | 2079 |
| | 2094 | | 2087 | 2086 | 2085 | 2090 |
| 2089 | | 2093 | 2098 | | 2091 | |
| 2095 | | 2099 | | 2097 | | |

Note: Table 4-5 is constructed from Table 3-7 by reversing the order of the years and then deleting the leap years.

**Table 4-6**
**Year Table for Leap Year Sheets for the 24-Sheet Design**

| 2000 | | 2004 | | | | |
|---|---|---|---|---|---|---|
| | 2016 | | | 2008 | | 2012 |
| | | | 2020 | | | |
| | | | | | 2024 | |
| 2028 | | 2032 | | | | |
| | 2044 | | | 2036 | | 2040 |
| | | | 2048 | | | |
| | | | | | 2052 | |
| 2056 | | 2060 | | | | |
| | 2072 | | | 2064 | | 2068 |
| | | | 2076 | | | |
| | | | | | 2080 | |
| 2084 | | 2088 | | | | |
| | | | | 2092 | | 2096 |

Note: Table 4-6 is constructed from Table 3-7 by reversing the order of the years and then deleting the common years.

## Development of the Year Table for the 14-Sheet Design

The development of the year table for the 14-sheet design is similar to the development of the year table for the single-sheet perpetual calendar where March through December is the same for common years and leap years. (See discussion regarding Tables 3-8 and 3-9 in Chapter 3.) Therefore, in the year table for the 14-sheet design, leap years must be in a column corresponding to *one day later in the week than the actual day of the week for January 1.* Common years are in the same column. As previously noted, Tables 4-5 and 4-6 are the reverse order of Table 3-7. Therefore, the year table section of Table 3-12 can be reversed to make the year table for the 14-sheet design. Table 4-7 is the resulting table. In this table, the columns from left to right are labeled *Saturday* to *Sunday.* Common years are in the day-of-week column that January 1 falls on, and leap years are in the day-of-week column *after* the day that January 1 falls on. In Table 4-7, leap years are in boldface.

**Table 4-7**
**Year Table for the 14-Sheet Design, and for March through December for the 12-Sheet Design**

| | | | | | | |
|---|---|---|---|---|---|---|
| 2005 | **2004** | 2009 | 2003 | 2002 | 2001 | **2000** |
| 2011 | 2010 | 2015 | **2008** | 2013 | 2007 | 2006 |
| **2016** | 2021 | **2020** | 2014 | 2019 | **2012** | 2017 |
| 2022 | 2027 | 2026 | 2025 | **2024** | 2018 | 2023 |
| 2033 | **2032** | 2037 | 2031 | 2030 | 2029 | **2028** |
| 2039 | 2038 | 2043 | **2036** | 2041 | 2035 | 2034 |
| **2044** | 2049 | **2048** | 2042 | 2047 | **2040** | 2045 |
| 2050 | 2055 | 2054 | 2053 | **2052** | 2046 | 2051 |
| 2061 | **2060** | 2065 | 2059 | 2058 | 2057 | **2056** |
| 2067 | 2066 | 2071 | **2064** | 2069 | 2063 | 2062 |
| **2072** | 2077 | **2076** | 2070 | 2075 | **2068** | 2073 |
| 2078 | 2083 | 2082 | 2081 | **2080** | 2074 | 2079 |
| 2089 | **2088** | 2093 | 2087 | 2086 | 2085 | **2084** |
| 2095 | 2094 | 2099 | **2092** | 2097 | 2091 | 2090 |
| | | | 2098 | | **2096** | |

Note: Leap years are in boldface.

Table 4-7 in its entirety (or only part of it if the calendar covers less than the entire 21st century) is on each month sheet for March to December. On the January common year and February common year sheets, only the common years are listed. Similarly, on the January leap year and the February leap year sheets, only the leap years are listed.

For both the 24-sheet and 14-sheet designs, the marker on the window lines up with the same column on each day-of-month table for every month for both common and leap years. The appropriate day-of-month tables to account for common years and leap years must be used. As noted previously, Tables 4-1 and 4-2 are used for the 24-sheet design, and Tables 4-1 and 4-3 are used for the 14-sheet design.

## Development of the Year Table for the 12-Sheet Design

A 12-sheet design of the multisheet perpetual calendar with a year table on each sheet is possible. This design uses the common year day-of month tables in Table 4-1, with February having 29 days instead of 28. The 29th is ignored for common years. Since March through December is the same for the 12-sheet design as for the 14-sheet design, Table 4-7 is used as the year table for these months. This table makes the days from March 1 to December 31 one day later in the week than the year before for common years, and two days later in the week for leap years. (As previously noted, in Table 4-7 common years are in the day-of-week column that January 1 falls on and leap years are in the day-of-week column *after* the day that January 1 falls on.) The days in January and February in a leap year are only one day later in the week than in the year before. In the 14-sheet design, additional sheets are used specifically for January leap year and February leap year to enable using the same year table for the whole year. With the 12-sheet design, a different year table must be used for January and February. Table 4-8 is the table. In this table, the columns from left to right are labeled *Saturday* to *Sunday*. Common years are under the day-of-week column that January 1 falls on, and leap years are also under the day of the week that January 1 falls on. A comparison of Tables 4-7 and 4-8 shows that common years are in the same columns in both tables but that leap years are in different columns. In Table 4-7, leap years are under the day *after* the day of the week that January 1 falls on.

### Table 4-8
### Year Table for January and February for the 12-Sheet Design

| **2000** | 2010 | **2004** | 2003 | 2002 | 2001 | 2006 |
|---|---|---|---|---|---|---|
| 2005 | **2016** | 2009 | 2014 | **2008** | 2007 | **2012** |
| 2011 | 2021 | 2015 | **2020** | 2013 | 2018 | 2017 |
| 2022 | 2027 | 2026 | 2025 | 2019 | **2024** | 2023 |
| **2028** | 2038 | **2032** | 2031 | 2030 | 2029 | 2034 |
| 2033 | **2044** | 2037 | 2042 | **2036** | 2035 | **2040** |
| 2039 | 2049 | 2043 | **2048** | 2041 | 2046 | 2045 |
| 2050 | 2055 | 2054 | 2053 | 2047 | **2052** | 2051 |
| **2056** | 2066 | **2060** | 2059 | 2058 | 2057 | 2062 |
| 2061 | **2072** | 2065 | 2070 | **2064** | 2063 | **2068** |
| 2067 | 2077 | 2071 | **2076** | 2069 | 2074 | 2073 |
| 2078 | 2083 | 2082 | 2081 | 2075 | **2080** | 2079 |
| **2084** | 2094 | **2088** | 2087 | 2086 | 2085 | 2090 |
| 2089 | | 2093 | 2098 | **2092** | 2091 | **2096** |
| 2095 | | 2099 | | 2097 | | |

Note: Leap years are in boldface.

A characteristic of the 12-sheet design is that the marker on the window lines up with the same column in the year table on each day-of-month sheet for every month for common years. In leap years, it lines up with one column for January and February and a column corresponding to one day later in the week for March to December. Thus, in a leap year, the window has to be moved on both January 1 and March 1.

Reducing the number of sheets saves material and simplifies design. However, if each sheet has a picture, the 24-sheet design provides a change in pictures for leap years. The 14-sheet design provides some variety with different sheets for January and February in leap years. See Chapter 6 for various applications of the multisheet perpetual calendar with a year table on each sheet.

## Multisheet Calendar with a Single Year Table—14 Sheets

On the multisheet calendars with a single year table, each sheet has a day-of-month table only. The process for developing the single year table is similar to the process used in Chapter 3 to develop the year tables for the single-sheet calendar.

Table 4-9 is the year table for the 14-sheet design of the multisheet calendar with a single year table. This table is the same as Table 3-9b and is the mirror image of Table 4-7. See Figures 7-1b, 7-1c and 7-1d in Chapter 7 for an example of this calendar.

**Table 4-9**
**Year Table for the Multisheet Calendar with a Single Year Table—14 Sheets**

| | | | | | | |
|---|---|---|---|---|---|---|
| **2000** | 2001 | 2002 | 2003 | 2009 | **2004** | 2005 |
| 2006 | 2007 | 2013 | **2008** | 2015 | 2010 | 2011 |
| 2017 | **2012** | 2019 | 2014 | **2020** | 2021 | **2016** |
| 2023 | 2018 | **2024** | 2025 | 2026 | 2027 | 2022 |
| **2028** | 2029 | 2030 | 2031 | 2037 | **2032** | 2033 |
| 2034 | 2035 | 2041 | **2036** | 2043 | 2038 | 2039 |
| 2045 | **2040** | 2047 | 2042 | **2048** | 2049 | **2044** |
| 2051 | 2046 | **2052** | 2053 | 2054 | 2055 | 2050 |
| **2056** | 2057 | 2058 | 2059 | 2065 | **2060** | 2061 |
| 2062 | 2063 | 2069 | **2064** | 2071 | 2066 | 2067 |
| 2073 | **2068** | 2075 | 2070 | **2076** | 2077 | **2072** |
| 2079 | 2074 | **2080** | 2081 | 2082 | 2083 | 2078 |
| **2084** | 2085 | 2086 | 2087 | 2093 | **2088** | 2089 |
| 2090 | 2091 | 2097 | **2092** | 2099 | 2094 | 2095 |
| | **2096** | | 2098 | | | |

I consider the 14-sheet design to be the best design of the multisheet calendar with a single year table. The day-of-month tables to use on the sheets when Table 4-9 is the single year table are as follows:

| | |
|---|---|
| Common year January and February, and all years March to December: | Table 4-1 |
| Leap year January and February: | Table 4-3 |

## Multisheet Calendar with a Single Year Table—24 Sheets

Instead of 14 sheets, 24 sheets can be used. For this design, the single year table is the year table part of Table 3-11. The day-of-month tables to use for the 24-sheet design are as follows:

| | |
|---|---|
| Common year all months: | Table 4-1 |
| Leap year all months: | Table 4-2 |

## Multisheet Calendar with a Single Year Table—12 Sheets

A 12-sheet design is also possible. In the 12-sheet design of a multisheet calendar with a year table on each sheet, the user is hardly aware that there are two different year tables, as he or she notices only having to move the window on March 1 in leap years. When there is a year table on the face only, when there are 12 sheets, and when the year is a leap year, the marker for January and February has to point to a different column in the year table than it does for the rest of the year. This can be achieved by adding a year table that applies to January leap year and February leap year only or by having two markers on the January and February sheets. However, the resulting calendar is confusing. Since a 12-sheet design would save only one double-sided sheet over a 14-sheet design, it offers little advantage.

## Extension of Single-Sheet to Multisheet with a Year Table on Each Sheet

The single-sheet calendar with a single slider in Table 3-12 can be made into a calendar that has some similarities to the 12-sheet design of the multisheet perpetual calendar with a year table on each sheet. This could be done by having 12 of these calendars and setting each one to a different month of the year. Each calendar could be the same, so that it could be set to any month. However, in a multisheet calendar, each sheet is unique to a particular month. In keeping with this philosophy, the slider in Table 3-12 is modified so that the months in the month table are replaced with markers that are for a particular month. Table 4-10 shows the slider part of Table 3-12 for reference.

**Table 4-10**
**Slider from Single-Slider Calendar with March through December Shared by Common Years and Leap Years**

| | | | | | | 1 | 2 | 3 | 4 | 5 | 6 | 7 |
|---|---|---|---|---|---|---|---|---|---|---|---|---|
| 2 | 3 | 4 | 5 | 6 | 7 | 8 | 9 | 10 | 11 | 12 | 13 | 14 |
| 9 | 10 | 11 | 12 | 13 | 14 | 15 | 16 | 17 | 18 | 19 | 20 | 21 |
| 16 | 17 | 18 | 19 | 20 | 21 | 22 | 23 | 24 | 25 | 26 | 27 | 28 |
| 23 | 24 | 25 | 26 | 27 | 28 | 29 | 30 | 31 | | | | |
| 30 | 31 | | | | | | | | | | | |
| **Jan.** | Leap yr | Leap yr | Leap yr | **Feb.** | Leap yr | Leap yr | **Jan.** | Leap yr | Leap yr | Leap yr | **Feb.** | Leap yr |
| Apr. | Sep. | Jun. | Mar. | Aug. | May | Oct. | Apr. | Sep. | Jun. | Mar. | Aug. | May |
| Jul. | Dec. | | Nov. | | | | Jul. | Dec. | | Nov. | | |
| Com yr | Com yr | Com yr | Feb. | Com yr | Com yr | Jan. | Com yr | Com yr | Com yr | Feb. | Com yr | Com yr |

Notes:

1. The top row of the month table part of the slider is for January and February in leap years. *Jan.* and *Feb.* are in boldface to indicate that they apply to leap years.
2. The bottom row of the month table part of the slider is for January and February in common years.

The slider in Table 4-10 applies to any month. To make a slider that applies to, say, November, look at Table 4-10 and note that November is under two columns that have the numbers 5, 12, 19 and 26. Replace the names of the months under these two columns with the cells filled in using black, and erase the names of all the other months. Since November has 30 days, also erase both number 31s from the day-of-month table. Follow the same procedure to make sliders that are unique to the other months. To avoid having one slider for January common year and another for January leap year, combine these sliders into one. February common year and February leap year are also combined into one. This slider displays 29 days; 29 is ignored in common years. Table 4-11 shows the resulting sliders. See Figure 6-8 for a calendar that uses these sliders.

**Table 4-11**
**Sliders for Extension of Single-Sheet Calendar to Multisheet Calendar**

| January | | | | | | 1 | 2 | 3 | 4 | 5 | 6 | 7 |
|---|---|---|---|---|---|---|---|---|---|---|---|---|
| 2 | 3 | 4 | 5 | 6 | 7 | 8 | 9 | 10 | 11 | 12 | 13 | 14 |
| 9 | 10 | 11 | 12 | 13 | 14 | 15 | 16 | 17 | 18 | 19 | 20 | 21 |
| 16 | 17 | 18 | 19 | 20 | 21 | 22 | 23 | 24 | 25 | 26 | 27 | 28 |
| 23 | 24 | 25 | 26 | 27 | 28 | 29 | 30 | 31 | | | | |
| 30 | 31 | | | | | | | | | | | |
| | Leap year | | | | | | | Leap year | | | | |
| Common year | | | | | | | Common year | | | | | |

| February | | | | | | 1 | 2 | 3 | 4 | 5 | 6 | 7 |
|---|---|---|---|---|---|---|---|---|---|---|---|---|
| 2 | 3 | 4 | 5 | 6 | 7 | 8 | 9 | 10 | 11 | 12 | 13 | 14 |
| 9 | 10 | 11 | 12 | 13 | 14 | 15 | 16 | 17 | 18 | 19 | 20 | 21 |
| 16 | 17 | 18 | 19 | 20 | 21 | 22 | 23 | 24 | 25 | 26 | 27 | 28 |
| 23 | 24 | 25 | 26 | 27 | 28 | 29 | | | | | | |
| | | | | | | | | | | | | |
| Leap year 29 days | | | | | Leap year 29 days | | | | | | | |
| Com. year 28 days | | | | Common year 28 days | | | | | | | | |

| March | | | | | | 1 | 2 | 3 | 4 | 5 | 6 | 7 |
|---|---|---|---|---|---|---|---|---|---|---|---|---|
| 2 | 3 | 4 | 5 | 6 | 7 | 8 | 9 | 10 | 11 | 12 | 13 | 14 |
| 9 | 10 | 11 | 12 | 13 | 14 | 15 | 16 | 17 | 18 | 19 | 20 | 21 |
| 16 | 17 | 18 | 19 | 20 | 21 | 22 | 23 | 24 | 25 | 26 | 27 | 28 |
| 23 | 24 | 25 | 26 | 27 | 28 | 29 | 30 | 31 | | | | |
| 30 | 31 | | | | | | | | | | | |
| | | | | | | | | | | | | |

| April | | | | | | 1 | 2 | 3 | 4 | 5 | 6 | 7 |
|---|---|---|---|---|---|---|---|---|---|---|---|---|
| 2 | 3 | 4 | 5 | 6 | 7 | 8 | 9 | 10 | 11 | 12 | 13 | 14 |
| 9 | 10 | 11 | 12 | 13 | 14 | 15 | 16 | 17 | 18 | 19 | 20 | 21 |
| 16 | 17 | 18 | 19 | 20 | 21 | 22 | 23 | 24 | 25 | 26 | 27 | 28 |
| 23 | 24 | 25 | 26 | 27 | 28 | 29 | 30 | | | | | |
| 30 | | | | | | | | | | | | |
| | | | | | | | | | | | | |

| May | | | | | | 1 | 2 | 3 | 4 | 5 | 6 | 7 |
|---|---|---|---|---|---|---|---|---|---|---|---|---|
| 2 | 3 | 4 | 5 | 6 | 7 | 8 | 9 | 10 | 11 | 12 | 13 | 14 |
| 9 | 10 | 11 | 12 | 13 | 14 | 15 | 16 | 17 | 18 | 19 | 20 | 21 |
| 16 | 17 | 18 | 19 | 20 | 21 | 22 | 23 | 24 | 25 | 26 | 27 | 28 |
| 23 | 24 | 25 | 26 | 27 | 28 | 29 | 30 | 31 | | | | |
| 30 | 31 | | | | | | | | | | | |

| June | | | | | | 1 | 2 | 3 | 4 | 5 | 6 | 7 |
|---|---|---|---|---|---|---|---|---|---|---|---|---|
| 2 | 3 | 4 | 5 | 6 | 7 | 8 | 9 | 10 | 11 | 12 | 13 | 14 |
| 9 | 10 | 11 | 12 | 13 | 14 | 15 | 16 | 17 | 18 | 19 | 20 | 21 |
| 16 | 17 | 18 | 19 | 20 | 21 | 22 | 23 | 24 | 25 | 26 | 27 | 28 |
| 23 | 24 | 25 | 26 | 27 | 28 | 29 | 30 | | | | | |
| 30 | | | | | | | | | | | | |

| July | | | | | | 1 | 2 | 3 | 4 | 5 | 6 | 7 |
|---|---|---|---|---|---|---|---|---|---|---|---|---|
| 2 | 3 | 4 | 5 | 6 | 7 | 8 | 9 | 10 | 11 | 12 | 13 | 14 |
| 9 | 10 | 11 | 12 | 13 | 14 | 15 | 16 | 17 | 18 | 19 | 20 | 21 |
| 16 | 17 | 18 | 19 | 20 | 21 | 22 | 23 | 24 | 25 | 26 | 27 | 28 |
| 23 | 24 | 25 | 26 | 27 | 28 | 29 | 30 | 31 | | | | |
| 30 | 31 | | | | | | | | | | | |

| August | | | | | | 1 | 2 | 3 | 4 | 5 | 6 | 7 |
|---|---|---|---|---|---|---|---|---|---|---|---|---|
| 2 | 3 | 4 | 5 | 6 | 7 | 8 | 9 | 10 | 11 | 12 | 13 | 14 |
| 9 | 10 | 11 | 12 | 13 | 14 | 15 | 16 | 17 | 18 | 19 | 20 | 21 |
| 16 | 17 | 18 | 19 | 20 | 21 | 22 | 23 | 24 | 25 | 26 | 27 | 28 |
| 23 | 24 | 25 | 26 | 27 | 28 | 29 | 30 | 31 | | | | |
| 30 | 31 | | | | | | | | | | | |

| September | | | | | | 1 | 2 | 3 | 4 | 5 | 6 | 7 |
|---|---|---|---|---|---|---|---|---|---|---|---|---|
| 2 | 3 | 4 | 5 | 6 | 7 | 8 | 9 | 10 | 11 | 12 | 13 | 14 |
| 9 | 10 | 11 | 12 | 13 | 14 | 15 | 16 | 17 | 18 | 19 | 20 | 21 |
| 16 | 17 | 18 | 19 | 20 | 21 | 22 | 23 | 24 | 25 | 26 | 27 | 28 |
| 23 | 24 | 25 | 26 | 27 | 28 | 29 | 30 | | | | | |
| 30 | | | | | | | | | | | | |

| October | | | | | | 1 | 2 | 3 | 4 | 5 | 6 | 7 |
|---|---|---|---|---|---|---|---|---|---|---|---|---|
| 2 | 3 | 4 | 5 | 6 | 7 | 8 | 9 | 10 | 11 | 12 | 13 | 14 |
| 9 | 10 | 11 | 12 | 13 | 14 | 15 | 16 | 17 | 18 | 19 | 20 | 21 |
| 16 | 17 | 18 | 19 | 20 | 21 | 22 | 23 | 24 | 25 | 26 | 27 | 28 |
| 23 | 24 | 25 | 26 | 27 | 28 | 29 | 30 | 31 | | | | |
| 30 | 31 | | | | | | | | | | | |

| November | | | | | | 1 | 2 | 3 | 4 | 5 | 6 | 7 |
|---|---|---|---|---|---|---|---|---|---|---|---|---|
| 2 | 3 | 4 | 5 | 6 | 7 | 8 | 9 | 10 | 11 | 12 | 13 | 14 |
| 9 | 10 | 11 | 12 | 13 | 14 | 15 | 16 | 17 | 18 | 19 | 20 | 21 |
| 16 | 17 | 18 | 19 | 20 | 21 | 22 | 23 | 24 | 25 | 26 | 27 | 28 |
| 23 | 24 | 25 | 26 | 27 | 28 | 29 | 30 | | | | | |
| 30 | | | | | | | | | | | | |

| December | | | | | | 1 | 2 | 3 | 4 | 5 | 6 | 7 |
|---|---|---|---|---|---|---|---|---|---|---|---|---|
| 2 | 3 | 4 | 5 | 6 | 7 | 8 | 9 | 10 | 11 | 12 | 13 | 14 |
| 9 | 10 | 11 | 12 | 13 | 14 | 15 | 16 | 17 | 18 | 19 | 20 | 21 |
| 16 | 17 | 18 | 19 | 20 | 21 | 22 | 23 | 24 | 25 | 26 | 27 | 28 |
| 23 | 24 | 25 | 26 | 27 | 28 | 29 | 30 | 31 | | | | |
| 30 | 31 | | | | | | | | | | | |

## Two Variations of Full-Year Perpetual Calendars

The full-year perpetual calendar also uses the day-of month tables in Tables 4-1, 4-2 and 4-3. However, all of the day-of-month tables are on the same page, so a full year is displayed. Two variations are possible.

One variation has Table 4-1 for common years on one side of the slider and Table 4-2 for leap years on the other side. The slider has to be turned over when switching from a common year to a leap year and vice versa. There are 12 windows to display the months, a window to display a marker for common years and a window to display a marker for leap years. The common year side of the slider is used for years in the common year window, and the leap year side is used for years in the leap year window.

The other variation has Tables 4-1 and 4-3 on the same side. The calendar has 14 windows for months, which are January common year, February common year, January leap year, February leap year and March to December shared for common and leap years. There is also a window for a marker to point to the applicable row in the year table. See Chapter 8 for additional details.

## An Impractical Full-Year Perpetual Calendar

In theory, a full-year perpetual calendar with 12 windows for the months that does not require the user to turn over the slider is possible. It would use Table 4-1 for the day-of-month tables. However, this calendar would be confusing for leap years and is not recommended. The face would require two windows to indicate the applicable years. One of the year windows would indicate the applicable common years for any month and the applicable leap years for March to December. The other year window would indicate the applicable leap years for January and February. The reason that every leap year would appear in both windows is because the day of the week that a date in a leap year falls on with respect to the previous year advances on both January 1 and March 1. Thus, in a leap year, the slider would have to be advanced on both January 1 and March 1. When the slider is advanced on January 1 of a leap year, the displays for January and February are correct for that year, and the displays for March to December do not apply. Similarly, when the slider is advanced on March 1 of a leap year, the displays for March to December are correct for that year, and the displays for January and February do not apply. Therefore, a full-year calendar with 12 windows for the months that does not require the user to turn over the slider would display common years correctly, but only January and February or March to December of leap years. This would be a serious deficiency.

## Seven-Column Multisheet Perpetual Calendar

All of the multisheet calendars previously discussed use the 13-column day-of-month table (Table 3-1). Either sheets with this table on them move in a window, or a window moves across the sheets. A calendar that has a seven-column day-of-month table, as in a conventional calendar, is possible. There are two styles, with one having a year table for each month and the other having a single year table. As noted in Chapter 1, I consider the single year table style to be one of three potential replacements for the conventional multisheet desk calendar. I do not consider the other style to have very much market potential, but I show how the tables for it are developed so as to make *Practical Perpetual Calendars* complete.

## Seven-Column Multisheet Perpetual Calendar with a Year Table for Each Month

The seven-column multisheet perpetual calendar with a year table for each month consists of two sets of sheets. The first is a set of 12 year-table sheets, one for each month. On each sheet, the columns in the table are arranged so that the leftmost column has the years when the first of that month falls on a Sunday. The next column has the years when the first of that month falls on a Monday, and so on, until the rightmost column has the years when the first of that month falls on a Saturday.

The second set of sheets consists of seven day-of-month sheets. The first sheet has the days arranged for the first of the month falling on a Sunday, the second on a Monday, and so on, until the seventh, which has the days arranged for the first of the month falling on a Saturday. Each sheet has 31 days, with 31, 30 and 29 being ignored when these days are not in the month of interest. Setting the calendar involves finding the month sheet of interest, checking this sheet to find which day of the week the first of the month falls on for the year of interest, and then finding the applicable day-of-month sheet. The two sheets are then put in a suitable holder. Tables 4-12a and 4-12b illustrate the concept.

### Table 4-12
### Concept of a Seven-Column Multisheet Perpetual Calendar

#### a. Contents and arrangement of a year-table sheet

| **Name of the month** | | | | | | |
|---|---|---|---|---|---|---|
| Years when 1st of this month is on a Sun. | Years when 1st of this month is on a Mon. | Years when 1st of this month is on a Tue. | Years when 1st of this month is on a Wed. | Years when 1st of this month is on a Thur. | Years when 1st of this month is on a Fri. | Years when 1st of this month is on a Sat. |
| | | | | | | |
| | | | | | | |
| | | | | | | |
| | | | | | | |
| | | | | | | |
| | | | | | | |
| | | | | | | |
| | | | | | | |

**b. A day-of-month sheet for a month when the first is on a Tuesday**

| Sun. | Mon. | Tue. | Wed. | Thu. | Fri. | Sat. |
|---|---|---|---|---|---|---|
| | | 1 | 2 | 3 | 4 | 5 |
| 6 | 7 | 8 | 9 | 10 | 11 | 12 |
| 13 | 14 | 15 | 16 | 17 | 18 | 19 |
| 20 | 21 | 22 | 23 | 24 | 25 | 26 |
| 27 | 28 | 29 | 30 | 31 | | |
| | | | | | | |

The year-table sheets can be double-sided to enable having more years in the tables, or they can have a different month on each side. The holder can be made so that the year-table sheet is above the day-of-month sheet. In this arrangement, all of the year-table sheet is visible, and the *1* on the day-of-month sheet is below the column that has the years that apply to that day-of-month sheet. Alternatively, the day-of-month sheet can cover the years so that only the name of the month is visible.

The contents of the year columns in the year-table sheets for January and February are the same as in Table 4-8 for the 12-sheet perpetual calendar, but the columns are in a different order. The contents of the year columns in the year-table sheets for March to December are the same as in Table 4-7 for the 12-sheet design, but the columns are also in a different order.

The year-table sheet for February is developed as follows. Table 4-13 is a duplicate of Table 4-8, with a row added at the top to number the columns and a row added at the bottom to indicate which day of the week February 1 falls on for the years in each column.

**Table 4-13**
**Development of the Year-Table Sheet for February for the Seven-Column Multisheet Perpetual Calendar**

| Column | | | | | | |
|---|---|---|---|---|---|---|
| 1 | 2 | 3 | 4 | 5 | 6 | 7 |
| **2000** | 2010 | **2004** | 2003 | 2002 | 2001 | 2006 |
| 2005 | **2016** | 2009 | 2014 | **2008** | 2007 | **2012** |
| 2011 | 2021 | 2015 | **2020** | 2013 | 2018 | 2017 |
| 2022 | 2027 | 2026 | 2025 | 2019 | **2024** | 2023 |
| **2028** | 2038 | **2032** | 2031 | 2030 | 2029 | 2034 |
| 2033 | **2044** | 2037 | 2042 | **2036** | 2035 | **2040** |
| 2039 | 2049 | 2043 | **2048** | 2041 | 2046 | 2045 |
| 2050 | 2055 | 2054 | 2053 | 2047 | **2052** | 2051 |
| **2056** | 2066 | **2060** | 2059 | 2058 | 2057 | 2062 |
| 2061 | **2072** | 2065 | 2070 | **2064** | 2063 | **2068** |
| 2067 | 2077 | 2071 | **2076** | 2069 | 2074 | 2073 |
| 2078 | 2083 | 2082 | 2081 | 2075 | **2080** | 2079 |
| **2084** | 2094 | **2088** | 2087 | 2086 | 2085 | 2090 |
| 2089 | | 2093 | 2098 | **2092** | 2091 | **2096** |
| 2095 | | 2099 | | 2097 | | |
| Tue. | Mon. | Sun. | Sat. | Fri. | Thu. | Wed. |

Note: Leap years are in boldface.

The year-table sheet must have the columns arranged with Sunday to Saturday going from left to right. Therefore, Table 4-13 must be rearranged so that, from left to right, the columns are in the order 3, 2, 1,7, 6, 5 and 4. Tables 4-14a and 4-14b show two formats for the rearranged table. Table 4-14a is a compact arrangement, which is the same as is used in Table 4-8 and many other tables in *Practical Perpetual Calendars.* Table 4-14b, which shows only the top five rows, has the years in sequence from row to row. The right-hand side of Table 4-14a shows the year table with the day-of-month sheet that applies to February 2017 placed in front of it. If the concepts in Table 4-14a were used to make a practical calendar with a pleasing appearance, the size of the year table would be reduced and/or the height of the day-of-month sheet would be increased so that the day-of-month sheet would cover the lower half of the year-table sheet. The part of the year-table sheet that is shown covered in the right-hand side of Table 4-14a could have the years written upside down with respect to the top. The sheet could then be rotated to display these years.

## Table 4-14
## Year Table Sheet for February

### a. Compact arrangement

Complete 21st-century year table

| February | | | | | | |
|---|---|---|---|---|---|---|
| **2004** | 2010 | **2000** | 2006 | 2001 | 2002 | 2003 |
| 2009 | **2016** | 2005 | **2012** | 2007 | **2008** | 2014 |
| 2015 | 2021 | 2011 | 2017 | 2018 | 2013 | **2020** |
| 2026 | 2027 | 2022 | 2023 | **2024** | 2019 | 2025 |
| **2032** | 2038 | **2028** | 2034 | 2029 | 2030 | 2031 |
| 2037 | **2044** | 2033 | **2040** | 2035 | **2036** | 2042 |
| 2043 | 2049 | 2039 | 2045 | 2046 | 2041 | **2048** |
| 2054 | 2055 | 2050 | 2051 | **2052** | 2047 | 2053 |
| **2060** | 2066 | **2056** | 2062 | 2057 | 2058 | 2059 |
| 2065 | **2072** | 2061 | **2068** | 2063 | **2064** | 2070 |
| 2071 | 2077 | 2067 | 2073 | 2074 | 2069 | **2076** |
| 2082 | 2083 | 2078 | 2079 | **2080** | 2075 | 2081 |
| **2088** | 2094 | **2084** | 2090 | 2085 | 2086 | 2087 |
| 2093 | | 2089 | **2096** | 2091 | **2092** | 2098 |
| 2099 | | 2095 | | | 2097 | |
| Sun. | Mon. | Tue. | Wed. | Thu. | Fri. | Sat. |

Note: Leap years are in boldface.

Year table with the day-of-month sheet that applies to February 2017 placed in front of it

| February | | | | | | |
|---|---|---|---|---|---|---|
| **2004** | 2010 | **2000** | 2006 | 2001 | 2002 | 2003 |
| 2009 | **2016** | 2005 | **2012** | 2007 | **2008** | 2014 |
| 2015 | 2021 | 2011 | 2017 | 2018 | 2013 | **2020** |
| 2026 | 2027 | 2022 | 2023 | **2024** | 2019 | 2025 |
| **2032** | 2038 | **2028** | 2034 | 2029 | 2030 | 2031 |
| 2037 | **2044** | 2033 | **2040** | 2035 | **2036** | 2042 |
| 2043 | 2049 | 2039 | 2045 | 2046 | 2041 | **2048** |
| 2054 | 2055 | 2050 | 2051 | **2052** | 2047 | 2053 |
| **2060** | 2066 | **2056** | 2062 | 2057 | 2058 | 2059 |
| 2065 | **2072** | 2061 | **2068** | 2063 | **2064** | 2070 |
| | | | 1 | 2 | 3 | 4 |
| 5 | 6 | 7 | 8 | 9 | 10 | 11 |
| 12 | 13 | 14 | 15 | 16 | 17 | 18 |
| 19 | 20 | 21 | 22 | 23 | 24 | 25 |
| 26 | 27 | 28 | 29 | 30 | 31 | |
| | | | | | | |

### b. Arrangement when years are in sequence from row to row

| | | | | | | |
|---|---|---|---|---|---|---|
| **2004** | | **2000** | | 2001 | 2002 | 2003 |
| 2009 | 2010 | 2005 | 2006 | 2007 | **2008** | |
| 2015 | **2016** | 2011 | **2012** | | 2013 | 2014 |
| | 2021 | 2022 | 2017 | 2018 | 2019 | **2020** |
| 2026 | 2027 | | 2023 | **2024** | | 2025 |
| Sun. | Mon. | Tue. | Wed. | Thu. | Fri. | Sat. |

Notes

1. Leap years are in boldface.
2. Only the first five lines (approximately 25 years) are shown.

With two sets of sheets to handle, this calendar is a little inconvenient to use. There is some acceptance of the concept of having two sets of sheets, as there are commercially available perpetual calendars that follow this concept. For an example, see Figure A-9a. To the best of my knowledge, none of the commercial calendars have year tables, so they are not stand-alone. Adding year tables based on the concepts in Table 4-14a or 4-14b to these calendars would make them stand-alone. However, with the years in different columns for each month, the year of interest can be difficult to find.

## Seven-Column Multisheet Perpetual Calendar with a Single Year Table

The seven-column multisheet perpetual calendar with a single year table uses concepts from Table 4-12b to develop a day-of-month sheet for each of the seven days of the week. These sheets are combined with the month and year table of the single-sheet dual-slider calendar. See Table 3-8 for the month table, which is on a slider, and Table 3-9a, 3-9b or 3-9c for the year table. The concept is similar to the hybrid calendar in Figure 5-17a. See Figures 1-3c, 1-3d, 7-6a, 7-6b and 7-6c for a practical calendar that uses this concept. This calendar is easier to use than the seven-column multisheet calendar with a year table for each month. Other than having to ignore the 29th, 30th and 31st days of the month when not applicable, this calendar is quite similar to a conventional multisheet calendar.

## Summary of Tables for Multisheet and Full-Year Perpetual Calendars

The tables developed in this chapter can be used to make the following calendars:

1. Multisheet with a year table on each sheet—24 sheets. (Use Tables 4-1, 4-2, 4-5 and 4-6.)
2. Multisheet with a year table on each sheet—14 sheets. (Use Tables 4-1, 4-3 and 4-7.)
3. Multisheet with a year table on each sheet—12 sheets. (Use Tables 4-1, 4-7 and 4-8, with the 29th added to February in Table 4-1.)
4. Multisheet with a single year table—14 sheets. (Use Tables 4-1, 4-3 and 4-9.)
5. Multisheet with a single year table—24 sheets. (Use the year table part of Table 3-11 with Tables 4-1 and 4-2.)
6. Extension of single-sheet to multisheet. (Use the year table part of Table 3-12, which is also Table 3-9c, along with the sliders in Table 4-11.)
7. Double-sided slider full-year calendar. (Use Tables 4-1 and 4-2 for the day-of-month tables, along with the year table in Chapter 8.)
8. Single-sided slider full-year calendar. (Use Tables 4-1 and 4-3 for the day-of-month tables, along with the year table in Chapter 8.)
9. Seven-column multisheet calendar with a year table for each month. (Use concepts from Tables 4-13 and 4-14 to develop a year-table sheet for each of the 12 months. Use concepts from Table 4-12b to develop a day-of-month sheet for each of the seven days of the week.)

10. Seven-column multisheet calendar with a single year table. (Use Table 3-8 for the month table, which is on a slider, and Table 3-9a, 3-9b or 3-9c for the year table. Use concepts from Table 4-12b to develop a day-of-month sheet for each of the seven days of the week. See Figure 7-6c for a complete set of day-of-month sheets.)

In addition to the two full-year calendars (items 7 and 8 of the foregoing list), there are the vertical full-year calendar and the single day-of-month table full-year calendar. Tables for these calendars are developed in Chapter 8. (See Figures 8-3, 8-4a and 8-4b.)

# CHAPTER 5

# SINGLE-SHEET PERPETUAL CALENDARS—APPLICATIONS AND PRODUCTS

## Applications

The single-sheet perpetual calendar is the simplest and most versatile type. This chapter describes many applications for this calendar type. I suggest looking at all the designs in this chapter and not just the one for the application of interest. For example, the key holder has a different design for the window, which may work for other applications.

Table 5-1 lists the applications for the single-sheet perpetual calendar that are described in this chapter. The one with the greatest potential for low-cost calendars for advertising is the single-window tent desk calendar shown in Figure 5-1a. A marvel of practicality and simplicity, it can be sold in the millions. The other applications do not have as large a potential for quantity, but they can be profitable in niche markets for both small and relatively large-scale manufacturers. Many of the calendars can be easily made in small quantities for personal use.

**Table 5-1**
**Applications for the Single-Sheet Perpetual Calendar**

| Application | Description | Figure |
|---|---|---|
| Single-window tent desk calendar | Single slider has day-of-month table above the month table, with both in the same window. The year table is below the slider. | 5-1a to 5-1e |
| Double-window desk calendar | Single slider has month table above the day-of-month table in separate windows. The year table is above the slider. | 5-2a to 5-2c |
| Pocket calendar | Credit-card-size calendar that has 50 years. Window moves instead of having a slider. | 5-3a |
| Pocket calendar | Similar to above, but slider moves. Slightly smaller font for same overall size. | 5-3b |
| Pocket/tent calendar | Calendar can be either a pocket calendar or a small tent calendar. | 5-3c |
| Pocket calendar | Calendar folds open to enable having a larger year table in the same width when folded. | 5-3d |
| Pocket calendar | Single slider with year tables beside day-of-month window. | 5-3e |
| Bookmark | Moving-slider type with a window on the front for day of month and a window on the back for the month table. | 5-4 |
| Notepad calendar | Similar to the first two pocket calendars above. | 5-3a, 5-3b |
| Planners | Calendar designs that can be modified for use in pocket planners and full-size planner that have undated pages that can be added or removed. | 5-1a, 5-2a, 5-2b, 5-3a, 5-3b, 5-3d, 5-3e |
| Lamp or pencil holder | Single-window calendar that wraps around a pencil holder or the base of a lamp. | 5-5 |
| Simple holder for 4 × 6 inch photograph | Dual-slider calendar made from cardstock. | 5-6a, 5-6b |
| Key holder | Dual-slider calendar with hooks for keys below it. | 5-7a |
| Key holder | Single-slider calendar with hooks for keys below it. The year table is on both sides of the day-of-month window. | 5-7b |
| Clock | Dual-slider calendar with clock above it. | 5-8 |
| Clock | Double-window calendar with clock above it. | 5-9 |

| Application | Description | Figure |
|---|---|---|
| Picture frame, 8 × 10 inches | Single-window calendar with a 5 × 7 inch photo in portrait orientation beside it, all in an 8 × 10 picture frame. | 5-10a, 5-10b |
| Picture frame, 8 × 10 inches | Single-window calendar with a 5 × 7 inch photo in landscape orientation above it, all in an 8 × 10 picture frame. | 5-11 |
| Picture frame, 5 × 7 inches | Dual-slider calendar below a 5 × 7 inch picture frame in landscape orientation. | 5-12 |
| Modified sliding-window commercial perpetual calendar | Commercial perpetual calendar that has year and month indication added to it. | 5-13a, 5-13b |
| Wall planner | A 13-column planner chart that has a window to select 7 columns according to which day of the week the first of the month falls on. | 5-14b |
| Wall planner | A planner that has 7 strips that are arranged according to which day of the week the first of the month falls on. | 5-15a, 5-15b |
| Wall planner | A planner that has 31 lines and a built-in perpetual calendar. The calendar has a single-slider vertical arrangement, which can also be used to make a wall calendar. | 5-16a |
| Day planner | A single-slider vertical calendar that can convert a standard 3-ring binder into a day planner. | 5-16b |
| Hybrid wall calendar | Conventional tile-type perpetual calendar that has a slider added to indicate which day of the week the first of the month falls on. | 5-17a to 5-17c |
| Stand with calendar | Single-slider calendar with year tables beside day-of-month window. Calendar is on the face of a block that a photo or a commercial perpetual desk calendar can sit on. | 5-18 |

## Tables

All of the calendars in Chapter 5 use tables from Chapter 3. Table 5-2 indicates which tables to use.

## Table 5-2
## Tables to Use for the Various Single-Sheet Perpetual Calendar Designs

| Calendar design | Day-of-month table | Year table | Month table | Leap year months and common year months (*see* note 1) |
|---|---|---|---|---|
| Single-slider with year table above or below window | Table 3-11 | Table 3-11 | Table 3-11 | Separate |
| Dual-slider | Table 3-1 | Table 3-7 | Table 3-6a | Separate |
| Single-slider with year table above or below window | Table 3-12 | Table 3-9 (Table 3-9b is used most often) | Table 3-12 | Combined |
| Dual-slider | Table 3-1 | Table 3-9 | Table 3-8 | Combined |
| Single-slider with year tables to side of window | Table 3-16 | Table 3-17 | Table 3-16 | Combined (*see* note 2) |
| Single-slider vertical calendar | Table 3-18 | Table 3-18 | Table 3-18 | Combined (*see* note 2) |

Notes:

1. *Separate* and *Combined*:

   *Separate* means that the month table has common and leap year months separate from each other. There are three rows for leap year months and three rows for common year months.

   *Combined* means that the month table has March to December the same for both common and leap years. The table has one row for January and February in leap years, one row for January and February in common years and two rows for March to December for both leap and common years. This arrangement requires four rows, compared to six when leap and common years are separate. All the designs in Chapter 5 use this arrangement, but they can be easily converted to having common and leap year months separate.

2. Chapter 3 does not have any tables for leap year months and common year months being separate for these two designs. Tables can be developed by using the same procedures as are used in Chapter 3 to develop Tables 3-16, 3-17 and 3-18.

## Single-Sheet, Single-Slider Desk Calendars

Figures 5-1a, 5-1b and 5-1c show details of the tent calendar depicted in Figure 1-1a, which is made from cardstock. One sheet of 8.5 × 11 inch paper (Figure 5-1a) is used to make the tent body, and a second sheet is used to make five sliders. The tent body is 6.5 inches wide by 11 inches long. The width is the minimum to keep the slider hidden behind the face when it is at the end of its travel. This width provides about two inches on each side of the calendar for pictures or text. If you wanted to avoid having to trim each side, you could make the width 8.5 inches. In this case, the discretionary area on each side of the calendar would be 3 inches wide by 4 inches high. A length of 11 inches is just enough to make a tent. As shown in Figure 5-1a, two slits are cut to hold the slider. For small quantities, the slits can be cut manually to save the cost of a die. Before folding, the back side of the tent should be scored along the fold lines with a blunt tool such as a small flat-blade screwdriver. However, a reasonably good fold can be made by scoring lightly on the front side, folding in the opposite direction and then folding in the correct direction after the fold line is visible on the back side. This avoids having to print or manually draw fold lines on the back side. Of course, for large-scale production, scoring and folding would be done by machine.

As shown in Figure 5-1b, there is enough extra material at the end of each slider to make a year table for the 20th century. The assembly instructions in Figure 5-1c show how a pocket can be made inside the tent to hold the 20th-century year table. It is taken out and held in front of the 21st-century table when it is used. Alternatively, a slit can be cut on either side of the 21st-century table to hold the 20th-century table if this table is to be used for an extended period. There is a dot above each year column on the front face. This is for inserting a pin to identify the current year, if desired. My experience is that a pin is not needed. Figure 5-1d shows a table of holidays as an alternative to a picture on the back of the calendar. Figure 5-1d also has some notes on how to use Excel for graphics.

Figure 5-1e illustrates a concept for making the calendar from wood or another rigid material. Since the slider would not be flexible, slits cannot be used to hold it. Instead, there has to be a window and a track. Although a calendar made from rigid material could have a back and a bottom like a tent calendar, an easier construction method is to use a prop or a base plate. Figure 5-1e shows an alternative to a single-piece front with a window cut in it. There is a top rectangular piece with abbreviations for the days of the week (SMTWTFS) printed on it and a bottom rectangular piece with the year table printed on it. The back is one piece with a groove cut in it. The depth of the groove is slightly greater than the thickness of the slider, and the width of the groove is slightly greater than the height of the slider. When the top and bottom rectangular pieces are attached to the back, there is a top and a bottom track for the slider. This alternative to a single-piece front is faster to construct and is also novel. However, with the full slider exposed, there is less room for pictures or text on the face, as there are no panels hiding the unused part of the slider. Most print shops do not have the capability of printing on rigid material. The easiest way for small-scale production is to print on paper and then glue the paper to the rigid material.

Figure 5-2a shows a double-window desk calendar made from only one 8.5 × 11 inch sheet of cardstock. As an alternative to the tent configuration, a back support is used. With the year table above the slider, two windows are needed. A track for the slider is made by using mounting tape to make a gap between the support and the front. The gap can also be made by gluing in strips of cardstock. Instead of having the slider move in a track, it can move in two slits, similar to the single-window desk calendar in Figure 5-1a. Figure 5-2b shows how to cut the slits and leave a strip with SMTWTFS between the two windows. This figure also lists the parts needed and provides some construction suggestions.

The double-window desk calendar can also be made from wood or another rigid material, as shown in Figure 5-2c. The construction is similar to that shown in Figure 5-1e, but the front is one piece with two windows cut in it instead of two pieces. The width of the back can be either slightly wider than the windows or equal to the width of the front. If it is the former, the slider can be moved from the back. If it is the latter, the slider will need a knob so that it can be moved from the front. The knob has to be in the same column as the numbers 1, 8, 15, 22 and 29, as this is the only column that is visible for all settings of the slider.

## Single-Sheet, Single-Slider Pocket Calendars

The single-sheet perpetual calendar with one slider is ideal for small-size calendars such as a pocket calendar, a calendar for a pocket notepad, or a bookmark. Figure 5-3a shows a credit-card-size pocket calendar that is approximately 1.875 inches wide by 3.5 inches long. It is designed to fit into a 2.375 × 3.5 inch envelope, which is the standard size used to hold credit cards, hotel key cards, business cards and ID cards. The prototype in Figure 5-3a covers the years 2000 to 2050. Since it is a little narrower than the envelope, another two rows of years could be added to extend the coverage to 2065. The tables are the same as the ones used in Figures 5-1a to 5-1e, and 5-2a to 5-2c. However, the window with the year table on it moves, and the month table and the day-of-month table are stationary.

A moving-window calendar for a pocket notepad can also be made from the prototype in Figure 5-3a. Only a table sheet and a window are required, as the inside of the front cover forms the back of the calendar. For a standard 3 × 5 inch notepad, the calendar can be slightly larger than the pocket calendar.

Figure 5-3b shows a moving-slider calendar for a pocket notepad. The operation of this calendar is similar to that of the single-window desk calendar shown in Figures 5-1a to 5-1e. However, the slider is moved from the front instead of the back. Therefore, there is a second slit on each side of the window to bring the slider up to the front. To fit this calendar in a 3 × 5 inch notepad, the image must be reduced to a smaller size than it is in the moving-window calendar in Figure 5-3a. However, the font size is still quite legible. The choice between a moving-window and a moving-slider notepad calendar is mainly personal preference.

The calendar in Figure 5-3b can be sized to fit into a standard 2.375 × 3.5 inch envelope to make a pocket calendar. It can also be made as a tent/fold-back calendar, as shown in Figure 5-3c. When it is used as a pocket calendar, the back flap is tucked in to protect the ends of the slider, eliminating the need for an envelope when put in a pocket. When the calendar is used as a tent calendar, the back flap is the back of the tent.

To make the calendars in Figures 5-3a, 5-3b and 5-3c, the following modifications are needed to the Excel settings described at the end of Chapter 2:

- Column widths are 2 instead of the usual 3.
- The row heights for the days of the month (numbers 1 to 31) are 10 instead of 15. The remaining row heights are 15.
- The font is Calibri, with the point size mainly a mix of 11 and 18.
- All three calendars are printed at 40 percent of normal size.

Figure 5-3d shows a fold-down moving-slider calendar that can also be carried in a pocket without an envelope. The calendar in Figure 5-3d is called a fold-down calendar because the top part folds down over the face. This is opposite to how the calendar in Figure 5-3c is folded. The folded-up size is 2 × 6.25 inches when printed at 50 percent of normal size. The size can be reduced by changing the column widths and row heights, and by printing to a smaller scale, as previously noted. The following features on this calendar are different from those in Figures 5-3a, 5-3b and 5-3c:

- SMTWTFS is below the slider rather than above it.
- The month table is above the day-of-month table.
- The year table folds over the slider to minimize the width when the calendar is stored in a pocket. This feature enables putting more years in the table for a specified width when folded.

The main purpose of Figure 5-3d is to illustrate different ways of designing a calendar. The folding feature in Figure 5-3d could be added to Figure 5-3b by making a fold above the year table.

Another way of making a pocket calendar is to use a single slider with the year tables beside the day-of-month window. Figure 5-3e shows the details. The calendar in Figure 5-3e has the month table below the day-of-month table and covers 100 years. The height of the calendar can be reduced by putting the month table on the back of the day-of-month table and by putting a year table that covers 70 years on the back face. The resulting calendar would be similar to the bookmark calendar in Figure 5-4, except the slider (instead of the window) would move. Because it has more pieces to glue, the calendar in Figure 5-3e is more difficult to make in small quantities than the calendars in Figures 5-3a to 5-3d. In large quantities, where gluing is done by machine, this calendar should not be significantly more difficult to make than the others.

Figure 5-4 shows a moving-window bookmark calendar. This calendar has the day-of-month table on the front, and the year table and month table on the back. With two windows to cut out and a body that has a few corners and spacers to glue, this calendar is more difficult to make than the others. Of course, for large-quantity production, it is not significantly more difficult once the production line has been set up.

In Figure 5-4, the entries in the year table and the month table are in reverse order when compared to the entries shown in Tables 3-9 and 3-12. This is because when the calendar is turned from front to back, it is turned on its left or right edge. Imagine taking a pin and punching holes from left to right from the front and then reading the entries found on the back. The entries would read in the same order as in Tables 3-9 and 3-12. The bookmark calendar can be designed so that when it is turned from front to back, it is turned on its top or bottom edge. In this case, the tables are not in reverse order.

## Planners and Appointment Books—General

In spite of cell phones, tablets and computers, there is still a large market for planners and appointment books. There is considerable waste in this area because products made for a particular year are not used or only partly used. Presently available perpetual planners can reduce some of the waste since they do not have the days of the week assigned to any particular day of the month. Typically, these planners have calendars in them that cover three years. After the three years, the usefulness of the planner is diminished, as it no longer has a built-in calendar for the current year. Even in the third year, the planner's usefulness is partially diminished, as a look ahead to the next year cannot be done without consulting an external calendar. Replacing the built-in calendars with a single perpetual calendar, similar to the notepad calendars previously described, would extend the shelf life of the planner from 3 years to 50 to 100 years, depending on the size of the year table. This would effectively eliminate having to throw away a whole planner on account of the fact that it has expired, but it may not eliminate having to discard a partially used planner, as planners typically do not have removable pages. The following shows how perpetual calendars can be used in planners and also makes some suggestions for page design to eliminate having to throw away partially used planners.

I believe that the two keys to making planners useful and versatile are to use looseleaf paper or another type of removable page, and to include a perpetual calendar in the planner. This provides the following advantages:

1. Unused pages from a year can be reused, provided the pages are designed to be general in that there are only one or two different page types other than dividers.
2. Used pages can be filed if desired, and pages without any information of interest can be discarded.
3. A new planner does not have to be purchased every year—only additional sheets if necessary.

4. Two planners do not have to be in use near the end of the year to record events that will occur in the next year. Instead, the sheets for the months that have passed in the current year can be removed and then be replaced with sheets for the next year. Sheets can be added at the end of the planner to record events that will take place more than a year in the future.

Some readers may feel that planners are not worth discussing in detail in *Practical Perpetual Calendars*, as the market for planners is a very competitive one that is dominated by a few major manufacturers. However, my perpetual calendars, along with my page concepts, have the potential of reducing waste. These ideas are worthy of consideration by small companies that want a product for a niche market, and also by large manufacturers. Unlike wall and desk calendars, where there may be some objection to using a perpetual calendar since the same pictures are displayed year after year, planners are plain and do not have pictures. In addition to reducing waste, a perpetual planner using my concepts has the advantage of eliminating the inconvenience of obtaining a new planner because the old one is obsolete.

## Pocket Planner / Notepad

A product that I would find very useful is a 3 × 5 inch pocket planner / notepad combination for carrying in a shirt pocket. The ideal product would have perpetual planner pages in the front and lined pages in the back for notes. The pages would be removable so that used pages could be replaced with new ones. Used pages could be recycled or saved in a separate binder. To minimize the width, the binding should be on the short (3-inch) side of the paper. A notepad with binding on the short side that allows for the addition and removal of pages is not a common item. I have found the following possibilities:

1. The only small commercially available notepad that I have found has room for 40 sheets, with a punch available for making your own sheets. The size is slightly smaller than the common non-refillable 3 × 5 inch notepad, but this notepad is large enough to be a useful product. The model number is LIHIT LAB N-1661-24 and it is made by Lihit Lab in Japan. More information can be obtained on the U.S. supplier's website: http://www.jetpens.com/Lihit-Lab-Aqua-Drops-Twist-Ring-Memo-Notepad-2.8-X-4.7-5-mm-Graph-40-Sheets-Black/pd/9482.
2. The Mead Vinyl Loose-Leaf Memo Book (46000), found at http://www.meaddirect.ca/meadCA/browse/product/Vinyl+Loose-Leaf+Memo+Book+%2846000%29/46000, is a 6-ring binder with the binding on the long side for holding up to 40 sheets of 3 × 5 inch paper. It is an ideal product for making a perpetual planner for a handbag, but is a little wide to fit into a shirt pocket. A similar product is available from All-Pro Software (https://www.allprosoftware.com/Binders/mini/). The Mead and All-Pro Software binders have different ring spacing.
3. Use plastic comb binding. Comb binding, which is sometimes referred to as Cerlox or Sure-Lox binding, is available in an 11-inch length for use with standard 8.5 × 11 inch paper. For small production runs, the binding can be cut to the desired length. For large

runs, the binding can be custom-made at the desired length, or an alternate binding system can be developed.

4. Use two Chicago screws to make a binder: A Chicago screw, which is also called a binding post and screw, or a screw post, consists of two parts. One part is a flange with a smaller-diameter barrel attached to it. The barrel is threaded on the inside, and the screw, which is similar to a bolt, threads into it. When assembled, the threads on the bolt are inside the barrel and the sheets are held in place by a flange on each end.
5. Use two brass paper fasteners, which are also called split-pin paper fasteners.
6. Use a prong paper fastener as an alternative to two brass paper fasteners. A prong paper fastener for a standard two-hole punch has a spacing of 2.75 inches between the prongs. The minimum width notepad for this hole spacing is about 3.5 inches, which will fit in a shirt pocket.
7. Use a binder clip or a bulldog clip to hold the sheets together.
8. Use a conventional coil binder. Usually, a coil binder's wires are bent at each end to prevent them from threading out of the sheets. One alternative is to not bend either end, and then attach a piece of thin tubing from one end to the other. Another alternative is to bend one end and put a removable plastic piece on the other end, or leave it uncovered.
9. Use small plastic tie wraps that are replaced when sheets are added or removed.
10. Use looseleaf rings. ScrewPost (https://www.screwpost.com/index.php?cPath=2) sells 1/2-inch diameter metal rings and 9/16-inch diameter plastic rings. They also sell metal and plastic Chicago screws. Binding 101 (https://www.binding101.com/binding-rings/plastic-snap-lock-binding-rings) sells 1/2-inch-diameter plastic rings and other binding supplies. The cost of looseleaf rings is about 15¢ each for plastic and 30¢ each for metal.
11. Bind with string using a knot (or knots) that can be easily untied. Some trial and error would be required to find a satisfactory way of threading the string and tying the knot, but this may be the easiest method for a small production run, where special order pieces such as Chicago screws want to be avoided.
12. Use non-opening binder rings, an alternative to rings, bolts or other devices that open to accept sheets. In this system, the sheets are pushed in and pulled out of the binder. The sheets have holes punched, with a cut to the edge of the paper starting at each hole. One supplier of this type of notebook is Staples, which sells the M by Staples Arc Notebook. See http://www.staples.com/sbd/cre/marketing/arc/. Staples has notebooks that measure nominally 8.5 × 11 inches and 5.5 × 8.5 inches. The 8.5 × 11 inch sheet has 11 holes punched on the long side. A punch is available for making your own sheets. If you wish to make a pocket planner, you can cut an 11-inch binder strip down to three 3-inch strips that have three holes. Of course, for large production runs, a special binder for 3 × 5 inch paper can be made. Unmodified Arc Notebooks can be used to make larger planners.

The pocket planner would have a perpetual calendar on the inside of the front cover. The concepts in Figures 5-3a and 5-3b would be used. Table 5-3 shows one way of making the planner pages, assuming the pages are to be bound on the short side. The table shows the front side of the sheet. The back side is similar, with the numbers 17 to 31 instead of 1 to 16.

**Table 5-3**
**Planner Page Concept for Pocket Notepad**

| This area is for the binding. Sheet size is approximately 3 inches wide by 5 inches high. If a screw or another type of binding that does not allow the pages to flip over is used, there will be a fold line at the bottom of this area. |
|---|
| Suggestion: Circle all Sundays |
| Year _________ Month _____________<br>1 |
| 2 |
| 3 |
| 4 |
| 5 |
| 6 |
| 7 |
| 8 |
| 9 |
| 10 |
| 11 |
| 12 |
| 13 |
| 14 |
| 15 |
| 16 |

Using the concept in Table 5-3, only one sheet is required for each month. If enough sheets are put in to cover two years and the notepad has room for 40 sheets, then up to 16 blank sheets can be included for notes. To have more space for appointments, two sheets can be used for each month. In this case, a 40-sheet notepad would have room for 20 months, or for 12 months plus 16 blank sheets for notes. With two sheets per month, the first sheet would have 1 to 8 on the front side and 9 to 16 on the back. The second sheet would have 17 to 24 on the front and 25 to 31 on the back.

## Improving Common Office Day Planners

Common office day planners use sheets that are 5.5 × 8.5 inches or 8.5 × 11 inches. Binders for 8.5 × 11 inch sheets are widely available. Binders for 5.5 × 8.5 inch sheets are not as widely available, but some are manufactured by Avery and other companies. See https://www.avery.ca/products/

mini-binders-and-accessories/minibinders.html. The M by Staples Arc Notebook is an alternative to a binder that has rings that open. Undated (or perpetual) planners are available with various page formats, such as one day per page or two days per page. Most of these planners are bound. Once they are started, the whole planner is used up, as pages cannot be replaced. Many of these planners have a calendar that covers three years, with the assumption that the planner will be used in one of the three years. If you wish to use the planner after the third year, an external calendar is required. The following modifications can enhance the usefulness of these planners and reduce waste:

1. Use a looseleaf binder instead of a bound book. In addition to affording the user the ability to replace pages and thereby reuse a planner that has many pages without any entries, this binder's used pages for many years can be filed in a single large binder.
2. Design the pages so that they are undated and apply to any day of the week. The abbreviations for the days of the week (SMTWTFS) can be at the top of the page for each day and the applicable day of the week circled or checked. There can be blanks to write in the year and the day of the month. There are many undated planners on the market that can be used as a guide. Of course, copyrights must be respected.
3. Add a full-year perpetual calendar to the front. See Figures 8-2a and 8-2b in Chapter 8 for a calendar designed for an 8.5 × 11 inch binder. If you want a 5.5 × 8.5 inch binder, this calendar can be reduced in size or modified to be on two pages. Alternatively, the perpetual calendar design in Figure 5-1a that displays only one month can be adapted to a binder.
4. Put a sheet at the front that lists special days. Instead of actual dates, the method of determining the date would be given. For example, Labour Day would be listed as the first Monday in September. See Figure 5-1d for a list of special days, including the dates for Easter Sunday for the entire 21st century. Instead of being on a separate sheet, the dates can be on the back of the full-year perpetual calendar.
5. Add a divider for each month that has a perpetual calendar on it. When adapted to a binder, the calendar in Figure 5-1a can be used. However, with each divider being for a particular month, the month table can be modified to display only the applicable month. See Figure 6-8 for a multisheet calendar based on Figure 5-1a. See Chapter 6 for other multisheet calendars that can be used for dividers.
6. If the planner is 8.5 × 11 inches or close to that size, add a full-year calendar divider ahead of the sheets that are for dates far in the future. A good choice would be the single-sided slider full-year perpetual calendar in Figures 8-2a and 8-2b. An alternative is the vertical full-year perpetual calendar in Figure 8-3. If the planner size is smaller than 8.5 × 11 inches, the single day-of-month full-year calendars in Figure 8-4a or 8-4b can be reduced in size to fit. Another option is to use a smaller calendar that displays only one month, such as the front of Figure 5-1a.
7. An alternative to the modifications discussed in no. 3 and no. 5 is to have a calendar based on the concept in Figure 5-16b. Such a calendar would be attached to a cardstock sheet at the back of the planner. The calendar would be on a flap that could cover part of the right-hand side of any page. For more information, see the discussion later in this chapter under *Other Applications for the Single-Slider Vertical Calendar.*

## Pencil Holder and Table Lamp

A pencil holder that has a perpetual calendar on it would be a useful item in any office. Figure 5-5 shows a design for a pencil holder that is 3.0 inches in diameter by 3.5 inches high. The calendar consists of an inner sleeve with the day-of-month and month tables on it, and an outer window sleeve. The inner sleeve is firmly attached to the outside of the pencil holder, and the window sleeve is wrapped over the first sleeve. The two ends of the window sleeve are joined together to make a snug fit that enables the window sleeve to be rotated with respect to the inner sleeve. The window sleeve has a year table, a list of special days and a table of dates for Easter Sunday that covers the entire 21st century. These tables occupy about three-quarters of the surface area, leaving an area approximately 3.5 inches square for a picture or some other discretionary use. If the Easter Sunday table is omitted, then an area approximately 3.5 inches high by 7 inches along the arc is available. The calendar is set by rotating the window instead of moving a slider. The month is set over the year, which is the same design as the calendar in Figure 5-1a. As shown in Figure 5-5, one 8.5 × 11 inch sheet has enough area to make the two sleeves. The inner sleeve can be paper, but the outer sleeve should be heavier material, such as 80 lb. cardstock. A raised piece or an area with friction grip can be put on the outer sleeve to provide grip for rotating. The cost of a simple cardstock calendar for a pencil holder is about $1. Pencil holders cost $2 or less at a dollar store and $5 to $10 at a stationery store.

The cardstock design is suitable for small production runs where a calendar is added to a commercially available pencil holder. For a large production run, the inner sleeve would be the outer surface of the pencil holder and the outer sleeve would be made of plastic instead of cardstock.

The same concept that is used to put a perpetual calendar on a pencil holder can be used to put a calendar on a table lamp. To have reasonably large numbers and letters that fit into an approximately 90-degree viewing area for the extremes of rotation, the stem of the lamp should be at least 3.0 inches in diameter. Although a low-cost calendar for a lamp can be made from cardstock, a more durable and aesthetically pleasing material, such as heavy plastic, would be preferable. For a mass-produced lamp, the extra cost for a calendar is estimated to be $5 to $10.

An alternative to using the design in Figure 5-5 for a lamp is to use the designs in Figure 5-16a or 5-16b, which are described later in this chapter. This would be for a lamp with a square stem rather than a round stem.

## Single-Sheet, Dual-Slider Calendar from Cardstock

Figures 5-6a and 5-6b show basic construction details for two slightly different single-sheet perpetual calendars with two sliders designed to hold a 4 × 6 inch landscape photo. The calendar in Figure 5-6b is depicted in Figure 1-1c. These calendars are made from cardstock, and the sliders are held in slits, the same as the single slider in Figure 5-1a. With this type of construction, the marker on the dual-slider calendar has to be in the month table, or above or below the month table. In Figure 5-6a, a marker is put on the month slider under *January* for a common year. The year columns are labeled SMTWTFS. The instructions for using this calendar are as follows:

1. Find the column that has the year of interest, and note the column heading.
2. Move the top slider to put the marker on it above the same day of the week as was found in Step 1.
3. Move the bottom slider to put the *1* under the month of interest.
4. Ignore the dates 29, 30 and 31 when applicable.
5. Note that common years are under the day of the week that January 1 falls on. Leap years are under the day of the week *after* the day of the week that January 1 falls on.

Having to look at which letter the marker is above and then find the year column corresponding to that letter makes checking the setting a bit awkward. When the top slider is made from rigid material and the slider moves in a track, the marker can be on the left-hand end of the slider and point to the applicable column in the year table. See Figures 5-7a, 5-8 and 5-12 for examples. The design in Figure 5-6b also eliminates the need to do a lookup. It has the year table above the top slider, which does not have to be made from rigid material.

The year table in Figures 5-6a and 5-6b is Table 3-9a. The tables in Table 3-9b or 3-9c could be used instead. The month table is Table 3-8, with January and February for common years in the next-to-top row instead of the bottom row.

The calendars in Figures 5-6a and 5-6b can be made as tent calendars, or with a back support similar to that shown in Figure 5-2a. Suggested dimensions of the support are 6.5 inches high (the height of the calendar) by 4.5 inches wide. Make the fold at 1.5 inches to leave 3.0 inches behind the calendar. Two supports can be made from one 8.5 × 11 inch sheet of cardstock. The support can be attached with glue or double-sided tape. As the sliders are in slits, mounting tape does not need to be used to make tracks for them.

## Key Holder

Figure 5-7a shows details of a dual-slider perpetual calendar built into a wall-mounted key holder. Adding a perpetual calendar to a key holder makes a useful and novel product that takes up little more space than a conventional key holder. The advantage of using a dual-slider calendar instead of one of the single-slider calendars (Figures 5-1e and 5-2c) is its lower height. The calendar in Figure 5-7a is designed to be easy to construct. The windows for the day-of-month and month sliders are made by using the edges of the left and right panels, the spacers and the key block to frame them, instead of cutting out windows in a panel. Thus, all the pieces are rectangles. As indicated in the parts list, the suggested material for the left and right panels, the back, the spacers and the sliders is 0.125-inch-thick hardboard. Thin plywood or a mix of materials can be used. A difficulty encountered when using the same thickness of material for the spacers as the sliders is that the gap for the slider to move in is the same as the thickness of the slider. If the sliders are covered with tables made from cardstock, then the gap is far too narrow. In Figure 5-7a, the suggestion is made to build up the thickness of the spacers with cardstock. Another alternative is to use 0.125-inch-thick material for the sliders and 0.25-inch-thick material for the spacers. These suggestions and those in Figure 5-7a apply to making a single key holder or a small production run. For large production runs, the tables can be printed directly on hardboard, plastic or another material instead of cardstock, and custom thicknesses of material can be used.

The year and month tables in Figure 5-7a are the same as in Figures 5-6a and 5-6b. The instructions for setting the calendar on the key holder are as follows:

1. Move the bottom slider so that its push knob is under the column that has the year of interest.
2. Move the top slider to line up its push knob with the month of interest.
3. Ignore dates 29, 30 and 31 when applicable.
4. As noted in the year table and the month table, use the top row of the month table for January and February in leap years, and the next-to-top row for January and February in common years.

If desired, the image or picture on the right-hand panel in Figure 5-7a can be replaced with these instructions.

Alternatives to using a dual-slider calendar for a key holder are to use a single-slider calendar, as described in the next paragraph, or to use a multisheet calendar with a single year table, as described in Chapter 7.

Figure 5-7b shows details of a single-slider perpetual calendar with year tables beside the day-of-month table built into a wall-mounted holder for keys. This calendar uses the slider in Table 3-16 and the year tables in Table 3-17. The construction is similar to the dual-slider key holder in Figure 5-7a. As there is one slider instead of two, this key holder is a little easier to build. In general, this design and the dual-slider design can be used interchangeably.

## Clock

A wall clock or desk clock with a perpetual calendar below the clock is another useful and novel product. Either a single- or a dual-slider calendar can be used. Figure 5-8 shows the concept for the face of a clock with a dual-slider calendar. The face has the following windows:

1. Marker window above the year table to point to applicable years
2. Month table window above SMTWTFS to show which day of the week the first of the month falls on
3. Day-of-month table window below SMTWTFS

The top slider is set at the beginning of the year (January 1), and the bottom slider is set on the first of each month. The detailed instructions are as follows:

1. Move the top slider so that the marker is over the column that has the year of interest.
2. Move the bottom slider to line up the *1* with the month of interest.
3. Ignore dates 29, 30 and 31 when applicable.
4. Use the top row for January and February of leap years, and the next-to-top row for January and February of common years. Leap years are in boldface.

In Figure 5-8, the marker on the top slider is set over the year column that has 2016. The *1* on the bottom slider is set under the months January leap year, April and July. Thus, the setting is for January, April or July of 2016. Only the applicable parts of the month and day-of-month tables are visible. These tables are the same as in Figure 5-7a. The year table is Table 3-9b.

If you imagine the letters SMTWTFS representing the days of the week written above the year columns, then common years are under the day of the week that January 1 falls on. Leap years are under the day of the week *after* the day of the week that January 1 falls on. The year table in Figure 5-8 has leap years and common years together to minimize height. Adding a dual-slider calendar to the bottom of a clock increases the height by about 2.5 inches, or approximately 35 percent.

The windows could be framed with panels and spacers, as is done for the key holder in Figure 5-7a. If this were done, the marker window and the month table window would become one, with a left-hand part and a right-hand part. A better method is to use one panel for the entire face and cut out the three windows as previously noted. The tracks for the sliders can be made with spacer strips as in Figure 5-7a. An alternate method of construction is to make a panel that goes between the front and back panels and that has windows cut out to make the tracks. In Figure 5-8, there is a black dot on the day-of-month slider below the number 29, and a white dot in the middle of the marker above the year table. These dots represent knobs for moving the sliders.

Figure 5-9 shows the concept for the face of a clock with a single-slider calendar. The calendar is similar to the rigid-material model shown in Figure 5-2c. This type of construction or one of the two alternatives at the bottom of Figure 5-9 can be used. The face has the following windows:

1. Month table window above SMTWTFS
2. Day-of-month table window below SMTWTFS

The instructions as printed on the face are as follows:

1. Set month under year.
2. Leap years are in boldface. Use top row of month table for January and February.
3. Ignore 29, 30 and 31 when applicable.

The clock hands sweep over the year table. To minimize the vertical space between the year table and the month table window, the number 6 is omitted from the clock face. It can be included by having the year table closer to the centre of the clock, with the overall height staying the same. With the year table under the clock hands, the single-slider calendar increases the height of the clock by about the same amount as the dual-slider calendar. Since it has one slider instead of two and two windows rather than three, a clock with a single-slider calendar is easier to construct.

Rather than using the single-slider design where a single year table is above the slider, one may use the design with a year table on each side of the day-of-month table. The construction of the calendar can be similar to that for the key holder in Figure 5-7b.

## Single-Sheet, Single-Slider Calendar in a Picture Frame

Many people have a picture frame holding a family photo or other favourite photo on their desk. A picture frame with a built-in perpetual calendar would be a very useful office accessory. For reference, the parts of a picture frame are as follows:

- the frame, which holds everything together and forms a border
- the glazing, which is the transparent front and is usually made of glass or acrylic
- the matting, which separates the glazing from the photo or artwork and highlights the photo or artwork
- the mounting board, which is behind the matting and is not seen
- the protective cover, which covers the back of the frame and the back of the mounting board to prevent dust from entering through the gap between the frame and the mounting board

Simple low-cost frames do not have matting or a protective cover. If the photo (or artwork) is the same size as the glazing, it is put between the glazing and the mounting board. If the photo is smaller than the glazing, a sheet of paper or cardstock is put behind it to cover the mounting board, which is usually some shade of brown and not pleasing to view. The following two paragraphs describe how to build a calendar into a standard 8 × 10 inch picture frame.

Figure 5-10a shows how a single-slider perpetual calendar can be incorporated into a standard 8 × 10 inch picture frame, along with a 5 × 7 inch photo in portrait orientation and a 2 × 3 inch photo in landscape orientation. The calendar is beside the 5 × 7 inch photo, and the 8 × 10 inch frame is in landscape orientation. There is room beside the calendar for a table of dates for Easter Sunday for the years 2000 to 2069 or a motif or picture. In the construction method shown in Figure 5-10a, the calendar and the Easter Sunday table are printed on an 8 × 10 inch sheet of cardstock and two slits are cut for the slider. This is similar to the construction in Figure 5-1a. The two photos are set between the cardstock and the glazing. They can be lightly glued to the cardstock for easier assembly. As shown in Figure 5-10b, two cutouts or one large cutout is made in the mounting board to enable reaching the slider to move it back and forth. Figure 5-10b also shows the slider and an alternate construction. In the alternate construction, there are two pieces of cardstock plus the slider. The front piece, which is in contact with the glass, is 8 × 10 inches and has the Easter Sunday table printed on it. The back piece of cardstock has the calendar printed on it. This piece is glued on the back of the mounting board, and a window is cut in the front cardstock and the mounting board so that the calendar can be seen.

Figure 5-11 shows how a single-slider perpetual calendar can be incorporated into a standard 8 × 10 inch picture frame, along with a 5 × 7 inch photo in landscape orientation. The calendar is below the 5 × 7 inch photo, and the 8 × 10 inch frame is in portrait orientation. Figure 5-11 implies that the construction details are the same as in Figure 5-10a. However, the calendar can be behind the mounting board as in Figure 5-10b. In Figure 5-11, the slider is shown set for May 2016. As can be seen in the figure, there is considerable space on each side of the calendar for a table of dates for Easter Sunday, small photos, motifs or other information. There is even a bit of space between the bottom of the photo and the calendar. This space can be increased by reducing the number of years in the year table. The arrangement in Figure 5-11 is ideal for a group photo. If the construction shown in Figure 5-10a is used, the photo can be printed on the same 8 × 10 inch sheet as the calendar. The names of those in the photo and other information or artwork can be on the same sheet as well.

Instead of putting the calendar and the photograph in the same picture frame, a commercial 5 × 7 inch frame can be used for the photo and a calendar can be attached to the frame. To minimize height, a dual-slider calendar is used, similar to that added to the clock in Figure 5-8. Figure 5-12 illustrates the concept. In Figure 5-12, the picture frame is in landscape orientation. The calendar can also be designed so that the picture frame is in portrait orientation. Another option is to make the calendar so that either a 5 × 7 inch photo or a 4 × 6 inch photo can be mounted in portrait or landscape orientation. However, making a universal calendar at a low cost and with a pleasing appearance may be difficult.

For a large quantity of picture frames with a calendar, a better approach than using a commercially available frame is to design one that has a calendar built in. Of the three designs previously discussed, the best one to use as a guide for doing this is the one in Figure 5-12. An alternative to a dual-slider calendar is the single-slider design, where there is a year table on each side of the day-of-month table. The construction of the calendar can be similar to that for the key holder in Figure 5-7b.

Sometimes picture frames are hinged together to display two photos. A perpetual calendar fits well into this arrangement. One of the frames can have a full-sized photo and the other a smaller photo and a calendar.

## Improving Commercial 13-Column Calendars

Some commercially available perpetual calendars use the basic 13-column day-of-month table that is common to all of my designs. On these calendars, a sliding window moves across the day-of-month table. The window is set at the beginning of each month to display the day of the week each day falls on, but there is no indication of the month or the year. One of the compact calendars shown in Figure 5-3a or 5-3b could be glued to the back, but this would not provide indication of the setting. Figure 5-13a shows two methods of adding stickers to these commercial calendars to provide month and year indication. The methods are as follows:

1. Put a moveable marker near the bottom of the face of the sliding window, a month table below the sliding window and a year table on the back. (The moveable marker can be as simple as a sticker that is moved each year. Another simple idea is a magnetic strip and a small washer that is moved.) The procedure for setting the calendar is as follows:
   a) Find the column that has the year of interest in the table on the back, and then set the marker on the sliding window under the same column.
   b) Set the month by moving the sliding window so that the marker is over the month.

2. Put a year table on the back of the sliding window and a month table below it on the back of the day-of-month table. (The year table moves with the window, whereas the month table is fixed.) The calendar is set by moving the window to put the year over the month. This is the same concept as in the bookmark calendar shown in Figure 5-4. Note that the year and month are only displayed on the back. As there is limited space where the year table is mounted, it has only 33 consecutive years.

If the first method is used for a large production run, the marker should be designed so that it is easily moved, solidly in place and not easily lost. One way of doing this is to glue a thick strip of plastic that has seven threaded holes to the bottom of the window. The marker would then be a small stud bolt that is put in the applicable hole for the year.

While either of these two methods can be used for large production runs, a better approach is to redesign the calendar. One way of doing this is to adapt the moving-window design shown in Figure 5-3a. A disadvantage of this approach is that the year table at the bottom of the window takes up considerable vertical space. Figure 5-13b shows a way that uses ideas from both methods. Following Method 1, a moveable marker is added near the bottom of the sliding window and a month table is added below the sliding window. The finished calendar then looks almost the same from the front as the calendar shown in Method 1 in Figure 5-13a. However, the marker is a bolt that goes right through to the back and there is a slot for the bolt to travel in. The back of the sliding window is extended so that it is the same height as the front and the bolt passes through the extension. Following Method 2, a year table is put on the back of the sliding window. With the sliding window extended, there is room for a full century. Since the bolt passes through the extension, it will point to a year column. Thus, the front end of the bolt will point to the applicable months, and the back end will point to the applicable years. As the bolt will usually be set only at the beginning of the year, having to look at the back of the calendar to check the year setting will not be an inconvenience.

## Wall Planners

Many offices use an erasable wall planner to display meetings and events. Figure 5-14a shows a typical example. There are seven columns labeled *Sunday* to *Saturday* that have day blocks. Each day block has a small box in the upper left-hand corner for writing in the day of the month. As the day of the week that a date falls on changes each month, the numbers in the small boxes have to be changed each month. Figure 5-14b shows a 13-column prenumbered erasable wall planner with a window that eliminates the need to write in the numbers. This planner uses the 13-column day-of-month table that is in most of my perpetual calendars and a moveable window to select the columns that apply for the current month. This table that is used for writing in events could be part of a large perpetual calendar that uses the previously described concept of the single-sheet perpetual calendar with a single slider or a dual slider. However, this would make an already large planner even larger, so a small perpetual calendar is incorporated into the upper left-hand corner of the moveable window. If the calendar uses the single-slider concepts of Figure 5-1a, it would add fewer than four inches to the height of the window for a calendar covering a full century. If it uses the dual-slider in the clock shown in Figure 5-8, it would add only 2.5 inches to the overall height.

The side view in Figure 5-14b illustrates a window that can be moved across the top of the planner sheet by sliding it in a track. This would make the planner considerably more complicated than the standard one that is simply taped to the wall. A simpler method would be to make the window from magnetic material and put a narrow strip of painted iron sheet metal above the planner. If this were done, then the perpetual calendar would be mounted separately from the window.

A typical planner with 7 columns is 24 inches high by 24 to 36 inches wide. After allowing an inch for a border on each side of these planners, the cell width is calculated to be 3.1 to 4.8 inches. For the same cell width and border in a 13-column planner, the overall width is 42 to 64 inches. For many offices, the overall width for a reasonable cell width would be too large. The width can be reduced by using seven strips for the planner rather than one large sheet. Each strip is one column of the planner and can be put under any day of the week. The top of each strip can be in either the first or the second row. The small perpetual calendar in the upper left-hand corner of the frame is set to the month to show how the strips are to be arranged. Figure 5-15a shows how the strips are arranged when the first of the month is on a Wednesday, and Figure 5-15b shows how they are arranged when the first of the month is on a Saturday. One way of hanging the strips is to make them from magnetic material and place a piece of iron sheet metal on the wall that they can be attached to.

Instead of making a planner look like a conventional calendar with seven columns, the planner can have lines numbered 1 to 31, as in the single-slider vertical calendar shown in Table 3-18. If the lines are spaced at 0.5 inches, the planning sheet would be only 24 inches high after allowance for slider travel. The overall width can be as desired. An option is to make a wide planner (say, 36 inches) and have light guidelines on it to enable the user to cut it down to size.

Figure 5-16a shows the line-style planner with a single-slider vertical perpetual calendar on the left-hand side. Having a full calendar instead of a slider with just the days of the week adds about five inches to the width. This planner can be 24 inches high by 30 to 36 inches wide, which is the same size as a typical planner. After allowing five inches for the calendar and three inches for the day-of-the-week and day-of-the-month columns, there would be a line about 20 inches long for writing events on the 30-inch-wide planner. Figure 5-16a does not show any method of moving the slider and holding it in place. The simplest method is to make the body of the planner from painted iron sheet metal and hold the slider in place with magnets.

In summary, Figures 5-14b, 5-15 and 5-16a illustrate three different methods of using perpetual calendar concepts to eliminate having to write the days of the month on a wall planner each month. The planner in Figure 5-14b is the easiest to use, but it has the disadvantage of being 13 columns wide, compared to 7 for a conventional planner. This increases the width by a factor of approximately 1.85 for the same block width, resulting in a planner that may be too large. The planner in Figures 5-15a and 5-15b increases the width slightly to allow for borders on the strips but requires more effort to change each month. Both of these planners have a separate perpetual calendar that must be looked at to verify which month is to be displayed. The planner in Figure 5-16a has a line instead of a rectangular block for writing in events, and has a built-in perpetual calendar that indicates the month and the year. Thus, there are advantages and disadvantages to each design. Even if none of these is attractive for an office, having a small wall-mounted perpetual calendar near a standard planner can be very useful.

## Other Applications for the Single-Slider Vertical Calendar

The design in Figure 5-16a can be reduced in size to make a wall calendar that holds 8.5 × 11 inch sheets of paper. Either blank sheets, which could be recycled paper, or lined sheets with the numbers 1 to 31 printed on them can be used. Blank sheets would be mounted to the right of the column that has the numbers 1 to 31. Sheets with numbers printed on them can cover the column. The sheets would be clamped along the right-hand side and at the upper and lower left corners. The corner clamps would be easily undone to enable looking at and writing on the sheets behind the top sheet. For both blank sheets and printed sheets, the user would have to at least write the month and year on the top of the sheet, and indicate which days are Sundays. When the sheets are blank, the user would also have to add the numbers 1 to 31, or some numbers to enable identification of the lines. The overall size of this calendar would be about 16 inches wide by 12 to 16 inches high. An advantage of having a calendar that enables adding sheets is that the calendar is not limited to 12 months. This is the same advantage previously noted for the monthly planners.

A second application for the design in Figure 5-16a is a lamp with a square stem. The minimum size of the stem is about 2.5 inches square by 8.0 inches high. For a stem this size, the slider and the numbers 1 to 31 would be on one face, and the year table would be on an adjacent face. If the stem is 5.0 inches or more square, then all of the calendar can be on one face.

A third application for the design in Figure 5-16a is to combine this concept with that of the magnetic type calendar in Figure A-7a. The calendar in Figure 5-16a would be rotated so that the slider moves horizontally instead of vertically. (With the change in direction, the calendar designation could be changed to single-slider linear calendar.) The rotated calendar, with the 1 to 31 number strip removed, would then be placed below the straight piece of material in Figure A-7a that has the numbers 1 to 31.

A fourth application for a single-slider vertical calendar is a day planner. Figure 5-16b shows a design that has the calendar on the right-hand side of the paper rather than on the left-hand side, as in Figure 5-16a. To install this calendar in a planner, put a piece of cardstock about 11 inches high by 12.5 inches wide in the back of the planner. Fold the cardstock along a line that is 3.0 inches from the right-hand edge. (When folded over, the cardstock will cover about 2.0 inches of the right-hand edge of the 8.5 × 11 inch sheets in the planner.) Then attach the calendar in Figure 5-16b to the folded-over cardstock.

## Hybrid Calendar

There are many commercially available perpetual wall calendars that have tiles for the date. The tiles are rearranged at the beginning of each month with reference to a current year calendar. Figures 5-17a to 5-17c illustrate a calendar design that uses tiles but incorporates a feature that eliminates the need to refer to another calendar. The feature, which is at the top of Figure 5-17a, uses both the month table slider and the year table from the dual-slider calendar. (See Figures 5-6a, 5-6b, 5-7a and 5-8, and Tables 3-8 and 3-9.) When the marker on the slider is lined up with the year of interest, the window below the year table indicates which day of the week the first of each month falls on. Most commercial calendars have a tile made of wood or other material for each day of the month (1, 2, 3, etc., to 31) plus tiles for the names of the months. To illustrate another way of making a tile calendar, Figure 5-17 has a tile for each column in the calendar. The first tile column has the numbers 1, 8, 15, 22 and 29; the next has 2, 9, 16, 23 and 30; and so on to the seventh tile column, which has the numbers 7, 14, 21 and 28. As shown in Figure 5-17b, there are actually 9 double-sided tiles to account for the first number in the column being in either the top or next-to-top row, and also for the fact that the number of days in a month can be 28, 29, 30 or 31. An alternative to using nine double-sided tiles made of thin material (up to 0.125 inches thick) is to use seven blocks that have a square cross-section. Five of the blocks would have printing on two sides, and two would have printing on all four sides. This alternative would work well if the columns were up to about 0.5 inches wide. However, for a column, say, 1.0 inch wide, the cross-section of the block would be 1.0 × 1.0 inches. This is a little large. Plus, each block would be heavy if it were made of wood.

The calendar is set by moving the slider so that the marker is under the column that has the year of interest. The user, after looking in the window to find which day of the week the first of the month of interest falls on, arranges the tiles appropriately. This is a bit more work than is required for the other calendars in this chapter that have the days of the month on a 13-column slider that is moved to display the 7 columns that apply to the month of interest, e.g. Figure 5-6. (Depending on the arrangement, the window, rather than the slider, can move.) In Figure 5-17a, there are no tiles to display the month, as the month can be determined by tracing from the day of the week that has *1* under it back to the window. If desired, tiles with the names of the months could be added. The tile with the name of the current month could be hung above the year table.

## Stand with Calendar

Figure 5-18 shows a perpetual calendar built into a block that can be either a stand-alone calendar or a stand for a commercial perpetual desk calendar or picture frame. In Figure 5-18, a single-slider calendar with side year tables is used for low height and simplicity. A dual-slider calendar (see Figure 5-7a or 5-8) or a multisheet calendar with a single year table could also be used (see Figure 1-3a and Chapter 7). Setting a non-stand-alone commercial perpetual calendar on top of a stand-alone perpetual calendar seems redundant; however, the commercial calendar has a larger display. As an alternative to mounting the calendar on a block or box as in Figure 5-18, the calendar could be flat like a pocket calendar and lie on the desk almost out of sight.

## Solving Date Problems

The single-sheet perpetual calendar is very useful for solving date problems. Some examples are as follows:

- You are at a meeting of a camping club that always has a weeklong outing around Canada Day, which is July 1. Someone asks when the outings will be held for the next few years. If only a conventional calendar for the current year is available, the day of the week that July 1 falls on could be determined. However, an error could be made by failing to account for a leap year. With a single-sheet perpetual calendar, the day of the week for July 1 can be quickly determined by setting *July* on the slider over each year of interest. The results are as follows:

| **Year** | 2017 | 2018 | 2019 | 2020 | 2021 |
|---|---|---|---|---|---|
| **Day of week** | Saturday | Sunday | Monday | Wednesday | Thursday |

- You find a sheet of paper dated Friday, February 4. What was the year? Set *4* under *Friday*. Under *February* for common years, you note that the year could have been 2005 or 2011. Under *February* for leap years, you find *2000*. You know that the paper is less than 10 years old, so you conclude that it is from 2011.

- You want to know which years have three Friday the thirteenths. Set *13* under *Friday*. Note that for common years, the only group of three months that begin on the same day of the week are February, March and November. The applicable years under these months are 2009, 2015, 2026, etc. For leap years, the only group of three months that begin on the same day of the week are January, April and July. The applicable years under these months are 2012, 2040, etc.

- You come across a newspaper article dated May 13, 2013, and it reports that an event took place on Sunday. What was the date of the event? Set the calendar for May 2013 and note that the 13th was on a Monday. Assuming that the article was written very soon after the event, you conclude that it must have taken place on Sunday, May 12, 2013.

- On June 22, 2017, a co-worker mentions that today is her wedding anniversary, but does not say which one. You remember that she was married on a Saturday but you forget the year. Set the calendar so that the 22nd is on Saturday. The recent years under June are 2002 and 2013. You know the wedding was later than 2002, so it must have been 2013.

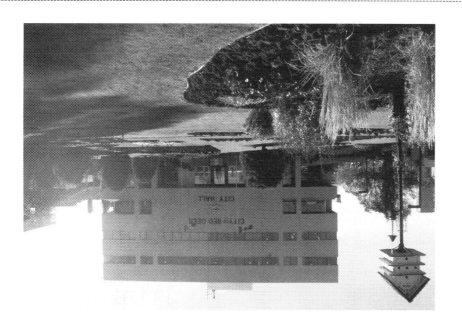

Fold along the dashed lines.

# RED DEER
# ALBERTA
# CANADA

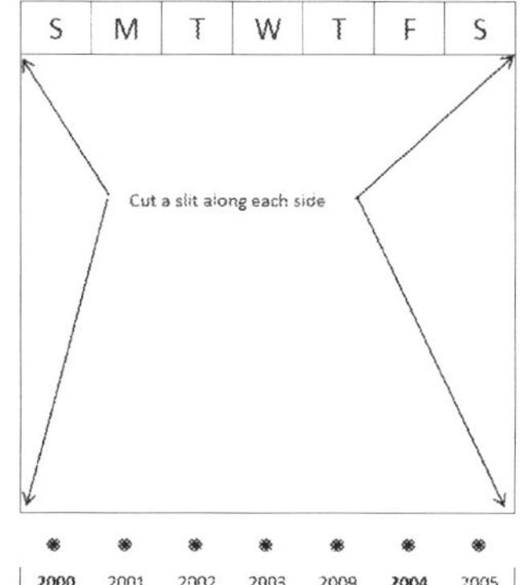

S
M
T
W
T
F
S
Cut a slit along each side


| | | | | | | |
|---|---|---|---|---|---|---|
| **2000** | 2001 | 2002 | 2003 | 2009 | **2004** | 2005 |
| 2006 | 2007 | 2013 | **2008** | 2015 | 2010 | 2011 |
| 2017 | **2012** | 2019 | 2014 | **2020** | 2021 | **2016** |
| 2023 | 2018 | **2024** | 2025 | 2026 | 2027 | 2022 |
| **2028** | 2029 | 2030 | 2031 | 2037 | **2032** | 2033 |
| 2034 | 2035 | 2041 | **2036** | 2043 | 2038 | 2039 |
| 2045 | **2040** | 2047 | 2042 | **2048** | 2049 | **2044** |
| 2051 | 2046 | **2052** | 2053 | 2054 | 2055 | 2050 |
| **2056** | 2057 | 2058 | 2059 | 2065 | **2060** | 2061 |
| 2062 | 2063 | 2069 | **2064** | 2071 | 2066 | 2067 |
| 2073 | **2068** | 2075 | 2070 | **2076** | 2077 | **2072** |
| 2079 | 2074 | **2080** | 2081 | 2082 | 2083 | 2078 |
| **2084** | 2085 | 2086 | 2087 | 2093 | **2088** | 2089 |
| 2090 | 2091 | 2097 | **2092** | 2099 | 2094 | 2095 |
| | **2096** | | 2098 | | | |

INSTRUCTIONS

1. Set month over year.
2. Leap years are bold. Use top row of month table for January and February.
3. Ignore 29, 30 and 31 when applicable.

To identify the current year, a pin can be put into the dot above the applicable column.

For 20th century, pull out table installed behind rear picture.
If desired, slits can be cut beside the 21st century table to hold the 20th century table.

A good website for finding holidays and phases of the moon is www.timeanddate.com/calendar

How the Year Table is Constructed

For Common Years, the year is under the day of the week that January 1 falls on. For example, January 1, 2001 was on a Monday.

For Leap Years, the year is under the day of the week after the day of the week that January 1 falls on. For example, January 1, 2000 was on a Saturday.

Figure 5-1a: Body of a single-window tent desk calendar made from cardstock

| | | | | | | | | | | | | |
|---|---|---|---|---|---|---|---|---|---|---|---|---|
| | | | | | | 1 | 2 | 3 | 4 | 5 | 6 | 7 |
| 2 | 3 | 4 | 5 | 6 | 7 | 8 | 9 | 10 | 11 | 12 | 13 | 14 |
| 9 | 10 | 11 | 12 | 13 | 14 | 15 | 16 | 17 | 18 | 19 | 20 | 21 |
| 16 | 17 | 18 | 19 | 20 | 21 | 22 | 23 | 24 | 25 | 26 | 27 | 28 |
| 23 | 24 | 25 | 26 | 27 | 28 | 29 | 30 | 31 | | | | |
| 30 | 31 | | | | | | | | | | | |
| **JAN** | LEAP YR | LEAP YR | LEAP YR | **FEB** | LEAP YR | LEAP YR | **JAN** | LEAP YR | LEAP YR | LEAP YR | **FEB** | LEAP YR |
| APR | SEP | JUN | MAR | AUG | MAY | OCT | APR | SEP | JUN | MAR | AUG | MAY |
| JUL | DEC | | NOV | | | | JUL | DEC | | NOV | | |
| COM YR | COM YR | COM YR | FEB | COM YR | COM YR | JAN | COM YR | COM YR | COM YR | FEB | COM YR | COM YR |

| | | | | | | |
|---|---|---|---|---|---|---|
| | 1900 | 1901 | 1902 | 1903 | 1909 | **1904** |
| 1905 | 1906 | 1907 | 1913 | **1908** | 1915 | 1910 |
| 1911 | 1917 | **1912** | 1919 | 1914 | **1920** | 1921 |
| **1916** | 1923 | 1918 | **1924** | 1925 | 1926 | 1927 |
| 1922 | **1928** | 1929 | 1930 | 1931 | 1937 | **1932** |
| 1933 | 1934 | 1935 | 1941 | **1936** | 1943 | 1938 |
| 1939 | 1945 | **1940** | 1947 | 1942 | **1948** | 1949 |
| **1944** | 1951 | 1946 | **1952** | 1953 | 1954 | 1955 |
| 1950 | **1956** | 1957 | 1958 | 1959 | 1965 | **1960** |
| 1961 | 1962 | 1963 | 1969 | **1964** | 1971 | 1966 |
| 1967 | 1973 | **1968** | 1975 | 1970 | **1976** | 1977 |
| 1972 | 1979 | 1974 | **1980** | 1981 | 1982 | 1983 |
| 1978 | **1984** | 1985 | 1986 | 1987 | 1993 | **1988** |
| 1989 | 1990 | 1991 | 1997 | **1992** | 1999 | 1994 |
| 1995 | | **1996** | | 1998 | | |

Figure 5-1b Slider and year table for 20th century

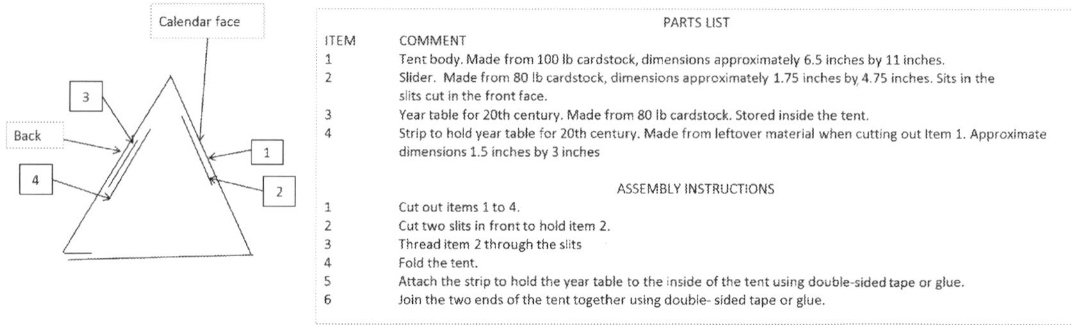
Calendar face
Back
1
2
3
4

PARTS LIST

| ITEM | COMMENT |
|---|---|
| 1 | Tent body. Made from 100 lb cardstock, dimensions approximately 6.5 inches by 11 inches. |
| 2 | Slider. Made from 80 lb cardstock, dimensions approximately 1.75 inches by 4.75 inches. Sits in the slits cut in the front face. |
| 3 | Year table for 20th century. Made from 80 lb cardstock. Stored inside the tent. |
| 4 | Strip to hold year table for 20th century. Made from leftover material when cutting out Item 1. Approximate dimensions 1.5 inches by 3 inches |

ASSEMBLY INSTRUCTIONS

1. Cut out items 1 to 4.
2. Cut two slits in front to hold item 2.
3. Thread item 2 through the slits
4. Fold the tent.
5. Attach the strip to hold the year table to the inside of the tent using double-sided tape or glue.
6. Join the two ends of the tent together using double- sided tape or glue.

Figure 5-1c Parts list and assembly instructions

INSTRUCTIONS
1. Move slider to set month over year.
2. Leap years are bold. Use top row of month table for January and February.
3. Ignore 29, 30 and 31 when applicable.

SPECIAL DAYS

| | |
|---|---|
| New Year's Day | January 1 |
| Family Day | 3rd Monday in Feb. |
| Ash Wednesday | 46 days before Easter Sunday |
| Easter Sunday | See table |
| Mother's Day | 2nd Sunday in May |
| Victoria Day | Monday preceding May 25 |
| Father's Day | 3rd Sunday in June |
| Canada Day | July 1 |
| Civic Holiday | 1st Monday in Aug. |
| Labour Day | 1st Monday in Sept. |
| Thanksgiving | 2nd Monday in Oct. |
| Remembrance Day | November 11 |
| Christmas Day | December 25 |
| Boxing Day | December 26 |

Advent begins on the 4th Sunday before Dec. 25
Epiphany begins on Jan. 6
Lent begins on Ash Wednesday
Pentecost Sunday is the 7th Sunday after Easter

Most of Canada and the United States observe Daylight Saving Time from the second Sunday in March to the first Sunday in November.

DATE OF EASTER SUNDAY

| YEAR | DATE | YEAR | DATE | YEAR | DATE |
|---|---|---|---|---|---|
| 2000 | April 23 | 2035 | March 25 | 2070 | March 30 |
| 2001 | April 15 | 2036 | April 13 | 2071 | April 19 |
| 2002 | March 31 | 2037 | April 5 | 2072 | April 10 |
| 2003 | April 20 | 2038 | April 25 | 2073 | March 26 |
| 2004 | April 11 | 2039 | April 10 | 2074 | April 15 |
| 2005 | March 27 | 2040 | April 1 | 2075 | April 7 |
| 2006 | April 16 | 2041 | April 21 | 2076 | April 19 |
| 2007 | April 8 | 2042 | April 6 | 2077 | April 11 |
| 2008 | March 23 | 2043 | March 29 | 2078 | April 3 |
| 2009 | April 12 | 2044 | April 17 | 2079 | April 23 |
| 2010 | April 4 | 2045 | April 9 | 2080 | April 7 |
| 2011 | April 24 | 2046 | March 25 | 2081 | March 30 |
| 2012 | April 8 | 2047 | April 14 | 2082 | April 19 |
| 2013 | March 31 | 2048 | April 5 | 2083 | April 4 |
| 2014 | April 20 | 2049 | April 18 | 2084 | March 26 |
| 2015 | April 5 | 2050 | April 10 | 2085 | April 15 |
| 2016 | March 27 | 2051 | April 2 | 2086 | March 31 |
| 2017 | April 16 | 2052 | April 21 | 2087 | April 20 |
| 2018 | April 1 | 2053 | April 6 | 2088 | April 11 |
| 2019 | April 21 | 2054 | March 29 | 2089 | April 3 |
| 2020 | April 12 | 2055 | April 18 | 2090 | April 16 |
| 2021 | April 4 | 2056 | April 2 | 2091 | April 8 |
| 2022 | April 17 | 2057 | April 22 | 2092 | March 31 |
| 2023 | April 9 | 2058 | April 14 | 2093 | April 12 |
| 2024 | March 31 | 2059 | March 30 | 2094 | April 04 |
| 2025 | April 20 | 2060 | April 18 | 2095 | April 24 |
| 2026 | April 5 | 2061 | April 10 | 2096 | April 15 |
| 2027 | March 28 | 2062 | March 26 | 2097 | March 31 |
| 2028 | April 16 | 2063 | April 15 | 2098 | April 20 |
| 2029 | April 1 | 2064 | April 6 | 2099 | April 12 |
| 2030 | April 21 | 2065 | March 29 | | |
| 2031 | April 13 | 2066 | April 11 | | |
| 2032 | March 28 | 2067 | April 3 | | |
| 2033 | April 17 | 2068 | April 22 | | |
| 2034 | April 9 | 2069 | April 14 | | |

A good website for finding holidays and phases of the moon is www.timeanddate.com/calendar

NOTES ON USING EXCEL FOR GRAPHICS
1. Except as noted, all rows are 15 high.
2. All column widths are 3 before any merging.
3. Tent face and back are 40 rows high. The bottom is the remainder of the 11 inch cardstock.
4. Tent width is 44 columns.
5. Slider width is 32 columns.
6. Slider height is 16 rows for the tables plus a row 3.7 high on the top and a row 3.7 high on the bottom to allow for cutting.
7. Make the slits for the slider 17 rows high to allow some room for tolerance.
8. The SMTWTFS heading and the numbers in the day of month table (1 to 31) are in merged cells that are 2 rows high by 2 columns wide. The font is Calibri 18.
9. The entries in the month table and the year table are in merged cells that are 1 row high by 2 columns wide. The font is Calibri 11 for most entries. The font for "LEAP YEAR" and "COM YEAR" is Calibri 9.
10. Wherever possible use cell outlines for lines and fill instead of lines and shapes in the drawing tools.
11. Print at 45% of normal size.

HINTS FOR SETTING HEIGHTS AND WIDTHS

HEIGHT: If a part that is N rows high starts in row M, it ends in row M + N - 1.

WIDTH: Make up a table with the letters A to Z in one column and the numbers 1 to 26 in another column and use this table to give the columns numbers. For example, we want something 32 columns wide that starts in Column B. From the table, Column B can be considered to be Column 2. Column B to Column Z is 25 columns. Therefore, we need 7 more columns. From the table, Column G can be considered to be Column 7. Therefore 7 columns after Column Z will be Column AG. Thus, start the item in Column B and end it in AG.

Figure 5-1d: An alternative to a picture on the back and notes on using Excel for graphics.

Figures 5-1b to 5-1d: Slider and other details for a single-window tent desk calendar

1
4
S M T W T F S
1 2 3 4 5 6 7
2 3 4 5 6 7 8 9 10 11 12 13 14
9 10 11 12 13 14 15 16 17 18 19 20 21
16 17 18 19 20 21 22 23 24 25 26 27 28
23 24 25 26 27 28 29 30 31
30 31
JAN LEAP YR LEAP YR LEAP YR FEB LEAP YR LEAP YR JAN LEAP YR LEAP YR LEAP YR FEB LEAP YR
APR SEP JUN MAR AUG MAY OCT APR SEP JUN MAR AUG MAY
JUL DEC NOV JUL DEC NOV
COM YR COM YR COM YR FEB COM YR COM YR JAN COM YR COM YR COM YR FEB COM YR COM YR
2000 2001 2002 2003 2009 2004 2005
2006 2007 2013 2008 2015 2010 2011
2017 2012 2019 2014 2020 2021 2016
2023 2018 2024 2025 2026 2027 2022
2028 2029 2030 2031 2037 2032 2033
2034 2035 2041 2036 2043 2038 2039
2045 2040 2047 2042 2048 2049 2044
2051 2046 2052 2053 2054 2055 2050
2056 2057 2058 2059 2065 2060 2061
2062 2063 2069 2064 2071 2066 2067
2073 2068 2075 2070 2076 2077 2072
2079 2074 2080 2081 2082 2083 2078
2084 2085 2086 2087 2093 2088 2089
2090 2091 2097 2092 2099 2094 2095
2096 2098
3
RED DEER
ALBERTA
CANADA
INSTRUCTIONS
1. Set month over year.
2. Leap years are bold. Use top row of month table for January and February.
3. Ignore 29, 30 and 31 when applicable.
2
PARTS LIST FOR WOOD MODEL BELOW
ITEM COMMENT
1 Front top strip, approx. 0.75 in. wide by 6.5 in. long. Suggested material 0.125 in. thick hardwood.
2 Front bottom strip, approx. 2.5 in. wide by 6.5 in long. Same material as item 1.
3 Slider, approx. 2.25 in. high by 4.75 in. long. Same material as item 1.
4 Back, approx. 6.5 in. wide by 4.0 in. high by 0.75 in. thick, with a groove approximately 0.2 in. deep by 2.25 in. wide cut for Item 3. Suggested material 1 by 4 spruce board or 0.75 in. plywood.
5 Back prop approx. 2.0 in. by 4.0 in. by 0.75 in. thick. Cut to shape to give desired tilt to front. Same material as item 4.
NOTE: All printed material is on thin cardstock which is glued to the faces of items 1, 2 and 3.
Cross-section through middle
5
Side view showing calendar on a table with prop holding it up.

Figure 5-1e: Single-window desk calendar made from wood

2000 2001 2002 2003 2009 2004 2005
2006 2007 2013 2008 2015 2010 2011
2017 2012 2019 2014 2020 2021 2016
2023 2018 2024 2025 2026 2027 2022
2028 2029 2030 2031 2037 2032 2033
2034 2035 2041 2036 2043 2038 2039
2045 2040 2047 2042 2048 2049 2044
2051 2046 2052 2053 2054 2055 2050
2056 2057 2058 2059 2065 2060 2061
2062 2063 2069 2064 2071 2066 2067
2073 2068 2075 2070 2076 2077 2072
2079 2074 2080 2081 2082 2083 2078
2084 2085 2086 2087 2093 2088 2089
2090 2091 2097 2092 2099 2094 2095
2096 2098
Cut out this window
S M T W T F S
Cut out this window
RED DEER
ALBERTA
CANADA
INSTRUCTIONS
1. Set month under year.
2. Leap years are bold. Use top row of month table for January and February.
3. Ignore 29, 30 and 31 when applicable.
JAN LEAP YR LEAP YR LEAP YR FEB LEAP YR LEAP YR JAN LEAP YR LEAP YR LEAP YR FEB LEAP YR
APR SEP JUN MAR AUG MAY OCT APR SEP JUN MAR AUG MAY
JUL DEC NOV JUL DEC NOV
COM YR COM YR COM YR FEB COM YR COM YR JAN COM YR COM YR COM YR FEB COM YR COM YR
1 2 3 4 5 6 7
2 3 4 5 6 7 8 9 10 11 12 13 14
9 10 11 12 13 14 15 16 17 18 19 20 21
16 17 18 19 20 21 22 23 24 25 26 27 28
23 24 25 26 27 28 29 30 31
30 31
PARTS LIST
ITEM COMMENT
1 Front piece
2 Slider
3 Back support
4 0.5 in. wide 1/16 in. thick mounting tape for attaching back support and for making a track for the slider
Same as window width
CONSTRUCTION NOTES
1. Cut items 1 to 3 from one 8.5 x 11 inch sheet of 80 or 100 lb piece of cardstock.
2. Cut out the two windows shown above.
3. Attach back support with mounting tape on bottom and top to provide a space for the slider to move in. The bottom strip of mounting tape must be accurately lined up with the bottom edge of the lower window. Locate the top strip of mounting tape so that slider moves freely.
4. Trim bottom edge of front as required.
5. Slip in slider.
FOLD
Notes
For years not shown, make a marker from a Sticky Note and put it above the day of week that applies to the year of interest. For common years not shown, the day of the week is the day that January 1 falls on. For leap years, the day of the week is the is the day after the day of the week that Jnauary 1 falls on.

See Figure 5-2b for an alternate window construction.

Figure 5-2a: Double-window desk calendar made from cardstock

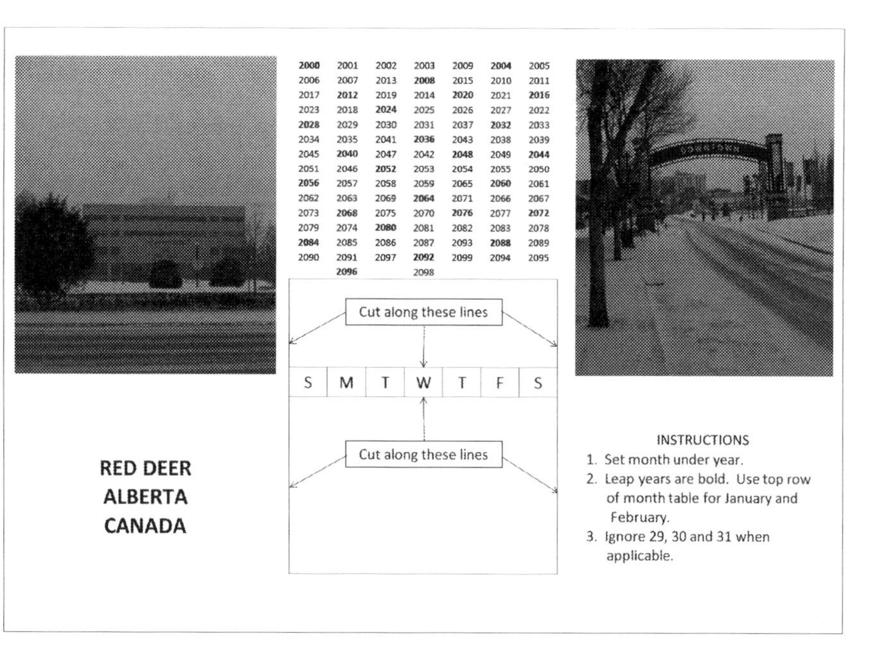

2000 2001 2002 2003 2009 2004 2005
2006 2007 2013 2008 2015 2010 2011
2017 2012 2019 2014 2020 2021 2016
2023 2018 2024 2025 2026 2027 2022
2028 2029 2030 2031 2037 2032 2033
2034 2035 2041 2036 2043 2038 2039
2045 2040 2047 2042 2048 2049 2044
2051 2046 2052 2053 2054 2055 2050
2056 2057 2058 2059 2065 2060 2061
2062 2063 2069 2064 2071 2066 2067
2073 2068 2075 2070 2076 2077 2072
2079 2074 2080 2081 2082 2083 2078
2084 2085 2086 2087 2093 2088 2089
2090 2091 2097 2092 2099 2094 2095
2096 2098
Cut along these lines
S M T W T F S
Cut along these lines
RED DEER
ALBERTA
CANADA
INSTRUCTIONS
1. Set month under year.
2. Leap years are bold. Use top row of month table for January and February.
3. Ignore 29, 30 and 31 when applicable.


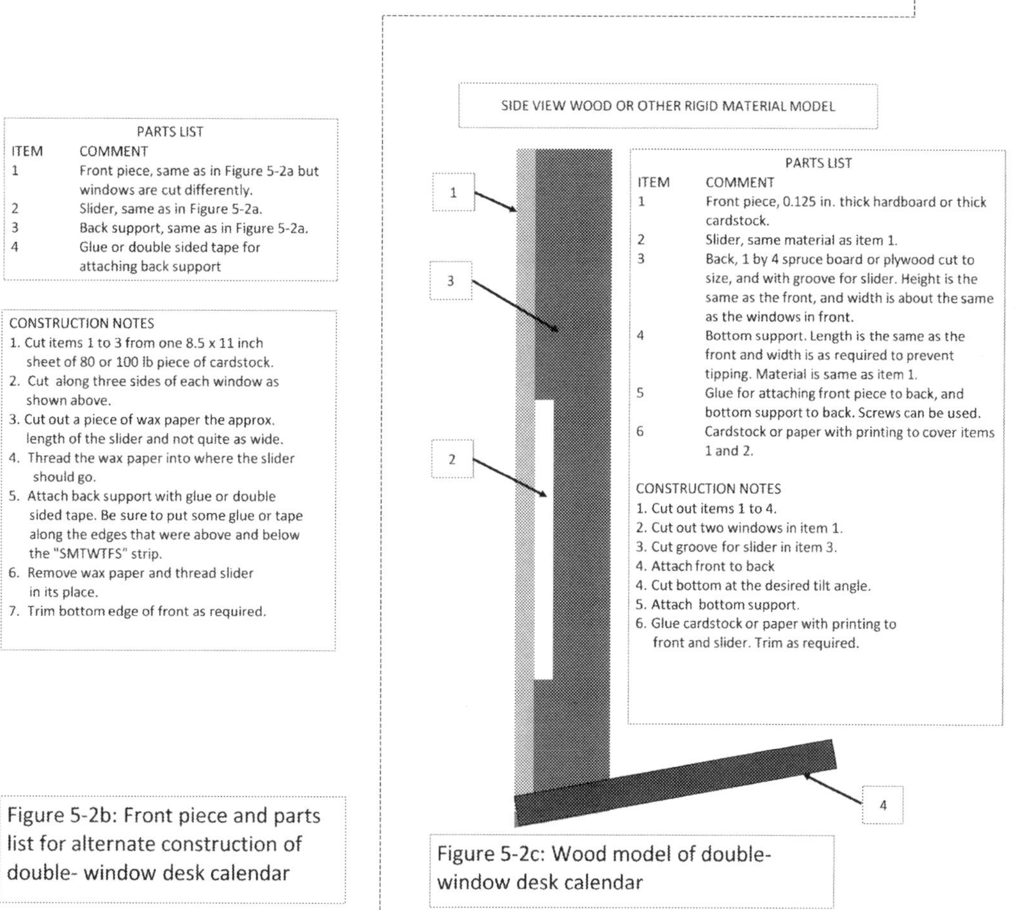

PARTS LIST
ITEM COMMENT
1 Front piece, same as in Figure 5-2a but windows are cut differently.
2 Slider, same as in Figure 5-2a.
3 Back support, same as in Figure 5-2a.
4 Glue or double sided tape for attaching back support
CONSTRUCTION NOTES
1. Cut items 1 to 3 from one 8.5 x 11 inch sheet of 80 or 100 lb piece of cardstock.
2. Cut along three sides of each window as shown above.
3. Cut out a piece of wax paper the approx. length of the slider and not quite as wide.
4. Thread the wax paper into where the slider should go.
5. Attach back support with glue or double sided tape. Be sure to put some glue or tape along the edges that were above and below the "SMTWTFS" strip.
6. Remove wax paper and thread slider in its place.
7. Trim bottom edge of front as required.
SIDE VIEW WOOD OR OTHER RIGID MATERIAL MODEL
1
3
2
4
PARTS LIST
ITEM COMMENT
1 Front piece, 0.125 in. thick hardboard or thick cardstock.
2 Slider, same material as item 1.
3 Back, 1 by 4 spruce board or plywood cut to size, and with groove for slider. Height is the same as the front, and width is about the same as the windows in front.
4 Bottom support. Length is the same as the front and width is as required to prevent tipping. Material is same as item 1.
5 Glue for attaching front piece to back, and bottom support to back. Screws can be used.
6 Cardstock or paper with printing to cover items 1 and 2.
CONSTRUCTION NOTES
1. Cut out items 1 to 4.
2. Cut out two windows in item 1.
3. Cut groove for slider in item 3.
4. Attach front to back
4. Cut bottom at the desired tilt angle.
5. Attach bottom support.
6. Glue cardstock or paper with printing to front and slider. Trim as required.


Figure 5-2b: Front piece and parts list for alternate construction of double- window desk calendar

Figure 5-2c: Wood model of double-window desk calendar

Figures 5-2b and 5-2c: Alternate construction of double-window desk calendar and wood model

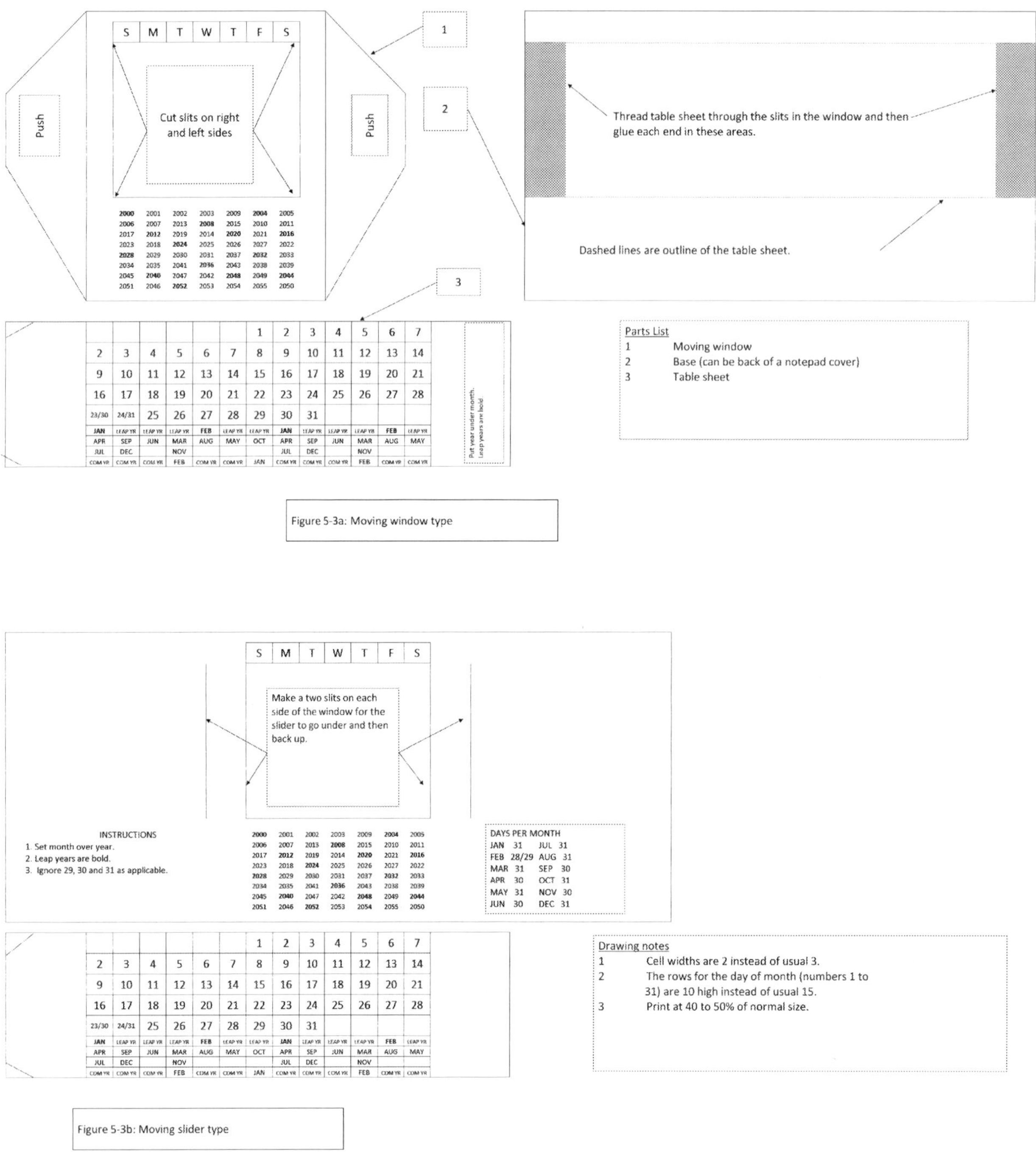
1
2
3
S M T W T F S
Cut slits on right and left sides
Push
Push
Thread table sheet through the slits in the window and then glue each end in these areas.
Dashed lines are outline of the table sheet.
Put year under month.
Leap years are bold.
Parts List
1 Moving window
2 Base (can be back of a notepad cover)
3 Table sheet
Figure 5-3a: Moving window type
Make a two slits on each side of the window for the slider to go under and then back up.
INSTRUCTIONS
1. Set month over year.
2. Leap years are bold.
3. Ignore 29, 30 and 31 as applicable.
DAYS PER MONTH
JAN 31 JUL 31
FEB 28/29 AUG 31
MAR 31 SEP 30
APR 30 OCT 31
MAY 31 NOV 30
JUN 30 DEC 31
Drawing notes
1 Cell widths are 2 instead of usual 3.
2 The rows for the day of month (numbers 1 to 31) are 10 high instead of usual 15.
3 Print at 40 to 50% of normal size.
Figure 5-3b: Moving slider type

| | | | | | | | |
|---|---|---|---|---|---|---|---|
| 2000 | 2001 | 2002 | 2003 | 2009 | 2004 | 2005 |
| 2006 | 2007 | 2013 | 2008 | 2015 | 2010 | 2011 |
| 2017 | 2012 | 2019 | 2014 | 2020 | 2021 | 2016 |
| 2023 | 2018 | 2024 | 2025 | 2026 | 2027 | 2022 |
| 2028 | 2029 | 2030 | 2031 | 2037 | 2032 | 2033 |
| 2034 | 2035 | 2041 | 2036 | 2043 | 2038 | 2039 |
| 2045 | 2040 | 2047 | 2042 | 2048 | 2049 | 2044 |
| 2051 | 2046 | 2052 | 2053 | 2054 | 2055 | 2050 |

| | | | | | | | | | | | | |
|---|---|---|---|---|---|---|---|---|---|---|---|---|
| | | | | | | 1 | 2 | 3 | 4 | 5 | 6 | 7 |
| 2 | 3 | 4 | 5 | 6 | 7 | 8 | 9 | 10 | 11 | 12 | 13 | 14 |
| 9 | 10 | 11 | 12 | 13 | 14 | 15 | 16 | 17 | 18 | 19 | 20 | 21 |
| 16 | 17 | 18 | 19 | 20 | 21 | 22 | 23 | 24 | 25 | 26 | 27 | 28 |
| 23/30 | 24/31 | 25 | 26 | 27 | 28 | 29 | 30 | 31 | | | | |
| JAN | LEAP YR | LEAP YR | LEAP YR | FEB | LEAP YR | LEAP YR | JAN | LEAP YR | LEAP YR | LEAP YR | FEB | LEAP YR |
| APR | SEP | JUN | MAR | AUG | MAY | OCT | APR | SEP | JUN | MAR | AUG | MAY |
| JUL | DEC | | NOV | | | | JUL | DEC | | NOV | | |
| COM YR | COM YR | COM YR | FEB | COM YR | COM YR | JAN | COM YR | COM YR | COM YR | FEB | COM YR | COM YR |

Figures 5-3a and 5-3b: Pocket calendars—moving-window type and moving-slider type

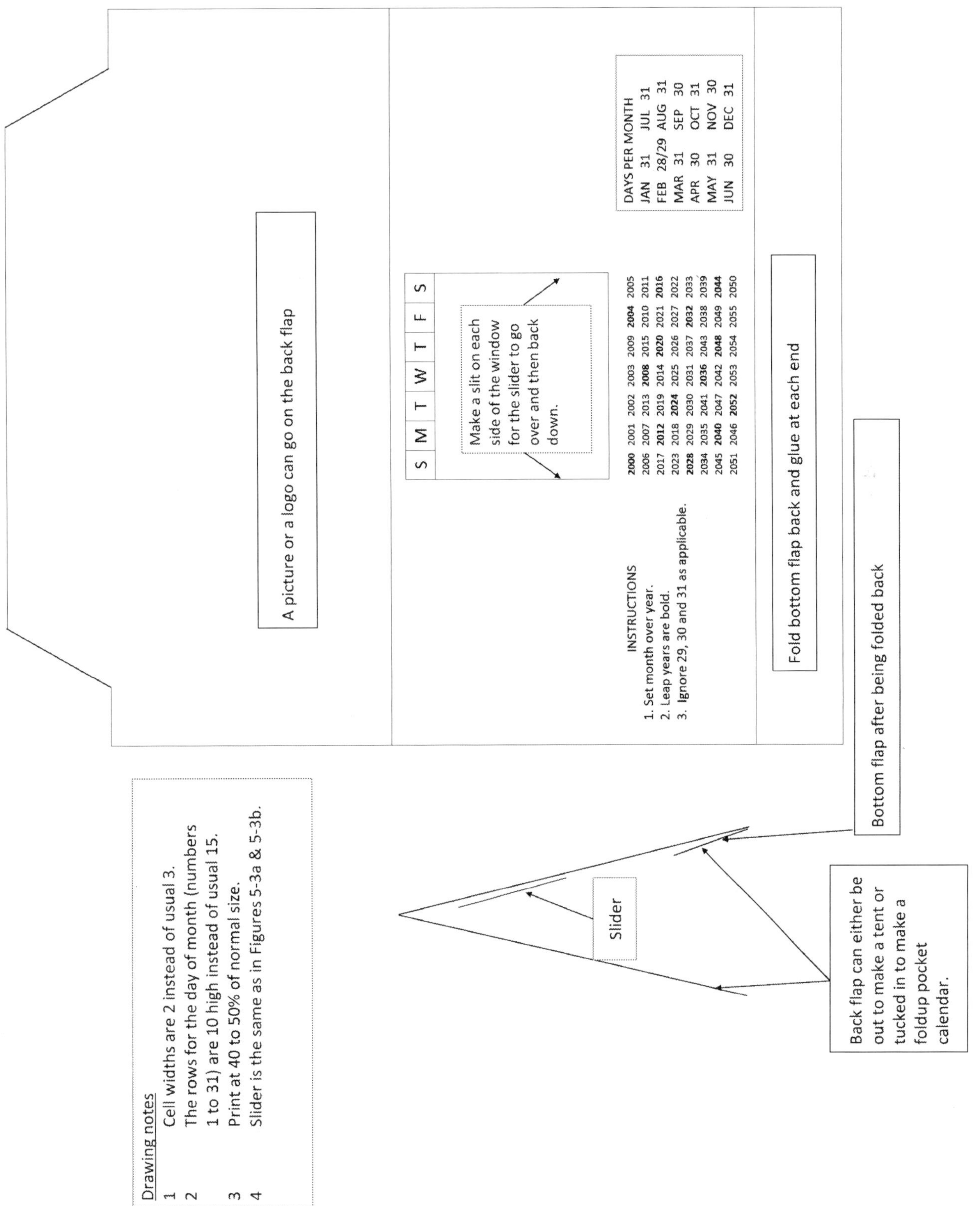

A picture or a logo can go on the back flap
S M T W T F S
Make a slit on each side of the window for the slider to go over and then back down.
INSTRUCTIONS
1. Set month over year.
2. Leap years are bold.
3. Ignore 29, 30 and 31 as applicable.
2000 2001 2002 2003 2009 2004 2005
2006 2007 2013 2008 2015 2010 2011
2017 2012 2019 2014 2020 2021 2016
2023 2018 2024 2025 2026 2027 2022
2028 2029 2030 2031 2037 2032 2033
2034 2035 2041 2036 2043 2038 2039
2045 2040 2047 2042 2048 2049 2044
2051 2046 2052 2053 2054 2055 2050
DAYS PER MONTH
JAN 31 JUL 31
FEB 28/29 AUG 31
MAR 31 SEP 30
APR 30 OCT 31
MAY 31 NOV 30
JUN 30 DEC 31
Fold bottom flap back and glue at each end
Bottom flap after being folded back
Slider
Back flap can either be out to make a tent or tucked in to make a foldup pocket calendar.
Drawing notes
1 Cell widths are 2 instead of usual 3.
2 The rows for the day of month (numbers 1 to 31) are 10 high instead of usual 15.
3 Print at 40 to 50% of normal size.
4 Slider is the same as in Figures 5-3a & 5-3b.


Figure 5-3c: Pocket/tent calendar

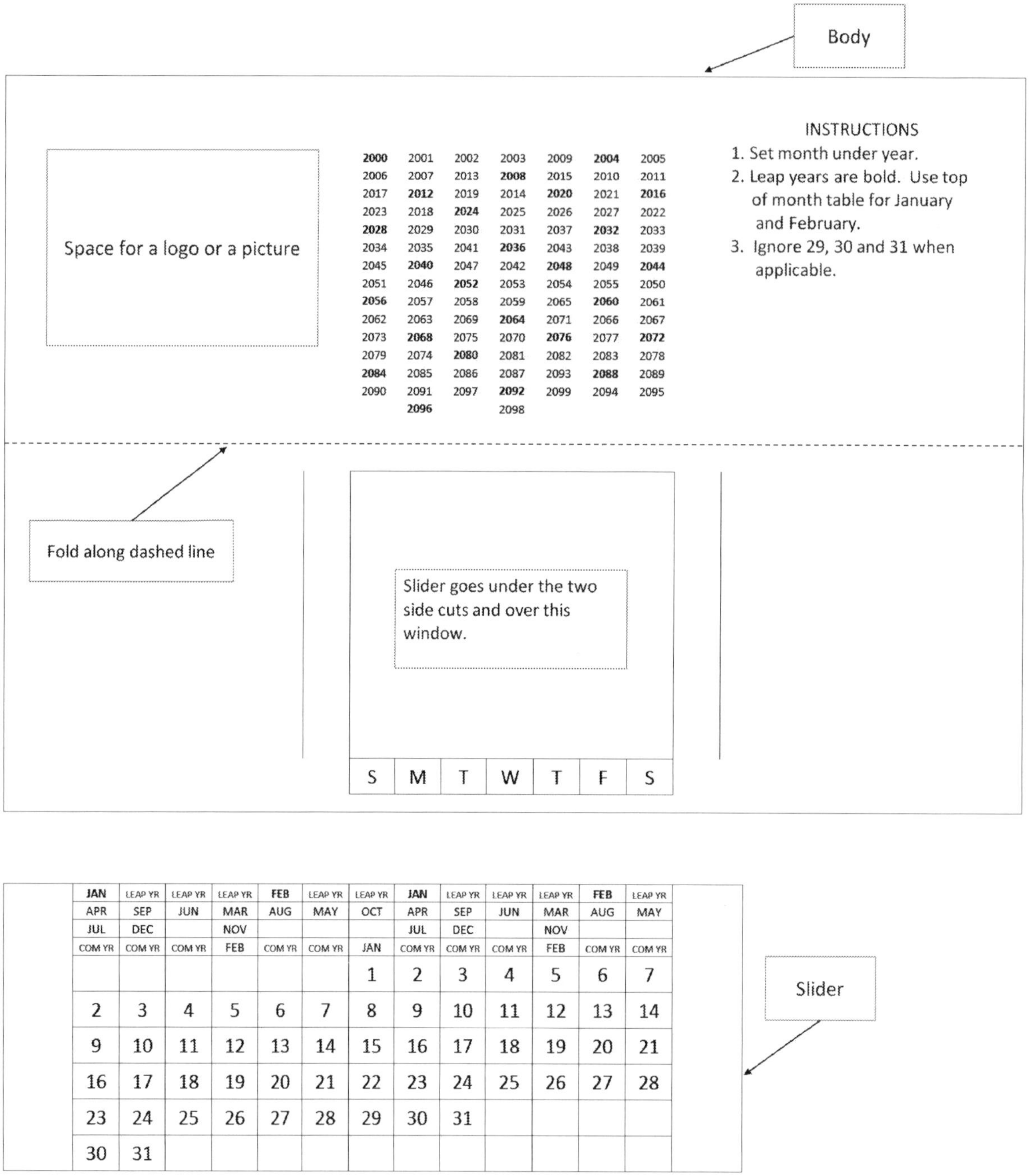

Body

Space for a logo or a picture

| **2000** | 2001 | 2002 | 2003 | 2009 | **2004** | 2005 |
|---|---|---|---|---|---|---|
| 2006 | 2007 | 2013 | **2008** | 2015 | 2010 | 2011 |
| 2017 | **2012** | 2019 | 2014 | **2020** | 2021 | **2016** |
| 2023 | 2018 | **2024** | 2025 | 2026 | 2027 | 2022 |
| **2028** | 2029 | 2030 | 2031 | 2037 | **2032** | 2033 |
| 2034 | 2035 | 2041 | **2036** | 2043 | 2038 | 2039 |
| 2045 | **2040** | 2047 | 2042 | **2048** | 2049 | **2044** |
| 2051 | 2046 | **2052** | 2053 | 2054 | 2055 | 2050 |
| **2056** | 2057 | 2058 | 2059 | 2065 | **2060** | 2061 |
| 2062 | 2063 | 2069 | **2064** | 2071 | 2066 | 2067 |
| 2073 | **2068** | 2075 | 2070 | **2076** | 2077 | **2072** |
| 2079 | 2074 | **2080** | 2081 | 2082 | 2083 | 2078 |
| **2084** | 2085 | 2086 | 2087 | 2093 | **2088** | 2089 |
| 2090 | 2091 | 2097 | **2092** | 2099 | 2094 | 2095 |
| | **2096** | | 2098 | | | |

INSTRUCTIONS

1. Set month under year.
2. Leap years are bold. Use top of month table for January and February.
3. Ignore 29, 30 and 31 when applicable.

Fold along dashed line

Slider goes under the two side cuts and over this window.

| S | M | T | W | T | F | S |
|---|---|---|---|---|---|---|

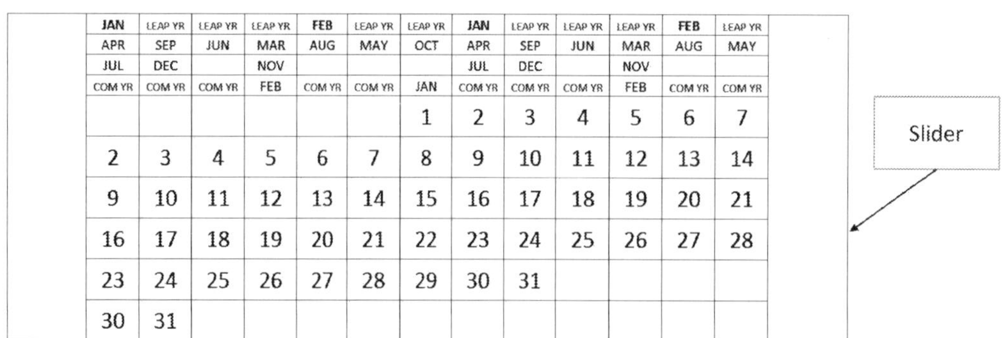

| **JAN** | LEAP YR | LEAP YR | LEAP YR | **FEB** | LEAP YR | LEAP YR | **JAN** | LEAP YR | LEAP YR | LEAP YR | **FEB** | LEAP YR |
|---|---|---|---|---|---|---|---|---|---|---|---|---|
| APR | SEP | JUN | MAR | AUG | MAY | OCT | APR | SEP | JUN | MAR | AUG | MAY |
| JUL | DEC | | NOV | | | | JUL | DEC | | NOV | | |
| COM YR | COM YR | COM YR | FEB | COM YR | COM YR | JAN | COM YR | COM YR | COM YR | FEB | COM YR | COM YR |
| | | | | | | 1 | 2 | 3 | 4 | 5 | 6 | 7 |
| 2 | 3 | 4 | 5 | 6 | 7 | 8 | 9 | 10 | 11 | 12 | 13 | 14 |
| 9 | 10 | 11 | 12 | 13 | 14 | 15 | 16 | 17 | 18 | 19 | 20 | 21 |
| 16 | 17 | 18 | 19 | 20 | 21 | 22 | 23 | 24 | 25 | 26 | 27 | 28 |
| 23 | 24 | 25 | 26 | 27 | 28 | 29 | 30 | 31 | | | | |
| 30 | 31 | | | | | | | | | | | |

Slider

Figure 5-3d: Fold-down moving-slider pocket calendar

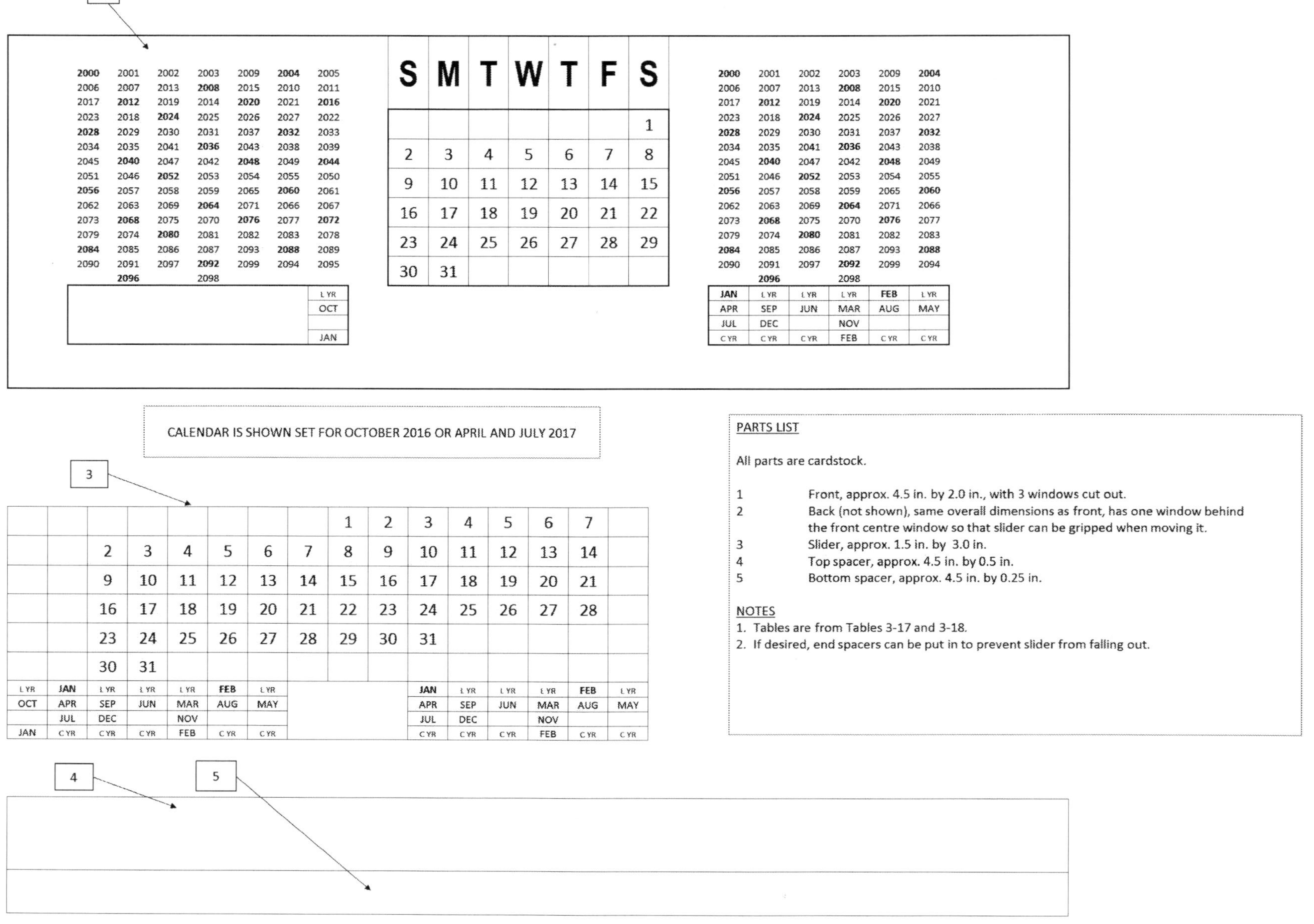
1
S M T W T F S
CALENDAR IS SHOWN SET FOR OCTOBER 2016 OR APRIL AND JULY 2017
3
4
5
PARTS LIST
All parts are cardstock.
1 Front, approx. 4.5 in. by 2.0 in., with 3 windows cut out.
2 Back (not shown), same overall dimensions as front, has one window behind the front centre window so that slider can be gripped when moving it.
3 Slider, approx. 1.5 in. by 3.0 in.
4 Top spacer, approx. 4.5 in. by 0.5 in.
5 Bottom spacer, approx. 4.5 in. by 0.25 in.
NOTES
1. Tables are from Tables 3-17 and 3-18.
2. If desired, end spacers can be put in to prevent slider from falling out.

Figure 5-3e: Pocket calendar with a single slider and year tables beside the window

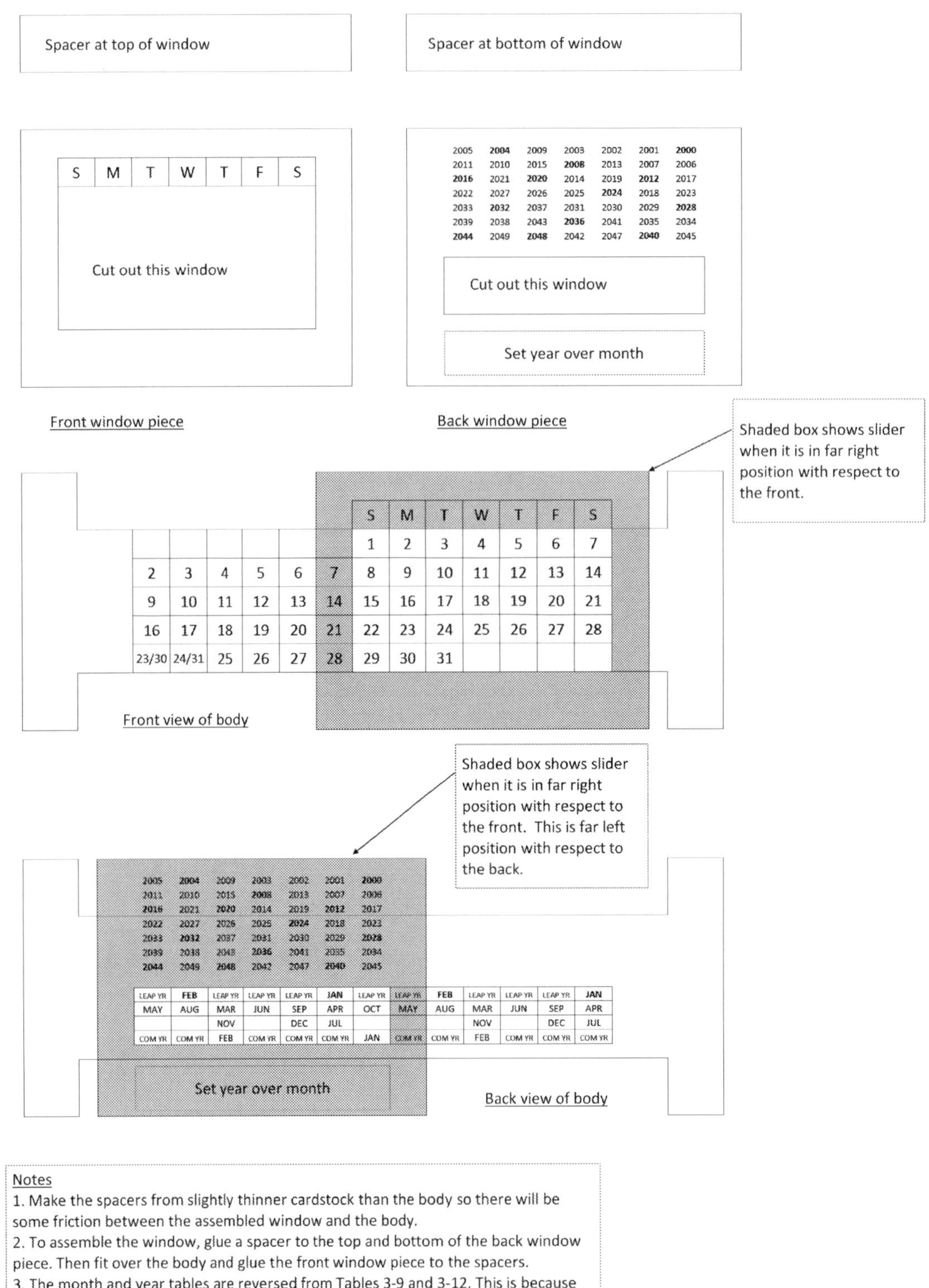

Spacer at top of window
Spacer at bottom of window
S M T W T F S
Cut out this window
2005 2004 2009 2003 2002 2001 2000
2011 2010 2015 2008 2013 2007 2006
2016 2021 2020 2014 2019 2012 2017
2022 2027 2026 2025 2024 2018 2023
2033 2032 2037 2031 2030 2029 2028
2039 2038 2043 2036 2041 2035 2034
2044 2049 2048 2042 2047 2040 2045
Cut out this window
Set year over month
Front window piece
Back window piece
Shaded box shows slider when it is in far right position with respect to the front.
Front view of body
Shaded box shows slider when it is in far right position with respect to the front. This is far left position with respect to the back.
Set year over month
Back view of body


Notes

1. Make the spacers from slightly thinner cardstock than the body so there will be some friction between the assembled window and the body.
2. To assemble the window, glue a spacer to the top and bottom of the back window piece. Then fit over the body and glue the front window piece to the spacers.
3. The month and year tables are reversed from Tables 3-9 and 3-12. This is because when the calendar is turned from front to back, it is turned on the left or right edge. The tables would not be reversed if the calendar were turned on the top or bottom edge.

Figure 5-4: Bookmark calendar

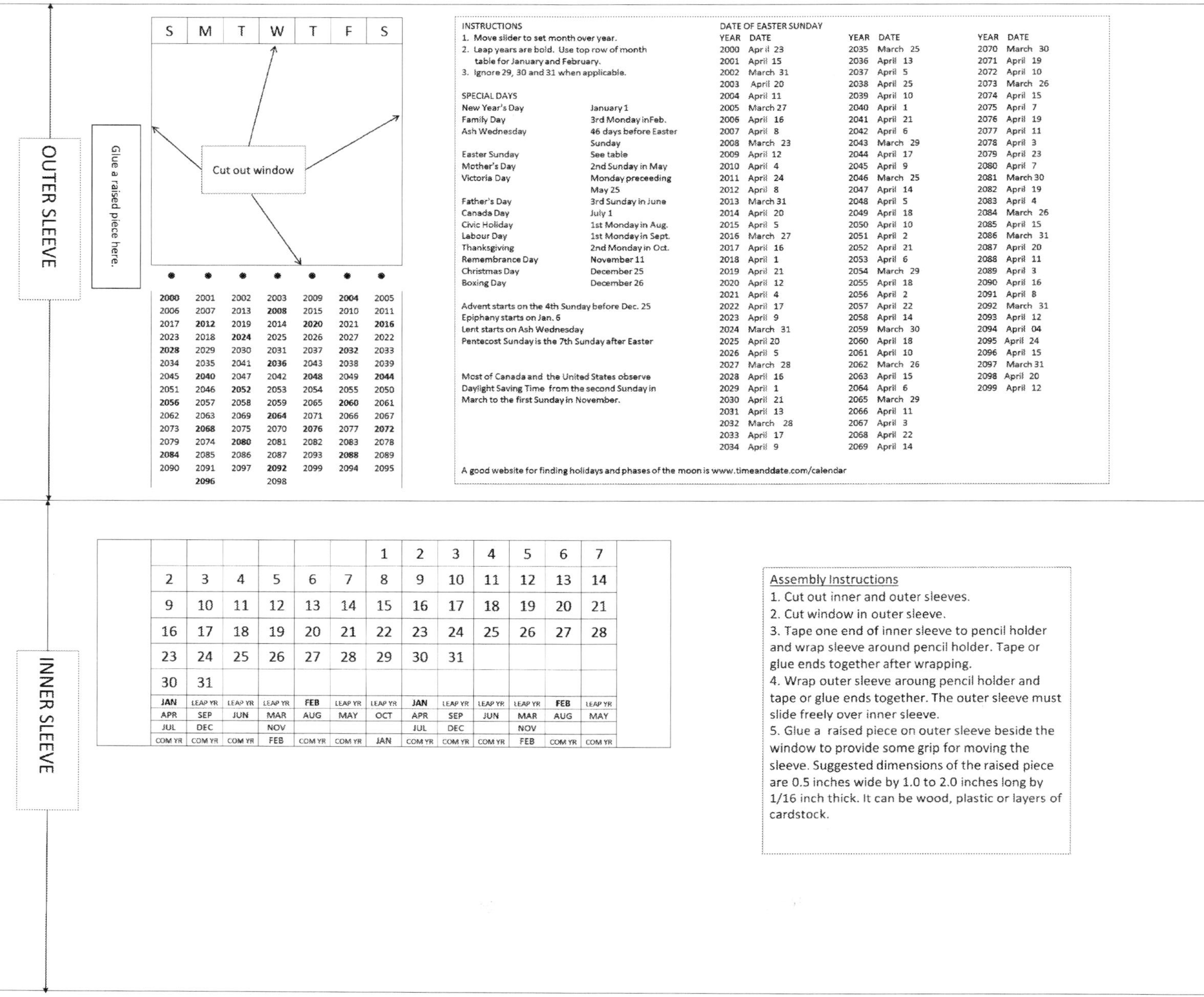

S M T W T F S
Cut out window
Glue a raised piece here.
OUTER SLEEVE
INNER SLEEVE
2000 2001 2002 2003 2009 2004 2005
2006 2007 2013 2008 2015 2010 2011
2017 2012 2019 2014 2020 2021 2016
2023 2018 2024 2025 2026 2027 2022
2028 2029 2030 2031 2037 2032 2033
2034 2035 2041 2036 2043 2038 2039
2045 2040 2047 2042 2048 2049 2044
2051 2046 2052 2053 2054 2055 2050
2056 2057 2058 2059 2065 2060 2061
2062 2063 2069 2064 2071 2066 2067
2073 2068 2075 2070 2076 2077 2072
2079 2074 2080 2081 2082 2083 2078
2084 2085 2086 2087 2093 2088 2089
2090 2091 2097 2092 2099 2094 2095
2096 2098
INSTRUCTIONS
1. Move slider to set month over year.
2. Leap years are bold. Use top row of month table for January and February.
3. Ignore 29, 30 and 31 when applicable.
SPECIAL DAYS
New Year's Day January 1
Family Day 3rd Monday inFeb.
Ash Wednesday 46 days before Easter Sunday
Easter Sunday See table
Mother's Day 2nd Sunday in May
Victoria Day Monday preceeding May 25
Father's Day 3rd Sunday in June
Canada Day July 1
Civic Holiday 1st Monday in Aug.
Labour Day 1st Monday in Sept.
Thanksgiving 2nd Monday in Oct.
Remembrance Day November 11
Christmas Day December 25
Boxing Day December 26
Advent starts on the 4th Sunday before Dec. 25
Epiphany starts on Jan. 6
Lent starts on Ash Wednesday
Pentecost Sunday is the 7th Sunday after Easter
Most of Canada and the United States observe Daylight Saving Time from the second Sunday in March to the first Sunday in November.
DATE OF EASTER SUNDAY
YEAR DATE
2000 April 23
2001 April 15
2002 March 31
2003 April 20
2004 April 11
2005 March 27
2006 April 16
2007 April 8
2008 March 23
2009 April 12
2010 April 4
2011 April 24
2012 April 8
2013 March 31
2014 April 20
2015 April 5
2016 March 27
2017 April 16
2018 April 1
2019 April 21
2020 April 12
2021 April 4
2022 April 17
2023 April 9
2024 March 31
2025 April 20
2026 April 5
2027 March 28
2028 April 16
2029 April 1
2030 April 21
2031 April 13
2032 March 28
2033 April 17
2034 April 9
YEAR DATE
2035 March 25
2036 April 13
2037 April 5
2038 April 25
2039 April 10
2040 April 1
2041 April 21
2042 April 6
2043 March 29
2044 April 17
2045 April 9
2046 March 25
2047 April 14
2048 April 5
2049 April 18
2050 April 10
2051 April 2
2052 April 21
2053 April 6
2054 March 29
2055 April 18
2056 April 2
2057 April 22
2058 April 14
2059 March 30
2060 April 18
2061 April 10
2062 March 26
2063 April 15
2064 April 6
2065 March 29
2066 April 11
2067 April 3
2068 April 22
2069 April 14
YEAR DATE
2070 March 30
2071 April 19
2072 April 10
2073 March 26
2074 April 15
2075 April 7
2076 April 19
2077 April 11
2078 April 3
2079 April 23
2080 April 7
2081 March 30
2082 April 19
2083 April 4
2084 March 26
2085 April 15
2086 March 31
2087 April 20
2088 April 11
2089 April 3
2090 April 16
2091 April 8
2092 March 31
2093 April 12
2094 April 04
2095 April 24
2096 April 15
2097 March 31
2098 April 20
2099 April 12
A good website for finding holidays and phases of the moon is www.timeanddate.com/calendar
1 2 3 4 5 6 7
2 3 4 5 6 7 8 9 10 11 12 13 14
9 10 11 12 13 14 15 16 17 18 19 20 21
16 17 18 19 20 21 22 23 24 25 26 27 28
23 24 25 26 27 28 29 30 31
30 31
JAN LEAP YR LEAP YR LEAP YR FEB LEAP YR LEAP YR JAN LEAP YR LEAP YR LEAP YR FEB LEAP YR
APR SEP JUN MAR AUG MAY OCT APR SEP JUN MAR AUG MAY
JUL DEC NOV JUL DEC NOV
COM YR COM YR COM YR FEB COM YR COM YR JAN COM YR COM YR COM YR FEB COM YR COM YR
Assembly Instructions
1. Cut out inner and outer sleeves.
2. Cut window in outer sleeve.
3. Tape one end of inner sleeve to pencil holder and wrap sleeve around pencil holder. Tape or glue ends together after wrapping.
4. Wrap outer sleeve aroung pencil holder and tape or glue ends together. The outer sleeve must slide freely over inner sleeve.
5. Glue a raised piece on outer sleeve beside the window to provide some grip for moving the sleeve. Suggested dimensions of the raised piece are 0.5 inches wide by 1.0 to 2.0 inches long by 1/16 inch thick. It can be wood, plastic or layers of cardstock.


Figure 5-5: Calendar for a lamp or a pencil holder

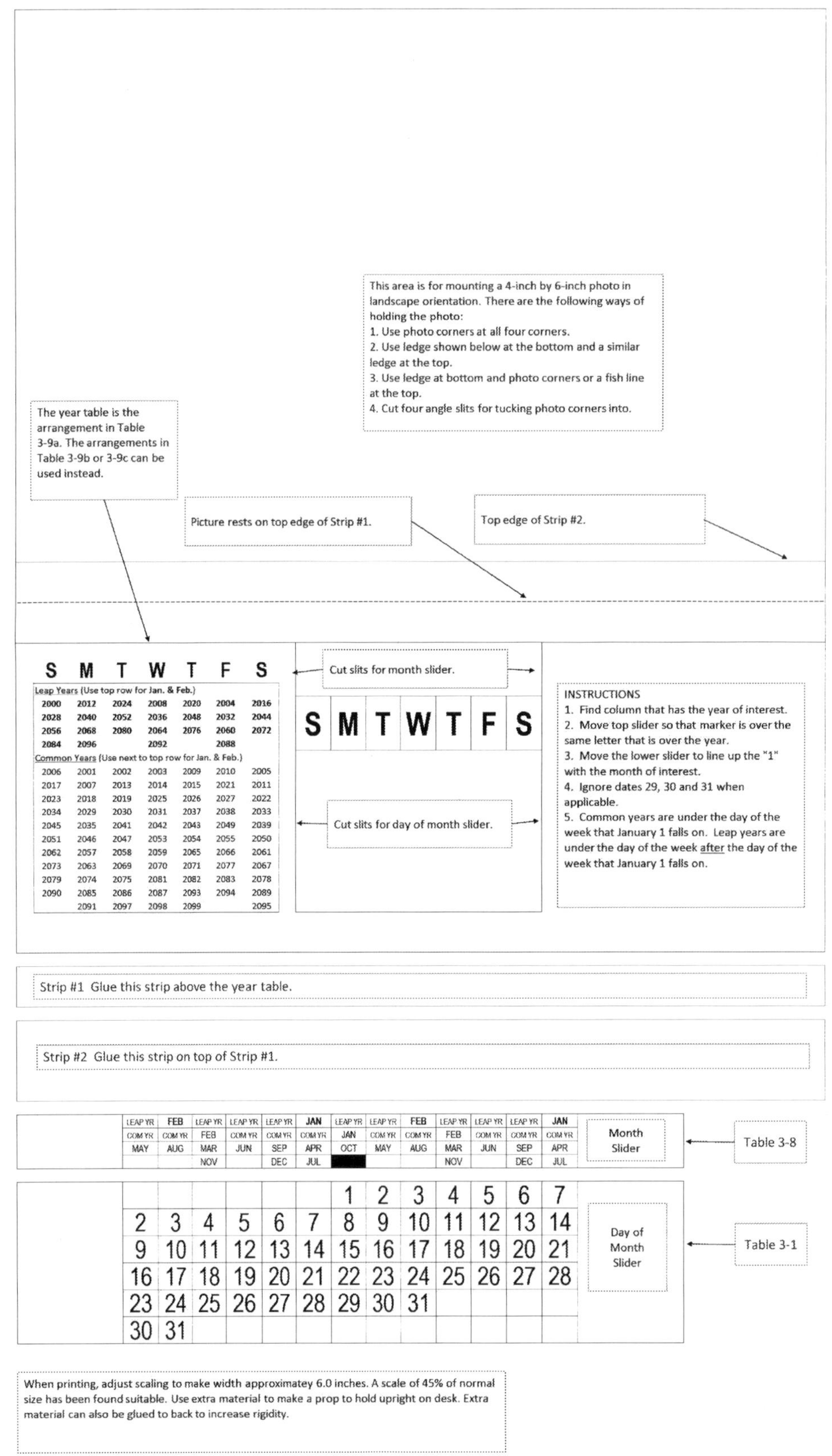
This area is for mounting a 4-inch by 6-inch photo in landscape orientation. There are the following ways of holding the photo:
1. Use photo corners at all four corners.
2. Use ledge shown below at the bottom and a similar ledge at the top.
3. Use ledge at bottom and photo corners or a fish line at the top.
4. Cut four angle slits for tucking photo corners into.
The year table is the arrangement in Table 3-9a. The arrangements in Table 3-9b or 3-9c can be used instead.
Picture rests on top edge of Strip #1.
Top edge of Strip #2.
Cut slits for month slider.
S M T W T F S
Cut slits for day of month slider.
INSTRUCTIONS
1. Find column that has the year of interest.
2. Move top slider so that marker is over the same letter that is over the year.
3. Move the lower slider to line up the "1" with the month of interest.
4. Ignore dates 29, 30 and 31 when applicable.
5. Common years are under the day of the week that January 1 falls on. Leap years are under the day of the week after the day of the week that January 1 falls on.
Strip #1 Glue this strip above the year table.
Strip #2 Glue this strip on top of Strip #1.
Month Slider
Table 3-8
Day of Month Slider
Table 3-1
When printing, adjust scaling to make width approximatey 6.0 inches. A scale of 45% of normal size has been found suitable. Use extra material to make a prop to hold upright on desk. Extra material can also be glued to back to increase rigidity.

| S | M | T | W | T | F | S |
|---|---|---|---|---|---|---|
| Leap Years (Use top row for Jan. & Feb.) | | | | | | |
| **2000** | **2012** | **2024** | **2008** | **2020** | **2004** | **2016** |
| **2028** | **2040** | **2052** | **2036** | **2048** | **2032** | **2044** |
| **2056** | **2068** | **2080** | **2064** | **2076** | **2060** | **2072** |
| **2084** | **2096** | | **2092** | | **2088** | |
| Common Years (Use next to top row for Jan. & Feb.) | | | | | | |
| 2006 | 2001 | 2002 | 2003 | 2009 | 2010 | 2005 |
| 2017 | 2007 | 2013 | 2014 | 2015 | 2021 | 2011 |
| 2023 | 2018 | 2019 | 2025 | 2026 | 2027 | 2022 |
| 2034 | 2029 | 2030 | 2031 | 2037 | 2038 | 2033 |
| 2045 | 2035 | 2041 | 2042 | 2043 | 2049 | 2039 |
| 2051 | 2046 | 2047 | 2053 | 2054 | 2055 | 2050 |
| 2062 | 2057 | 2058 | 2059 | 2065 | 2066 | 2061 |
| 2073 | 2063 | 2069 | 2070 | 2071 | 2077 | 2067 |
| 2079 | 2074 | 2075 | 2081 | 2082 | 2083 | 2078 |
| 2090 | 2085 | 2086 | 2087 | 2093 | 2094 | 2089 |
| | 2091 | 2097 | 2098 | 2099 | | 2095 |

| | | | | | | | | | | | | |
|---|---|---|---|---|---|---|---|---|---|---|---|---|
| LEAP YR | **FEB** | LEAP YR | LEAP YR | LEAP YR | **JAN** | LEAP YR | LEAP YR | **FEB** | LEAP YR | LEAP YR | LEAP YR | **JAN** |
| COM YR | COM YR | FEB | COM YR | COM YR | COM YR | JAN | COM YR | COM YR | FEB | COM YR | COM YR | COM YR |
| MAY | AUG | MAR | JUN | SEP | APR | OCT | MAY | AUG | MAR | JUN | SEP | APR |
| | | NOV | | DEC | JUL | ■ | | | NOV | | DEC | JUL |

| | | | | | | | | | | | | |
|---|---|---|---|---|---|---|---|---|---|---|---|---|
| | | | | | | 1 | 2 | 3 | 4 | 5 | 6 | 7 |
| 2 | 3 | 4 | 5 | 6 | 7 | 8 | 9 | 10 | 11 | 12 | 13 | 14 |
| 9 | 10 | 11 | 12 | 13 | 14 | 15 | 16 | 17 | 18 | 19 | 20 | 21 |
| 16 | 17 | 18 | 19 | 20 | 21 | 22 | 23 | 24 | 25 | 26 | 27 | 28 |
| 23 | 24 | 25 | 26 | 27 | 28 | 29 | 30 | 31 | | | | |
| 30 | 31 | | | | | | | | | | | |

Figure 5-6a: Cardstock 4 × 6 inch photo holder with dual sliders—design "A"

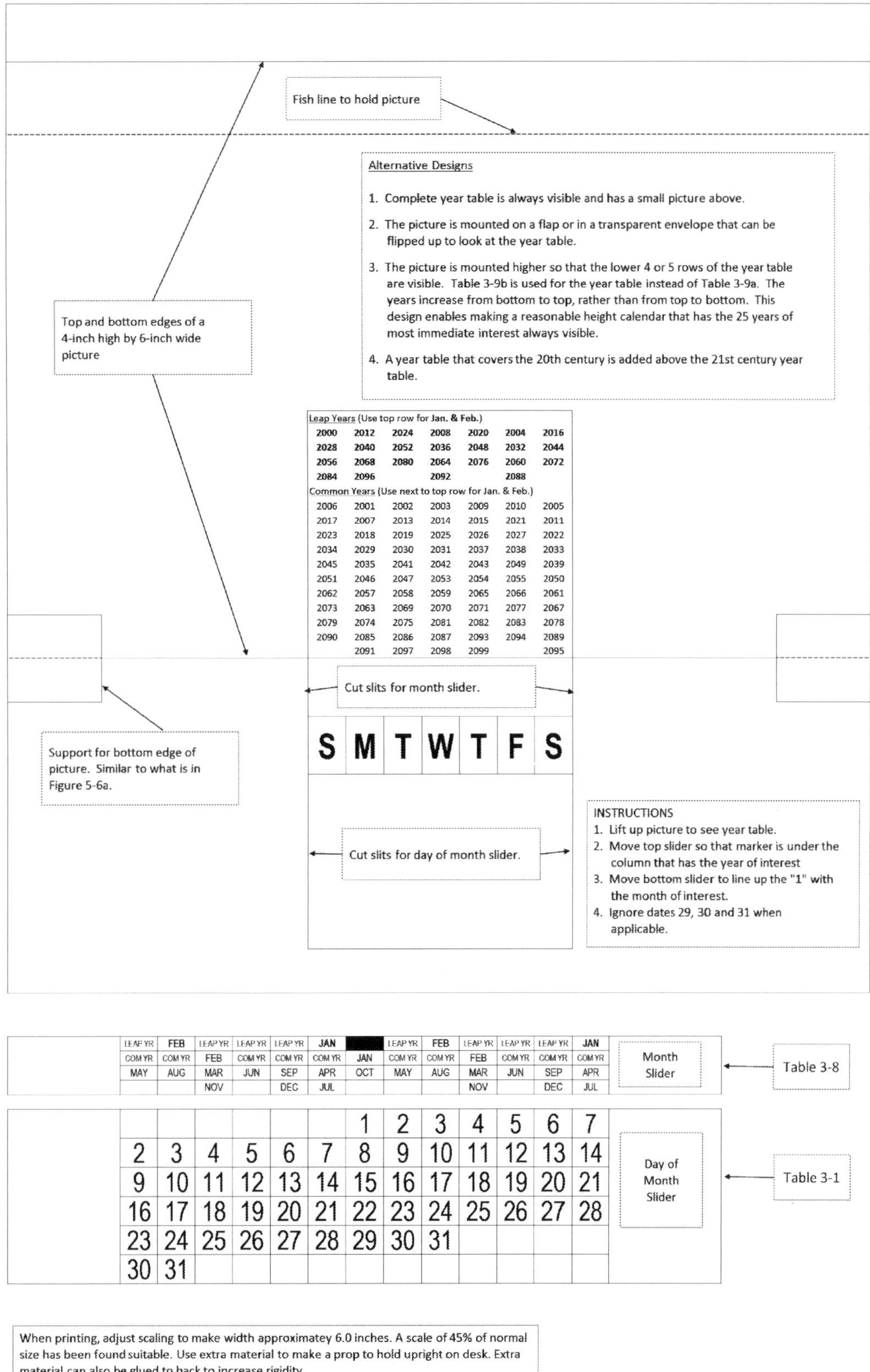
Fish line to hold picture
Alternative Designs
1. Complete year table is always visible and has a small picture above.
2. The picture is mounted on a flap or in a transparent envelope that can be flipped up to look at the year table.
3. The picture is mounted higher so that the lower 4 or 5 rows of the year table are visible. Table 3-9b is used for the year table instead of Table 3-9a. The years increase from bottom to top, rather than from top to bottom. This design enables making a reasonable height calendar that has the 25 years of most immediate interest always visible.
4. A year table that covers the 20th century is added above the 21st century year table.
Top and bottom edges of a 4-inch high by 6-inch wide picture
Cut slits for month slider.
Support for bottom edge of picture. Similar to what is in Figure 5-6a.
S M T W T F S
Cut slits for day of month slider.
INSTRUCTIONS
1. Lift up picture to see year table.
2. Move top slider so that marker is under the column that has the year of interest
3. Move bottom slider to line up the "1" with the month of interest.
4. Ignore dates 29, 30 and 31 when applicable.
Month Slider
Table 3-8
Day of Month Slider
Table 3-1
When printing, adjust scaling to make width approximatey 6.0 inches. A scale of 45% of normal size has been found suitable. Use extra material to make a prop to hold upright on desk. Extra material can also be glued to back to increase rigidity.

| Leap Years (Use top row for Jan. & Feb.) | | | | | | |
|---|---|---|---|---|---|---|
| **2000** | **2012** | **2024** | **2008** | **2020** | **2004** | **2016** |
| **2028** | **2040** | **2052** | **2036** | **2048** | **2032** | **2044** |
| **2056** | **2068** | **2080** | **2064** | **2076** | **2060** | **2072** |
| **2084** | **2096** | | **2092** | | **2088** | |
| Common Years (Use next to top row for Jan. & Feb.) | | | | | | |
| 2006 | 2001 | 2002 | 2003 | 2009 | 2010 | 2005 |
| 2017 | 2007 | 2013 | 2014 | 2015 | 2021 | 2011 |
| 2023 | 2018 | 2019 | 2025 | 2026 | 2027 | 2022 |
| 2034 | 2029 | 2030 | 2031 | 2037 | 2038 | 2033 |
| 2045 | 2035 | 2041 | 2042 | 2043 | 2049 | 2039 |
| 2051 | 2046 | 2047 | 2053 | 2054 | 2055 | 2050 |
| 2062 | 2057 | 2058 | 2059 | 2065 | 2066 | 2061 |
| 2073 | 2063 | 2069 | 2070 | 2071 | 2077 | 2067 |
| 2079 | 2074 | 2075 | 2081 | 2082 | 2083 | 2078 |
| 2090 | 2085 | 2086 | 2087 | 2093 | 2094 | 2089 |
| | 2091 | 2097 | 2098 | 2099 | | 2095 |

| LEAP YR | **FEB** | LEAP YR | LEAP YR | LEAP YR | **JAN** | | LEAP YR | **FEB** | LEAP YR | LEAP YR | LEAP YR | **JAN** |
|---|---|---|---|---|---|---|---|---|---|---|---|---|
| COM YR | COM YR | FEB | COM YR | COM YR | COM YR | JAN | COM YR | COM YR | FEB | COM YR | COM YR | COM YR |
| MAY | AUG | MAR | JUN | SEP | APR | OCT | MAY | AUG | MAR | JUN | SEP | APR |
| | | NOV | | DEC | JUL | | | | NOV | | DEC | JUL |

| | | | | | | | | | | | | |
|---|---|---|---|---|---|---|---|---|---|---|---|---|
| | | | | | | 1 | 2 | 3 | 4 | 5 | 6 | 7 |
| 2 | 3 | 4 | 5 | 6 | 7 | 8 | 9 | 10 | 11 | 12 | 13 | 14 |
| 9 | 10 | 11 | 12 | 13 | 14 | 15 | 16 | 17 | 18 | 19 | 20 | 21 |
| 16 | 17 | 18 | 19 | 20 | 21 | 22 | 23 | 24 | 25 | 26 | 27 | 28 |
| 23 | 24 | 25 | 26 | 27 | 28 | 29 | 30 | 31 | | | | |
| 30 | 31 | | | | | | | | | | | |

Figure 5-6b: Cardstock 4 × 6 inch photo holder with dual sliders—design "B"

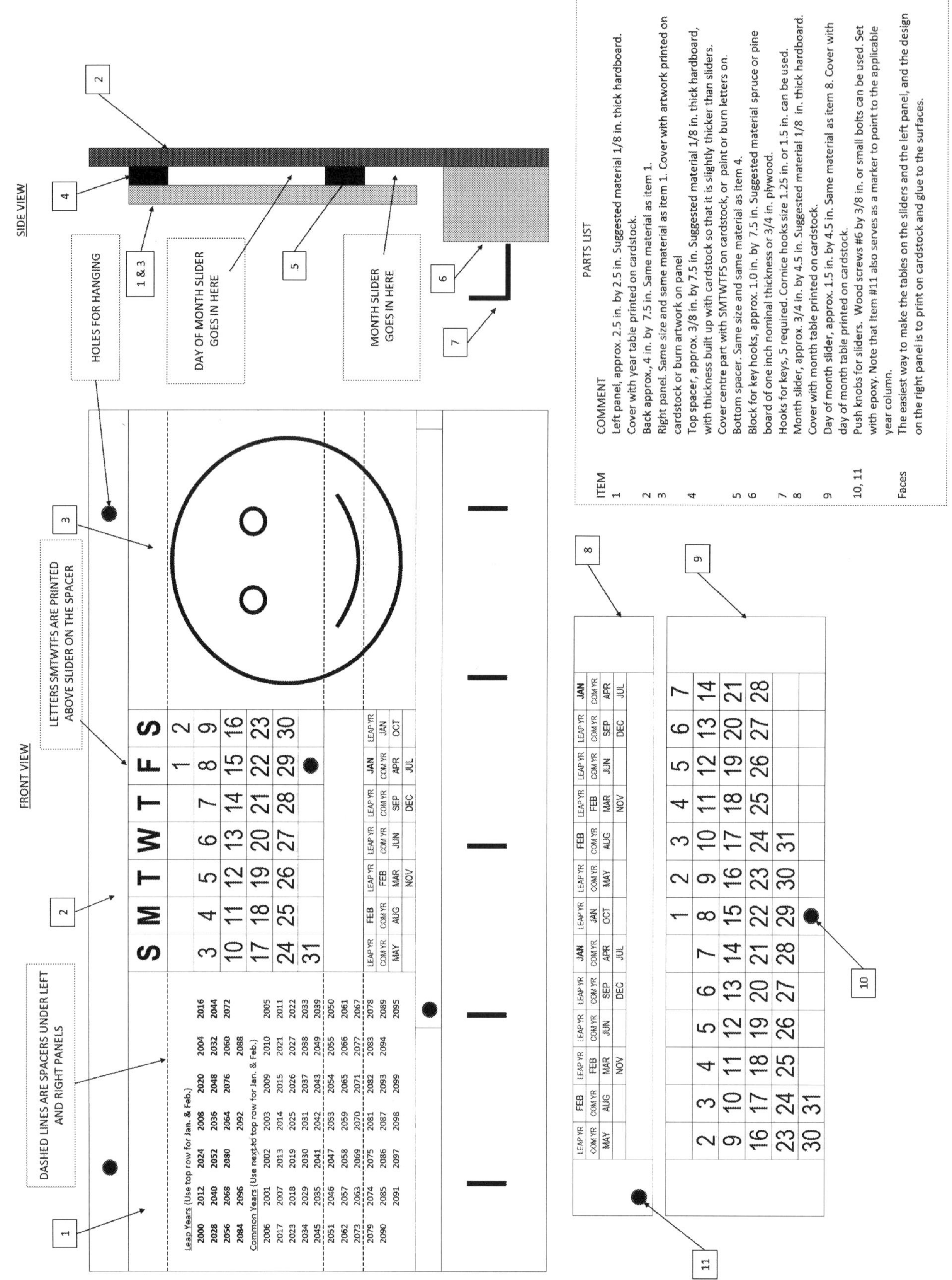
FRONT VIEW
SIDE VIEW
DASHED LINES ARE SPACERS UNDER LEFT AND RIGHT PANELS
LETTERS SMTWTFS ARE PRINTED ABOVE SLIDER ON THE SPACER
HOLES FOR HANGING
DAY OF MONTH SLIDER GOES IN HERE
MONTH SLIDER GOES IN HERE
1 & 3
Leap Years (Use top row for Jan. & Feb.)
Common Years (Use next to top row for Jan. & Feb.)
S M T W T F S
LEAP YR
COM YR
PARTS LIST
ITEM COMMENT
1 Left panel, approx. 2.5 in. by 2.5 in. Suggested material 1/8 in. thick hardboard. Cover with year table printed on cardstock.
2 Back approx., 4 in. by 7.5 in. Same material as item 1.
3 Right panel. Same size and same material as item 1. Cover with artwork printed on cardstock or burn artwork on panel
4 Top spacer, approx. 3/8 in. by 7.5 in. Suggested material 1/8 in. thick hardboard, with thickness built up with cardstock so that it is slightly thicker than sliders. Cover centre part with SMTWTFS on cardstock, or paint or burn letters on.
5 Bottom spacer. Same size and same material as item 4.
6 Block for key hooks, approx. 1.0 in. by 7.5 in. Suggested material spruce or pine board of one inch nominal thickness or 3/4 in. plywood.
7 Hooks for keys, 5 required. Cornice hooks size 1.25 in. or 1.5 in. can be used.
8 Month slider, approx. 3/4 in. by 4.5 in. Suggested material 1/8 in. thick hardboard. Cover with month table printed on cardstock.
9 Day of month slider, approx. 1.5 in. by 4.5 in. Same material as item 8. Cover with day of month table printed on cardstock.
10, 11 Push knobs for sliders. Wood screws #6 by 3/8 in. or small bolts can be used. Set with epoxy. Note that Item #11 also serves as a marker to point to the applicable year column.
Faces The easiest way to make the tables on the sliders and the left panel, and the design on the right panel is to print on cardstock and glue to the surfaces.

Figure 5-7a: Key holder with a dual-slider calendar

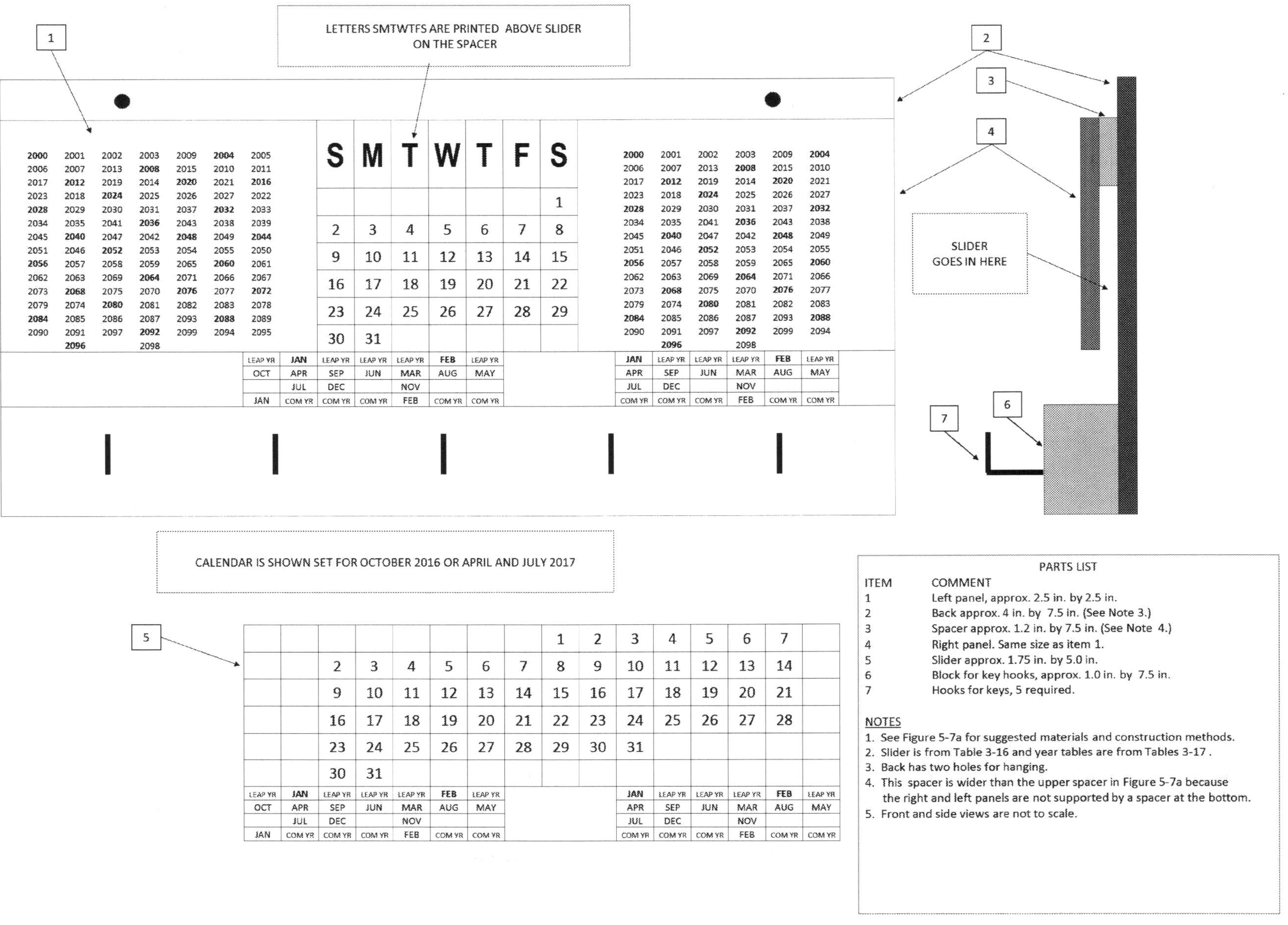
LETTERS SMTWTFS ARE PRINTED ABOVE SLIDER ON THE SPACER
S M T W T F S
SLIDER GOES IN HERE
CALENDAR IS SHOWN SET FOR OCTOBER 2016 OR APRIL AND JULY 2017
1
2
3
4
5
6
7
PARTS LIST
ITEM COMMENT
1 Left panel, approx. 2.5 in. by 2.5 in.
2 Back approx. 4 in. by 7.5 in. (See Note 3.)
3 Spacer approx. 1.2 in. by 7.5 in. (See Note 4.)
4 Right panel. Same size as item 1.
5 Slider approx. 1.75 in. by 5.0 in.
6 Block for key hooks, approx. 1.0 in. by 7.5 in.
7 Hooks for keys, 5 required.
NOTES
1. See Figure 5-7a for suggested materials and construction methods.
2. Slider is from Table 3-16 and year tables are from Tables 3-17 .
3. Back has two holes for hanging.
4. This spacer is wider than the upper spacer in Figure 5-7a because the right and left panels are not supported by a spacer at the bottom.
5. Front and side views are not to scale.

Figure 5-7b: Key holder with single-slider calendar

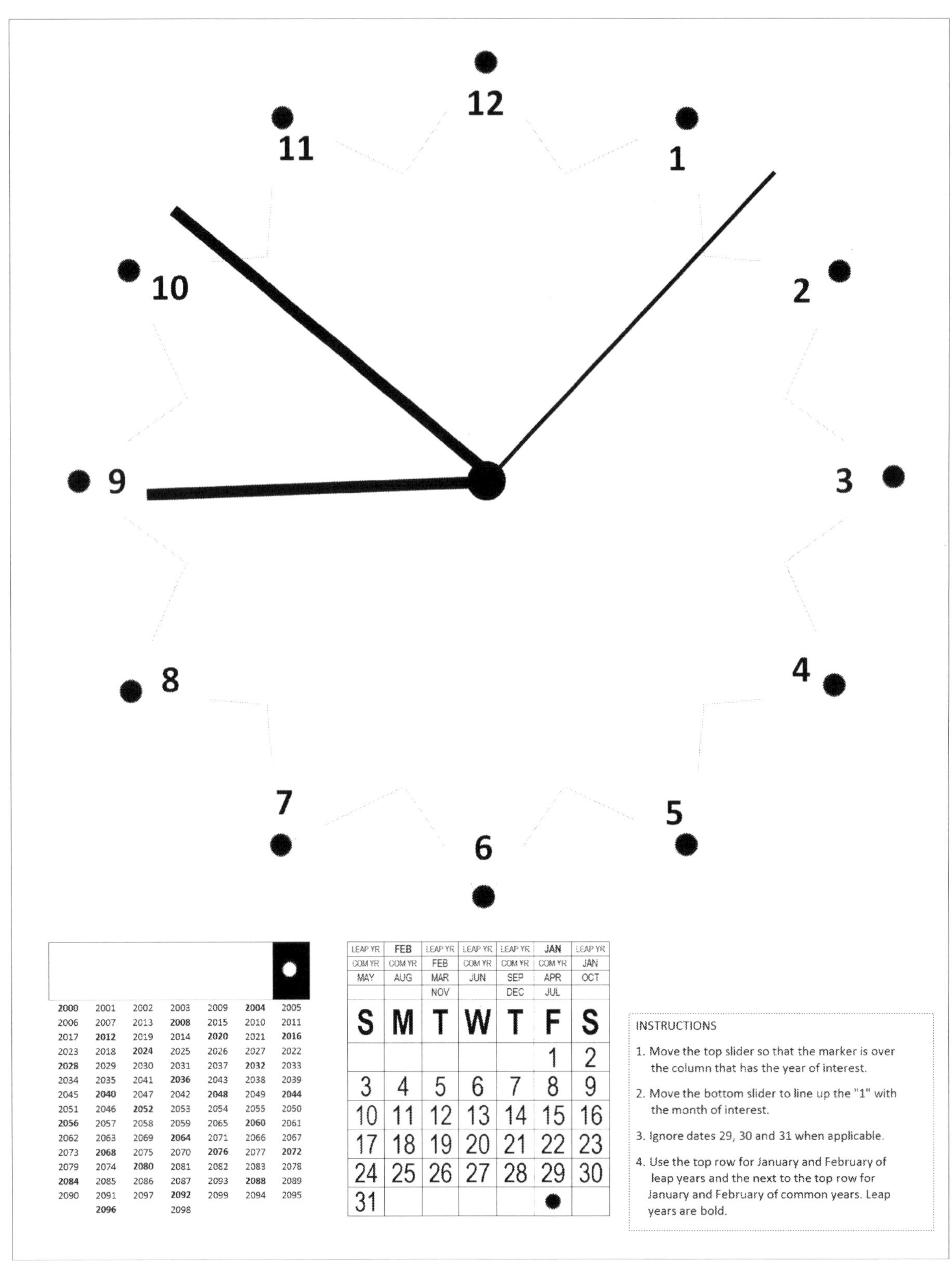
12
1
2
3
4
5
6
7
8
9
10
11
INSTRUCTIONS
1. Move the top slider so that the marker is over the column that has the year of interest.
2. Move the bottom slider to line up the "1" with the month of interest.
3. Ignore dates 29, 30 and 31 when applicable.
4. Use the top row for January and February of leap years and the next to the top row for January and February of common years. Leap years are bold.

| | | | | | | |
|---|---|---|---|---|---|---|
| **2000** | 2001 | 2002 | 2003 | 2009 | **2004** | 2005 |
| 2006 | 2007 | 2013 | **2008** | 2015 | 2010 | 2011 |
| 2017 | **2012** | 2019 | 2014 | **2020** | 2021 | **2016** |
| 2023 | 2018 | **2024** | 2025 | 2026 | 2027 | 2022 |
| **2028** | 2029 | 2030 | 2031 | 2037 | **2032** | 2033 |
| 2034 | 2035 | 2041 | **2036** | 2043 | 2038 | 2039 |
| 2045 | **2040** | 2047 | 2042 | **2048** | 2049 | **2044** |
| 2051 | 2046 | **2052** | 2053 | 2054 | 2055 | 2050 |
| **2056** | 2057 | 2058 | 2059 | 2065 | **2060** | 2061 |
| 2062 | 2063 | 2069 | **2064** | 2071 | 2066 | 2067 |
| 2073 | **2068** | 2075 | 2070 | **2076** | 2077 | **2072** |
| 2079 | 2074 | **2080** | 2081 | 2082 | 2083 | 2078 |
| **2084** | 2085 | 2086 | 2087 | 2093 | **2088** | 2089 |
| 2090 | 2091 | 2097 | **2092** | 2099 | 2094 | 2095 |
| | **2096** | | 2098 | | | |

| LEAP YR | **FEB** | LEAP YR | LEAP YR | LEAP YR | **JAN** | LEAP YR |
|---|---|---|---|---|---|---|
| COM YR | COM YR | FEB | COM YR | COM YR | COM YR | JAN |
| MAY | AUG | MAR | JUN | SEP | APR | OCT |
| | | NOV | | DEC | JUL | |
| **S** | **M** | **T** | **W** | **T** | **F** | **S** |
| | | | | | 1 | 2 |
| 3 | 4 | 5 | 6 | 7 | 8 | 9 |
| 10 | 11 | 12 | 13 | 14 | 15 | 16 |
| 17 | 18 | 19 | 20 | 21 | 22 | 23 |
| 24 | 25 | 26 | 27 | 28 | 29 | 30 |
| 31 | | | | | ● | |

Month slider is from Table 3-8, year table is from Table 3-9b, and day -of-month slider is from Table 3-1.

Figure 5-8: Clock with a dual-slider calendar

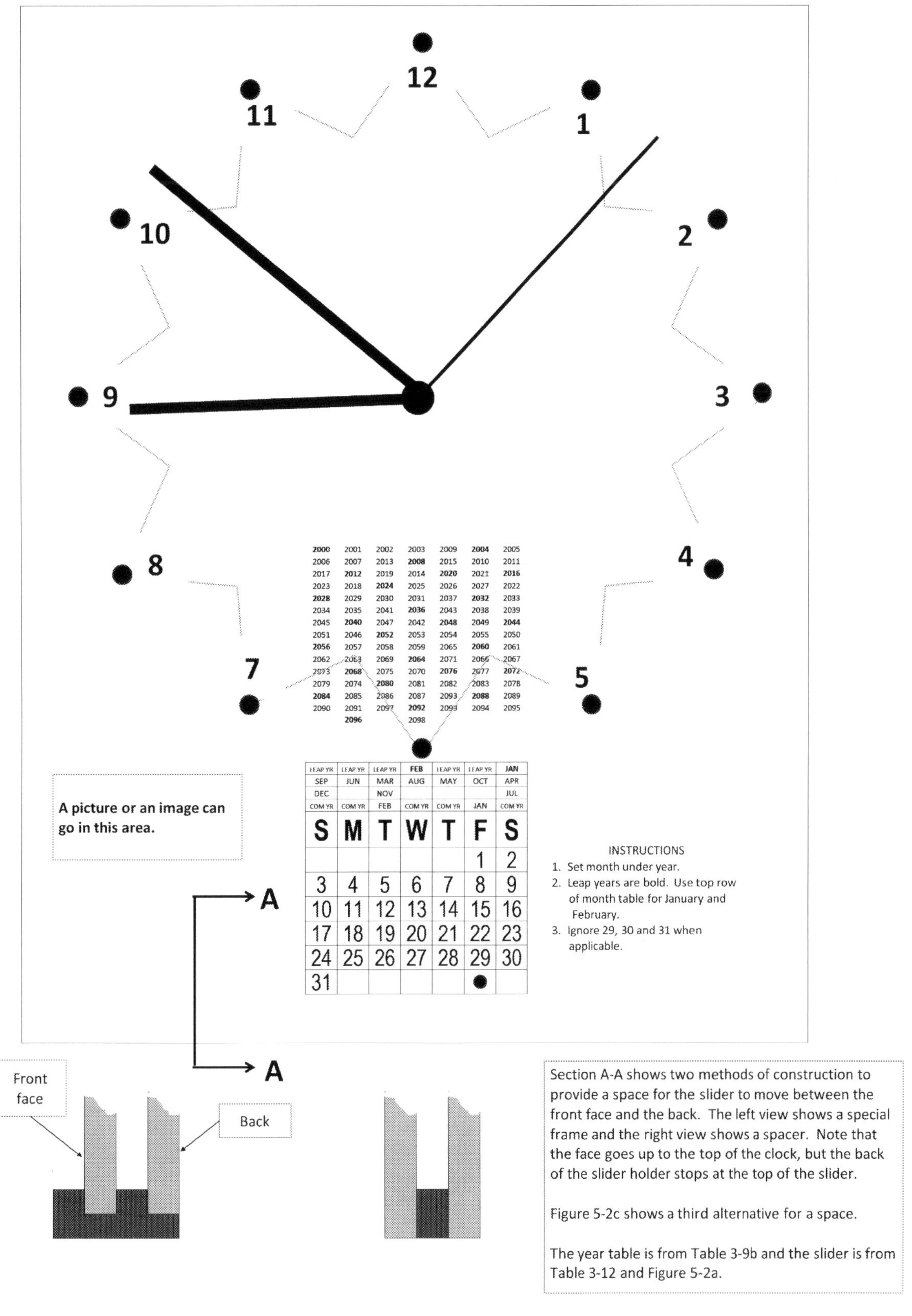
12
1
2
3
4
5
7
8
9
10
11
2000 2001 2002 2003 2009 2004 2005
2006 2007 2013 2008 2015 2010 2011
2017 2012 2019 2014 2020 2021 2016
2023 2018 2024 2025 2026 2027 2022
2028 2029 2030 2031 2037 2032 2033
2034 2035 2041 2036 2043 2038 2039
2045 2040 2047 2042 2048 2049 2044
2051 2046 2052 2053 2054 2055 2050
2056 2057 2058 2059 2065 2060 2061
2062 2063 2069 2064 2071 2066 2067
2073 2068 2075 2070 2076 2077 2072
2079 2074 2080 2081 2082 2083 2078
2084 2085 2086 2087 2093 2088 2089
2090 2091 2097 2092 2099 2094 2095
2096 2098
LEAP YR LEAP YR LEAP YR FEB LEAP YR LEAP YR JAN
SEP JUN MAR AUG MAY OCT APR
DEC NOV JUL
COM YR COM YR FEB COM YR COM YR JAN COM YR
S M T W T F S
1 2
3 4 5 6 7 8 9
10 11 12 13 14 15 16
17 18 19 20 21 22 23
24 25 26 27 28 29 30
31
A picture or an image can go in this area.
INSTRUCTIONS
1. Set month under year.
2. Leap years are bold. Use top row of month table for January and February.
3. Ignore 29, 30 and 31 when applicable.
A
A
Front face
Back
Section A-A shows two methods of construction to provide a space for the slider to move between the front face and the back. The left view shows a special frame and the right view shows a spacer. Note that the face goes up to the top of the clock, but the back of the slider holder stops at the top of the slider.
Figure 5-2c shows a third alternative for a space.
The year table is from Table 3-9b and the slider is from Table 3-12 and Figure 5-2a.

Figure 5-9: Clock with a single-slider double-window calendar

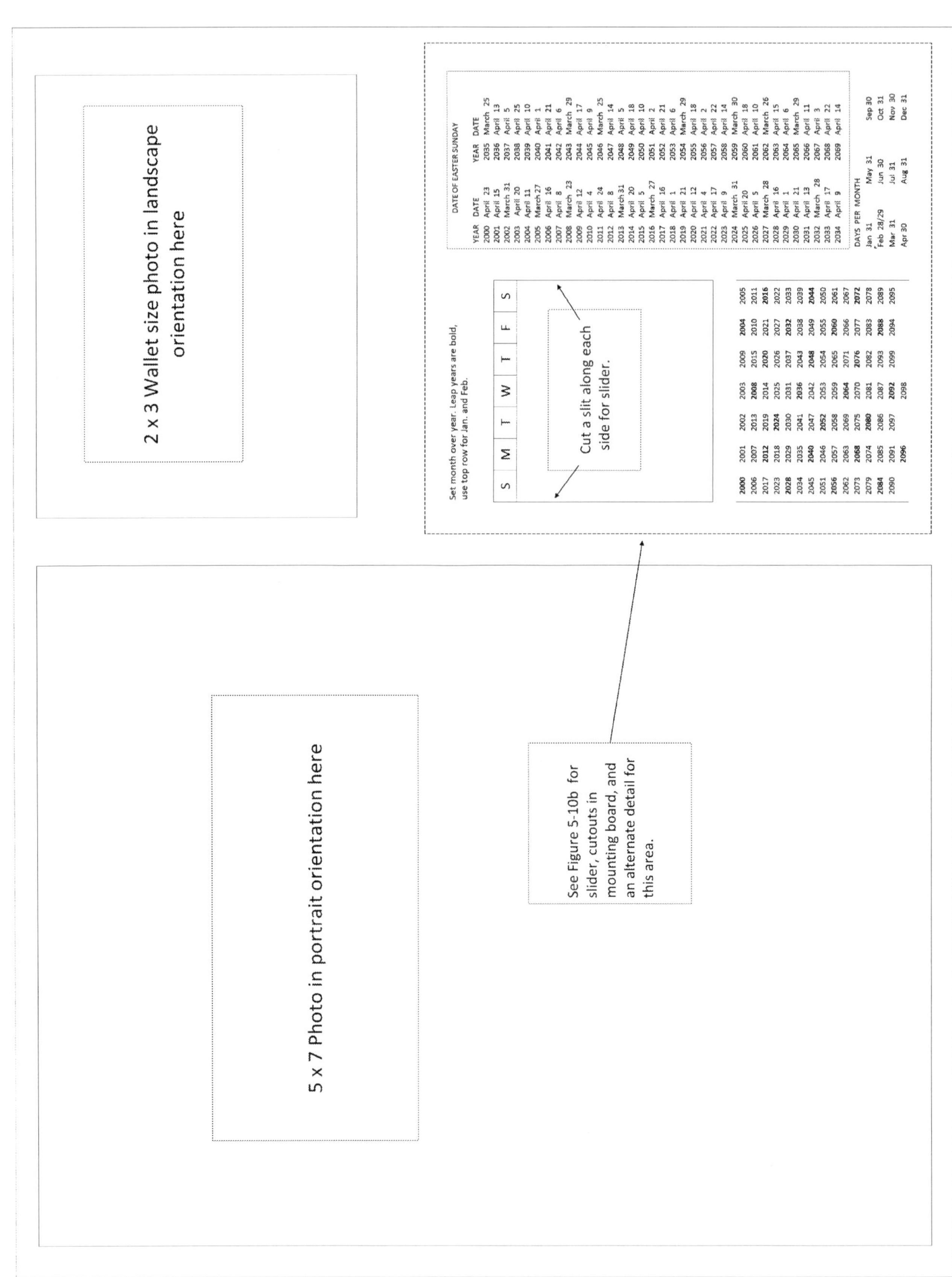
2 x 3 Wallet size photo in landscape orientation here
5 x 7 Photo in portrait orientation here
See Figure 5-10b for slider, cutouts in mounting board, and an alternate detail for this area.
Set month over year. Leap years are bold, use top row for Jan. and Feb.
S M T W T F S
Cut a slit along each side for slider.

| S | M | T | W | T | F | S |
|---|---|---|---|---|---|---|
| **2000** | 2001 | 2002 | 2003 | 2009 | **2004** | 2005 |
| 2006 | 2007 | 2013 | **2008** | 2015 | 2010 | 2011 |
| 2017 | **2012** | 2019 | 2014 | **2020** | 2021 | **2016** |
| 2023 | 2018 | **2024** | 2025 | 2026 | 2027 | 2022 |
| **2028** | 2029 | 2030 | 2031 | 2037 | **2032** | 2033 |
| 2034 | 2035 | 2041 | **2036** | 2043 | 2038 | 2039 |
| 2045 | **2040** | 2047 | 2042 | **2048** | 2049 | **2044** |
| 2051 | 2046 | **2052** | 2053 | 2054 | 2055 | 2050 |
| **2056** | 2057 | 2058 | 2059 | 2065 | **2060** | 2061 |
| 2062 | 2063 | 2069 | **2064** | 2071 | 2066 | 2067 |
| 2073 | **2068** | 2075 | 2070 | **2076** | 2077 | **2072** |
| 2079 | 2074 | **2080** | 2081 | 2082 | 2083 | 2078 |
| **2084** | 2085 | 2086 | 2087 | 2093 | **2088** | 2089 |
| 2090 | 2091 | 2097 | **2092** | 2099 | 2094 | 2095 |
| | **2096** | | 2098 | | | |

DATE OF EASTER SUNDAY

| YEAR | DATE | YEAR | DATE |
|---|---|---|---|
| 2000 | April 23 | 2035 | March 25 |
| 2001 | April 15 | 2036 | April 13 |
| 2002 | March 31 | 2037 | April 5 |
| 2003 | April 20 | 2038 | April 25 |
| 2004 | April 11 | 2039 | April 10 |
| 2005 | March 27 | 2040 | April 1 |
| 2006 | April 16 | 2041 | April 21 |
| 2007 | April 8 | 2042 | April 6 |
| 2008 | March 23 | 2043 | March 29 |
| 2009 | April 12 | 2044 | April 17 |
| 2010 | April 4 | 2045 | April 9 |
| 2011 | April 24 | 2046 | March 25 |
| 2012 | April 8 | 2047 | April 14 |
| 2013 | March 31 | 2048 | April 5 |
| 2014 | April 20 | 2049 | April 18 |
| 2015 | April 5 | 2050 | April 10 |
| 2016 | March 27 | 2051 | April 2 |
| 2017 | April 16 | 2052 | April 21 |
| 2018 | April 1 | 2053 | April 6 |
| 2019 | April 21 | 2054 | March 29 |
| 2020 | April 12 | 2055 | April 18 |
| 2021 | April 4 | 2056 | April 2 |
| 2022 | April 17 | 2057 | April 22 |
| 2023 | April 9 | 2058 | April 14 |
| 2024 | March 31 | 2059 | March 30 |
| 2025 | April 20 | 2060 | April 18 |
| 2026 | April 5 | 2061 | April 10 |
| 2027 | March 28 | 2062 | March 26 |
| 2028 | April 16 | 2063 | April 15 |
| 2029 | April 1 | 2064 | April 6 |
| 2030 | April 21 | 2065 | March 29 |
| 2031 | April 13 | 2066 | April 11 |
| 2032 | March 28 | 2067 | April 3 |
| 2033 | April 17 | 2068 | April 22 |
| 2034 | April 9 | 2069 | April 14 |

DAYS PER MONTH

| | | |
|---|---|---|
| Jan 31 | May 31 | Sep 30 |
| Feb 28/29 | Jun 30 | Oct 31 |
| Mar 31 | Jul 31 | Nov 30 |
| Apr 30 | Aug 31 | Dec 31 |

Figure 5-10a: Picture frame with calendar beside photo

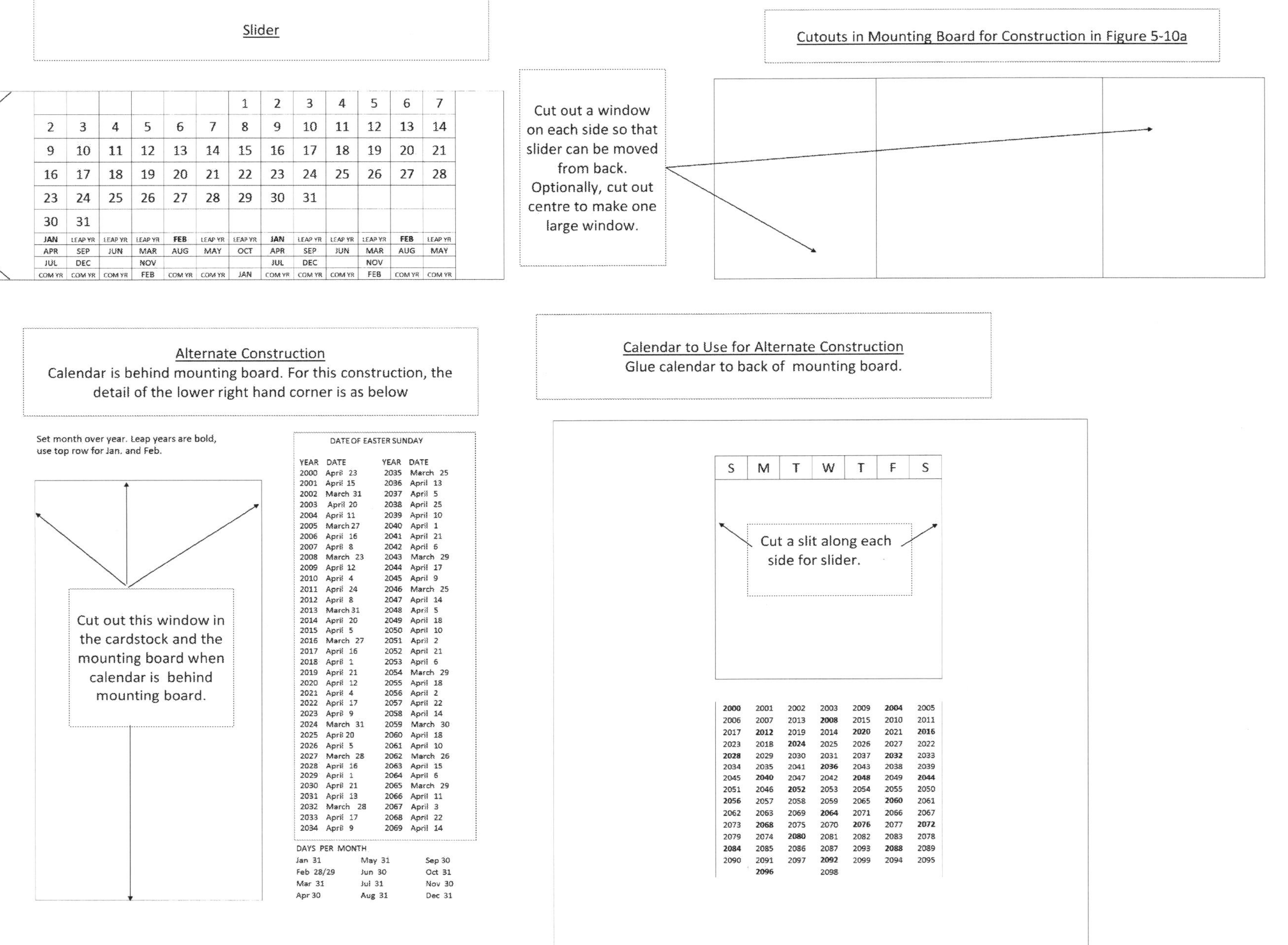

Slider
1 2 3 4 5 6 7
2 3 4 5 6 7 8 9 10 11 12 13 14
9 10 11 12 13 14 15 16 17 18 19 20 21
16 17 18 19 20 21 22 23 24 25 26 27 28
23 24 25 26 27 28 29 30 31
30 31
JAN LEAP YR LEAP YR LEAP YR FEB LEAP YR LEAP YR JAN LEAP YR LEAP YR LEAP YR FEB LEAP YR
APR SEP JUN MAR AUG MAY OCT APR SEP JUN MAR AUG MAY
JUL DEC NOV JUL DEC NOV
COM YR COM YR COM YR FEB COM YR COM YR JAN COM YR COM YR COM YR FEB COM YR COM YR
Cutouts in Mounting Board for Construction in Figure 5-10a
Cut out a window on each side so that slider can be moved from back. Optionally, cut out centre to make one large window.
Alternate Construction
Calendar is behind mounting board. For this construction, the detail of the lower right hand corner is as below
Calendar to Use for Alternate Construction
Glue calendar to back of mounting board.
Set month over year. Leap years are bold, use top row for Jan. and Feb.
Cut out this window in the cardstock and the mounting board when calendar is behind mounting board.
DATE OF EASTER SUNDAY
YEAR DATE YEAR DATE
2000 April 23 2035 March 25
2001 April 15 2036 April 13
2002 March 31 2037 April 5
2003 April 20 2038 April 25
2004 April 11 2039 April 10
2005 March 27 2040 April 1
2006 April 16 2041 April 21
2007 April 8 2042 April 6
2008 March 23 2043 March 29
2009 April 12 2044 April 17
2010 April 4 2045 April 9
2011 April 24 2046 March 25
2012 April 8 2047 April 14
2013 March 31 2048 April 5
2014 April 20 2049 April 18
2015 April 5 2050 April 10
2016 March 27 2051 April 2
2017 April 16 2052 April 21
2018 April 1 2053 April 6
2019 April 21 2054 March 29
2020 April 12 2055 April 18
2021 April 4 2056 April 2
2022 April 17 2057 April 22
2023 April 9 2058 April 14
2024 March 31 2059 March 30
2025 April 20 2060 April 18
2026 April 5 2061 April 10
2027 March 28 2062 March 26
2028 April 16 2063 April 15
2029 April 1 2064 April 6
2030 April 21 2065 March 29
2031 April 13 2066 April 11
2032 March 28 2067 April 3
2033 April 17 2068 April 22
2034 April 9 2069 April 14
DAYS PER MONTH
Jan 31 May 31 Sep 30
Feb 28/29 Jun 30 Oct 31
Mar 31 Jul 31 Nov 30
Apr 30 Aug 31 Dec 31
S M T W T F S
Cut a slit along each side for slider.
2000 2001 2002 2003 2009 2004 2005
2006 2007 2013 2008 2015 2010 2011
2017 2012 2019 2014 2020 2021 2016
2023 2018 2024 2025 2026 2027 2022
2028 2029 2030 2031 2037 2032 2033
2034 2035 2041 2036 2043 2038 2039
2045 2040 2047 2042 2048 2049 2044
2051 2046 2052 2053 2054 2055 2050
2056 2057 2058 2059 2065 2060 2061
2062 2063 2069 2064 2071 2066 2067
2073 2068 2075 2070 2076 2077 2072
2079 2074 2080 2081 2082 2083 2078
2084 2085 2086 2087 2093 2088 2089
2090 2091 2097 2092 2099 2094 2095
2096 2098


Figure 5-10b: Picture frame with calendar beside photo (detail)

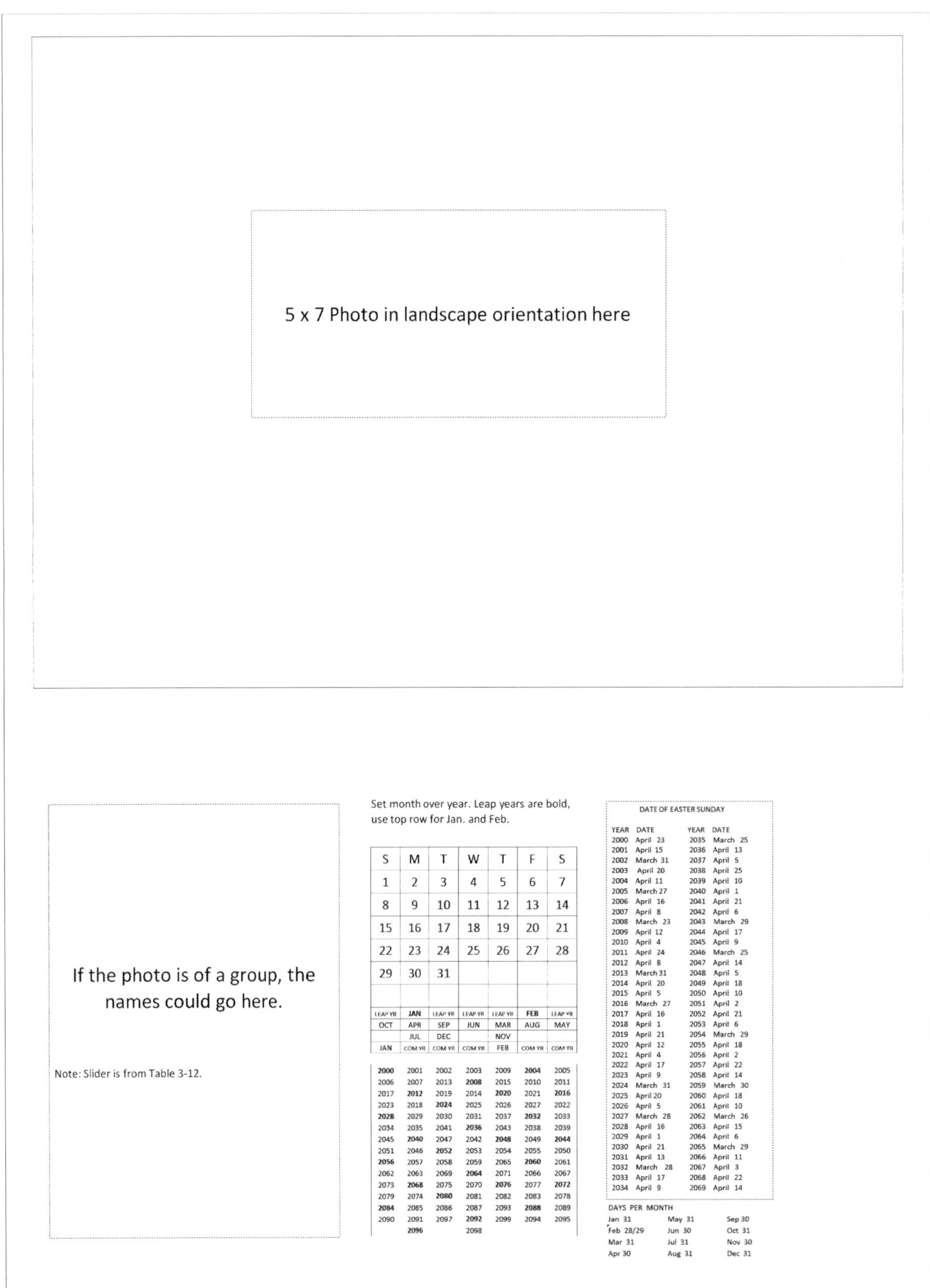

5 x 7 Photo in landscape orientation here

If the photo is of a group, the names could go here.

Note: Slider is from Table 3-12.

Set month over year. Leap years are bold, use top row for Jan. and Feb.

| S | M | T | W | T | F | S |
|---|---|---|---|---|---|---|
| 1 | 2 | 3 | 4 | 5 | 6 | 7 |
| 8 | 9 | 10 | 11 | 12 | 13 | 14 |
| 15 | 16 | 17 | 18 | 19 | 20 | 21 |
| 22 | 23 | 24 | 25 | 26 | 27 | 28 |
| 29 | 30 | 31 | | | | |
| | | | | | | |
| LEAP YR | **JAN** | LEAP YR | LEAP YR | LEAP YR | **FEB** | LEAP YR |
| OCT | APR | SEP | JUN | MAR | AUG | MAY |
| | JUL | DEC | | NOV | | |
| JAN | COM YR | COM YR | COM YR | FEB | COM YR | COM YR |

| | | | | | | |
|---|---|---|---|---|---|---|
| **2000** | 2001 | 2002 | 2003 | 2009 | **2004** | 2005 |
| 2006 | 2007 | 2013 | **2008** | 2015 | 2010 | 2011 |
| 2017 | **2012** | 2019 | 2014 | **2020** | 2021 | **2016** |
| 2023 | 2018 | **2024** | 2025 | 2026 | 2027 | 2022 |
| **2028** | 2029 | 2030 | 2031 | 2037 | **2032** | 2033 |
| 2034 | 2035 | 2041 | **2036** | 2043 | 2038 | 2039 |
| 2045 | **2040** | 2047 | 2042 | **2048** | 2049 | **2044** |
| 2051 | 2046 | **2052** | 2053 | 2054 | 2055 | 2050 |
| **2056** | 2057 | 2058 | 2059 | 2065 | **2060** | 2061 |
| 2062 | 2063 | 2069 | **2064** | 2071 | 2066 | 2067 |
| 2073 | **2068** | 2075 | 2070 | **2076** | 2077 | **2072** |
| 2079 | 2074 | **2080** | 2081 | 2082 | 2083 | 2078 |
| **2084** | 2085 | 2086 | 2087 | 2093 | **2088** | 2089 |
| 2090 | 2091 | 2097 | **2092** | 2099 | 2094 | 2095 |
| | **2096** | | 2098 | | | |

DATE OF EASTER SUNDAY

| YEAR | DATE | YEAR | DATE |
|---|---|---|---|
| 2000 | April 23 | 2035 | March 25 |
| 2001 | April 15 | 2036 | April 13 |
| 2002 | March 31 | 2037 | April 5 |
| 2003 | April 20 | 2038 | April 25 |
| 2004 | April 11 | 2039 | April 10 |
| 2005 | March 27 | 2040 | April 1 |
| 2006 | April 16 | 2041 | April 21 |
| 2007 | April 8 | 2042 | April 6 |
| 2008 | March 23 | 2043 | March 29 |
| 2009 | April 12 | 2044 | April 17 |
| 2010 | April 4 | 2045 | April 9 |
| 2011 | April 24 | 2046 | March 25 |
| 2012 | April 8 | 2047 | April 14 |
| 2013 | March 31 | 2048 | April 5 |
| 2014 | April 20 | 2049 | April 18 |
| 2015 | April 5 | 2050 | April 10 |
| 2016 | March 27 | 2051 | April 2 |
| 2017 | April 16 | 2052 | April 21 |
| 2018 | April 1 | 2053 | April 6 |
| 2019 | April 21 | 2054 | March 29 |
| 2020 | April 12 | 2055 | April 18 |
| 2021 | April 4 | 2056 | April 2 |
| 2022 | April 17 | 2057 | April 22 |
| 2023 | April 9 | 2058 | April 14 |
| 2024 | March 31 | 2059 | March 30 |
| 2025 | April 20 | 2060 | April 18 |
| 2026 | April 5 | 2061 | April 10 |
| 2027 | March 28 | 2062 | March 26 |
| 2028 | April 16 | 2063 | April 15 |
| 2029 | April 1 | 2064 | April 6 |
| 2030 | April 21 | 2065 | March 29 |
| 2031 | April 13 | 2066 | April 11 |
| 2032 | March 28 | 2067 | April 3 |
| 2033 | April 17 | 2068 | April 22 |
| 2034 | April 9 | 2069 | April 14 |

DAYS PER MONTH

| | | |
|---|---|---|
| Jan 31 | May 31 | Sep 30 |
| Feb 28/29 | Jun 30 | Oct 31 |
| Mar 31 | Jul 31 | Nov 30 |
| Apr 30 | Aug 31 | Dec 31 |

Figure 5-11: Picture frame with calendar below photo

2000 2001 2002 2003 2009 2004 2005
2006 2007 2013 2008 2015 2010 2011
2017 2012 2019 2014 2020 2021 2016
2023 2018 2024 2025 2026 2027 2022
2028 2029 2030 2031 2037 2032 2033
2034 2035 2041 2036 2043 2038 2039
2045 2040 2047 2042 2048 2049 2044
2051 2046 2052 2053 2054 2055 2050
2056 2057 2058 2059 2065 2060 2061
2062 2063 2069 2064 2071 2066 2067
2073 2068 2075 2070 2076 2077 2072
2079 2074 2080 2081 2082 2083 2078
2084 2085 2086 2087 2093 2088 2089
2090 2091 2097 2092 2099 2094 2095
2096 2098
LEAP YR FEB LEAP YR LEAP YR LEAP YR JAN LEAP YR
COM YR COM YR FEB COM YR COM YR COM YR JAN
MAY AUG MAR JUN SEP APR OCT
NOV DEC JUL
S M T W T F S
1 2
3 4 5 6 7 8 9
10 11 12 13 14 15 16
17 18 19 20 21 22 23
24 25 26 27 28 29 30
31
INSTRUCTIONS
1. Move the top slider so that the marker is over the column that has the year of interest.
2. Move the lower slider to line up the "1" with the month of interest.
3. Ignore dates 29, 30 and 31 when applicable.
4. Use the top row for January and February for leap years and the next to the top row for common years. Leap years are bold.
1
2
3
4
5
6
7
8


PARTS LIST

| ITEM | COMMENT |
|---|---|
| 1 | Commercial 5-inch by 7-inch photo frame |
| 2 | Back, suggested material 1/8 inch hardboard. See Notes 1 to 3. |
| 3 | Upper spacer, suggested material 1/8 inch hardboard built up to be thicker than sliders |
| 4 | Calendar face, suggested material 1/8 inch hardboard covered with cardstock. Has windows for upper slider marker, month table and day of month. |
| 5 | Upper slider (Table 3-8), suggested material 1/8 inch hardboard covered with cardstock |
| 6 | Middle spacer, same material as upper spacer |
| 7 | Lower slider (Table 3-1), same material as upper slider |
| 8 | Lower spacer, same material as upper spacer |

NOTES

1. For wall mounting, back can extend above picture frame and have holes for mouting, or there can be holes behind the picture frame or a hanging device behind the picture frame.
2. Picture frame is attached to back with screws
3. For desk mounting, a prop is required. An easy way to make one is to use a board or piece of plywood that is 0.75 inches by 0.75 inches by about 6 inches long, Round the bottom end, cut the top end at the desired angle and attach to the back with a screw.

Figure 5-12: Dual-slider calendar with 5 × 7 inch picture frame above it

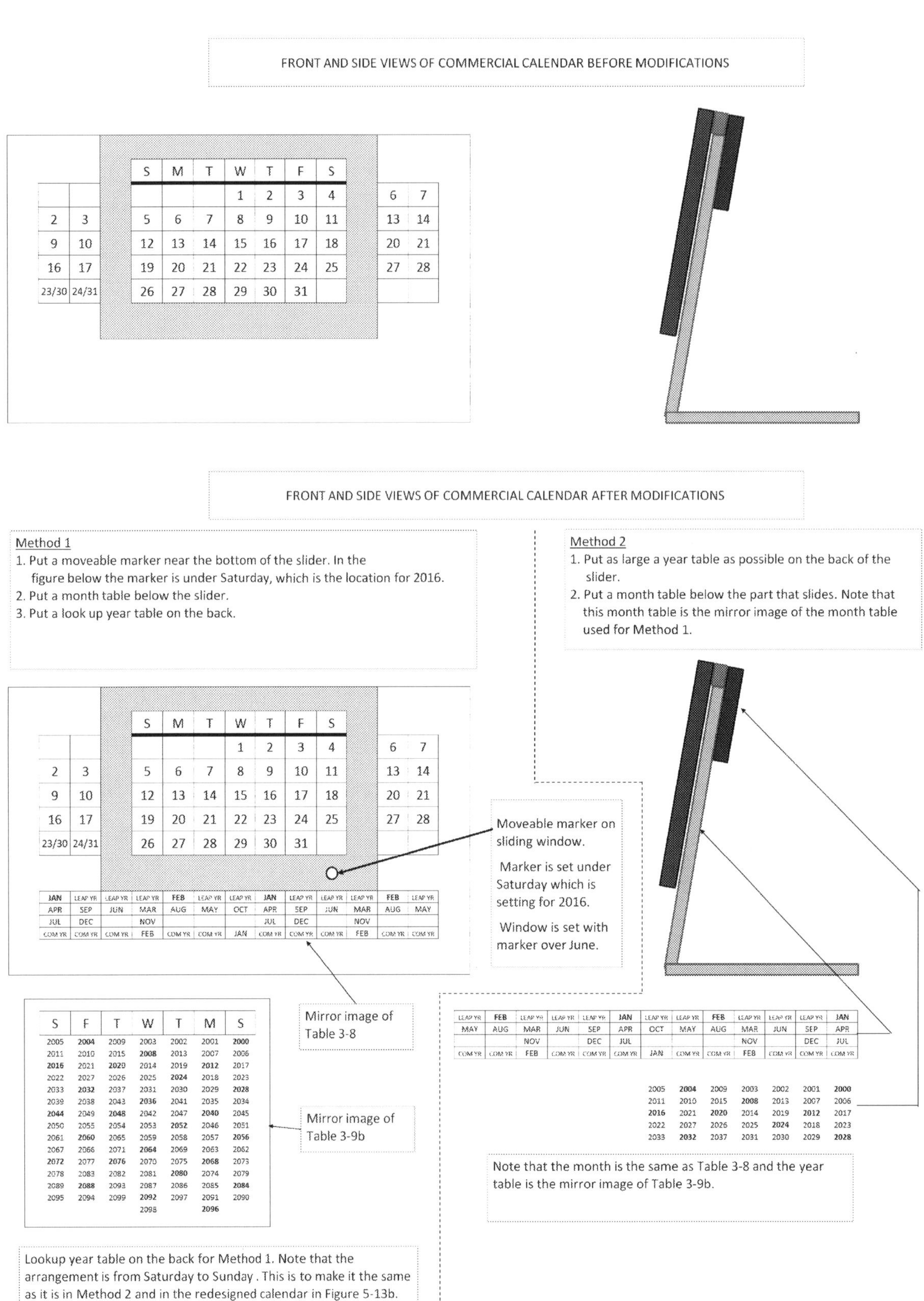
FRONT AND SIDE VIEWS OF COMMERCIAL CALENDAR BEFORE MODIFICATIONS
FRONT AND SIDE VIEWS OF COMMERCIAL CALENDAR AFTER MODIFICATIONS
Method 1
1. Put a moveable marker near the bottom of the slider. In the figure below the marker is under Saturday, which is the location for 2016.
2. Put a month table below the slider.
3. Put a look up year table on the back.
Method 2
1. Put as large a year table as possible on the back of the slider.
2. Put a month table below the part that slides. Note that this month table is the mirror image of the month table used for Method 1.
Moveable marker on sliding window.
Marker is set under Saturday which is setting for 2016.
Window is set with marker over June.
Mirror image of Table 3-8
Mirror image of Table 3-9b
Note that the month is the same as Table 3-8 and the year table is the mirror image of Table 3-9b.
Lookup year table on the back for Method 1. Note that the arrangement is from Saturday to Sunday . This is to make it the same as it is in Method 2 and in the redesigned calendar in Figure 5-13b.

Figure 5-13a: Modifications to commercial sliding-window 13-column calendar

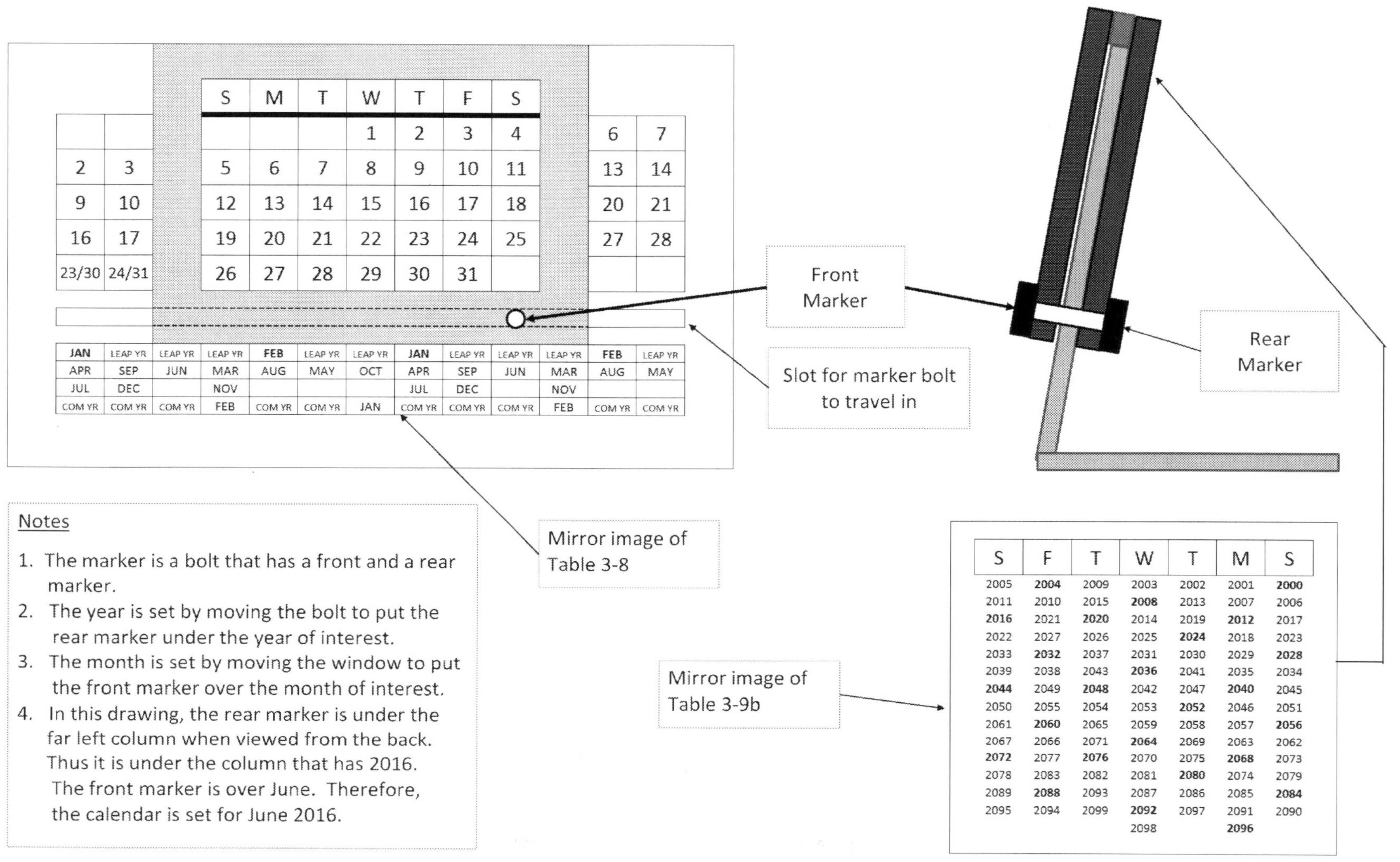
S M T W T F S
1 2 3 4
5 6 7 8 9 10 11
12 13 14 15 16 17 18
19 20 21 22 23 24 25
26 27 28 29 30 31
2 3 6 7
9 10 13 14
16 17 20 21
23/30 24/31 27 28
JAN APR JUL COM YR | LEAP YR SEP DEC COM YR | LEAP YR JUN COM YR | LEAP YR MAR NOV FEB | FEB AUG COM YR | LEAP YR MAY COM YR | LEAP YR OCT JAN | JAN APR JUL COM YR | LEAP YR SEP DEC COM YR | LEAP YR JUN COM YR | LEAP YR MAR NOV FEB | FEB AUG COM YR | LEAP YR MAY COM YR
Front Marker
Slot for marker bolt to travel in
Rear Marker
Mirror image of Table 3-8
Mirror image of Table 3-9b
S F T W T M S
2005 2004 2009 2003 2002 2001 2000
2011 2010 2015 2008 2013 2007 2006
2016 2021 2020 2014 2019 2012 2017
2022 2027 2026 2025 2024 2018 2023
2033 2032 2037 2031 2030 2029 2028
2039 2038 2043 2036 2041 2035 2034
2044 2049 2048 2042 2047 2040 2045
2050 2055 2054 2053 2052 2046 2051
2061 2060 2065 2059 2058 2057 2056
2067 2066 2071 2064 2069 2063 2062
2072 2077 2076 2070 2075 2068 2073
2078 2083 2082 2081 2080 2074 2079
2089 2088 2093 2087 2086 2085 2084
2095 2094 2099 2092 2097 2091 2090
2098 2096
Notes
1. The marker is a bolt that has a front and a rear marker.
2. The year is set by moving the bolt to put the rear marker under the year of interest.
3. The month is set by moving the window to put the front marker over the month of interest.
4. In this drawing, the rear marker is under the far left column when viewed from the back. Thus it is under the column that has 2016. The front marker is over June. Therefore, the calendar is set for June 2016.

Figure 5-13b: Redesigned commercial sliding-window 13-column calendar

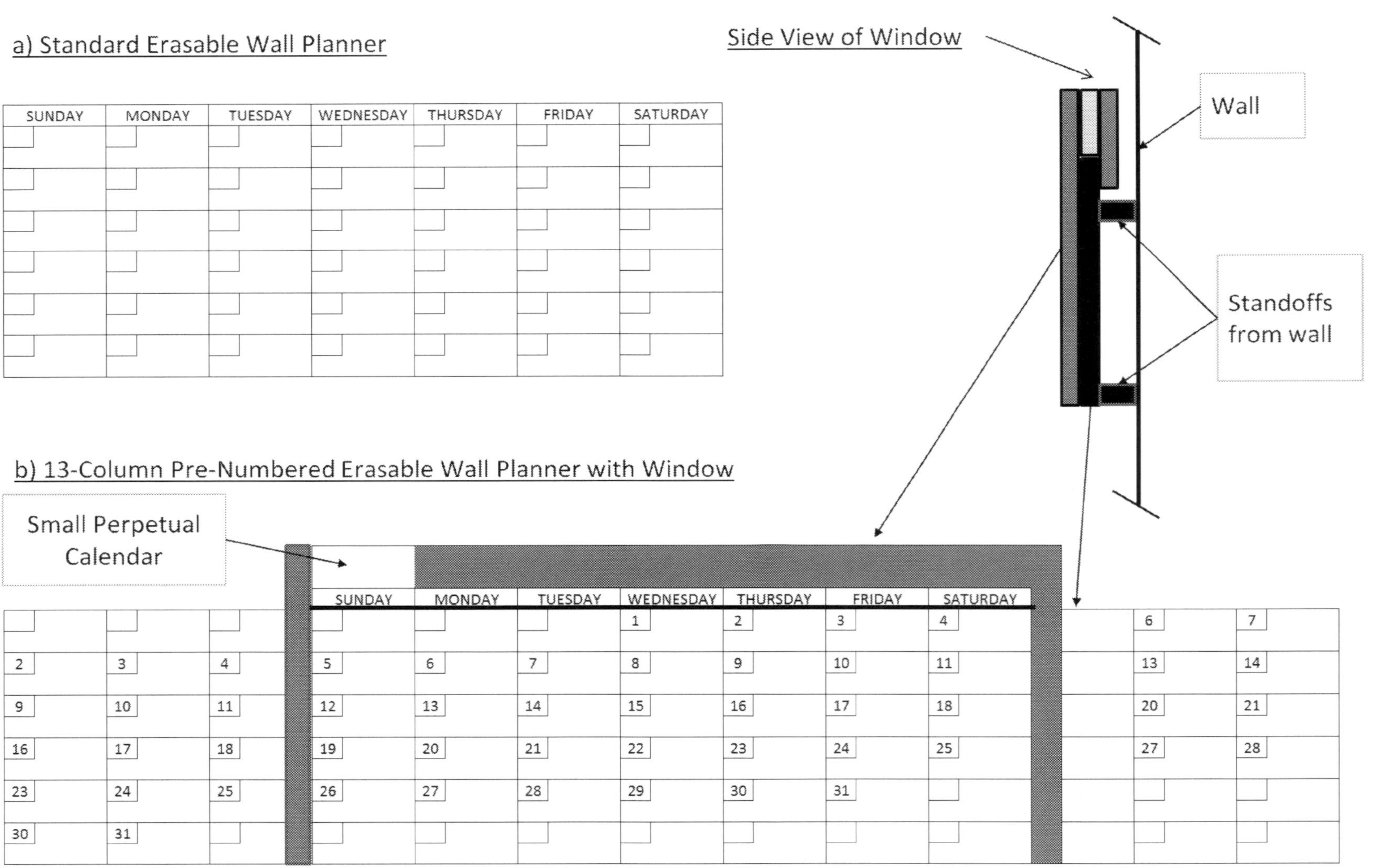
a) Standard Erasable Wall Planner
SUNDAY
MONDAY
TUESDAY
WEDNESDAY
THURSDAY
FRIDAY
SATURDAY
Side View of Window
Wall
Standoffs from wall
b) 13-Column Pre-Numbered Erasable Wall Planner with Window
Small Perpetual Calendar

Figures 5-14a and 5-14b: Monthly wall planner with 13 columns

a) Arrangement when first of month is on Wednesday

Small Perpetual Calendar

| SUNDAY | MONDAY | TUESDAY | WEDNESDAY | THURSDAY | FRIDAY | SATURDAY |
|---|---|---|---|---|---|---|
| | | | 1 | 2 | 3 | 4 |
| 5 | 6 | 7 | 8 | 9 | 10 | 11 |
| 12 | 13 | 14 | 15 | 16 | 17 | 18 |
| 19 | 20 | 21 | 22 | 23 | 24 | 25 |
| 26 | 27 | 28 | 29 | 30 | 31 | |
| | | | | | | |

b) Arrangement when first of month is on Saturday

Small Perpetual Calendar

| SUNDAY | MONDAY | TUESDAY | WEDNESDAY | THURSDAY | FRIDAY | SATURDAY |
|---|---|---|---|---|---|---|
| | | | | | | 1 |
| 2 | 3 | 4 | 5 | 6 | 7 | 8 |
| 9 | 10 | 11 | 12 | 13 | 14 | 15 |
| 16 | 17 | 18 | 19 | 20 | 21 | 22 |
| 23 | 24 | 25 | 26 | 27 | 28 | 29 |
| 30 | 31 | | | | | |

Figures 5-15a and 5-15b: Monthly wall planner with 7 strips

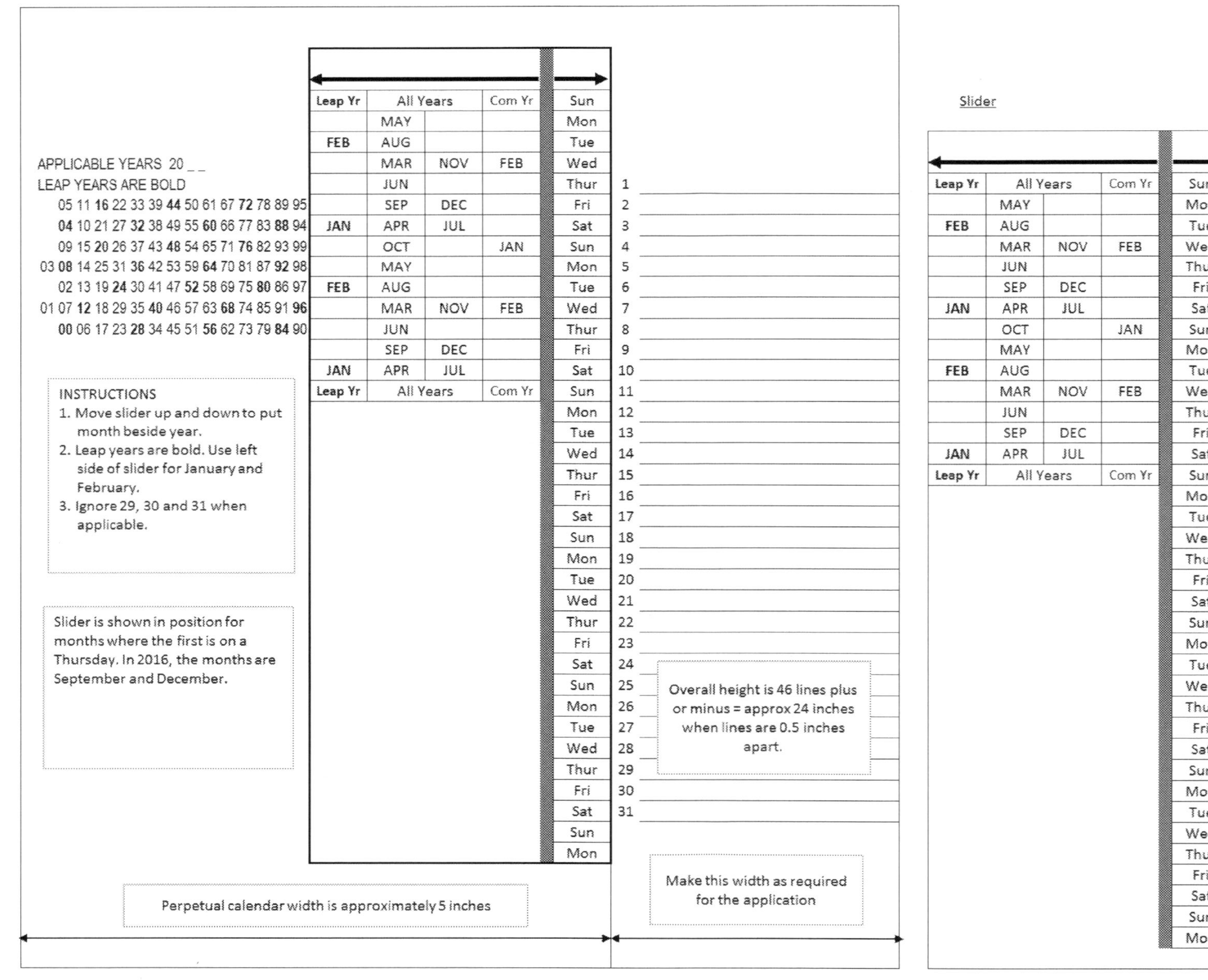
Main Body with Slider Outlined
APPLICABLE YEARS 20 _ _
LEAP YEARS ARE BOLD
05 11 16 22 33 39 44 50 61 67 72 78 89 95
04 10 21 27 32 38 49 55 60 66 77 83 88 94
09 15 20 26 37 43 48 54 65 71 76 82 93 99
03 08 14 25 31 36 42 53 59 64 70 81 87 92 98
02 13 19 24 30 41 47 52 58 69 75 80 86 97
01 07 12 18 29 35 40 46 57 63 68 74 85 91 96
00 06 17 23 28 34 45 51 56 62 73 79 84 90
INSTRUCTIONS
1. Move slider up and down to put month beside year.
2. Leap years are bold. Use left side of slider for January and February.
3. Ignore 29, 30 and 31 when applicable.
Slider is shown in position for months where the first is on a Thursday. In 2016, the months are September and December.
Perpetual calendar width is approximately 5 inches
Overall height is 46 lines plus or minus = approx 24 inches when lines are 0.5 inches apart.
Make this width as required for the application
Slider
Leap Yr
All Years
Com Yr

Figure 5-16a: Line-style monthly wall planner

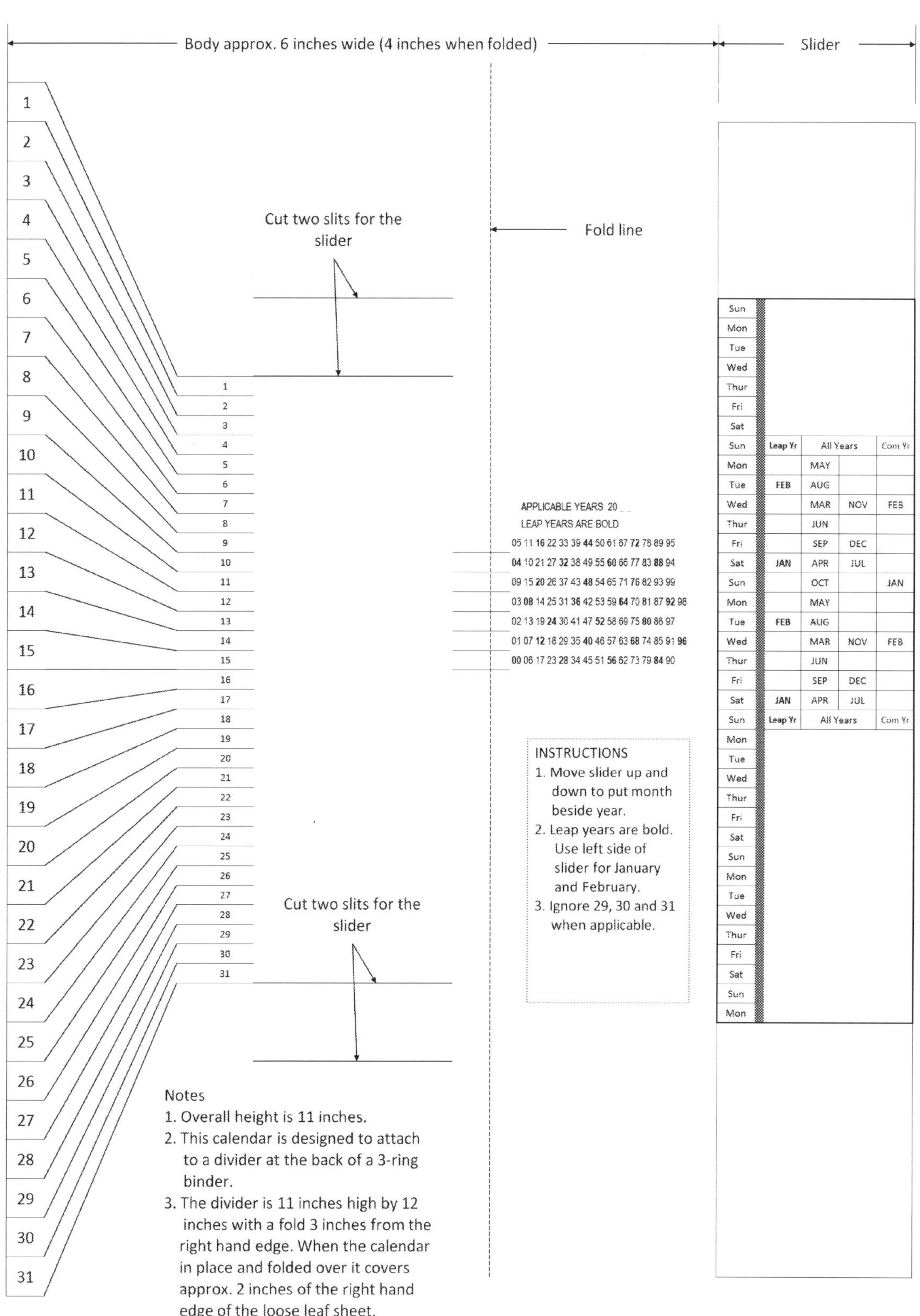

Body approx. 6 inches wide (4 inches when folded)
Slider
1 2 3 4 5 6 7 8 9 10 11 12 13 14 15 16 17 18 19 20 21 22 23 24 25 26 27 28 29 30 31
Cut two slits for the slider
Fold line
1 2 3 4 5 6 7 8 9 10 11 12 13 14 15 16 17 18 19 20 21 22 23 24 25 26 27 28 29 30 31
APPLICABLE YEARS 20_ _
LEAP YEARS ARE BOLD
05 11 **16** 22 33 39 **44** 50 61 67 **72** 78 89 95
**04** 10 21 27 **32** 38 49 55 **60** 66 77 83 **88** 94
09 15 **20** 26 37 43 **48** 54 65 71 **76** 82 93 99
03 **08** 14 25 31 **36** 42 53 59 **64** 70 81 87 **92** 98
02 13 19 **24** 30 41 47 **52** 58 69 75 **80** 86 97
01 07 **12** 18 29 35 **40** 46 57 63 **68** 74 85 91 **96**
**00** 06 17 23 **28** 34 45 51 **56** 62 73 79 **84** 90
INSTRUCTIONS
1. Move slider up and down to put month beside year.
2. Leap years are bold. Use left side of slider for January and February.
3. Ignore 29, 30 and 31 when applicable.
Cut two slits for the slider
Notes
1. Overall height is 11 inches.
2. This calendar is designed to attach to a divider at the back of a 3-ring binder.
3. The divider is 11 inches high by 12 inches with a fold 3 inches from the right hand edge. When the calendar in place and folded over it covers approx. 2 inches of the right hand edge of the loose leaf sheet.
Sun Mon Tue Wed Thur Fri Sat
Sun | Leap Yr | All Years | Com Yr
Mon | MAY
Tue | FEB | AUG
Wed | MAR | NOV | FEB
Thur | JUN
Fri | SEP | DEC
Sat | JAN | APR | JUL
Sun | OCT | JAN
Mon | MAY
Tue | FEB | AUG
Wed | MAR | NOV | FEB
Thur | JUN
Fri | SEP | DEC
Sat | JAN | APR | JUL
Sun | Leap Yr | All Years | Com Yr
Mon Tue Wed Thur Fri Sat Sun Mon Tue Wed Thur Fri Sat Sun Mon


Figure 5-16b: Vertical-slider 3-ring binder planner

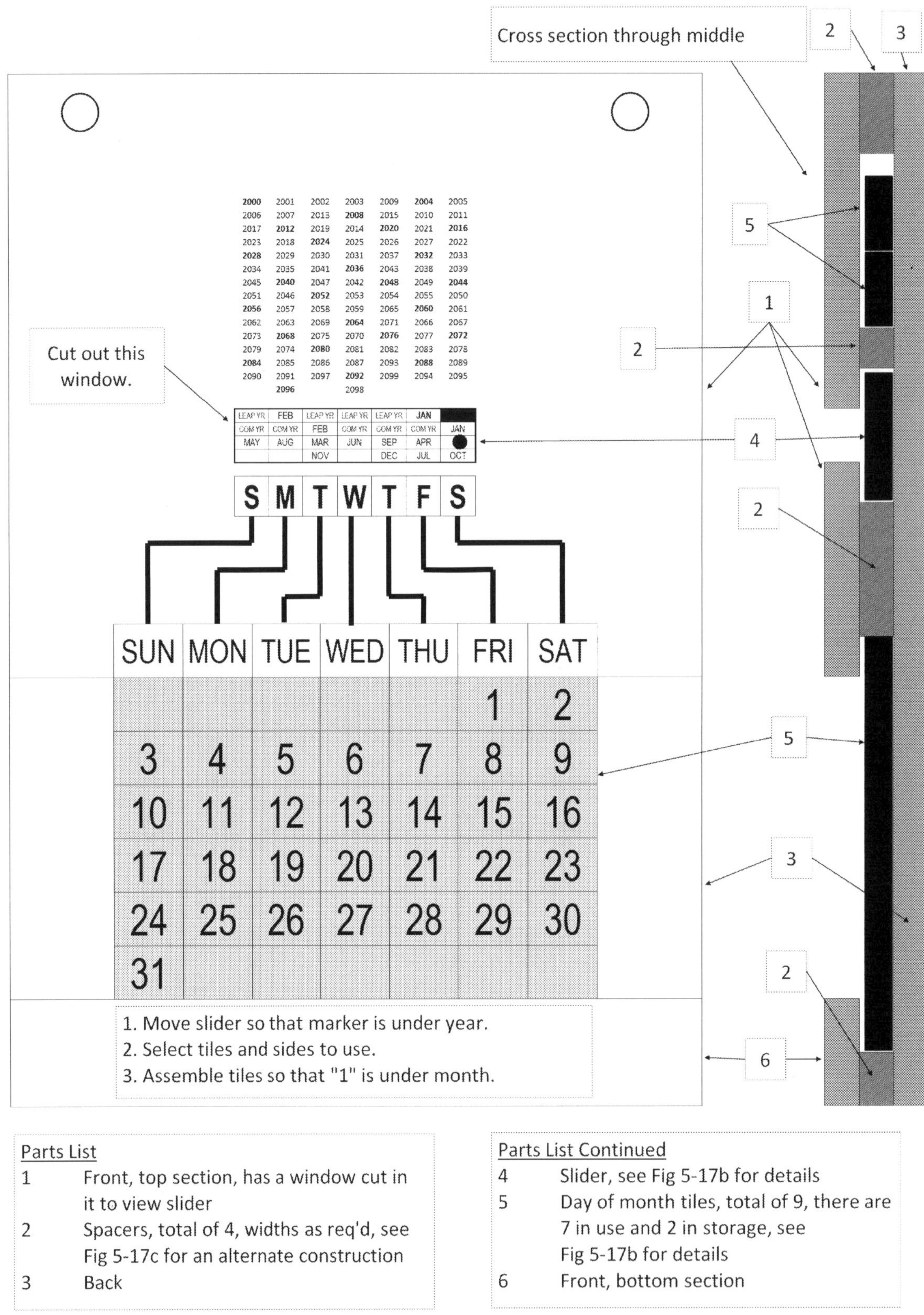
Cross section through middle
Cut out this window.
S M T W T F S
SUN MON TUE WED THU FRI SAT
1. Move slider so that marker is under year.
2. Select tiles and sides to use.
3. Assemble tiles so that "1" is under month.
Parts List
1 Front, top section, has a window cut in it to view slider
2 Spacers, total of 4, widths as req'd, see Fig 5-17c for an alternate construction
3 Back
Parts List Continued
4 Slider, see Fig 5-17b for details
5 Day of month tiles, total of 9, there are 7 in use and 2 in storage, see Fig 5-17b for details
6 Front, bottom section

Figure 5-17a: Ornate hybrid wall calendar, sheet 1 of 3

Slider

| | | | | | | | | | | | | |
|---|---|---|---|---|---|---|---|---|---|---|---|---|
| LEAP YR | **FEB** | LEAP YR | LEAP YR | LEAP YR | **JAN** | | LEAP YR | **FEB** | LEAP YR | LEAP YR | LEAP YR | **JAN** |
| COM YR | COM YR | FEB | COM YR | COM YR | COM YR | JAN | COM YR | COM YR | FEB | COM YR | COM YR | COM YR |
| MAY | AUG | MAR | JUN | SEP | APR | ● | MAY | AUG | MAR | JUN | SEP | APR |
| | | NOV | | DEC | JUL | OCT | | | NOV | | DEC | JUL |

Slider notes

1. The black dot between JAN & OCT is a push knob.
2. Only the applicable 7 columns of the slider are visible in the window.

Front sides of the 9 tiles

| | | | | | | | | |
|---|---|---|---|---|---|---|---|---|
| 1 | 2 | 2 | 3 | 3 | 4 | 5 | 6 | 7 |
| 8 | 9 | 9 | 10 | 10 | 11 | 12 | 13 | 14 |
| 15 | 16 | 16 | 17 | 17 | 18 | 19 | 20 | 21 |
| 22 | 23 | 23 | 24 | 24 | 25 | 26 | 27 | 28 |
| 29 | 30 | | 31 | | | | | |
| | | | | | | | | |
| | Note 3 | | Note 3 | | | | | |

Tile notes

1. When the number at the top of the tile is in the top row, use the front side.
2. When the number at the top of the tile is in the second row, use the back side.
3. These four tiles are two pairs. Only one tile from each pair is in use and the other is stored behind the year table.
4. An alternative to having 9 tiles is to have 7 and have sleeves to cover 30 and 31 when these dates are not applicable.

Back sides of the 9 tiles

| | | | | | | | | |
|---|---|---|---|---|---|---|---|---|
| 1 | | | | | | | | |
| 8 | 2 | 2 | 3 | 3 | 4 | 5 | 6 | 7 |
| 15 | 9 | 9 | 10 | 10 | 11 | 12 | 13 | 14 |
| 22 | 16 | 16 | 17 | 17 | 18 | 19 | 20 | 21 |
| | 23 | 23 | 24 | 24 | 25 | 26 | 27 | 28 |
| | 30 | | 31 | | | | | |
| | Note 3 | | Note 3 | | | | | |

Figure 5-17b: Ornate hybrid wall calendar, sheet 2 of 3

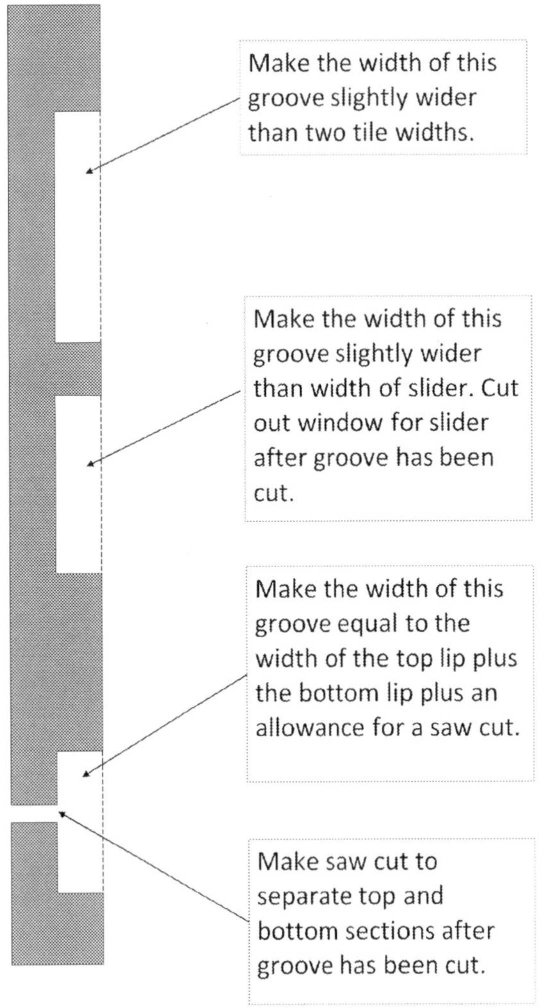
Make the width of this groove slightly wider than two tile widths.
Make the width of this groove slightly wider than width of slider. Cut out window for slider after groove has been cut.
Make the width of this groove equal to the width of the top lip plus the bottom lip plus an allowance for a saw cut.
Make saw cut to separate top and bottom sections after groove has been cut.

Alternate Construction for Face and Spacers

The sketch in Figure 5-17a implies that the front top section, front bottom section and the four spacers are all separate pieces. This construction is difficult to assemble. A simpler method is to use one thick piece for the front and cut out grooves in the back. After the grooves have been cut out, the piece is cut to make the front top and bottom sections. Suggested material is 3/8 inch plywood for the front and 1/8 inch plywood for the slider and tiles. Cut all grooves slightly deeper than 1/8 inch to allow for free movement of the slider and tiles.

Figure 5-17c: Ornate hybrid wall calendar, sheet 3 of 3

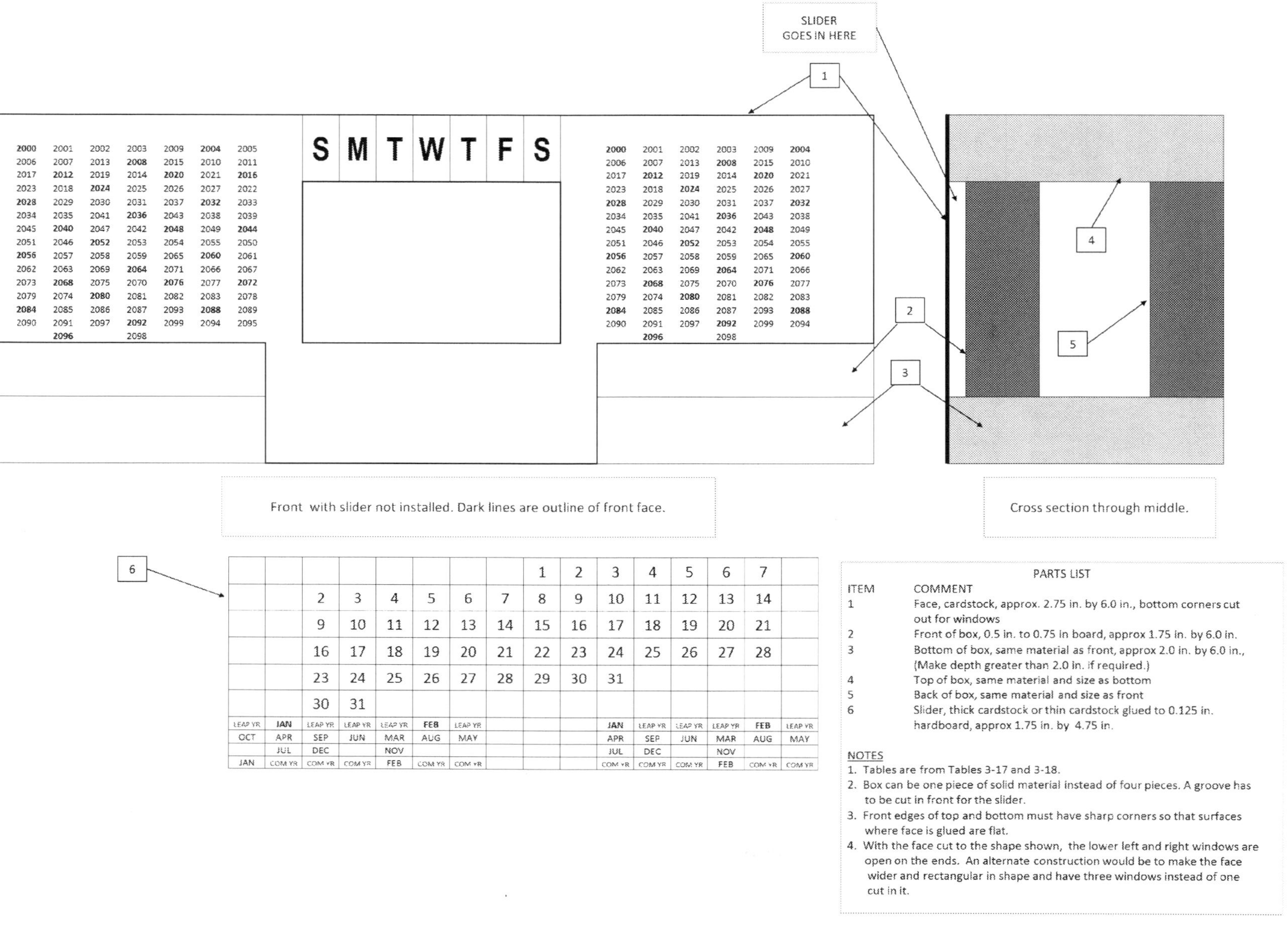
SLIDER GOES IN HERE
1
2
3
4
5
6
S M T W T F S
Front with slider not installed. Dark lines are outline of front face.
Cross section through middle.
PARTS LIST
ITEM COMMENT
1 Face, cardstock, approx. 2.75 in. by 6.0 in., bottom corners cut out for windows
2 Front of box, 0.5 in. to 0.75 in board, approx 1.75 in. by 6.0 in.
3 Bottom of box, same material as front, approx 2.0 in. by 6.0 in., (Make depth greater than 2.0 in. if required.)
4 Top of box, same material and size as bottom
5 Back of box, same material and size as front
6 Slider, thick cardstock or thin cardstock glued to 0.125 in. hardboard, approx 1.75 in. by 4.75 in.
NOTES
1. Tables are from Tables 3-17 and 3-18.
2. Box can be one piece of solid material instead of four pieces. A groove has to be cut in front for the slider.
3. Front edges of top and bottom must have sharp corners so that surfaces where face is glued are flat.
4. With the face cut to the shape shown, the lower left and right windows are open on the ends. An alternate construction would be to make the face wider and rectangular in shape and have three windows instead of one cut in it.

Figure 5-18: Stand for commercial perpetual desk calendar

## CHAPTER 6

# MULTISHEET PERPETUAL CALENDARS WITH A YEAR TABLE ON EACH SHEET—APPLICATIONS AND PRODUCTS

### Applications

The multisheet perpetual calendar with a year table on each sheet is ideal for replacing conventional multisheet desk calendars. In this application, it has the following advantages over the calendar that is in almost every office:

- It does not have to be replaced every year.
- It enables looking forward or back many years, compared to only one or two years.
- It is very attractive for giving away as advertising, because calendars not given out in one year do not expire until many years in the future. Also, a calendar that costs only one and a half to twice as much as a one-year calendar will be on the recipient's desk for many years.
- It saves resources. A perpetual calendar that requires no more than 1.5 times the amount of material as a conventional calendar will last 5 to 10 years or longer before it wears out.
- It is a calendar that is both novel and practical.

Two minor advantages that a conventional calendar has over a perpetual calendar are space for larger pictures or larger font and the ability to feature fresh new pictures every year. However, a perpetual calendar can be made quite attractive, and if new pictures are preferred each year, designs can have pockets or another arrangement for adding and removing photos.

Table 6-1 lists the applications for the multisheet perpetual calendar with a year table on each sheet that are described in this chapter. Of all the various designs of multisheet perpetual calendars listed in the table, the flip-down-window desk calendar probably has the most potential for widespread use. However, the other designs are worth investigating, particularly for ideas for small production runs and niche markets. For example, the holders for the lift-out-pad calendars require less development effort than the style with the flip-down window. There is also a market for perpetual wall calendars in applications where the user does not write on the calendar sheets.

**Table 6-1**
**Applications for the Multisheet Perpetual Calendar with a Year Table on Each Sheet**

| Application | Description | Figure |
|---|---|---|
| Flip-down-window desk calendar | Standard tent calendar with a moving window that flips down to change the month. Can be made with 12, 14 or 24 sheets. | 6-1a and 6-1b |
| Lift-out-pad desk calendar | Pad lifts out of holder for changing the month. Can be made with 12, 14 or 24 sheets and with various types of holders. | 6-2 |
| Wall calendar format | Various methods of displaying permanent notes on a wall calendar. | 6-3 |
| Flip-down-window wall calendar | Wall calendar based on the flip-down-window desk calendar. | 6-4 |
| Clip-on-window wall calendar | Similar to flip-down-window wall calendar, but the window clips on rather than flipping down. | 6-5 |
| Lift-out-pad wall calendar | Wall calendar based on lift-out-pad desk calendar. Can be designed with calendar pages and pictures on separate pads to enable the reuse of old calendar pictures. | 6-6 |
| Window-on-each-sheet wall calendar | Has a window on each sheet. Each window is set at the beginning of the year, and the calendar sheets with the preset window are turned over each month as in a conventional wall calendar. The concept can be used for new calendars, a photo album calendar and planner divider sheets, or to reuse an expired calendar. The reference figure shows two different designs. | 6-7a and 6-7b |
| Extension of single-sheet calendar to multisheet | Uses Table 4-11 and Figure 5-1a to make a calendar that has a sheet per month. The resulting calendar is similar to the 12-sheet design of the multisheet perpetual calendar with a year table on each sheet. Can be used to make dividers in a planner or a flip-over desk calendar. | 6-8 |
| Seven-column multisheet calendar | Uses concepts in Tables 4-12, 4-13 and 4-14. This calendar is inconvenient to use. Note that a design based on these concepts is not developed in Chapter 6. See Figures 7-6a to 7-6c for a seven-column multisheet calendar with a single year table that is practical. | none |

## Tables for 12-, 14- and 24-Sheet Designs

The calendars in Figures 6-1a to 6-7b can be made with 12, 14 or 24 sheets for the months. Table 6-2 lists the year and day-of-month tables to use for each of these three designs.

### Table 6-2
### Tables to Use for 12-Sheet, 14-Sheet and 24-Sheet Designs

| Calendar design | Year table | Day-of-month table |
|---|---|---|
| 12-sheet | Table 4-8 for January and February<br><br>Table 4-7 for March to December | Table 4-1 with 29 added to February<br><br>(A note can be put on the sheet to indicate that 29 applies only to leap years.) |
| 14-sheet | Table 4-7<br><br>The year tables for January and February of common years show only common years.<br><br>The year tables for January and February of leap years show only leap years. | Table 4-1 for January and February of common years, and March to December for both leap years and common years<br><br>Table 4-3 for January and February of leap years |
| 24-sheet | Table 4-5 for all months in a common year<br><br>Table 4-6 for all months in a leap year | Table 4-1 for common years<br><br>Table 4-2 for leap years |

## Flip-Down-Window Desk Calendar

Figure 6-1a shows three typical month sheets for the 14-sheet design flip-down-window desk calendar, which is depicted in Figure 1-2a. This figure also shows the moving window set for July 2016. In keeping with a common office-size calendar, the sheets are 7.0 inches wide by 4.5 inches high. The year tables on the sheets are from Table 4-7; the day-of-month tables for January and February in a leap year are from Table 4-3; and the day-of-month tables for the other months are from Table 4-1. The year tables on the sheets for January and February of common years show only the common years in Table 4-7, and the sheets for January and February of leap years show only leap years. To leave space for a reasonable-size font in the day-of-the-month table, the year table has 65 years rather than a full century. The month sheets are made from standard paper, which has a weight of around 20 pounds. They are bound with double-loop binding that has the trade name Wire-O. In addition to attaching the sheets to each other, the binding attaches the sheets to a tent made from cardstock. There are 14 sheets for the calendar, plus optional sheets, which may have tables for holidays, advertising, pictures or other information. Typical one-year conventional calendars have 12 sheets for the calendar, plus one or two additional sheets. On some, the months are printed on the back sides of the calendar sheets so that the calendar looks the same from either side. On others, the back has pictures or small calendars for the month before and the month after the current month. The only options for the back sides of the perpetual calendar sheets are to leave them blank or to include pictures. Some conventional calendars have pictures on the front along with the days of the month. As the month requires only 7 columns, compared to 13 for the perpetual calendar, there is more room for a picture on a sheet of the same width. Figure 6-1a does not show any pictures or artwork on the front, but there is a small amount of unused space under the name of the month.

To change the month, the knob below the window is turned, the window is flipped down, the sheet for the current month is flipped over to put it at the back of the tent and the window is put back in place. (Some development work is required to make a window that is easy to flip down and that also presses against the sheets when flipped up. See Figure 6-4 for some concepts.) At the beginning of the year, the window is moved left or right as required to make the marker point to the desired column of the year table. The calendar sheets are flipped from the back to the front, and the appropriate sheet (January of a common year or January of a leap year) is selected for the first month of the year. The window is held in its horizontal position by friction rather than mechanical stops for each position. This design, which is simpler to build, enables making small adjustments to bring the marker in line with a year table column.

Figure 6-1b shows concepts for the window and the cardstock tent. Except for what is printed on them, the tent and the calendar sheets are the same as in a conventional one-year multisheet tent calendar. The extra material required for the perpetual function includes the window and the pieces associated with it. This is equivalent to 50 percent or less extra material. As noted in Figure 6-1b, strips are glued to the back of the calendar's front to stiffen it. To be able to clearly see which columns of the day-of-month table are in the window, the front must be stiff so that it will not bow out and push the window away from the calendar sheets. With a bit of trial and error, the concepts in Figure 6-1b should be able to be perfected.

The same construction shown in Figures 6-1a and 6-1b can be used for the 12-sheet and 24-sheet designs. Whether to use 14 sheets or 12 sheets is a matter of personal preference. I like the 14-sheet design because February 29 does not have to be ignored in common years and it provides the opportunity to have different pictures for January and February in leap years. A minor inconvenience of the 12-sheet design is that for a leap year, the window has to be moved on March 1 as well as on January 1. (See discussion on Table 4-8 in Chapter 4.)

The 24-sheet design can be made by printing the months for a common year on one side of the paper and the months for a leap year on the other side. If this is done, the window is moved from the front to the back of the tent when changing from common year to leap year. Alternatively, the 24-sheet design can have 24 pieces of paper to provide a different set of pictures on the back for leap years. Given the need to move the window or the extra material required, the 24-sheet design may not be attractive for many applications.

## Lift-Out-Pad Desk Calendar

Figure 6-2 shows details of two holders for the lift-out-pad configuration. Holder no. 1 is a simple design with a fixed window. Holder no. 2, which is depicted in Figure 1-2c, has a moving window. In both holders, the sheets rest on the holder, as they are not held up by a tent. (The back of the holder could have a hanger for the sheets, but having them rest on their bottom edges is simpler.) Therefore, the sheets should be made from cardstock instead of standard paper to minimize curling. Cardstock with a weight of 80 lb. is sufficiently stiff if the pad fits reasonably tight into the holder. I recommend that the gap behind the window for the pad be equal to the pad thickness, plus 1/16th of an inch. There are two options for making the window in the holder:

1. Make the window so that the 7 columns of the day-of-month table that are applicable to the current month are visible and the other columns are hidden. This is what the single-sheet tent calendar in Figure 5-1a displays. With this design, the holder displays 7 columns in the window and has space to hide up to 6 columns on each side of the window. The holder is then 19 columns wide, plus borders.
2. Make the window similar to that in Figure 6-1b, where columns in the day-of-month table beyond the edges of the window frame are visible. The holder is then the width of the calendar sheets, which is 13 columns plus borders.

To maximize font size in a given width, the second option is preferred. This is important for multisheet calendars that are competing with calendars printed with a large font. It is not as important for the single-sheet tent calendar when it competes with a calendar that has 6 or 12 months on the face.

The calendar shown in Figure 6-2 has a face 3.5 inches high by 8.5 inches wide. This size was selected so that three calendar sheets can be printed on each side of an 8.5 × 11 inch sheet of cardstock. The tables on the sheets are the same as on the calendar shown in Figure 6-1a. The font is a little smaller, and there is a 3 × 2.25 inch picture on each sheet. Double-sided printing is used. Table 6-3 shows how the printing is done for the 14-sheet design.

## Table 6-3
## How the Printing Is Done for a 14-Sheet Design

| Piece number | Front side | Back side |
|---|---|---|
| 1 | January, leap year | December |
| 2 | February, leap year | November |
| 3 | January, common year | October |
| 4 | February, common year | September |
| 5 | March | August |
| 6 | April | July |
| 7 | May | June |

The lift-out-pad perpetual calendar can also be made with 12 calendar sheets. In this case, the front sides have January to June and the back sides have July to December.

There are two holder designs shown in Figure 6-2. Holder no. 1 is very simple. The pad moves instead of the window. The location of the window and the width of the holder are determined as follows:

1. Line up the right-hand edge of the pad with the right-hand edge of the holder. Locate the window so that the marker points to the far right column of the year table.
2. Line up the far left column of the year table with the marker. Cut the holder so that the left-hand edge of the holder lines up with the left-hand edge of the pad.

When this procedure is followed, the right edge of the window frame is about 0.5 inches from the right edge of the holder, and the holder is about 6.5 inches wide.

Holder no. 2 has a moving window and is slightly more complicated. It is the same width as the calendar sheets. As shown in Figure 6-2, the calendar pad sits on the top edge of a support, and the bottom edge of the support is a guide for the window. A bolt holds the window in position. To simplify construction, the slot in which the bolt moves is cut all the way to the right-hand edge of the holder. This enables cutting most of the slot with a bandsaw or a table saw and doing only a bit of finishing with a coping saw and file. The window is U-shaped, so that a hole does not have to be drilled to get a saw blade into the opening. A U-shaped window could also be used on holder no. 1. Holder no. 2 does not have a guide on the left-hand edge to push the pad against. Instead, the pad is put in so that its left edge is close to the left edge of the holder. Then the pad is adjusted slightly in order to centre the appropriate columns of the day-of-month table in the window. A guide would complicate construction by requiring greater precision in printing the calendar sheets (especially with double-sided sheets) and would complicate setup by requiring the window to be set in an exact position. In a mass-produced calendar that has stops for window positions and adequate precision in manufacturing, a guide would eliminate having to check the window whenever the month is changed.

The lift-out-pad perpetual desk calendar is an ideal product for a small craft shop to manufacture. The pad is a simple print job that any print shop can do. In fact, it can be done on a home printer. Ideally, the pad would be bound with Wire-O double-loop binding. Many print shops do not have this capability, in which case one hole in an upper corner for a small ring or string does an adequate job of holding the sheets together. The sheets can be loose, but binding keeps them in the correct order. The only printing on the holder is the days of the week above the window. A strip with SMTWTFS on it can be glued above the window, or the lettering can be done by hand. Either holder design in Figure 6-2 can be put into production with very little effort to work out details, or a more ornate design can be developed.

An alternative to a moving window on holder no. 2 is to have seven different windows, with the six unused windows kept in a built-in storage space. This concept could be attractive if the sheets do not have a picture on them, as is the case for the sheets shown in Figure 6-1a. Instead of seeing columns of the day-of-month table on either side of the window, the user would see a wider window piece with suitable artwork on each side of the opening. Although having seven different windows would make a more attractive front, it would also make the design and use more complicated. This would increase production cost and detract from the simplicity that is inherent in the basic concept.

## Perpetual Wall Calendar Formats

Wall calendars are used in both offices and homes. Although many, particularly home kitchen calendars, are used to record appointments and other information, there is still a very large market for wall calendars that never get written on. In a kitchen, there are often two calendars—one for notes, and the other left untouched. Where there is wall space available in an office, a wall calendar that can be read from a distance may be preferable to a desk calendar. Thus, if a perpetual wall calendar can be made that is easy to set and read and is a reasonable cost, there would be a large potential market for it.

A very common size for wall calendars is 11 inches wide by 17 inches high. They typically fold in the centre, with one half displaying the days of the month in 8.5 × 11 inch format and the other half showing a picture. The discussion in this chapter is slanted towards the common size, but it could also apply to calendars 8.5 inches wide by 11 inches high. Small wall calendars are not written on as much as larger ones, so the market for small perpetual wall calendars could be quite large.

The concepts for the flip-down-window and lift-out-pad desk calendars can be adapted to make wall calendars. Although these and all of my calendars have a 13-column day-of-month table, compared to 7 for conventional calendars, a perpetual calendar that does not have space for writing in information can be made with a font that is as large as or larger than the one used for a conventional calendar. By using a slightly smaller font, there can be space for writing in recurring events such as birthdays and anniversaries. Figure 6-3 shows the month of March's calendar sheet from a perpetual calendar made in the common size of 8.5 × 11 inches. The figure illustrates four different styles of writing the numbers in the day-of-month table, as follows:

1. Make each box 2 Excel spreadsheet cells wide by 3 cells high. (As noted in Chapter 2, the row height on my spreadsheets is 15 and the column width is 3.) Write the numbers in as large a font as will fit in the box, which in the figure is Arial Narrow 34. The 1st and 15th of the month illustrate this style. Limited trials with different fonts and optimizing box size have been done. There may be a better font. However, the figure does show that the font in a 13-column table on an 11-inch-wide sheet can be made quite large.
2. Make the font a little smaller so that there is a line below the number to write in limited information. As for the first style, a box two cells wide by three cells high is allowed for each date. The numbers are set in Arial Narrow 28 in boxes two cells wide by two cells high, and there is a space (in Arial 9) two cells wide by one cell high below each number for information. Most of the numbers in the top four rows in Figure 6-3 are in this style. To illustrate how much information can be entered, see the 17th, which has *St. Patrick* (for "St. Patrick's Day") written below the *17*. The numbers for the days of the month are reasonably large, and the space below has room for abbreviated information.
3. Make the font even smaller so that there is space for two lines below the number. In Figure 6-3, the font size for these numbers is Arial Narrow 16 and the lines below are Arial Narrow 9. The 3rd and the 8th of the month illustrate this style. This doubles the space for information, but the numbers for the days of the month are a bit small.
4. Write the information for recurring events below the day-of-month table instead of below each number. As in the second style, the numbers are written in Arial Narrow 28 in boxes two cells wide by two cells high. The boxes are shaded for dates that have a note below the table. The bottom two rows in Figure 6-3 have this style, with the 27th and 29th illustrating how information can be entered. This enables making much better use of the space for information than the second style affords.

A point to note in Figure 6-3 is that when a day of the month is not in the centre column, the information associated with it must be written twice for the second and third styles, and two boxes must be shaded for the fourth style. Of the four styles illustrated in Figure 6-3, the first is the one to use if no information is to be written on the calendar. The fourth style is better for information than the second or third. A minor disadvantage of the fourth style is that the bottom frame of the window covers part of the information in the notes below the table. In many cases, the user knows what is associated with a shaded date without referring to a footnote. If the hiding of information is a concern, the window can be a piece of tinted transparent material with SMTWTFS printed across the top. Figure 6-3 clearly shows that perpetual wall calendar sheets can be made by using the same concepts as perpetual desk calendars use.

## Flip-Down-Window Wall Calendar

Figure 6-4 shows how the concepts in the flip-down-window desk calendar can be adapted to make a wall calendar. This wall calendar is a common size, 11 inches wide by 17 inches high when unfolded. The back sheet is cardstock, and the other sheets are standard paper with a weight of about 20 lb. The sheets are stapled at the fold in the middle. The bottom of each sheet has a calendar sheet similar to the sheets for March and July in Figure 6-1a. The top of each sheet has a picture. Assume that the 12-sheet design is used. (The construction in Figure 6-4 would be the same for the 14-sheet design, but the operating instructions would be slightly different.) Following are the differences between the flip-down-window desk calendar and this wall calendar:

1. As shown in Figure 6-4, the wall calendar is glued to a stiff back that is approximately 13 inches wide by 19 inches high to provide a 1-inch border all around the calendar. The figure suggests using hardboard, but thick cardstock or cardboard could also be used. The back performs the same function as the tent in the flip-down-window desk calendar.
2. The wall calendar has a top knob or clip to hold the sheets in place when they are flipped up. In the desk calendar, the sheets are simply flipped over. In a conventional wall calendar, the nail that holds the calendar up also holds the sheets in place. With the calendar glued to a back, a knob or clip must be used instead of a nail to hold the sheets in place.
3. The wall calendar has a wire frame and a side knob to press the window against the calendar sheets. With the sheets stapled in the middle, they will tend not to lie flat against the back, so something is needed to press the window against the sheets. In the desk calendar, the sheets are bound with Wire-O binding, which makes them lie flat. On the desk calendar, the one knob at the bottom is assumed to provide any pressure that may be required. The wall calendar also has this knob.

Instructions for using the 12-sheet wall calendar are as follows.

At the beginning of the year, do the following things:

1. Turn the three knobs aside and flip down the wire frame and window.
2. Turn the calendar page to January and set the window to the column that has the year of interest.
3. Flip up the window and wire frame, and turn the three knobs into place. Tighten or loosen the wing nut as required so that the wire frame pushes the window and calendar sheets firmly against the backing.

At the beginning of each month, do the following things:

1. Turn the three knobs aside and flip down the wire frame and window.
2. Turn the calendar page to the month of interest, and move the window to align with columns, if required. When changing from February to March in a leap year, the window will have to be set to a different column in the year table.
3. Flip up the window and wire frame, and turn the three knobs into place. Tighten or loosen the wing nut as required so that the wire frame pushes the window and calendar sheets firmly against the backing.

I have identified three different ways of pressing the window against the calendar sheets. The first is the three knobs. This is the easiest to construct in a home workshop with limited tools and capability.

The second way is shown in Figure 6-4 in the sketch beside the wire frame. The window is spring-loaded, and the side knob, bottom knob and wire frame are not required. The spring-loading is based on the same principle as the fold-up handle for winding a measuring tape. On a measuring tape, when the handle is folded up for storage, a flat spring pushes against it to hold it in this position. As the handle is unfolded to wind up the tape, the resistance of the spring increases until the handle makes a 90-degree angle with the case. At this point, the resistance begins to decrease. There is no resistance when the handle is at 180 degrees for winding up the tape. Similar to the measuring tape handle, the window of this calendar turns on a pivot point. When the window is in the *up* position, the flat spring pushes against the bottom of the window to hold it against the back. When the window is flipped down, the spring offers increasing resistance until the window reaches the 90-degree mark. Then the resistance decreases. There is no resistance when the window is down at approximately 180 degrees. If a flat spring pushes against the bottom of the window, the face of the window must be made of rigid material. Alternatively, the spring could push against a rigid piece that pushes against the window, similar to the wire frame. In this case, the face of the window can be cardstock. Figure 6-4 shows only a brief outline of the concept. Many details need to be worked out.

The third way of pressing the window against the calendar sheets is to employ the same concept as is used to press the folding handles of a binder clip against a bundle of papers. This would eliminate the side knob, but the bottom knob may still be needed to hold the bottom of the window in place. An examination of a binder clip shows that the concept is simple and the cost should be low. However, some development effort would be required. Of the three ways, this one may be the best. The development cost is estimated to be $5,000, which is a cost of 10¢ per calendar for a production run of 50,000.

## Clip-on-Window Wall Calendar

A clip-on window is an alternative to the holder in Figure 6-4. In this design, two clips similar to hair-sectioning clips are used to attach the window to the bottom of the calendar sheets. In fact, as shown in Figure 6-5, hair-sectioning clips can be used. They are available in a variety of sizes and colours. Common flat styles have an overall length of 2.0 inches. The finger grip and spring take up about 0.5 inches, leaving a clamping surface of 1.5 inches. Other styles have an overall length of about 3.5 inches, but these tend to have a curved clamping surface. For large production runs of calendars, a special clamp can be developed. Instead of using two clamps, a single clamp similar to that on a clipboard may be better. However, two 2.0-inch-long flat-style clamps are suitable for production runs of a few thousand. Tests show that the spring in these clips can hold the window in place when there is anywhere between 1 and 12 calendar sheets, plus the window, in the clip. The preferred way of installing the clip is to clamp the window, the current month, all the sheets from the current month through to the end of the year, and the back cover together. Alternatively, the window can be clamped to just the current month. However, the picture for the next month is on the back side of the current month, so there would be a risk of scratching the pictures.

When a window is clipped onto a calendar, two holes are required to hang the calendar. Otherwise, it would be at an angle with the centre of the window not directly below a single nail. The concepts in Figure 6-5 can be used to make an existing conventional calendar into a perpetual calendar by gluing a perpetual calendar sheet on top of each sheet. Although this may not be practical for a company to salvage unsold calendars, it is practical for an individual to extend the life of a calendar that has favourite pictures. The following section on the lift-out-pad wall calendar shows another way of extending the life of pictures by having them separate from the calendar sheets.

A comparison of Figures 6-4 and 6-5 shows that the clip-on-window wall calendar is much simpler to build and hence would be lower-cost. However, changing the month in the flip-down-window design in Figure 6-4 requires less effort to line up the window. As with all the alternative concepts in *Practical Perpetual Calendars*, there are pros and cons and personal preferences to consider when designing a calendar.

## Lift-Out-Pad Wall Calendar

Figure 6-6 shows how the concepts in the lift-out-pad desk calendar can be adapted to make a wall calendar. The holder for the wall calendar is based on holder no. 2 in Figure 6-2. The common wall calendar that is stapled at the fold in the middle could be used in the holder. However, the number of sheets between the window and the back would vary from 12 at the beginning of the year to 1 at the end of the year. With the gap between the window and the back fixed, there would be a snug fit at the beginning and a loose fit at the end. This could result in the day-of-month table for the last few months of the year not being as easy to read as desired. Therefore, a calendar that is bound along the top with Wire-O binding is preferred. With this construction, the pages are flipped over to change the month and there is always the same number of pages between the window and the back. As for the flip-down-window wall calendar in Figure 6-4, the concepts in Figure 6-6 can be used for either the 12- or 14-sheet design. They can also be used for the 24-sheet design, but this would require up to twice as much paper and does not offer any advantages other than a different set of pictures for leap years.

Instead of having the calendar sheet and the picture printed on the same page, the two can be on separate pages, as described in the alternate construction in Figure 6-6. The calendar sheets would then form one pad for the bottom of the holder, and the pictures would form another pad for the top of the holder. To keep the calendar sheets in order, they should be bound with Wire-O binding. The calendar sheets should be made from cardstock so that they will not curl if they are supported by the window guide instead of being hung. Binding the pictures together is optional. In fact, having them unbound may be preferable, as this would enable the adding and removing of pictures. The pictures can hang from a hole in the middle of the top edge as they do in a conventional calendar. This type of construction enables reusing favourite pictures from expired calendars. It would also enable using photographs.

## Window-on-Each-Sheet Wall Calendar

The multisheet perpetual calendars with a year table on each sheet discussed thus far have one window to view each sheet in turn. An alternative is to have a window on each sheet. Each window is set at the beginning of the year and the calendar sheets with the preset windows are turned over each month as in a conventional wall calendar. The window-on-each-sheet concept is ideal for the 12-sheet design, but it can also be used with the 14- and 24-sheet designs. An advantage to having a window on each sheet is that the window is easier to make than in a flip-down-window or lift-out-pad configuration. The major disadvantage is that the back side of the day-of-month table has part of the window on it and must be covered with a sheet of paper or cardstock if a picture or something else is to be printed there.

Figures 6-7a and 6-7b show two patterns for making a one-window-per-sheet calendar. These windows are similar to the windows in Figures 5-2b and 5-1a, respectively. The top pattern (Figure 6-7a) can be used to change the clip-on window shown in Figure 6-5 to a window on each sheet. All that is needed is to cut some slits in the window instead of cutting it out, and to cut some slits on the calendar sheet. In the top pattern, the day-of-month table is in the window and a marker on the top of the window points to the applicable column in the year table. The bottom pattern has both the day-of-month table and the year table in the window. A marker at the bottom of the window points to the applicable column in the year table.

To make a calendar that has a window on each sheet, follow the same procedure as for making a conventional wall calendar. Leave blank or print a background colour on the areas where the calendar pages would normally be printed. Make up the perpetual calendar pages, install the windows and glue the assembled pages over the blank or coloured areas as follows. The calendar sheet in Figure 6-7a is glued about 0.5 inches all around the perimeter. The calendar sheet in Figure 6-7b is glued along a 0.5-inch strip at each end only. The main pages in the calendar that have the pictures and provide the backing for the perpetual calendar pages can be paper. The calendar sheets and the windows should be made from 80 lb. cardstock or its equivalent to have some rigidity when moving the window. Making the window from cardstock is especially important if you want it to be easy to move. Prototypes have been made using paper for the calendar sheets and the windows. These paper sheets work, but they are flimsy and easily torn (although, with care, paper may last 10 years or longer). As is the case for the clip-on-window wall calendar, two holes are required to hang this calendar. Otherwise, it would be at an angle when the centres of all the windows were not directly below a single hanging hole.

Either of the two patterns can be used to convert a conventional wall calendar into a perpetual wall calendar. The assembled pages are simply glued on top of the existing calendar sheets. I converted a conventional calendar that is 11 inches wide by 17 inches high when unfolded. The design in Figure 6-7a was simply printed on 8.5 by 11 inch sheets in landscape orientation, and put on top of the conventional calendar sheets using double-sided tape. In addition to being used to make wall calendars, the window-on-each-sheet concept can be used to make dividers in a planner. In this application, there is no picture above the calendar sheet. One way of covering the back of the calendar sheet would be to make it double height and fold it in half like the front and back of a tent. Another application of a window-on-each-sheet calendar is in a photo album. The calendar sheets would be made without backing and would be inserted into the pouches in the album. The photos and calendar sheets would be arranged so that when the album is opened with the spine horizontal, there would be a photo on the upper page and a calendar sheet on the lower page.

## Extension of Single-Sheet Calendar to Multisheet

Table 4-11 shows how the single-sheet calendar with a single slider in Table 3-12 can be made into a calendar that has some similarities to the 12-sheet design of the multisheet perpetual calendar with a year table on each sheet. The result is the extension of the single-sheet calendar to a multisheet calendar. This design uses ideas from the single-sheet calendar in Figure 5-1a. Figure 6-8 shows two applications for this design. One is for making dividers for a planner, where each divider is for a particular month. Instead of setting the month over the year, a marker is set over the year. The other is a flip-over desk calendar that uses the same sheets as the dividers. Figure 6-8 shows the concept for a stand for such a calendar. The stand has a base and an upright with rings on top. There is a protrusion on the front face of the upright to give the sheets a slight tilt so as to make them easier to read. Figure 6-8 shows the face for January and the sliders for January, February and March. Sliders for the remaining months can be made by copying data from Table 4-11.

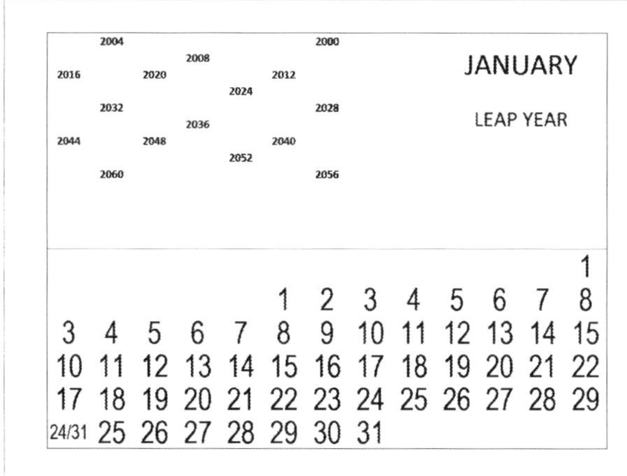
JANUARY
LEAP YEAR

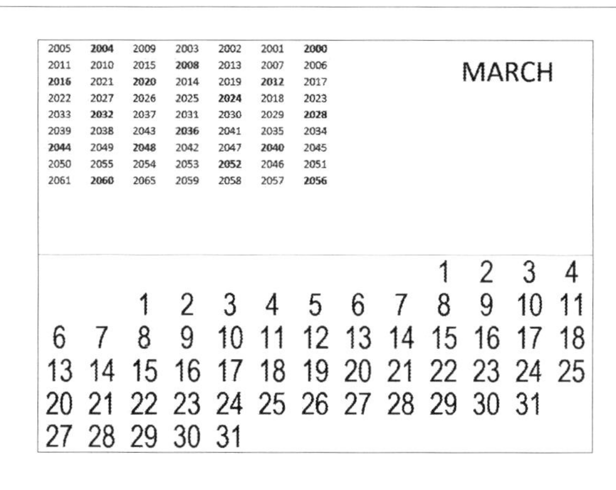
MARCH

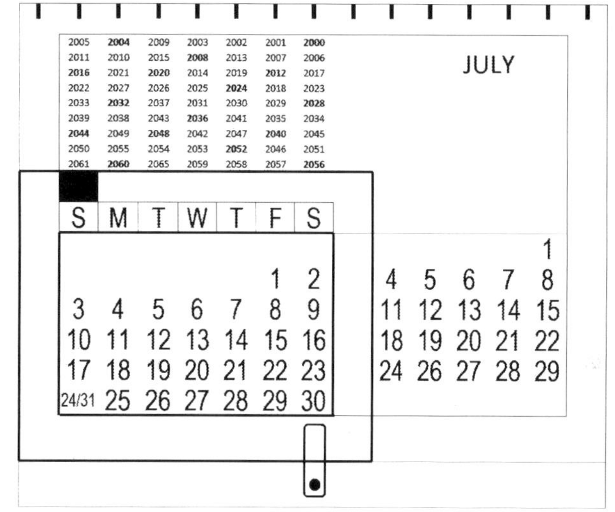
JULY
S M T W T F S

Notes

1. These sheets are for the 14-sheet design
2. The year tables are from Table 4-7. For January and February common years, only common years are shown. For January and February leap years, only leap years are shown.
3. The day of month tables are as follows:
   Table 4-1 for January and February common years and March to December all years
   Table 4-3 for January and February leap years
4. The sheet for July is shown in the assembled tent calendar. The window is set for 2016.

Figure 6-1a: Typical month sheets for a 14-sheet flip-down-window desk calendar

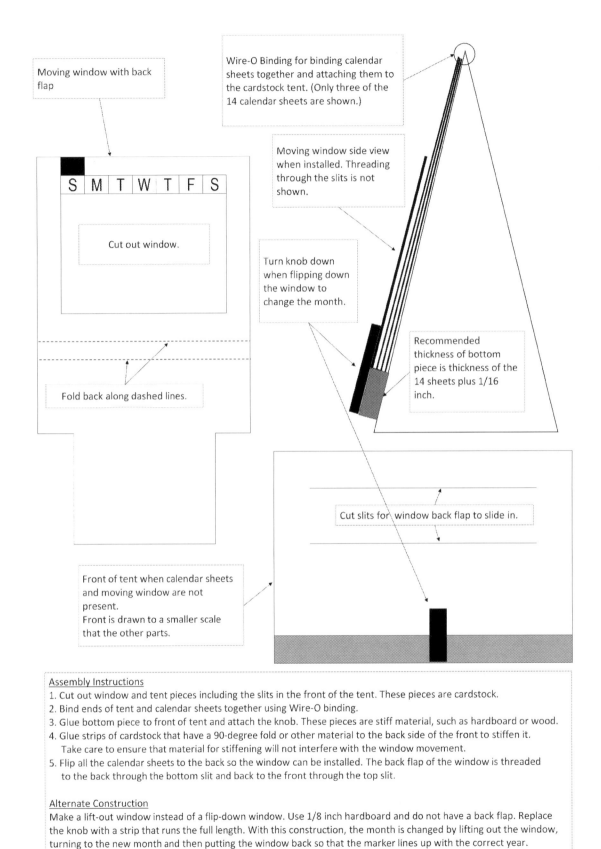

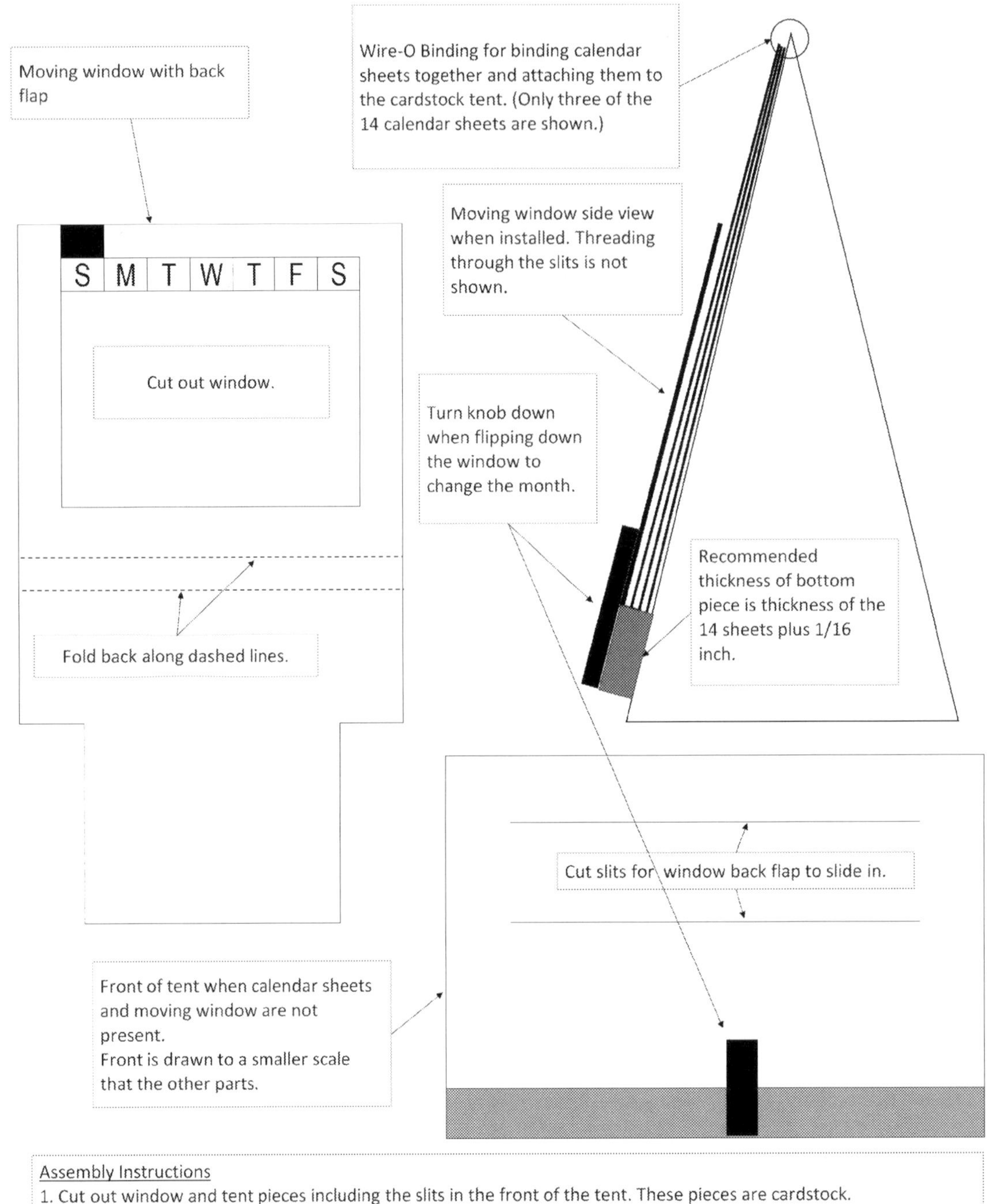
Moving window with back flap
Wire-O Binding for binding calendar sheets together and attaching them to the cardstock tent. (Only three of the 14 calendar sheets are shown.)
Moving window side view when installed. Threading through the slits is not shown.
S M T W T F S
Cut out window.
Turn knob down when flipping down the window to change the month.
Recommended thickness of bottom piece is thickness of the 14 sheets plus 1/16 inch.
Fold back along dashed lines.
Cut slits for window back flap to slide in.
Front of tent when calendar sheets and moving window are not present.
Front is drawn to a smaller scale that the other parts.

Assembly Instructions

1. Cut out window and tent pieces including the slits in the front of the tent. These pieces are cardstock.
2. Bind ends of tent and calendar sheets together using Wire-O binding.
3. Glue bottom piece to front of tent and attach the knob. These pieces are stiff material, such as hardboard or wood.
4. Glue strips of cardstock that have a 90-degree fold or other material to the back side of the front to stiffen it. Take care to ensure that material for stiffening will not interfere with the window movement.
5. Flip all the calendar sheets to the back so the window can be installed. The back flap of the window is threaded to the back through the bottom slit and back to the front through the top slit.

Alternate Construction

Make a lift-out window instead of a flip-down window. Use 1/8 inch hardboard and do not have a back flap. Replace the knob with a strip that runs the full length. With this construction, the month is changed by lifting out the window, turning to the new month and then putting the window back so that the marker lines up with the correct year.

Figure 6-1b: Flip-down-window desk calendar made from cardstock

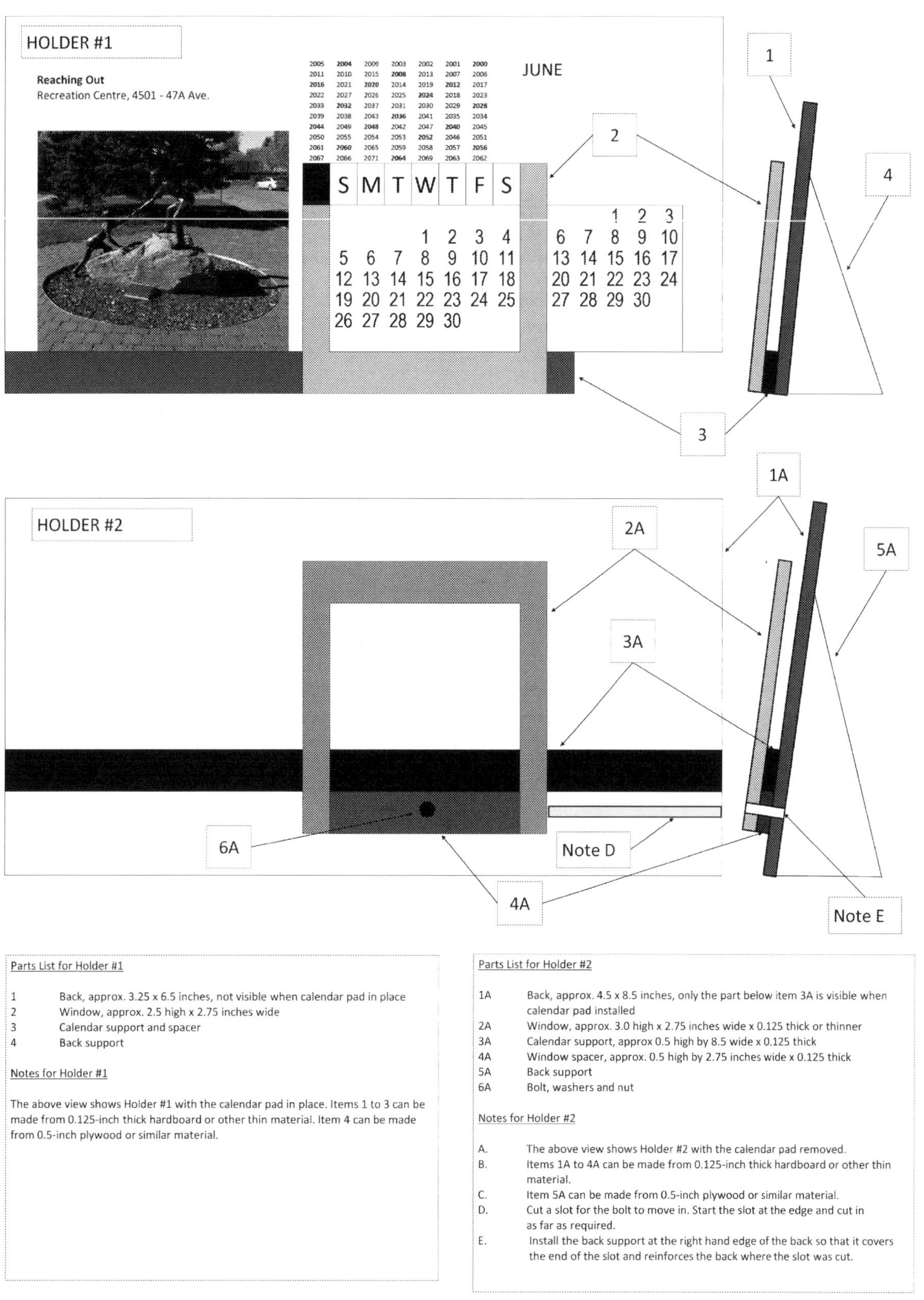
HOLDER #1
Reaching Out
Recreation Centre, 4501 - 47A Ave.
JUNE
S M T W T F S
1 2 3 4
5 6 7 8 9 10 11
12 13 14 15 16 17 18
19 20 21 22 23 24 25
26 27 28 29 30
1 2 3
6 7 8 9 10
13 14 15 16 17
20 21 22 23 24
27 28 29 30
1
2
3
4
HOLDER #2
1A
2A
3A
4A
5A
6A
Note D
Note E
Parts List for Holder #1
1 Back, approx. 3.25 x 6.5 inches, not visible when calendar pad in place
2 Window, approx. 2.5 high x 2.75 inches wide
3 Calendar support and spacer
4 Back support
Notes for Holder #1
The above view shows Holder #1 with the calendar pad in place. Items 1 to 3 can be made from 0.125-inch thick hardboard or other thin material. Item 4 can be made from 0.5-inch plywood or similar material.
Parts List for Holder #2
1A Back, approx. 4.5 x 8.5 inches, only the part below item 3A is visible when calendar pad installed
2A Window, approx. 3.0 high x 2.75 inches wide x 0.125 thick or thinner
3A Calendar support, approx 0.5 high by 8.5 wide x 0.125 thick
4A Window spacer, approx. 0.5 high by 2.75 inches wide x 0.125 thick
5A Back support
6A Bolt, washers and nut
Notes for Holder #2
A. The above view shows Holder #2 with the calendar pad removed.
B. Items 1A to 4A can be made from 0.125-inch thick hardboard or other thin material.
C. Item 5A can be made from 0.5-inch plywood or similar material.
D. Cut a slot for the bolt to move in. Start the slot at the edge and cut in as far as required.
E. Install the back support at the right hand edge of the back so that it covers the end of the slot and reinforces the back where the slot was cut.

Figure 6-2: Two holder designs for the lift-out-pad desk calendar

| | | | | | | |
|---|---|---|---|---|---|---|
| 2005 | **2004** | 2009 | 2003 | 2002 | 2001 | **2000** |
| 2011 | 2010 | 2015 | **2008** | 2013 | 2007 | 2006 |
| **2016** | 2021 | **2020** | 2014 | 2019 | **2012** | 2017 |
| 2022 | 2027 | 2026 | 2025 | **2024** | 2018 | 2023 |
| 2033 | **2032** | 2037 | 2031 | 2030 | 2029 | **2028** |
| 2039 | 2038 | 2043 | **2036** | 2041 | 2035 | 2034 |
| **2044** | 2049 | **2048** | 2042 | 2047 | **2040** | 2045 |
| 2050 | 2055 | 2054 | 2053 | **2052** | 2046 | 2051 |
| 2061 | **2060** | 2065 | 2059 | 2058 | 2057 | **2056** |

# MARCH

| Format Type | Example Dates |
|---|---|
| #1 Font 34 | 1st & 15th |
| #2 Font 28 | All dates in top 4 rows, except 1, 3, 8 & 15. Only the 17th has text. |
| #3 Font 16 | 3rd & 8th |
| #4 Font 28 | All dates in bottom 2 rows |

All number fonts are Arial Narrow. All boxes 2 cells wide. Boxes in top 4 rows are 3 cells high. Boxes in bottom 2 rows are 2 cells high.

| | | | | | | | | | | | | |
|---|---|---|---|---|---|---|---|---|---|---|---|---|
| | | | | | | | | | 1 | 2 | 3 Jill b. 1925 | 4 |
| | | 1 | 2 | 3 Jill b. 1925 | 4 | 5 | 6 | 7 | 8 John 1961 B & K 1980 | 9 | 10 | 11 |
| 6 | 7 | 8 John 1961 B & K 1980 | 9 | 10 | 11 | 12 | 13 | 14 | 15 | 16 | 17 St. Patrick | 18 |
| 13 | 14 | 15 | 16 | 17 St. Patrick | 18 | 19 | 20 | 21 | 22 | 23 | 24 | 25 |
| 20 | 21 | 22 | 23 | 24 | 25 | 26 | 27 | 28 | 29 | 30 | 31 | |
| 27 | 28 | 29 | 30 | 31 | | | | | | | | |

27 Joe & Amy 1995, Matt 1965

29 Jill d. 2011

Figure 6-3: Four different formats for wall calendar sheets

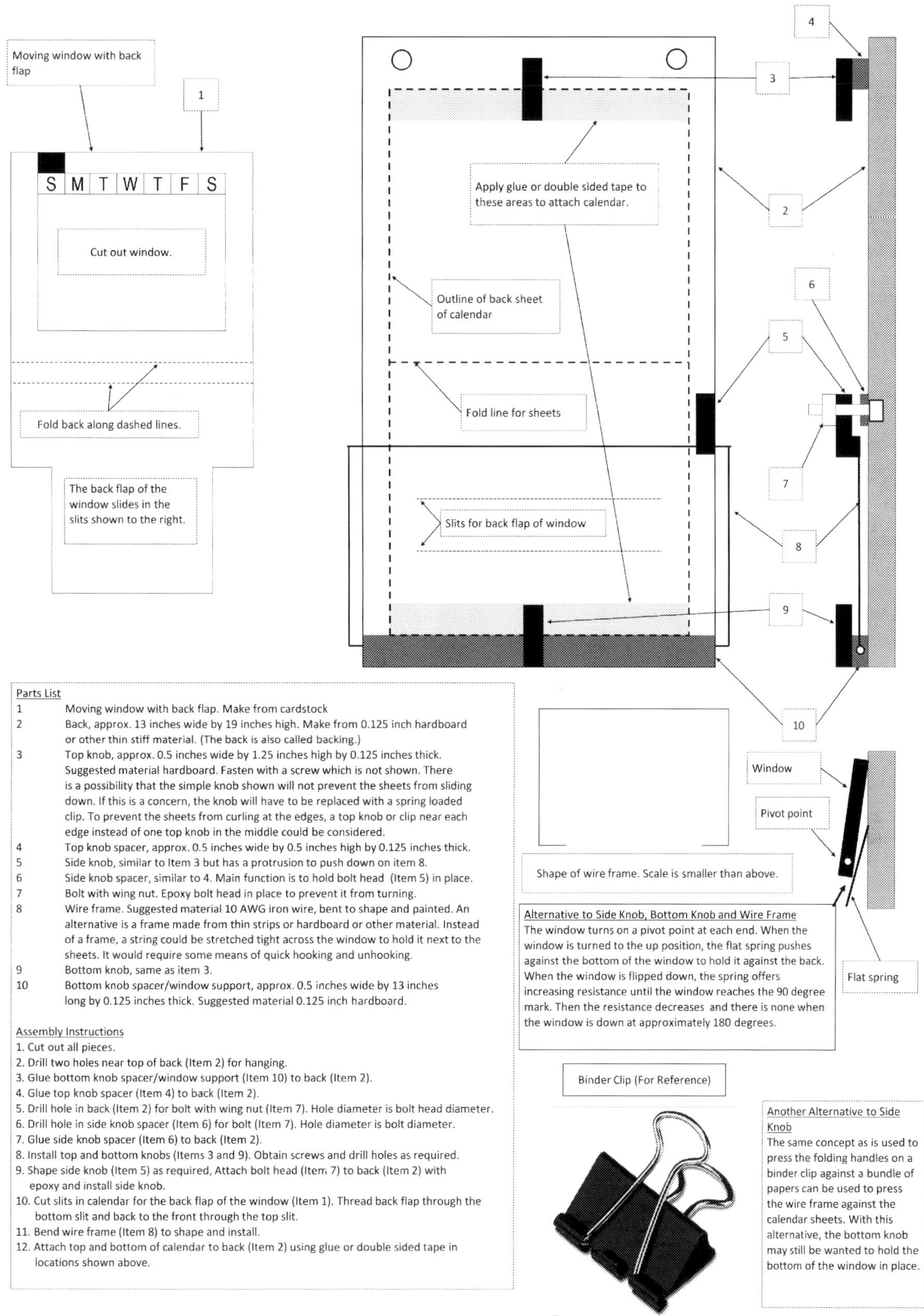

Moving window with back flap
1
S M T W T F S
Cut out window.
Fold back along dashed lines.
The back flap of the window slides in the slits shown to the right.
Apply glue or double sided tape to these areas to attach calendar.
Outline of back sheet of calendar
Fold line for sheets
Slits for back flap of window
4
3
2
6
5
7
8
9
10
Window
Pivot point
Shape of wire frame. Scale is smaller than above.
Flat spring
Parts List
1 Moving window with back flap. Make from cardstock
2 Back, approx. 13 inches wide by 19 inches high. Make from 0.125 inch hardboard or other thin stiff material. (The back is also called backing.)
3 Top knob, approx. 0.5 inches wide by 1.25 inches high by 0.125 inches thick. Suggested material hardboard. Fasten with a screw which is not shown. There is a possibility that the simple knob shown will not prevent the sheets from sliding down. If this is a concern, the knob will have to be replaced with a spring loaded clip. To prevent the sheets from curling at the edges, a top knob or clip near each edge instead of one top knob in the middle could be considered.
4 Top knob spacer, approx. 0.5 inches wide by 0.5 inches high by 0.125 inches thick.
5 Side knob, similar to Item 3 but has a protrusion to push down on item 8.
6 Side knob spacer, similar to 4. Main function is to hold bolt head (Item 5) in place.
7 Bolt with wing nut. Epoxy bolt head in place to prevent it from turning.
8 Wire frame. Suggested material 10 AWG iron wire, bent to shape and painted. An alternative is a frame made from thin strips or hardboard or other material. Instead of a frame, a string could be stretched tight across the window to hold it next to the sheets. It would require some means of quick hooking and unhooking.
9 Bottom knob, same as item 3.
10 Bottom knob spacer/window support, approx. 0.5 inches wide by 13 inches long by 0.125 inches thick. Suggested material 0.125 inch hardboard.
Assembly Instructions
1. Cut out all pieces.
2. Drill two holes near top of back (Item 2) for hanging.
3. Glue bottom knob spacer/window support (Item 10) to back (Item 2).
4. Glue top knob spacer (Item 4) to back (Item 2).
5. Drill hole in back (Item 2) for bolt with wing nut (Item 7). Hole diameter is bolt head diameter.
6. Drill hole in side knob spacer (Item 6) for bolt (Item 7). Hole diameter is bolt diameter.
7. Glue side knob spacer (Item 6) to back (Item 2).
8. Install top and bottom knobs (Items 3 and 9). Obtain screws and drill holes as required.
9. Shape side knob (Item 5) as required, Attach bolt head (Item 7) to back (Item 2) with epoxy and install side knob.
10. Cut slits in calendar for the back flap of the window (Item 1). Thread back flap through the bottom slit and back to the front through the top slit.
11. Bend wire frame (Item 8) to shape and install.
12. Attach top and bottom of calendar to back (Item 2) using glue or double sided tape in locations shown above.
Alternative to Side Knob, Bottom Knob and Wire Frame
The window turns on a pivot point at each end. When the window is turned to the up position, the flat spring pushes against the bottom of the window to hold it against the back. When the window is flipped down, the spring offers increasing resistance until the window reaches the 90 degree mark. Then the resistance decreases and there is none when the window is down at approximately 180 degrees.
Binder Clip (For Reference)
Another Alternative to Side Knob
The same concept as is used to press the folding handles on a binder clip against a bundle of papers can be used to press the wire frame against the calendar sheets. With this alternative, the bottom knob may still be wanted to hold the bottom of the window in place.


Figure 6-4: Flip-down-window wall calendar

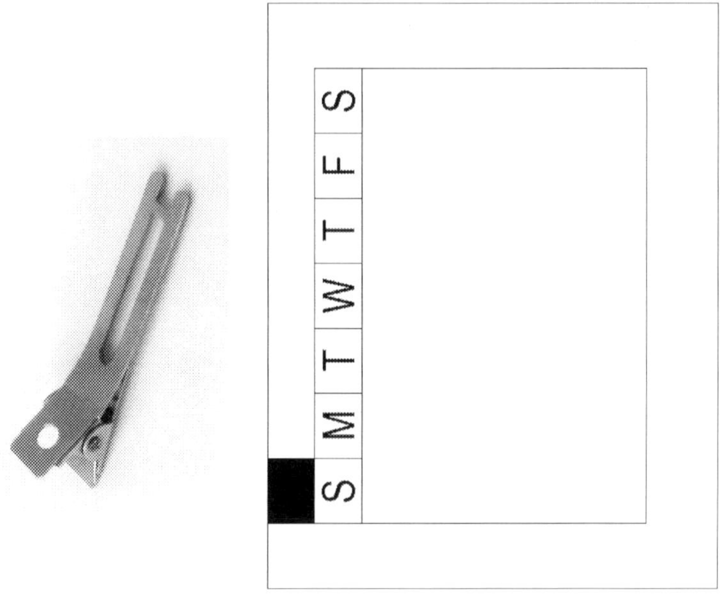
S
M
T
W
T
F
S

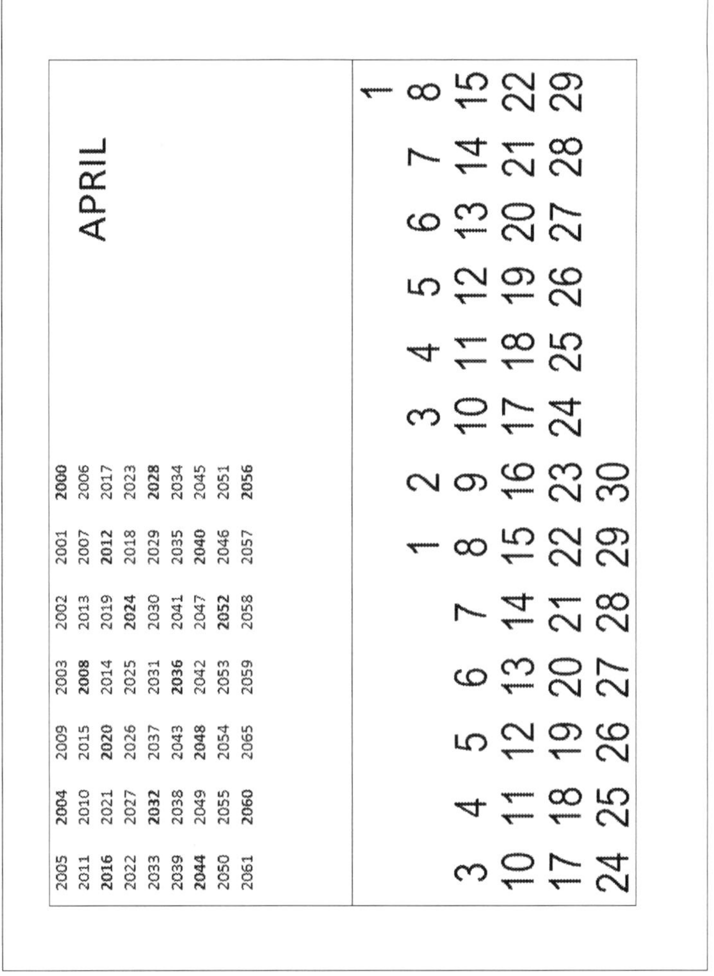
2005 2004 2009 2003 2002 2001 2000
2011 2010 2015 2008 2013 2007 2006
2016 2021 2020 2014 2019 2012 2017
2022 2027 2026 2025 2024 2018 2023
2033 2032 2037 2031 2030 2029 2028
2039 2038 2043 2036 2041 2035 2034
2044 2049 2048 2042 2047 2040 2045
2050 2055 2054 2053 2052 2046 2051
2061 2060 2065 2059 2058 2057 2056
APRIL

Figure 6-5: Clip-on-window wall calendar

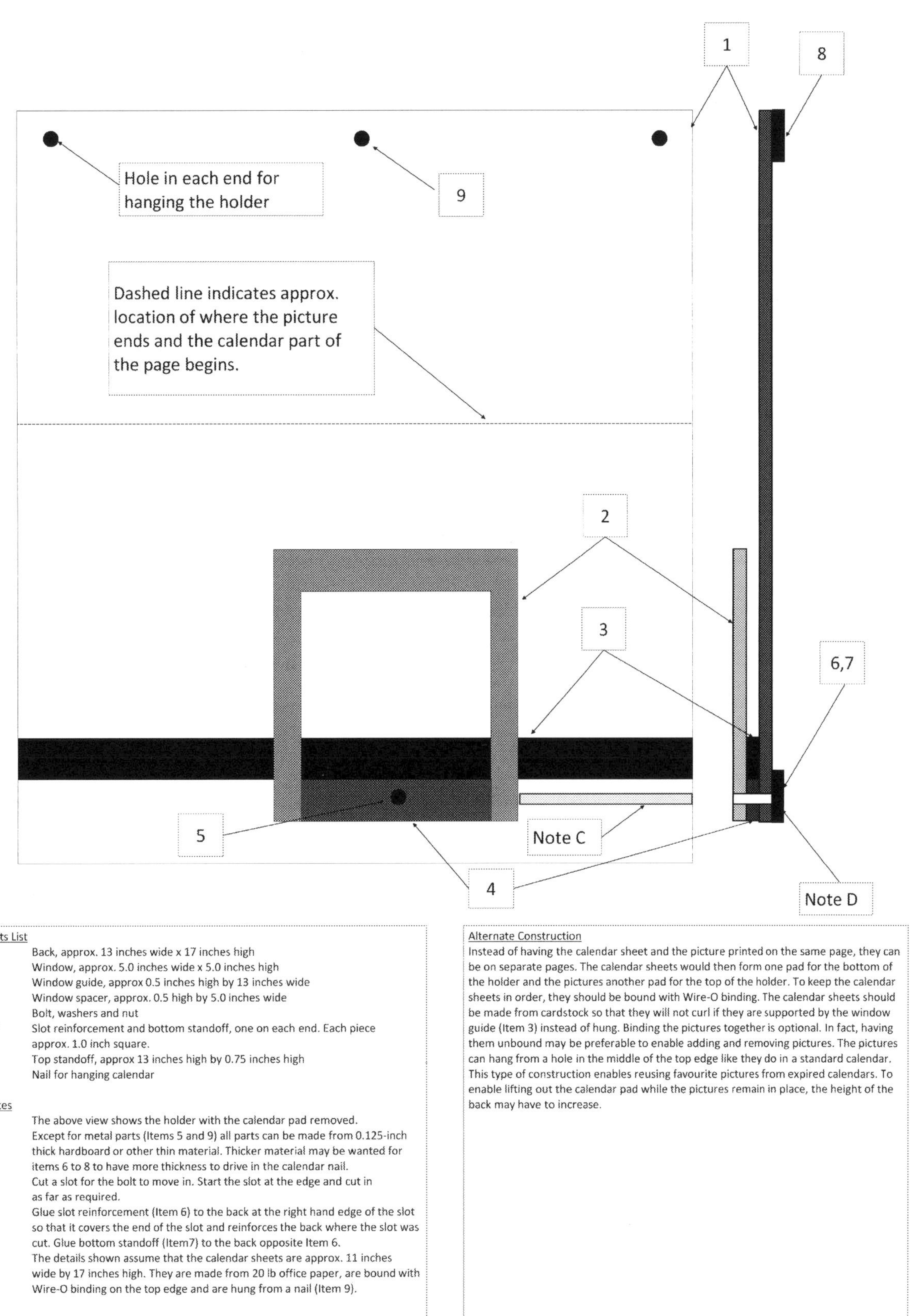
1
8
Hole in each end for hanging the holder
9
Dashed line indicates approx. location of where the picture ends and the calendar part of the page begins.
2
3
6,7
5
Note C
4
Note D
Parts List
1 Back, approx. 13 inches wide x 17 inches high
2 Window, approx. 5.0 inches wide x 5.0 inches high
3 Window guide, approx 0.5 inches high by 13 inches wide
4 Window spacer, approx. 0.5 high by 5.0 inches wide
5 Bolt, washers and nut
6,7 Slot reinforcement and bottom standoff, one on each end. Each piece approx. 1.0 inch square.
8 Top standoff, approx 13 inches high by 0.75 inches high
9 Nail for hanging calendar
Notes
A. The above view shows the holder with the calendar pad removed.
B. Except for metal parts (Items 5 and 9) all parts can be made from 0.125-inch thick hardboard or other thin material. Thicker material may be wanted for items 6 to 8 to have more thickness to drive in the calendar nail.
C. Cut a slot for the bolt to move in. Start the slot at the edge and cut in as far as required.
D. Glue slot reinforcement (Item 6) to the back at the right hand edge of the slot so that it covers the end of the slot and reinforces the back where the slot was cut. Glue bottom standoff (Item7) to the back opposite Item 6.
E. The details shown assume that the calendar sheets are approx. 11 inches wide by 17 inches high. They are made from 20 lb office paper, are bound with Wire-O binding on the top edge and are hung from a nail (Item 9).
Alternate Construction
Instead of having the calendar sheet and the picture printed on the same page, they can be on separate pages. The calendar sheets would then form one pad for the bottom of the holder and the pictures another pad for the top of the holder. To keep the calendar sheets in order, they should be bound with Wire-O binding. The calendar sheets should be made from cardstock so that they will not curl if they are supported by the window guide (Item 3) instead of hung. Binding the pictures together is optional. In fact, having them unbound may be preferable to enable adding and removing pictures. The pictures can hang from a hole in the middle of the top edge like they do in a standard calendar. This type of construction enables reusing favourite pictures from expired calendars. To enable lifting out the calendar pad while the pictures remain in place, the height of the back may have to increase.

Figure 6-6: Lift-out-pad wall calendar

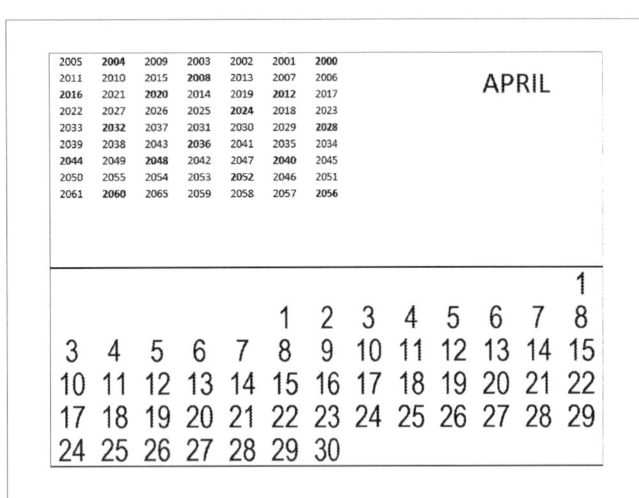
APRIL

Instructions
1. Cut out the calendar sheet and window along their outside borders.
2. Cut slits along the dark lines. There are two horizontal slits on the calendar sheet and one "H" shaped slit on the window.
3.Tuck the top and bottom window flaps behind the day of month table and tape the ends together.

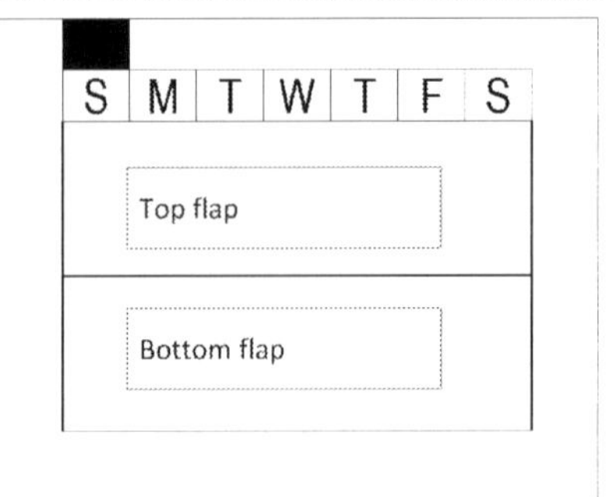
S M T W T F S
Top flap
Bottom flap

a) Year table above day of month table

Instructions
1. Cut out the calendar sheet and window along their outside borders.
2. Cut the two window slits along the dark lines.
3. Thread calendar sheet through the two slits
4. Glue each end of calendar sheet to base.

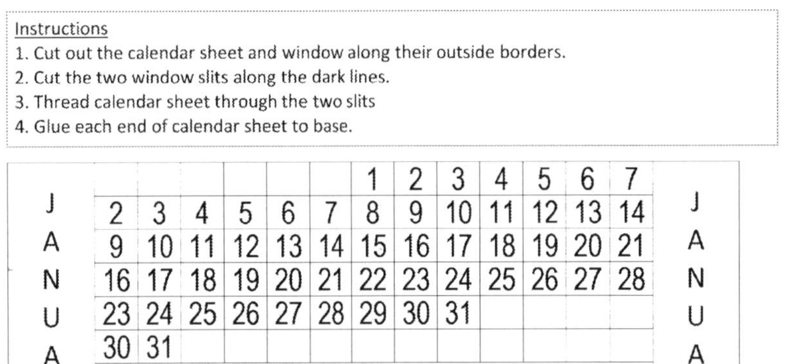
JANUARY
Leap years are bold.
JANUARY

S M T W T F S

b) Year table below day of month table

Figures 6-7a and 6-7b: Two patterns for a window-on-each-sheet wall calendar

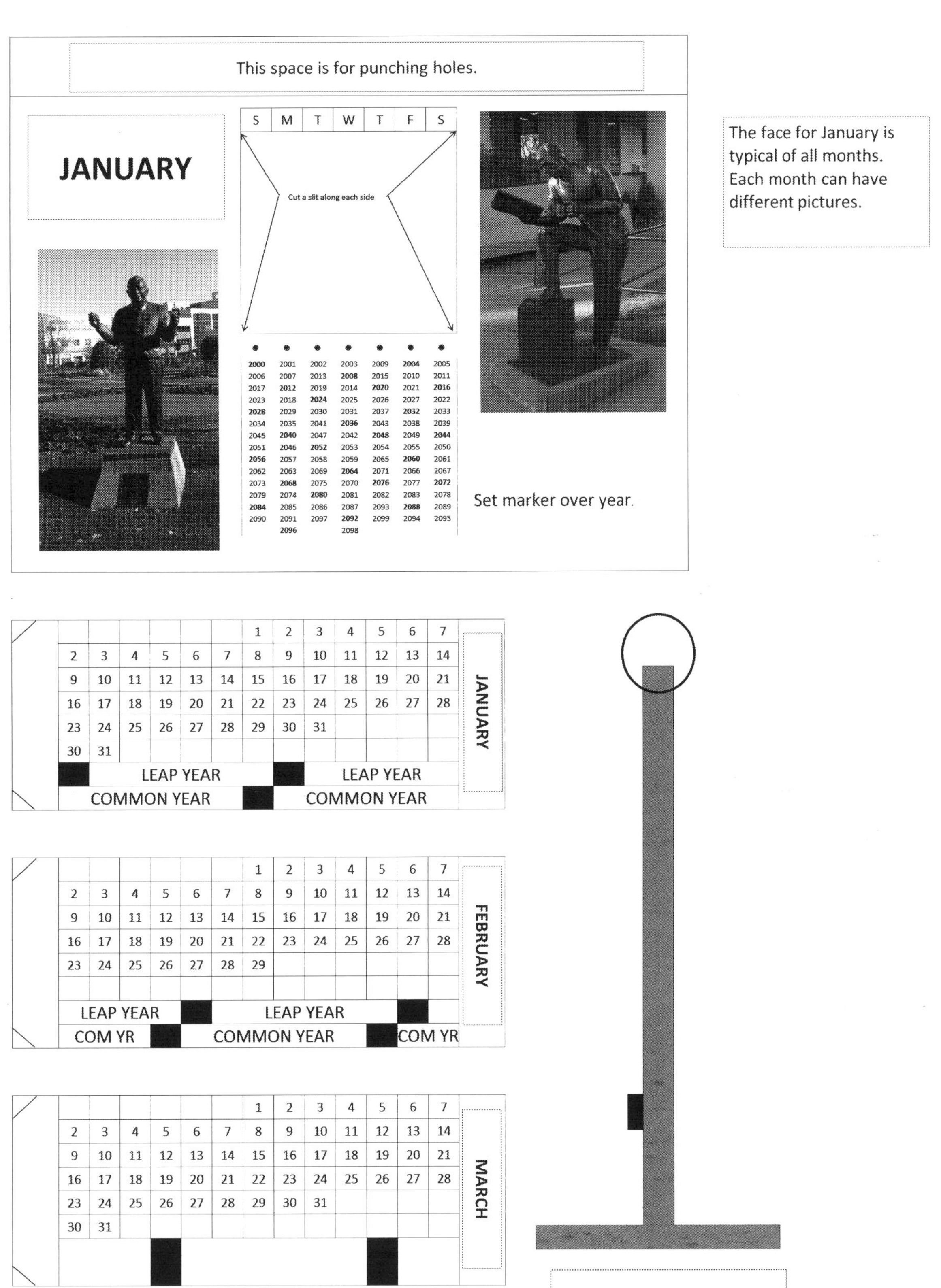

This space is for punching holes.
JANUARY
S M T W T F S
Cut a slit along each side
2000 2001 2002 2003 2009 2004 2005
2006 2007 2013 2008 2015 2010 2011
2017 2012 2019 2014 2020 2021 2016
2023 2018 2024 2025 2026 2027 2022
2028 2029 2030 2031 2037 2032 2033
2034 2035 2041 2036 2043 2038 2039
2045 2040 2047 2042 2048 2049 2044
2051 2046 2052 2053 2054 2055 2050
2056 2057 2058 2059 2065 2060 2061
2062 2063 2069 2064 2071 2066 2067
2073 2068 2075 2070 2076 2077 2072
2079 2074 2080 2081 2082 2083 2078
2084 2085 2086 2087 2093 2088 2089
2090 2091 2097 2092 2099 2094 2095
2096 2098
Set marker over year.
The face for January is typical of all months. Each month can have different pictures.
1 2 3 4 5 6 7
2 3 4 5 6 7 8 9 10 11 12 13 14
9 10 11 12 13 14 15 16 17 18 19 20 21
16 17 18 19 20 21 22 23 24 25 26 27 28
23 24 25 26 27 28 29 30 31
30 31
LEAP YEAR
LEAP YEAR
COMMON YEAR
COMMON YEAR
JANUARY
1 2 3 4 5 6 7
2 3 4 5 6 7 8 9 10 11 12 13 14
9 10 11 12 13 14 15 16 17 18 19 20 21
16 17 18 19 20 21 22 23 24 25 26 27 28
23 24 25 26 27 28 29
LEAP YEAR
LEAP YEAR
COM YR
COMMON YEAR
COM YR
FEBRUARY
1 2 3 4 5 6 7
2 3 4 5 6 7 8 9 10 11 12 13 14
9 10 11 12 13 14 15 16 17 18 19 20 21
16 17 18 19 20 21 22 23 24 25 26 27 28
23 24 25 26 27 28 29 30 31
30 31
MARCH
Stand for Desk Calendar


Figure 6-8: Extension of single-sheet calendar to multisheet

# CHAPTER 7

# MULTISHEET PERPETUAL CALENDARS WITH A SINGLE YEAR TABLE—APPLICATIONS AND PRODUCTS

## Applications

The fixed-window-style multisheet perpetual calendar with a single year table, which is shown in Figures 1-3a and 7-1b, is very similar in appearance to the single-sheet perpetual calendar with two sliders shown in Figures 5-8 and 5-12. Figures 7-1a and 7-1b compare the two and show construction details for the multisheet calendar with a single year table. This calendar is also similar in appearance to the single-sheet perpetual calendar with a single slider and with year tables to the sides of the window. (See Figures 5-3e and 5-18.) One characteristic that distinguishes these three calendars from the single-sheet calendar with a single slider and the year table below the window and from the multisheet calendar with a year table on each sheet is the shorter vertical height. This makes these types useful for applications such as under a picture frame, under a clock or above a row of key hooks, where a low-profile calendar enhances the appearance of the product.

In Figures 7-1a and 7-1b, both the single-sheet perpetual calendar with two sliders and the multisheet perpetual calendar with a single year table are the same size. A comparison of the two shows that, for a given font size for the day-of-month table, the sizes have to be almost the same. The multisheet with a single year table can possibly be reduced in height by allowing less space for binding, but the reduction would not be significant. Which type to use for a given application depends on personal preference. I prefer the appearance of the multisheet calendar with a single year table. I also like the characteristic of each sheet's having the correct number of days for the month, so that 29, 30 and 31 do not have to be ignored. However, having to lift out and turn a sheet to change the month is not as convenient as moving a slider. In addition to personal preference, another consideration in choosing which type to use is the ease and cost of construction. Except for the spacers, all the material in the multisheet calendar shown in Figure

7-1b is cardstock. This makes for easier and lower-cost construction than the single-sheet calendar with two sliders in Figure 7-1a, which requires rigid material for the sliders.

Table 7-1 lists applications for the multisheet perpetual calendar with a single year table. Applications such as a small calendar mounted below a picture or photo may have considerable market potential. The table lists five ways of doing this. (See descriptions for Figures 7-2 to 7-5 and the description for the commercial 8 × 10 picture frame.)

The seven-column multisheet calendar with a single year table, which is shown in Figures 1-3c, 1-3d, and 7-6a to 7-6c, may also have considerable market potential as both a desk calendar and a wall calendar. It is an alternative to the flip-down-window (Figures 1-2a, 6-1a and 6-1b) and lift-out-pad desk calendars (Figures 1-2c and 6-2). The underlying concepts of the seven-column calendar are different from the concepts of the other calendars in this chapter.

**Table 7-1**
**Applications for the Multisheet Perpetual Calendar with a Single Year Table**

| Application | Description | Figure |
|---|---|---|
| Basic desk calendar | Calendar sheets in a holder that is approximately 6.5 inches wide by 2.5 inches high. Can be made in 14- and 24-sheet designs. | 7-1b and 7-1c |
| Key holder | Basic desk calendar with a block of key hooks below it. | 7-1d |
| J-style wall/desk calendar | Calendar made from cardstock that can be either a wall or desk calendar. The picture can be preprinted or mounted. | 7-2 |
| Reverse J-style desk calendar | Calendar similar to J-style, but the calendar sheets are loaded from the back rather than the front. | 7-3 |
| Wooden frame desk calendar | Similar to reverse J-style, but with a wooden frame for the calendar and picture. Can also be made with a commercial 5 × 7 inch frame to hold the picture. | 7-4 |
| Commercial 8 × 10 picture frame | Calendar can be either glued to the outside surface of the glass below the picture or placed behind the glass. | none |
| Wall/desk calendar | Commercial 5 × 7 inch frame with calendar below it that has a flip-down front. | 7-5 |
| Seven-column desk calendar | Seven-column multisheet calendar with a single year table. | 7-6a to 7-6c |
| Seven-column wall calendar | Similar to above, but made for hanging on a wall rather than for sitting on a desk. | 7-6a to 7-6c |

## Tables for These Calendars

The calendars in Figures 7-1b to 7-5 can be made with either 14 or 24 sheets for the months. Each month has its own unique sheet. The seven-column calendar in Figures 7-6a, 7-6b and 7-6c has seven sheets. Table 7-2 lists the year and day-of-month tables to use for each of these three designs.

## Table 7-2
## Tables to Use for the Multisheet Perpetual Calendar with a Single Year Table

| Calendar design | Year table | Day-of-month table |
|---|---|---|
| 14-sheet | Table 4-9 | Table 4-1 for January and February in common years, and March to December for both leap years and common years<br><br>Table 4-3 for January and February in leap years |
| 24-sheet | The year table part of Table 3-11 | Table 4-1 for common years<br><br>Table 4-2 for leap years |
| 7-column | Table 3-9<br><br>In addition to the year table, there is a slider with the month table from Table 3-8 on it | Table 4-12b (This table shows the first of month falling on a Tuesday. There are seven similar tables, with each one for the first of the month falling on a different day of the week.) |

## Basic Multisheet Desk Calendar

Figures 7-1b and 7-1c show construction details for a basic multisheet desk calendar with a single year table. This is the calendar shown in Figure 1-3a. The front and back are separated by three spacers made from rigid material such as thin wood, hardboard or cardboard. Using rigid spacers ensures that the front and back will not bow out or in, even if they are made from thin cardstock. For a large production run, one piece of thick cardstock can be cut and folded like a box so that the front and back are one piece and spacers are not needed. These figures illustrate the parts of this calendar, but a plain calendar like this has limited appeal.

Figure 7-1b is a 14-sheet design, which I prefer to the 24-sheet design. The figure shows the sheet with the day-of-month table for July. The sheets for the other months can be made using Tables 4-1 and 4-3. The sheets are double-sided. The arrangement as to which month is on which side of the sheet is the same as shown in Table 6-3 in Chapter 6.

For my prototypes, I used one small plastic tie wrap to bind the calendar sheets. This worked well, but for a large production run, standard Wire-O binding may be preferred. However, Wire-O is more expensive and many print shops do not have this capability. Most print shops can do spiral wire binding, which can substitute.

## Key Holder

Figure 7-1d shows a key holder that has a multisheet perpetual calendar with a single year table. This is an alternative to the key holders in Figures 5-7a and 5-7b. As noted on the figure, the main parts are as follows:

1. The back, which ties everything together and has two holes for hanging. Suggested material is 0.125-inch-thick hardboard.
2. The calendar pad, which is bound with Wire-O binding or some other suitable binding.
3. Spacer no. 1 creates a gap between the calendar pad and the back to provide space for the binding. A spacer is needed to prevent the visible side of the back from being scratched when the pad is lifted out or set in.
4. Spacers on each side and the bottom, which provide a pocket for the calendar pad. The thickness of the spacers is equal to the thickness of the calendar pad plus 1/16 inch for some play.
5. The front, which is made from thick cardstock or hardboard covered with thin cardstock.
6. Block for the key hooks.
7. Hooks for keys.

Cornice hooks or cup hooks work well for holding keys, but these hooks are unattractive. There are many hooks made, but they may be difficult to obtain in small quantities unless you buy a key holder with many hooks on it. An alternative to mounting hooks on a block as shown in Figure 7-1d is to buy a ready-made key holder and attach a calendar to it.

## J-Style Calendars

Figure 7-2 shows the J-style wall/desk calendar. The main body is a piece of 8.5 × 11 inch cardstock folded into a *J* shape to accommodate a pocket for the calendar on the front side. There is enough space above the calendar to mount a 4 × 6 inch photo in either portrait or landscape orientation, or a 5 × 7 inch photo in landscape. A souvenir for sale in a tourist gift shop is an ideal application. The calendar can be designed to accept a favourite postcard or to be preprinted with a scene. For this application, the potential purchasers are probably willing to spend a little time doing assembly, especially if the calendar is sold as a kit that appeals to children.

Figure 7-3 shows the reverse J-style desk calendar, which is similar to the J-style wall/desk calendar. The sheets are loaded from the back rather than from the front. This type is more suited for a desk calendar than a wall calendar, the latter of which would have to be taken down to change the month. Since the top of the calendar pad is not visible in the reverse J-style, a window is required to display the marker and the name of the month. The reverse J-style desk calendar has the same amount of space for mounting a picture or photo as the J-style and is also ideal as a souvenir for sale in a tourist gift shop.

An assembly advantage of both the J-style and the reverse J-style calendars is that the body is one piece, with the spacers made from cardstock rather than rigid material. This type of construction requires precise folds to prevent the front from bowing out after assembly. It should be a practical matter to set up machinery to make the folds for large-quantity production. For small-quantity production, a design that uses rigid spacers as in Figure 7-1c can be used.

## Wooden Frame Desk Calendar

Figure 7-4 shows the wooden frame desk calendar. It is similar to the reverse J-style in that the calendar pad is inserted from the back. However, the front of the photo holder and the front of the calendar are glued to a wooden frame to provide stiffness. There is a gap between the top of the calendar front and the bottom of the photo holder so that a window does not have to be cut out to display the marker and the month at the top of the calendar pad. The area available for a photo is 7.5 inches wide by 5.0 inches high. This size was selected to accommodate 5 × 7 inch or 4 × 6 inch photos in landscape orientation. If the user does not mind having part of the photo above the frame, either size can also be in portrait orientation. The photo rests on a bottom support and is prevented from tipping over by fish line strung across in two places. This unique arrangement enables changing photo size or photo orientation without moving photo corners. The arrangement in Figure 7-4 is excellent for displaying postcards or photos when the picture is changed fairly often and does not need to be behind glass.

## Calendar Attached to Picture Frame

Instead of building a holder for a photo or a postcard as in Figures 7-2 to 7-4, a calendar can be added to a picture frame. The most suitable frame size is 8 × 10 inches in portrait orientation. The size of the glass that is not covered by the frame is approximately 7.5 inches wide by 9.5 inches high. The calendar shown in Figures 7-1b and 7-1c is about 7.5 inches wide by 2.5 inches high. This calendar can be attached near the bottom of the glass with mounting tape. The uncovered space above the calendar is approximately 7.5 inches wide by 7.0 inches high, which is suitable for a 5 × 7 inch postcard or photo in either portrait or landscape orientation. A calendar made this way can be used either as a wall calendar or desk calendar. To make a wall calendar easy to read, the angle between the floor of the room and the face of the calendar pad should be greater than 90 degrees, say, about 95 degrees. This can be achieved by mounting the calendar so that the bottom of the face is a little farther out from the glass than the top. Alternatively, a spacer can be put on the bottom of the back of the picture frame to bring the bottom out a bit from the wall. Since the calendar pad moves from side to side in the holder depending on the month, the centre of gravity of the picture frame will not always be in line with the top-to-bottom centre line of the frame. To keep the picture frame vertical, it needs to be hung from two points along the top, instead of only one. A figure showing a multisheet perpetual calendar with a single year table on an 8 × 10 inch picture frame is not included in *Practical Perpetual Calendars.*

The calendar can be mounted behind the glass rather than in front, as is done for the single-slider calendar in Figures 5-10a, 5-10b and 5-11. One way of doing this is to print the calendar face on an 8 × 10 inch sheet of paper that is between the mounting board and the glass. Two windows similar to those shown in Figure 7-3 are cut in the paper and the mounting board to view the calendar pad, which is behind the mounting board. Three spacers as in Figure 7-1c are glued to the back of the mounting board, and a piece of cardstock is glued to the back of the spacers, to make a pocket for the calendar pad. Mounting the pocket for the calendar pad so that the pad is lined up with the face may be difficult. Cutting windows with sharp edges in the mounting board may also be difficult. Another way of mounting the calendar behind the glass is to cut a strip off the bottom of the mounting board and attach an assembled calendar similar to the one shown in Figures 7-1b and 7-1c in the space where the strip was. The calendar can be attached to the back of the glass or to the back of the frame.

An alternative to mounting a calendar in a picture frame is to mount a calendar below it. The ideal size for this is a 5 × 7 inch frame in landscape orientation. Figure 7-5 shows details. The picture frame is attached to the top of a rectangular piece of hardboard and the calendar is attached to the bottom. To minimize the overall height, there is just enough gap between the bottom of the picture frame and the calendar pad to allow the pad to sit in the pocket without rubbing against the picture frame. To lift out the pad to change the month, the front of the calendar is folded down. As indicated in the notes for Figure 7-5, two alternatives to folding down the front of the calendar are as follows:

1. Hang the picture frame with two hinges (or one piano hinge) at the top so that the bottom of the frame can be moved out to enable lifting out the pad to change the month.
2. Use spacers to bring the calendar out so that the picture frame does not interfere with lifting out the pad.

## Seven-Column Multisheet Perpetual Calendar with a Single Year Table

The seven-column multisheet perpetual calendar with a single year table in Figures 7-6a to 7-6c is based on an underlying concept that differs from that of the other multisheet calendars with a single year table. This is the calendar depicted in Figures 1-3c and 1-3d. When it is built to be a replacement for conventional multisheet desk calendars, this calendar is an alternative to the flip-down-window and lift-out-pad desk perpetual calendars in Figures 6-1a, 6-1b and 6-2. Figure 7-6a shows the year table and slider, and Figure 7-6b shows an assembled calendar. If the pad were flipped up in Figure 7-6b, the marker on the slider would be seen pointing to the column in the year table that has 2016. The day-of-month table shown in Figure 7-6b is for months that begin on a Friday. The marker on the day-of-month table points to the labels ***Jan*** (boldface means leap year), *Apr* and *Jul*. Thus, the calendar is set for January, April and July of 2016. Figure 7-6c shows the seven different day-of-month tables. All of the tables are numbered 1 to 31, with 29, 30 and 31 ignored as applicable. Each table has a marker at the bottom of the column that has *1* in the top row. With the exception of the slider at the bottom, the construction of this calendar is identical to that for the conventional multisheet desk calendar. The additional cost per calendar for the slider is estimated to be 50¢ or less. Table 7-3 compares the seven-column multisheet calendar with the alternatives in Chapter 6.

## Table 7-3
## Comparison of Seven-Column Multisheet Calendar with Alternatives in Chapter 6

| **Feature** | **Seven-column in Figures 7-6a to 7-6c** | **Alternatives in Figures 6-1a, 6-1b and 6-2** |
|---|---|---|
| Extra cost for making perpetual | 50¢ or less per unit | $1 per unit |
| Size of numbers | Same as conventional | Approx. 60 percent of conventional |
| Location of year table | Hidden under calendar pad | On each sheet |
| Size of year table | 100 years | 60 years |
| Month name | Small letters on the slider | Large letters on each sheet |
| Need to ignore 29, 30 and 31? | Yes | No |
| Development/setup effort | Minimal | Some, but not excessive |

As can be seen in the table, the seven-column multisheet perpetual calendar has some advantages and some disadvantages compared to the others. There are also advantages and disadvantages when the flip-down window in Figures 6-1a and 6-1b is compared to the lift-out pad in Figure 6-2. All three designs are very attractive when compared to conventional desk calendars, which must be replaced each year. When perpetual multisheet calendars begin to replace conventional multisheet calendars, one of these designs may emerge as a clear winner—or all of them may equally share the market.

A feature that is not listed in Table 7-3 is the capability of designing the calendar so that the back side of the tent displays the same month as the front side. The potentials of the conventional multisheet tent calendar and the alternatives for having this feature are as follows:

- Conventional multisheet tent calendars are usually designed so that the same month is on both sides of the tent. This requires 13 sheets for a year, whereas only 12 would be needed if the back sides of the sheets were blank or had a picture.
- The seven-column multisheet perpetual calendar in Figures 7-6a to 7-6c can be designed so that the same month is on both sides of the tent. This requires a slider on each side of

the tent, and eight sheets rather than seven. As the slider is low-cost and does not interfere with the flipping over of a page, this is practical.

- If there is a window on each side of the tent, the flip-down-window desk calendar in Figures 6-1a and 6-1b can be designed to display the same month on both sides of the tent. With two windows to flip down when changing the month and with a significant extra cost for the second window, adding this feature is not as practical as for the seven-column calendar.
- The nature of the lift-out-pad desk calendar in Figure 6-2 is that the back sides of the sheets are not seen, so this feature cannot be added.

The seven-column multisheet perpetual calendar with a single year table in Figures 7-6a to 7-6c can be modified to be a wall calendar. In this configuration, the sheets would flip up as in a conventional wall calendar instead of over as in a tent desk calendar. Ideally, there would be a holding device to push the calendar sheets against the back. This would enable the user to clearly see which marker above the month table lines up with the marker on the day-of-month table sheet. However, the holding device can be omitted to save money. The seven-column multisheet perpetual wall calendar can be designed to salvage sheets from a conventional wall calendar. The resulting calendar would be an alternative to the designs discussed in Chapter 6.

## Seven-Column, 21-Sheet Perpetual Calendar with a Single Year Table

One inconvenience when using a calendar with seven day-of-month sheets is that when changing from the current month to the next, the sheet is not simply flipped over. Instead, the sheet with the correct day-of-month table must be found. For example, if the first of October is on a Saturday, then the first of November is on a Tuesday. In this case, with seven sheets for the day of the month, October would use sheet no. 7 and November would use sheet no. 3. The need to flip backwards or forwards to find the correct sheet can be eliminated by having more than one sheet for each day of the week that a month can start on. In any year, up to three months can begin on the same day of the week. Therefore, three sheets are required for each day of the week, for a total of 21 sheets. At the beginning of each year, the 12 sheets that apply to the year would be selected and arranged in the correct order. Two disadvantages of this concept are that (1) the sheets must be bound in such a way that they can be easily rearranged and (2) the calendar must be set up at the beginning of each year.

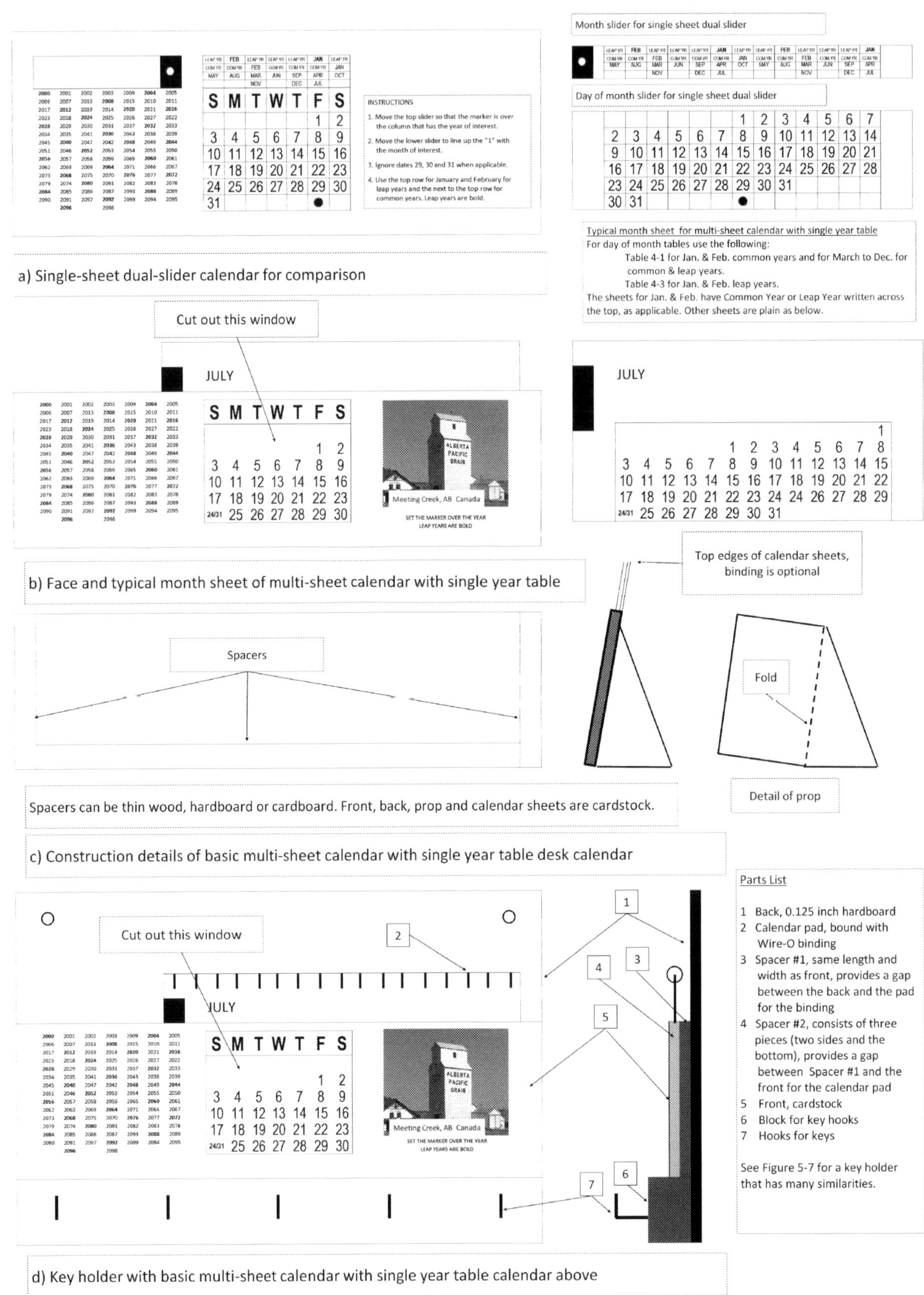

Month slider for single sheet dual slider
Day of month slider for single sheet dual slider
INSTRUCTIONS
1. Move the top slider so that the marker is over the column that has the year of interest.
2. Move the lower slider to line up the "1" with the month of interest.
3. Ignore dates 29, 30 and 31 when applicable.
4. Use the top row for January and February for leap years and the next to the top row for common years. Leap years are bold.
a) Single-sheet dual-slider calendar for comparison
Typical month sheet for multi-sheet calendar with single year table
For day of month tables use the following:
Table 4-1 for Jan. & Feb. common years and for March to Dec. for common & leap years.
Table 4-3 for Jan. & Feb. leap years.
The sheets for Jan. & Feb. have Common Year or Leap Year written across the top, as applicable. Other sheets are plain as below.
Cut out this window
JULY
Meeting Creek, AB Canada
SET THE MARKER OVER THE YEAR
LEAP YEARS ARE BOLD
b) Face and typical month sheet of multi-sheet calendar with single year table
Top edges of calendar sheets, binding is optional
Spacers
Fold
Detail of prop
Spacers can be thin wood, hardboard or cardboard. Front, back, prop and calendar sheets are cardstock.
c) Construction details of basic multi-sheet calendar with single year table desk calendar
Parts List
1 Back, 0.125 inch hardboard
2 Calendar pad, bound with Wire-O binding
3 Spacer #1, same length and width as front, provides a gap between the back and the pad for the binding
4 Spacer #2, consists of three pieces (two sides and the bottom), provides a gap between Spacer #1 and the front for the calendar pad
5 Front, cardstock
6 Block for key hooks
7 Hooks for keys
See Figure 5-7 for a key holder that has many similarities.
d) Key holder with basic multi-sheet calendar with single year table calendar above


Figures 7-1a to 7-1d: Multisheet calendar with a single year table

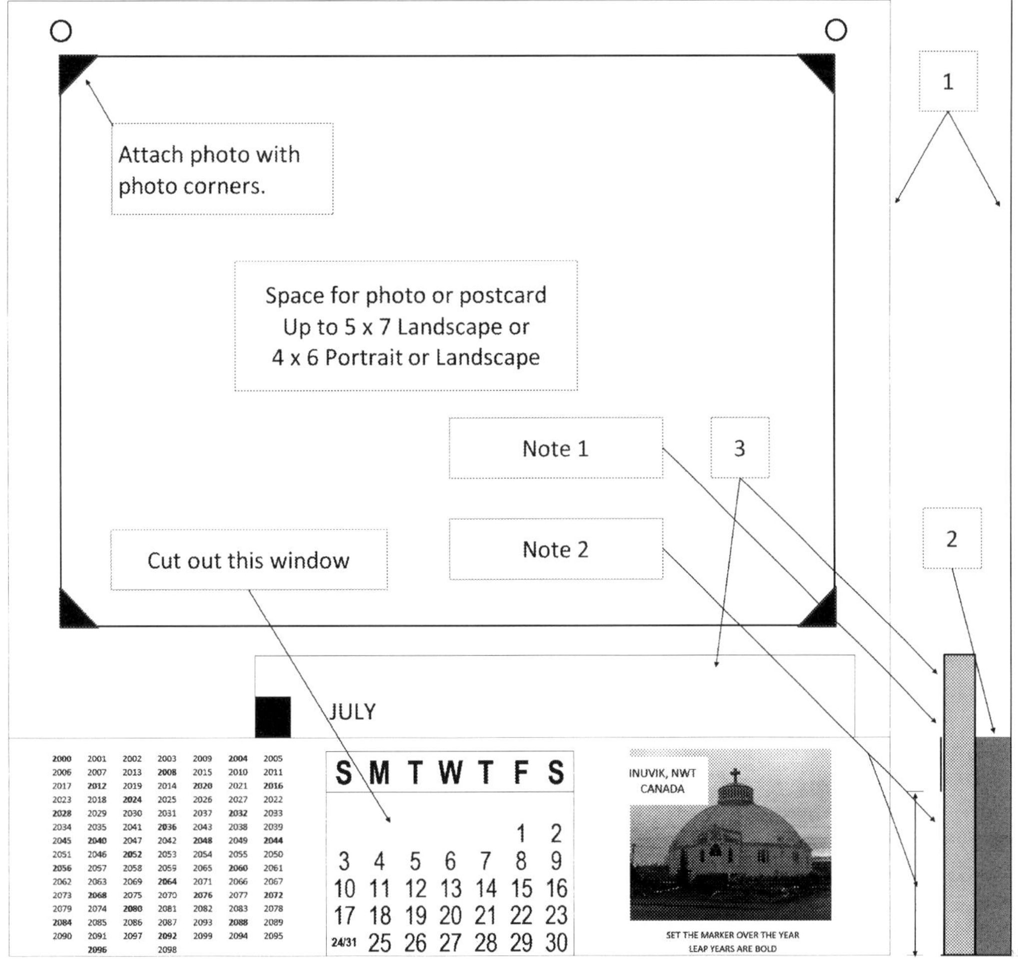
Attach photo with photo corners.
Space for photo or postcard
Up to 5 x 7 Landscape or
4 x 6 Portrait or Landscape
Note 1
Note 2
Cut out this window
1
2
3
JULY
S M T W T F S
1 2
3 4 5 6 7 8 9
10 11 12 13 14 15 16
17 18 19 20 21 22 23
24/31 25 26 27 28 29 30
INUVIK, NWT
CANADA
SET THE MARKER OVER THE YEAR
LEAP YEARS ARE BOLD

<u>Parts List</u>

1 Cardstock piece 8.5 inches by 11 inches folded to a "J" shape to make photo holder and calendar face. Trim as required so that overall dimensions after folding are approximately 7.5 inches wide by 8.5 inches high.

2 Filler to provide a gap between back of calendar pad and photo holder. Suggested material is cardboard.

3 Calendar pad

<u>Notes</u>

1 Method of joining the calendar face to the back after folding to be determined. Suggested method is to use strips of cardstock folded to shape and glued in place. Alternatively, use side spacers. If there is difficulty, make front and photo holder separate pieces and use side and bottom spacers as in Figures 7-1c and 7-1d.

2 The side view is a cross-section through the middle. The line with the two arrow heads shows the height of the window. (Note that the bottom of the window is along the fold line.)

3 Cut out window in front before folding.

4 When using as a wall calendar, a spacer at the bottom of the back may be wanted to give the calendar a slight tilt to make the numbers easier to read.

5 When using as a desk calendar, make a prop from cardstock shaped similar to the one in Figure 7-1c. Make height of prop at least two thirds of the overall height and extend 3.0 inches behind calendar.

Figure 7-2: J-style wall/desk calendar

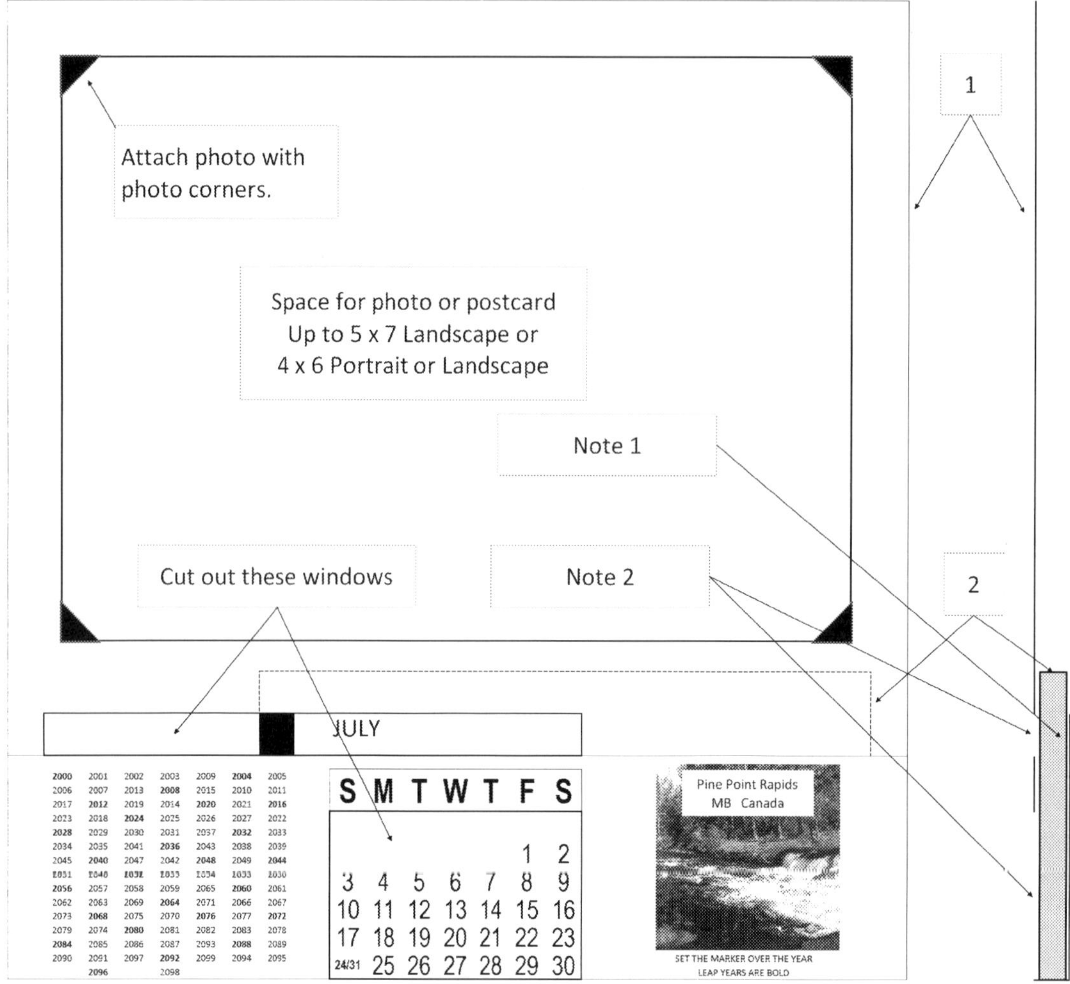
Attach photo with photo corners.
Space for photo or postcard Up to 5 x 7 Landscape or 4 x 6 Portrait or Landscape
Note 1
Cut out these windows
Note 2
1
2
JULY
S M T W T F S
Pine Point Rapids MB Canada
SET THE MARKER OVER THE YEAR
LEAP YEARS ARE BOLD

Parts List

1 Cardstock piece 8.5 inches by 11 inches folded to a "J" shape to make photo holder and calendar face. Trim as required so that overall dimensions after folding are approximately 7.5 inches wide by 8.5 inches high.

2 Calendar pad shown in far right position. There is no spacer as in Figure 7-2.

3 Prop, not shown. See Note 3 for a description.

Notes

1 Method of joining the calendar face to the back after folding to be determined. Suggested method is to use strips of cardstock folded to shape and glued in place. Alternatively, use side spacers. If there is difficulty, make front and photo holder separate pieces and use side and bottom spacers as in Figures 7-1c and 7-1d.

2 The side view is a cross-section through the middle. The top gap is the window to view the marker and the name of the month. The bottom gap is the window to view the day of month table.

2 Cut out windows in front before folding.

3 Make a prop from cardstock shaped similar to the one in Figure 7-1c. Make height of prop at least two thirds of the overall height and extend 3.0 inches behind calendar. Attach prop to back of main body at top and to back of calendar holder at bottom. Cut a window in the prop so that calendar pad can be lifted out.

Figure 7-3: Reverse J-style desk calendar

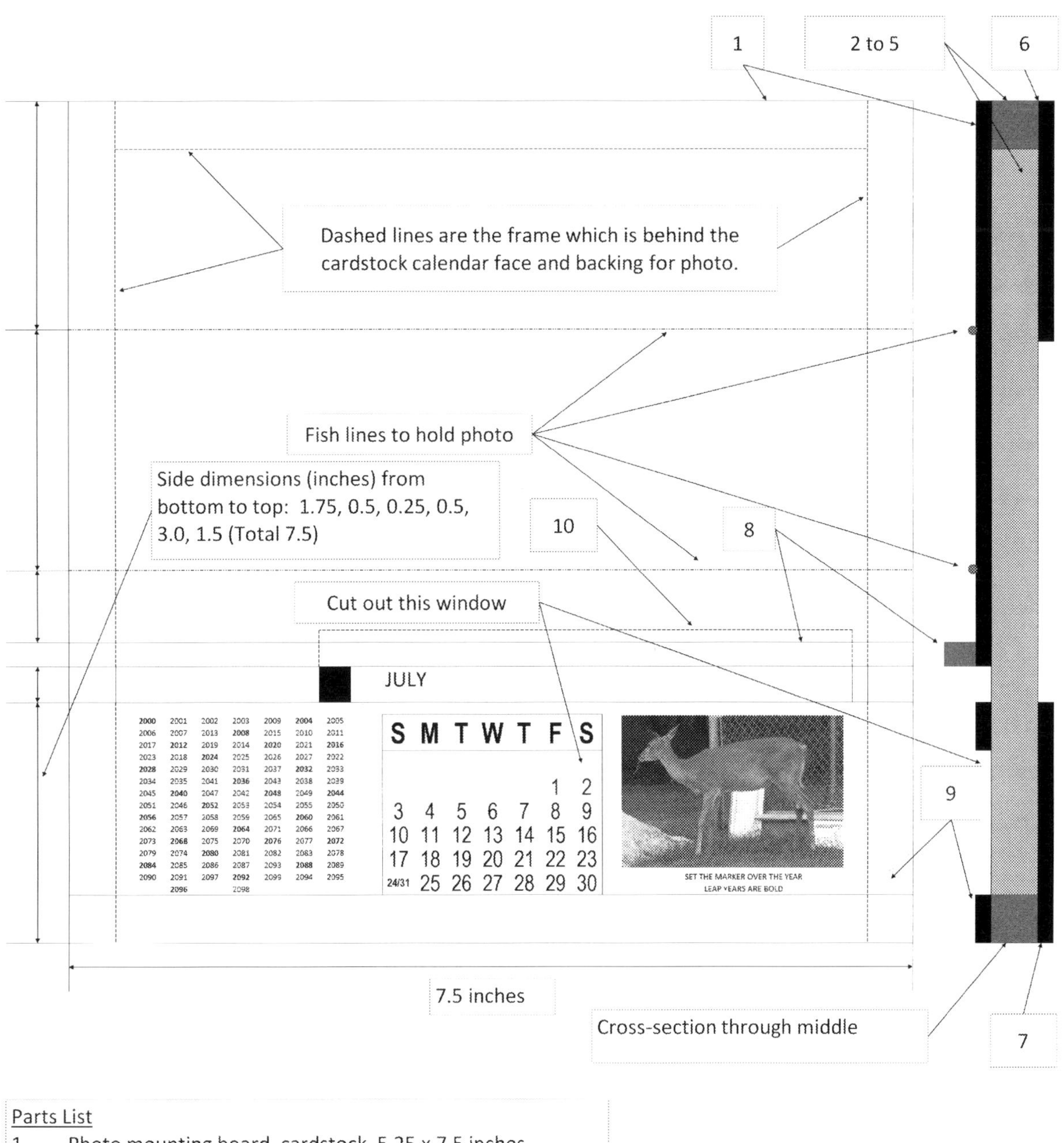
1
2 to 5
6
Dashed lines are the frame which is behind the cardstock calendar face and backing for photo.
Fish lines to hold photo
Side dimensions (inches) from bottom to top: 1.75, 0.5, 0.25, 0.5, 3.0, 1.5 (Total 7.5)
10
8
Cut out this window
JULY
S M T W T F S
1 2
3 4 5 6 7 8 9
10 11 12 13 14 15 16
17 18 19 20 21 22 23
24/31 25 26 27 28 29 30
9
SET THE MARKER OVER THE YEAR
LEAP YEARS ARE BOLD
7.5 inches
Cross-section through middle
7

Parts List

| | |
|---|---|
| 1 | Photo mounting board, cardstock, 5.25 x 7.5 inches |
| 2 - 5 | Frame, 0.5 x 0.5 wood, top & bottom each 6.5 in. long, sides each 7.5 in. long |
| 6, 7 | Top and bottom back bracing, cardstock, each 2 x 7.5 in. |
| 8 | Photo bottom support, wood 0.25 x 0.25 x 7.5 inches |
| 9 | Calendar front, cardstock 1.75 x 7.5 in. |
| 10 | Calendar pad, behind front, slips in from back |
| 11 | Prop (not shown), same material as frame, 7.5 in. long, attach to top corner of one side with a screw |
| 12 | Filler (not shown), cardboard to reduce the depth of the pocket behind the front as required so the calendar pad fits in snugly |

Figure 7-4: Wooden frame desk calendar

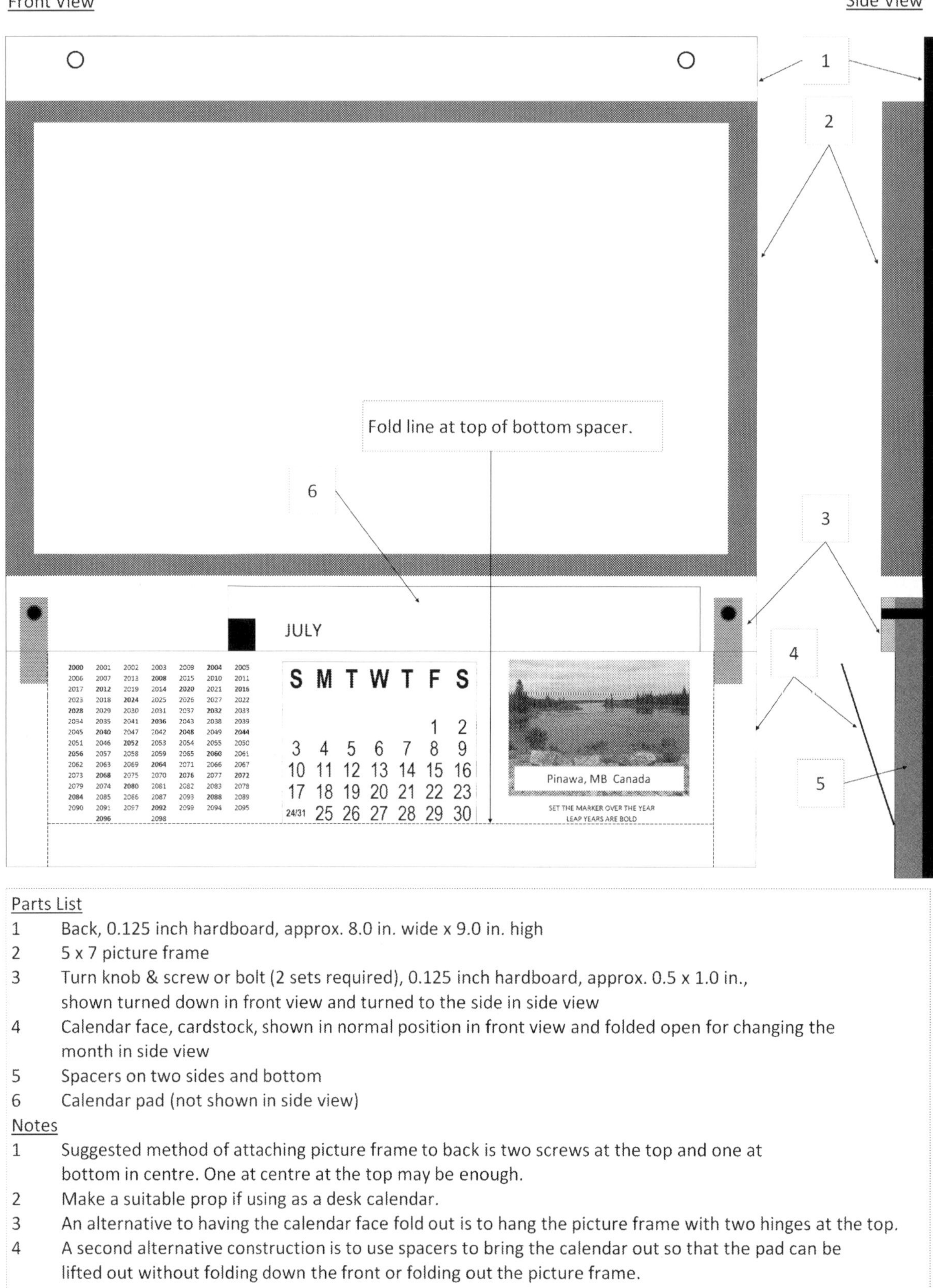

Front View
Side View
1
2
Fold line at top of bottom spacer.
6
3
JULY
4
S M T W T F S
1 2
3 4 5 6 7 8 9
10 11 12 13 14 15 16
17 18 19 20 21 22 23
24/31 25 26 27 28 29 30
Pinawa, MB Canada
SET THE MARKER OVER THE YEAR
LEAP YEARS ARE BOLD
5


Parts List

1 Back, 0.125 inch hardboard, approx. 8.0 in. wide x 9.0 in. high
2 5 x 7 picture frame
3 Turn knob & screw or bolt (2 sets required), 0.125 inch hardboard, approx. 0.5 x 1.0 in., shown turned down in front view and turned to the side in side view
4 Calendar face, cardstock, shown in normal position in front view and folded open for changing the month in side view
5 Spacers on two sides and bottom
6 Calendar pad (not shown in side view)

Notes

1 Suggested method of attaching picture frame to back is two screws at the top and one at bottom in centre. One at centre at the top may be enough.
2 Make a suitable prop if using as a desk calendar.
3 An alternative to having the calendar face fold out is to hang the picture frame with two hinges at the top.
4 A second alternative construction is to use spacers to bring the calendar out so that the pad can be lifted out without folding down the front or folding out the picture frame.

Figure 7-5: Multisheet single-year table calendar below a 5 × 7 inch picture frame

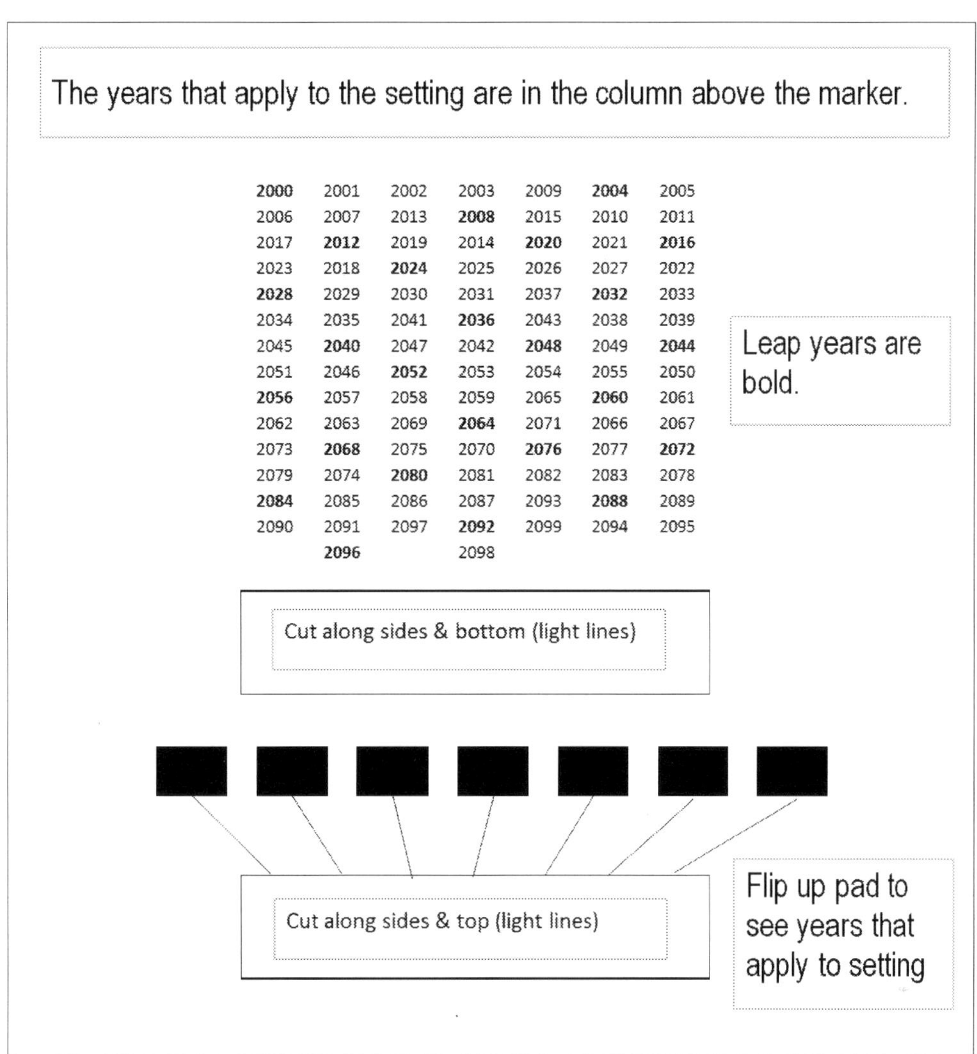
The years that apply to the setting are in the column above the marker.
2000 2001 2002 2003 2009 2004 2005
2006 2007 2013 2008 2015 2010 2011
2017 2012 2019 2014 2020 2021 2016
2023 2018 2024 2025 2026 2027 2022
2028 2029 2030 2031 2037 2032 2033
2034 2035 2041 2036 2043 2038 2039
2045 2040 2047 2042 2048 2049 2044
2051 2046 2052 2053 2054 2055 2050
2056 2057 2058 2059 2065 2060 2061
2062 2063 2069 2064 2071 2066 2067
2073 2068 2075 2070 2076 2077 2072
2079 2074 2080 2081 2082 2083 2078
2084 2085 2086 2087 2093 2088 2089
2090 2091 2097 2092 2099 2094 2095
2096 2098
Leap years are bold.
Cut along sides & bottom (light lines)
Cut along sides & top (light lines)
Flip up pad to see years that apply to setting

Body, showing year table and cutouts for slider

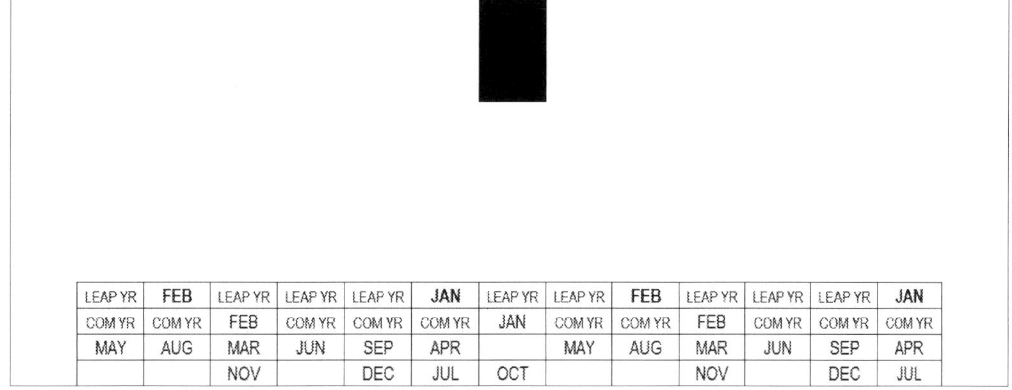
LEAP YR FEB LEAP YR LEAP YR LEAP YR JAN LEAP YR LEAP YR FEB LEAP YR LEAP YR LEAP YR JAN
COM YR COM YR FEB COM YR COM YR COM YR JAN COM YR COM YR FEB COM YR COM YR COM YR
MAY AUG MAR JUN SEP APR MAY AUG MAR JUN SEP APR
NOV DEC JUL OCT NOV DEC JUL

Slider

Figure 7-6a: Seven-column multisheet calendar with a single year table—body and slider

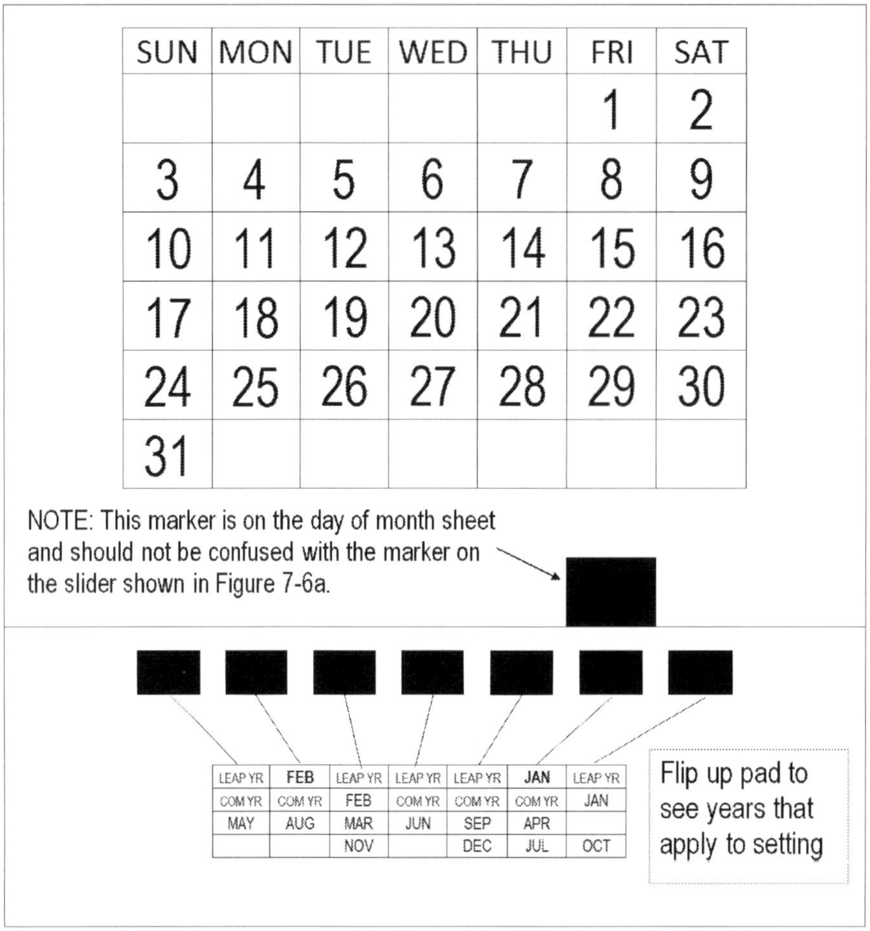

| SUN | MON | TUE | WED | THU | FRI | SAT |
|---|---|---|---|---|---|---|
| | | | | | 1 | 2 |
| 3 | 4 | 5 | 6 | 7 | 8 | 9 |
| 10 | 11 | 12 | 13 | 14 | 15 | 16 |
| 17 | 18 | 19 | 20 | 21 | 22 | 23 |
| 24 | 25 | 26 | 27 | 28 | 29 | 30 |
| 31 | | | | | | |

NOTE: This marker is on the day of month sheet and should not be confused with the marker on the slider shown in Figure 7-6a.

| LEAP YR | **FEB** | LEAP YR | LEAP YR | LEAP YR | **JAN** | LEAP YR |
|---|---|---|---|---|---|---|
| COM YR | COM YR | FEB | COM YR | COM YR | COM YR | JAN |
| MAY | AUG | MAR | JUN | SEP | APR | |
| | | NOV | | DEC | JUL | OCT |

Flip up pad to see years that apply to setting

<u>Operating Notes</u>

1. Flip up pad of day of month sheets so that year table can be seen.
2. Set black marker on slider under the column that has the year of interest.. Note that leap years are bold.
3. Flip down pad. Find month of interest in window. Use top row for January and February of leap years and next to top row for common years.
4. Turn to the calendar sheet that has a black mark that lines up with the black mark for the month of interest.

<u>Construction Notes for Windows and Installing Slider</u>

1. Cut along three sides of each window as shown in Figure 6-9a.
2. Cut a piece of wax paper the approximate length of the slider and not quite as wide.
3. Thread the wax paper into where the slider should go.
4. Cut a piece of cardstock the width of the slider and the length of the windows.
5. Glue the cardstock to the backs of the two window flaps.
6. Remove the wax paper and thread the slider in its place.

Slider set in the position that applies to 2016 (far right). The day of month sheet applies to January, April and July of 2016

Figure 7-6b: Seven-column multisheet calendar with a single year table—assembled

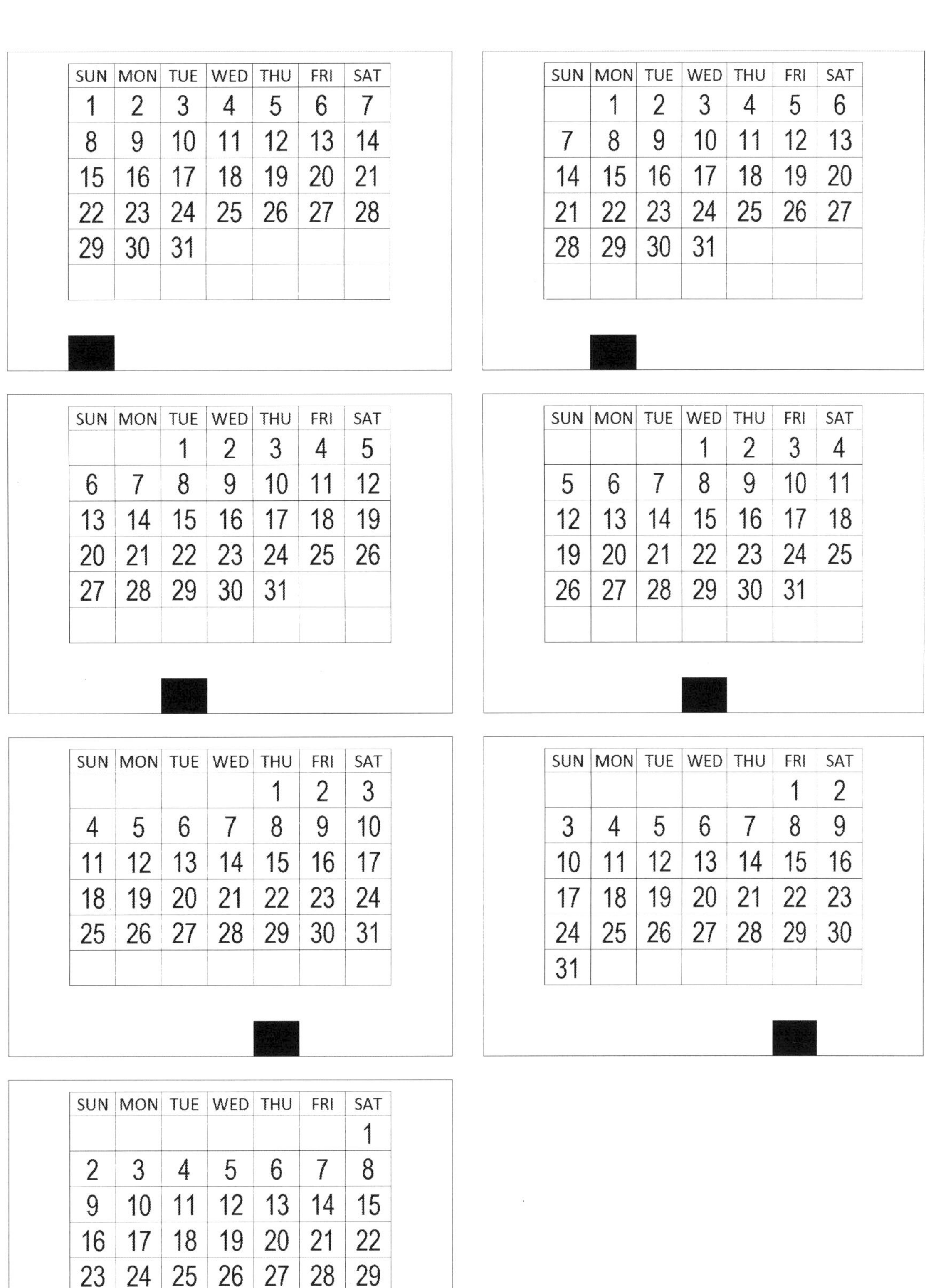

| SUN | MON | TUE | WED | THU | FRI | SAT |
|---|---|---|---|---|---|---|
| 1 | 2 | 3 | 4 | 5 | 6 | 7 |
| 8 | 9 | 10 | 11 | 12 | 13 | 14 |
| 15 | 16 | 17 | 18 | 19 | 20 | 21 |
| 22 | 23 | 24 | 25 | 26 | 27 | 28 |
| 29 | 30 | 31 | | | | |
| | | | | | | |

| SUN | MON | TUE | WED | THU | FRI | SAT |
|---|---|---|---|---|---|---|
| | 1 | 2 | 3 | 4 | 5 | 6 |
| 7 | 8 | 9 | 10 | 11 | 12 | 13 |
| 14 | 15 | 16 | 17 | 18 | 19 | 20 |
| 21 | 22 | 23 | 24 | 25 | 26 | 27 |
| 28 | 29 | 30 | 31 | | | |
| | | | | | | |

| SUN | MON | TUE | WED | THU | FRI | SAT |
|---|---|---|---|---|---|---|
| | | 1 | 2 | 3 | 4 | 5 |
| 6 | 7 | 8 | 9 | 10 | 11 | 12 |
| 13 | 14 | 15 | 16 | 17 | 18 | 19 |
| 20 | 21 | 22 | 23 | 24 | 25 | 26 |
| 27 | 28 | 29 | 30 | 31 | | |
| | | | | | | |

| SUN | MON | TUE | WED | THU | FRI | SAT |
|---|---|---|---|---|---|---|
| | | | 1 | 2 | 3 | 4 |
| 5 | 6 | 7 | 8 | 9 | 10 | 11 |
| 12 | 13 | 14 | 15 | 16 | 17 | 18 |
| 19 | 20 | 21 | 22 | 23 | 24 | 25 |
| 26 | 27 | 28 | 29 | 30 | 31 | |
| | | | | | | |

| SUN | MON | TUE | WED | THU | FRI | SAT |
|---|---|---|---|---|---|---|
| | | | | 1 | 2 | 3 |
| 4 | 5 | 6 | 7 | 8 | 9 | 10 |
| 11 | 12 | 13 | 14 | 15 | 16 | 17 |
| 18 | 19 | 20 | 21 | 22 | 23 | 24 |
| 25 | 26 | 27 | 28 | 29 | 30 | 31 |
| | | | | | | |

| SUN | MON | TUE | WED | THU | FRI | SAT |
|---|---|---|---|---|---|---|
| | | | | | 1 | 2 |
| 3 | 4 | 5 | 6 | 7 | 8 | 9 |
| 10 | 11 | 12 | 13 | 14 | 15 | 16 |
| 17 | 18 | 19 | 20 | 21 | 22 | 23 |
| 24 | 25 | 26 | 27 | 28 | 29 | 30 |
| 31 | | | | | | |

| SUN | MON | TUE | WED | THU | FRI | SAT |
|---|---|---|---|---|---|---|
| | | | | | | 1 |
| 2 | 3 | 4 | 5 | 6 | 7 | 8 |
| 9 | 10 | 11 | 12 | 13 | 14 | 15 |
| 16 | 17 | 18 | 19 | 20 | 21 | 22 |
| 23 | 24 | 25 | 26 | 27 | 28 | 29 |
| 30 | 31 | | | | | |

Figure 7-6c: Seven-column multisheet calendar with a single year table—day-of-month sheets

# CHAPTER 8

# FULL-YEAR PERPETUAL CALENDARS—APPLICATIONS AND PRODUCTS

## Applications and Designs

The two applications with the greatest market potential are a full-year perpetual calendar for a binder and one for an office wall. There are four designs described in this chapter that can be easily adapted to these applications. The designs are (1) double-sided slider, (2) single-sided slider, (3) vertical and (4) single day-of-month table. A full-year wall planner where the calendar sheet is rolled up is also described. It uses the same tables as the single-sided slider full-year perpetual calendar.

The double-sided slider and single-sided slider full-year calendars are effectively multisheet perpetual calendars that display all the months on one page. The double-sided slider is a full-year equivalent of the 24-sheet design, and the single-sided slider is a full-year equivalent of the 14-sheet design. As explained in Chapter 4, a full-year equivalent of the 12-sheet design is not possible. This is because in a leap year it would display either January and February, or March to December, but not the full year.

## Double-Sided Slider Full-Year Perpetual Calendar

The double-sided slider has one side for common years and one side for leap years. Table 4-1 is used for common years and Table 4-2 is used for leap years. The calendar face has 14 windows: one for each month, one to indicate applicable common years and one to indicate applicable leap years. (These last two windows could be combined into one with one year table.) A disadvantage of this type is that the slider must be turned over when going from a common year to a leap year and vice versa. Figure 8-1a shows the face of the full-year calendar with a double-sided slider; Figure 8-1b shows the common year side of the slider; and Figure 8-1c shows the leap year side of the slider.

The full-year calendar with a double-sided slider is assembled by cutting out all the windows on the face and then gluing the face to a plain back of the same size. The front and back are separated by spacers at the top and bottom to allow the slider to move freely. The bottom spacer is positioned so that it provides a guide to keep the slider at the correct height.

## Single-Sided Slider Full-Year Perpetual Calendar

The single-sided slider full-year perpetual calendar is the most practical design and is also easy to use. It has 14 windows for the months, and 1 window to indicate the applicable years. The windows for the months are as follows: January in a common year, February in a common year, January in a leap year, February in a leap year and 10 windows to cover March to December. Tables 4-1 and 4-3 are used to make this calendar, which is set by moving the slider so that the marker is beside the row that contains the year of interest. If the year is listed in boldface, then the leap year windows for January and February are used. Otherwise, the common year windows for January and February are used. A user may be a bit confused when deciding which January and February windows apply to the year of interest, but this is a minor disadvantage when compared to having to turn over the slider when switching between leap years and common years on the full-year calendar that is the equivalent of the 24-sheet style.

Figure 8-2a shows the slider and Figure 8-2b shows the face of a simple full-year perpetual calendar for a three-ring binder. This is the calendar depicted in Figure 1-4a. Each piece is made from an 8.5 × 11 inch sheet of cardstock. The face has two slits to guide the slider so that a back and spacers are not required, as is the case for the double-sided-slider calendar previously described. Figure 1-4a shows the assembled calendar, with the ends of the slider to the left and right of the window. The face has 14 windows to display the applicable columns of the day-of-month tables, and 1 window to display the marker for year indication. The windows are in five rows and three columns. Table 8-1 indicates the purpose of each window.

**Table 8-1**
**Purpose of Each Window of a Single-Sided Slider Full-Year Perpetual Calendar**

| Row | Column A | Column B | Column C |
|---|---|---|---|
| 1 | Marker for year indication | January, leap year | February, leap year |
| 2 | January, common year | February, common year | March |
| 3 | April | May | June |
| 4 | July | August | September |
| 5 | October | November | December |

In the year table, common years in the top row are years when January 1 is on a Sunday. Common years in the second row are years when January 1 is on a Monday, common years in the third row are years when January 1 is on a Tuesday, etc. Leap years in the top row are years when January

1 is on a Saturday. Leap years in the second row are years when January 1 is on a Sunday, leap years in the third row are years when January 1 is on a Monday, etc. Thus, leap years are in a row corresponding to the day after the day of the week that January 1 falls on. This is done so that the same windows for March to December can be used for both common years and leap years. Note that in a leap year, January 1 is one day ahead in the week with respect to January 1 of the previous year, but March 1 is two days ahead in the week with respect to March 1 of the previous year. When the year table is set up this way, the day-of-month tables for January and February are different for common years and leap years.

The face arrangement in Figure 8-2b is a fairly logical arrangement and makes a calendar with the correct proportions for a three-ring binder. One change that could be considered is to put the year table at the right-hand end of the top row so that January of a leap year would be above January of a common year and February of a leap year would be above February of a common year. If covers are used to blank out windows that are not applicable, this arrangement would enable sliding or hinging one cover up or down to blank out two windows at once. Otherwise, having the year indication in the top left window rather than at the top right seems more logical. Many arrangements are possible, depending on the user's preference.

## Single-Sided Slider Full-Year Perpetual Calendar—Cutting Out and Assembling

The steps to cut out and assemble the three-ring binder calendar in Figures 8-2a and 8-2b are as follows:

1. Cut out the 14 month windows on the face, which is Figure 8-2b.
2. Cut out the year-indicator window on Figure 8-2b.
3. Cut along the two vertical lines that are at the left- and right-hand sides of Figure 8-2b.
4. Cut from edge to edge along the top and bottom lines on Figure 8-2a. Note that when the page is printed, these lines will not quite reach from edge to edge.
5. Insert the slider, which is the piece cut from Figure 8-2a, into the left cut on the face so that it goes under the windows.
6. Bring the slider back up through the right cut on the face.
7. Move the slider back and forth to determine how much runs past the face on each side when the slider is at each extreme of its travel. Cut off this extra, which is about 0.5 inches on each end.

Rather than cutting out each window individually on its four sides, all the horizontal lines that line up can be cut at one time. Similarly, vertical lines can be cut at one time. For example, a straight edge is put at the bottom of October, November and December, and then the bottom of each window is cut in turn. This saves time and results in a neater job. Of course, in a large production run, a die is made and all cutting is done by machine.

The face in Figure 8-2b can be punched for putting in a three-ring binder. However, putting it in a three-ring-binder sheet protector will make it last longer. An examination of the face in Figure 8-2b shows that there is considerable blank space, to which graphics or other information can be added. The graphics can be pictures or artwork, and the other information can be things of interest to the user, such as metric conversion tables. A calendar given out for advertising purposes can have the company name at the top or bottom and pictures of products in the centre.

## Single-Sided Slider Full-Year Wall Calendar

Many offices have a full-year calendar on the wall. The concepts in Figures 8-2a and 8-2b can be used to make calendars that last many years, rather than just one year. For a low-cost calendar, the slider can be placed in slits cut in the face, as in Figure 8-2b. Calendars made from cardstock can be expected to last 5 to 10 years, and calendars made from plastic sheet can last 10 to 20 years. For either material, the quantity required would be about twice of what would be required to make a conventional calendar of the same dimensions. The cost is expected to be about twice as much. This is easily justified by an expected life of 5 to 20 times as long—and the versatility of the perpetual feature is a free bonus.

Tables 8-2 and 8-3 show the arrangement of two commercially available wall calendars.

**Table 8-2**
**Face Arrangement of a 24-Inch Wide × 36-Inch High Commercially Available Wall Calendar**

| Row | Column A | Column B | Column C |
|---|---|---|---|
| 1 | January | February | March |
| 2 | April | May | June |
| 3 | July | August | September |
| 4 | October | November | December |

**Table 8-3**
**Face Arrangement of a 24-Inch Wide × 18-Inch High Commercially Available Wall Calendar**

| Row | Column A | Column B | Column C | Column D |
|---|---|---|---|---|
| 1 | January | February | March | April |
| 2 | May | June | July | August |
| 3 | September | October | November | December |

A comparison of Table 8-1 with Table 8-2 shows that the perpetual calendar has a special top row and four bottom rows that are the same as those of the conventional calendar. By decreasing the font size to accommodate the additional row, the overall height of 36 inches can be the same. As each day-of-month table in a perpetual calendar has 13 columns, compared to 7 in a conventional calendar, the width may have to be increased to 30 or 36 inches. If the width cannot be more than 24 inches, a calendar of the same width-to-height proportion as in Figures 8-2a and 8-2b can be made, i.e. 11:8.5. If the width is 24 inches, the height would be 18.5 inches (8.5/11 × 24 = 18.5 inches). A perpetual calendar 24 inches wide by 18.5 inches high would require about the same amount of material and would cost the same as the commercial 24-inch wide by 36-inch high calendar. Of course, the font would be smaller, but obtaining a perpetual calendar for the same price may be a good tradeoff.

To replace the commercial calendar in Table 8-3, a row would also need to be added to the top. January of a leap year could be above January of a common year, and February of a leap year could be above February of a common year. The year indication could be above March and April. Since the commercial calendar in an 18-inch height has three rows, the additional row could add as much as six inches to the height if the font size is kept the same. The width of the perpetual calendar can be estimated by comparing the number of horizontal spaces the perpetual calendar requires to the number of horizontal spaces the commercial calendar requires. For this comparison, a space is regarded as the width required for one day of the week. Borders along the ends and between months are regarded as one space. A conventional full-year calendar that is four months wide requires 28 spaces for the days of the month, three spaces between the months and one space on each end. This is a total width of 33 spaces. An examination of Figures 8-2a and 8-2b shows that a perpetual calendar requires 13 spaces instead of seven for each month, and requires seven spaces on each end instead of one. Therefore, a perpetual calendar that is four months wide requires 52 spaces for the days of the week, three spaces between the months and seven spaces on each end. This is a total width of 69 spaces, which is approximately double that of a conventional calendar. Thus, converting the commercial full-year calendar in Table 8-3 to a perpetual calendar with the same font size would increase the width from 24 inches to 48 inches, and the height from 18 inches to 24 inches.

A full-year perpetual calendar for an office can also be made from rigid material such as hardboard or fine plywood. The construction details would be similar to those described in Chapter 5 for the single-sheet calendar. The cost would be considerably higher than for a calendar made from thin-sheet flexible material. However, using rigid material would enable making calendars that would be showpieces in boardrooms.

## Single-Sided Slider Full-Year Wall Planner

Table 8-4 illustrates the concept of a full-year wall planner that uses Tables 4-1 and 4-3 for the day-of-month tables. These are the same tables that are used to make the single-sided slider full-year three-ring-binder and wall calendars. Each cell in the day-of-month table has the number in the upper left-hand corner, which allows space for notes. This format is similar to that used in the 13-column wall planner in Figure 5-14b. The months are printed on a long sheet that can be rolled up. The order of months on the sheet is January of leap year, February of leap year, January of common year, February of common year and March to December for both leap years and common years. There is an upper roller and a lower roller with space between them for a moving window that outlines an area seven columns wide by seven rows high. The window, which has the same role as a slider, is positioned so that the marker on it points to the column in the year table that has the year of interest. The year table is Table 4-7, which is the same as is used for the 14-sheet perpetual calendar with a year table on each sheet. There is a hard surface behind the window so that the cells in the window can be written on. The rollers can be turned so that the seven rows in the window are all of one month or parts of two months.

**Table 8-4**
**Full-Year Wall Planner Concept**

Seven-column year table on top of upper roller

Operating instructions or a picture on top of upper roller

| | | | | | | | | | | | | | | |
|---|---|---|---|---|---|---|---|---|---|---|---|---|---|---|
| | | | | | | | | | | | | | | |
| | | S | M | T | W | T | F | S | | | | | | |
| September | | | | | | | | | | | | | 1 | 2 |
| | | | | | | 1 | 2 | 3 | 4 | 5 | 6 | 7 | 8 | 9 |
| | | 4 | 5 | 6 | 7 | 8 | 9 | 10 | 11 | 12 | 13 | 14 | 15 | 16 |
| | | 11 | 12 | 13 | 14 | 15 | 16 | 17 | 18 | 19 | 20 | 21 | 22 | 23 |
| | | 18 | 19 | 20 | 21 | 22 | 23 | 24 | 25 | 26 | 27 | 28 | 29 | 30 |
| | | 25 | 26 | 27 | 28 | 29 | 30 | | | | | | | |
| | | | | | | | | | | | | | | |
| | | | | | | | | | | | | | | |

Operating instructions or a picture on top of lower roller

In Table 8-4, the window frame is shown shaded in its far left position, which outlines the columns that apply to 2016. September is shown as a typical month. The full-year wall planner is included in this chapter more to show what is possible than to show what is practical. If each cell is 3 inches wide, then the total width for 13 columns plus 1-inch borders is 41 inches, compared to about 24 inches for a conventional planner with the same cell width. With rollers and a long sheet for the months, the cost of this planner could be 10 to 20 times that of a conventional one. However, it has the following advantages:

- no need to write out the numbers each month
- stand-alone, with no need to consult another calendar
- can display parts of two months
- holds data for an entire year

## Vertical Full-Year Perpetual Calendar

The concepts for the single-slider vertical calendar in Table 3-18 and Figures 5-16a and 5-16b, and the concepts for the day-of-month tables in Table 4-1, Table 4-3 and Figure 8-2a, can be used to make a vertical full-year perpetual calendar. The first of two steps is to eliminate the months on the slider in Figure 5-16a and to put a marker where January of a common year was. The next and last step is to replace the column that has the numbers 1 to 31 with 14 columns for the months. The columns are for January of a leap year, February of a leap year, January of a common year, February of a common year and March to December, which are the same for both leap years and common years. In the columns, the first of each month is offset from the first of January in a common year by the same amount as in Table 4-1, Table 4-3 and Figure 8-2a. Figure 8-3 shows the resulting calendar, which can be made for a wall or to fit in a three-ring binder.

## Single Day-of-Month Table Full-Year Perpetual Calendar

Figures 8-4a and 8-4b show two designs for a single day-of-month table full-year perpetual calendar, one with a horizontal slider and the other with a vertical slider. Both are made from cardstock with the slider held in slits. The horizontal design uses the same year and month tables as does the hybrid calendar in Figure 5-17a. A day-of-week table and a day-of-month table are added to the side. The day-of-week table has seven rows. The bottom row has *Sun., Mon., Tue., Wed., Thu., Fri.* and *Sat.* in the cells. The next row up has *Mon., Tue., Wed.,* etc. The vertical design uses the same tables as the horizontal design, with the month and year tables rotated counterclockwise 90 degrees. With this change, the month table is straight across from the day-of-week table, and the complicated lines in Figure 8-4a are replaced by straight lines. The idea of having a day-of-week table with seven rows came from United States Patent 1,784,117, December 9, 1930. This patent, which is discussed in the Appendix, describes a full-year calendar that has a rotating disk to bring the months into position, whereas I use a slider. My single day-of-month table full-year perpetual calendar is the only design for which I have used all the parts from another calendar without independently developing the overall concept on my own. The designs in both Figures 8-4a and 8-4b were not developed until much of *Practical Perpetual Calendars* had been written. These calendars are not as convenient to use as the full-year calendars in Figures 8-1 (a to c), 8-2 (a and b) and 8-3, where there is a table for each month. However, these calendars are easier to manufacture.

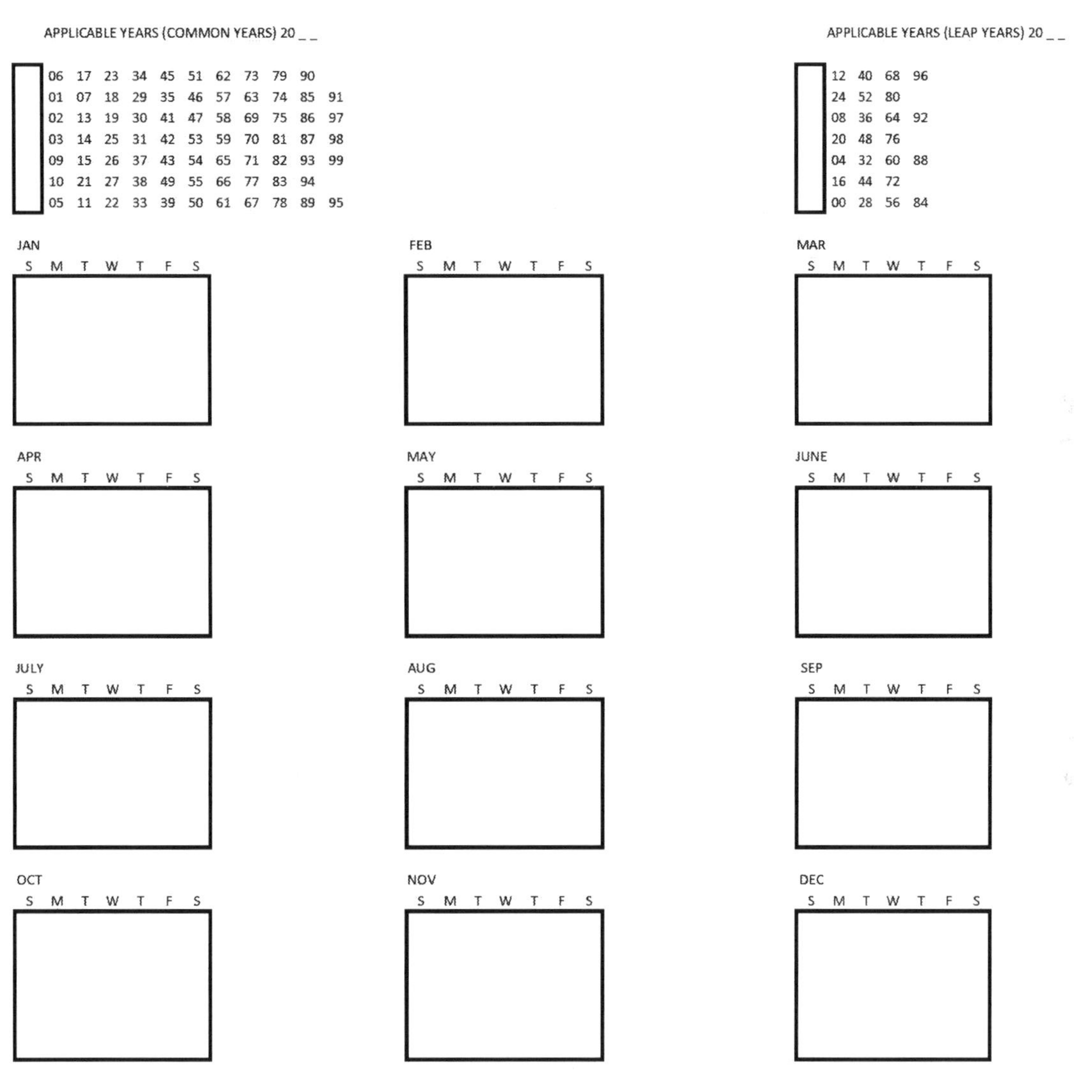
APPLICABLE YEARS (COMMON YEARS) 20 _ _
06 17 23 34 45 51 62 73 79 90
01 07 18 29 35 46 57 63 74 85 91
02 13 19 30 41 47 58 69 75 86 97
03 14 25 31 42 53 59 70 81 87 98
09 15 26 37 43 54 65 71 82 93 99
10 21 27 38 49 55 66 77 83 94
05 11 22 33 39 50 61 67 78 89 95
APPLICABLE YEARS (LEAP YEARS) 20 _ _
12 40 68 96
24 52 80
08 36 64 92
20 48 76
04 32 60 88
16 44 72
00 28 56 84
JAN
S M T W T F S
FEB
S M T W T F S
MAR
S M T W T F S
APR
S M T W T F S
MAY
S M T W T F S
JUNE
S M T W T F S
JULY
S M T W T F S
AUG
S M T W T F S
SEP
S M T W T F S
OCT
S M T W T F S
NOV
S M T W T F S
DEC
S M T W T F S

Figure 8-1a: Face of the full-year calendar with a double-sided slider

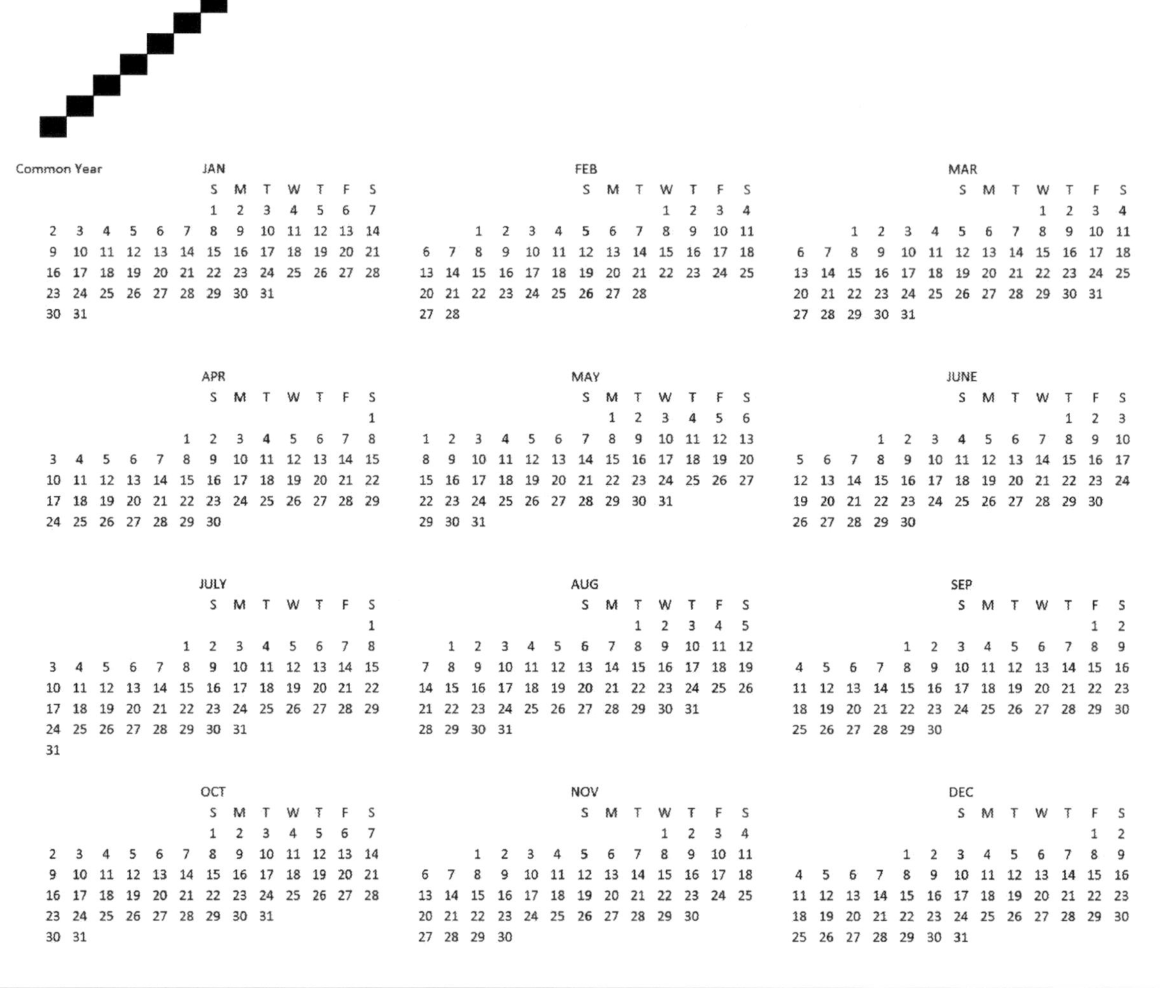
Common Year
JAN
S M T W T F S
1 2 3 4 5 6 7
2 3 4 5 6 7 8 9 10 11 12 13 14
9 10 11 12 13 14 15 16 17 18 19 20 21
16 17 18 19 20 21 22 23 24 25 26 27 28
23 24 25 26 27 28 29 30 31
30 31
FEB
S M T W T F S
1 2 3 4
1 2 3 4 5 6 7 8 9 10 11
6 7 8 9 10 11 12 13 14 15 16 17 18
13 14 15 16 17 18 19 20 21 22 23 24 25
20 21 22 23 24 25 26 27 28
27 28
MAR
S M T W T F S
1 2 3 4
1 2 3 4 5 6 7 8 9 10 11
6 7 8 9 10 11 12 13 14 15 16 17 18
13 14 15 16 17 18 19 20 21 22 23 24 25
20 21 22 23 24 25 26 27 28 29 30 31
27 28 29 30 31
APR
S M T W T F S
1
1 2 3 4 5 6 7 8
3 4 5 6 7 8 9 10 11 12 13 14 15
10 11 12 13 14 15 16 17 18 19 20 21 22
17 18 19 20 21 22 23 24 25 26 27 28 29
24 25 26 27 28 29 30
MAY
S M T W T F S
1 2 3 4 5 6
1 2 3 4 5 6 7 8 9 10 11 12 13
8 9 10 11 12 13 14 15 16 17 18 19 20
15 16 17 18 19 20 21 22 23 24 25 26 27
22 23 24 25 26 27 28 29 30 31
29 30 31
JUNE
S M T W T F S
1 2 3
1 2 3 4 5 6 7 8 9 10
5 6 7 8 9 10 11 12 13 14 15 16 17
12 13 14 15 16 17 18 19 20 21 22 23 24
19 20 21 22 23 24 25 26 27 28 29 30
26 27 28 29 30
JULY
S M T W T F S
1
1 2 3 4 5 6 7 8
3 4 5 6 7 8 9 10 11 12 13 14 15
10 11 12 13 14 15 16 17 18 19 20 21 22
17 18 19 20 21 22 23 24 25 26 27 28 29
24 25 26 27 28 29 30 31
31
AUG
S M T W T F S
1 2 3 4 5
1 2 3 4 5 6 7 8 9 10 11 12
7 8 9 10 11 12 13 14 15 16 17 18 19
14 15 16 17 18 19 20 21 22 23 24 25 26
21 22 23 24 25 26 27 28 29 30 31
28 29 30 31
SEP
S M T W T F S
1 2
1 2 3 4 5 6 7 8 9
4 5 6 7 8 9 10 11 12 13 14 15 16
11 12 13 14 15 16 17 18 19 20 21 22 23
18 19 20 21 22 23 24 25 26 27 28 29 30
25 26 27 28 29 30
OCT
S M T W T F S
1 2 3 4 5 6 7
2 3 4 5 6 7 8 9 10 11 12 13 14
9 10 11 12 13 14 15 16 17 18 19 20 21
16 17 18 19 20 21 22 23 24 25 26 27 28
23 24 25 26 27 28 29 30 31
30 31
NOV
S M T W T F S
1 2 3 4
1 2 3 4 5 6 7 8 9 10 11
6 7 8 9 10 11 12 13 14 15 16 17 18
13 14 15 16 17 18 19 20 21 22 23 24 25
20 21 22 23 24 25 26 27 28 29 30
27 28 29 30
DEC
S M T W T F S
1 2
1 2 3 4 5 6 7 8 9
4 5 6 7 8 9 10 11 12 13 14 15 16
11 12 13 14 15 16 17 18 19 20 21 22 23
18 19 20 21 22 23 24 25 26 27 28 29 30
25 26 27 28 29 30 31

Figure 8-1b: Common year side of the double-sided slider for the full-year calendar

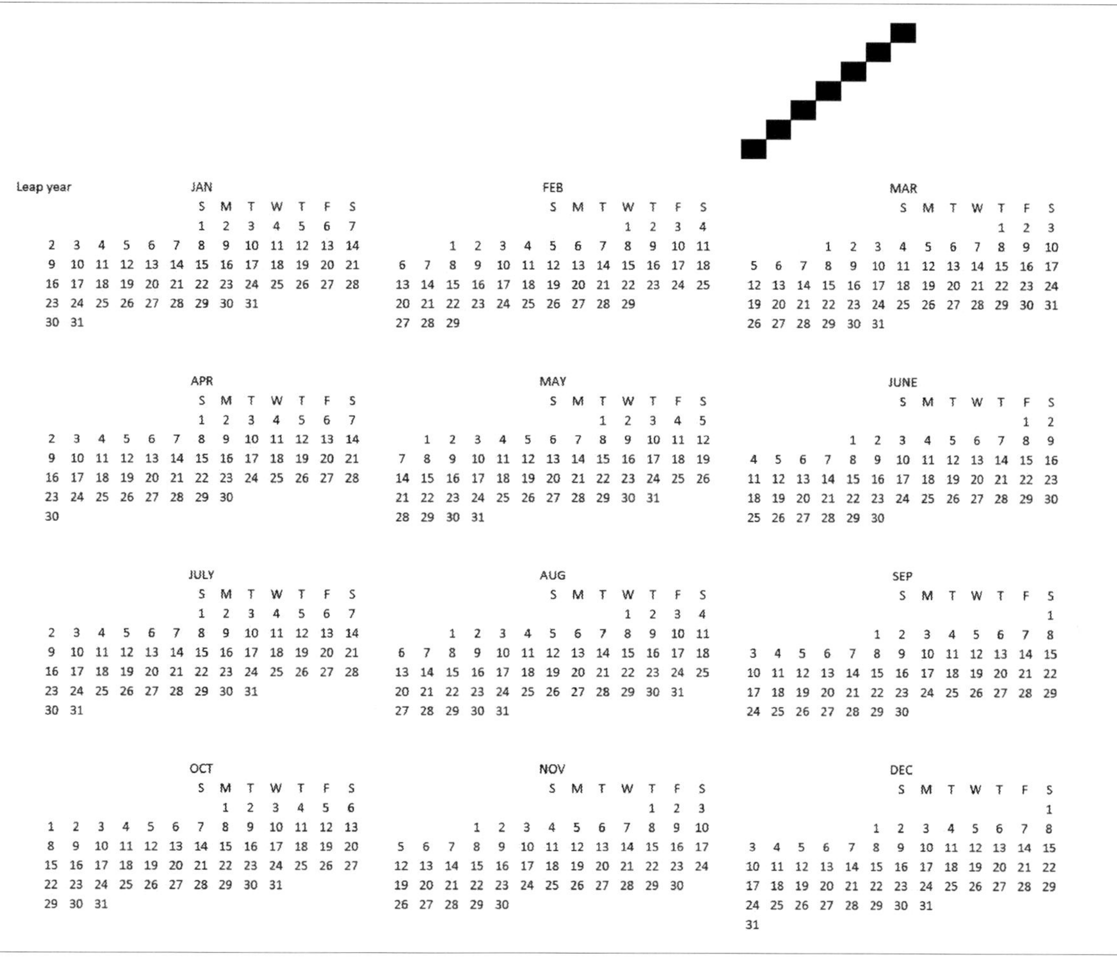
Leap year
JAN
S M T W T F S
1 2 3 4 5 6 7
2 3 4 5 6 7 8 9 10 11 12 13 14
9 10 11 12 13 14 15 16 17 18 19 20 21
16 17 18 19 20 21 22 23 24 25 26 27 28
23 24 25 26 27 28 29 30 31
30 31
FEB
S M T W T F S
1 2 3 4
1 2 3 4 5 6 7 8 9 10 11
6 7 8 9 10 11 12 13 14 15 16 17 18
13 14 15 16 17 18 19 20 21 22 23 24 25
20 21 22 23 24 25 26 27 28 29
27 28 29
MAR
S M T W T F S
1 2 3
1 2 3 4 5 6 7 8 9 10
5 6 7 8 9 10 11 12 13 14 15 16 17
12 13 14 15 16 17 18 19 20 21 22 23 24
19 20 21 22 23 24 25 26 27 28 29 30 31
26 27 28 29 30 31
APR
S M T W T F S
1 2 3 4 5 6 7
2 3 4 5 6 7 8 9 10 11 12 13 14
9 10 11 12 13 14 15 16 17 18 19 20 21
16 17 18 19 20 21 22 23 24 25 26 27 28
23 24 25 26 27 28 29 30
30
MAY
S M T W T F S
1 2 3 4 5
1 2 3 4 5 6 7 8 9 10 11 12
7 8 9 10 11 12 13 14 15 16 17 18 19
14 15 16 17 18 19 20 21 22 23 24 25 26
21 22 23 24 25 26 27 28 29 30 31
28 29 30 31
JUNE
S M T W T F S
1 2
1 2 3 4 5 6 7 8 9
4 5 6 7 8 9 10 11 12 13 14 15 16
11 12 13 14 15 16 17 18 19 20 21 22 23
18 19 20 21 22 23 24 25 26 27 28 29 30
25 26 27 28 29 30
JULY
S M T W T F S
1 2 3 4 5 6 7
2 3 4 5 6 7 8 9 10 11 12 13 14
9 10 11 12 13 14 15 16 17 18 19 20 21
16 17 18 19 20 21 22 23 24 25 26 27 28
23 24 25 26 27 28 29 30 31
30 31
AUG
S M T W T F S
1 2 3 4
1 2 3 4 5 6 7 8 9 10 11
6 7 8 9 10 11 12 13 14 15 16 17 18
13 14 15 16 17 18 19 20 21 22 23 24 25
20 21 22 23 24 25 26 27 28 29 30 31
27 28 29 30 31
SEP
S M T W T F S
1
1 2 3 4 5 6 7 8
3 4 5 6 7 8 9 10 11 12 13 14 15
10 11 12 13 14 15 16 17 18 19 20 21 22
17 18 19 20 21 22 23 24 25 26 27 28 29
24 25 26 27 28 29 30
OCT
S M T W T F S
1 2 3 4 5 6
1 2 3 4 5 6 7 8 9 10 11 12 13
8 9 10 11 12 13 14 15 16 17 18 19 20
15 16 17 18 19 20 21 22 23 24 25 26 27
22 23 24 25 26 27 28 29 30 31
29 30 31
NOV
S M T W T F S
1 2 3
1 2 3 4 5 6 7 8 9 10
5 6 7 8 9 10 11 12 13 14 15 16 17
12 13 14 15 16 17 18 19 20 21 22 23 24
19 20 21 22 23 24 25 26 27 28 29 30
26 27 28 29 30
DEC
S M T W T F S
1
1 2 3 4 5 6 7 8
3 4 5 6 7 8 9 10 11 12 13 14 15
10 11 12 13 14 15 16 17 18 19 20 21 22
17 18 19 20 21 22 23 24 25 26 27 28 29
24 25 26 27 28 29 30 31
31

Figure 8-1c: Leap year side of the double-sided slider for the full-year calendar

Cut along this line

All headings above the numbers are for reference only.

JAN LEAP YEAR
S M T W T F S
1
1 2 3 4 5 6 7 8
3 4 5 6 7 8 9 10 11 12 13 14 15
10 11 12 13 14 15 16 17 18 19 20 21 22
17 18 19 20 21 22 23 24 25 26 27 28 29
24 25 26 27 28 29 30 31
31

FEB LEAP YEAR
S M T W T F S
1 2 3 4 5
1 2 3 4 5 6 7 8 9 10 11 12
7 8 9 10 11 12 13 14 15 16 17 18 19
14 15 16 17 18 19 20 21 22 23 24 25 26
21 22 23 24 25 26 27 28 29
28 29

JAN COMMON YEAR
S M T W T F S
1 2 3 4 5 6 7
2 3 4 5 6 7 8 9 10 11 12 13 14
9 10 11 12 13 14 15 16 17 18 19 20 21
16 17 18 19 20 21 22 23 24 25 26 27 28
23 24 25 26 27 28 29 30 31
30 31

FEB COMMON YEAR
S M T W T F S
1 2 3 4
1 2 3 4 5 6 7 8 9 10 11
6 7 8 9 10 11 12 13 14 15 16 17 18
13 14 15 16 17 18 19 20 21 22 23 24 25
20 21 22 23 24 25 26 27 28
27 28

MAR
S M T W T F S
1 2 3 4
1 2 3 4 5 6 7 8 9 10 11
6 7 8 9 10 11 12 13 14 15 16 17 18
13 14 15 16 17 18 19 20 21 22 23 24 25
20 21 22 23 24 25 26 27 28 29 30 31
27 28 29 30 31

APR
S M T W T F S
1
1 2 3 4 5 6 7 8
3 4 5 6 7 8 9 10 11 12 13 14 15
10 11 12 13 14 15 16 17 18 19 20 21 22
17 18 19 20 21 22 23 24 25 26 27 28 29
24 25 26 27 28 29 30

MAY
S M T W T F S
1 2 3 4 5 6
1 2 3 4 5 6 7 8 9 10 11 12 13
8 9 10 11 12 13 14 15 16 17 18 19 20
15 16 17 18 19 20 21 22 23 24 25 26 27
22 23 24 25 26 27 28 29 30 31
29 30 31

JUNE
S M T W T F S
1 2 3
1 2 3 4 5 6 7 8 9 10
5 6 7 8 9 10 11 12 13 14 15 16 17
12 13 14 15 16 17 18 19 20 21 22 23 24
19 20 21 22 23 24 25 26 27 28 29 30
26 27 28 29 30

JULY
S M T W T F S
1
1 2 3 4 5 6 7 8
3 4 5 6 7 8 9 10 11 12 13 14 15
10 11 12 13 14 15 16 17 18 19 20 21 22
17 18 19 20 21 22 23 24 25 26 27 28 29
24 25 26 27 28 29 30 31
31

AUG
S M T W T F S
1 2 3 4 5
1 2 3 4 5 6 7 8 9 10 11 12
7 8 9 10 11 12 13 14 15 16 17 18 19
14 15 16 17 18 19 20 21 22 23 24 25 26
21 22 23 24 25 26 27 28 29 30 31
28 29 30 31

SEP
S M T W T F S
1 2
1 2 3 4 5 6 7 8 9
4 5 6 7 8 9 10 11 12 13 14 15 16
11 12 13 14 15 16 17 18 19 20 21 22 23
18 19 20 21 22 23 24 25 26 27 28 29 30
25 26 27 28 29 30

Cut along bottom line

OCT
S M T W T F S
1 2 3 4 5 6 7
2 3 4 5 6 7 8 9 10 11 12 13 14
9 10 11 12 13 14 15 16 17 18 19 20 21
16 17 18 19 20 21 22 23 24 25 26 27 28
23 24 25 26 27 28 29 30 31
30 31

NOV
S M T W T F S
1 2 3 4
1 2 3 4 5 6 7 8 9 10 11
6 7 8 9 10 11 12 13 14 15 16 17 18
13 14 15 16 17 18 19 20 21 22 23 24 25
20 21 22 23 24 25 26 27 28 29 30
27 28 29 30

DEC
S M T W T F S
1 2
1 2 3 4 5 6 7 8 9
4 5 6 7 8 9 10 11 12 13 14 15 16
11 12 13 14 15 16 17 18 19 20 21 22 23
18 19 20 21 22 23 24 25 26 27 28 29 30
25 26 27 28 29 30 31

Figure 8-2a: Slider for the single-sided slider full-year calendar

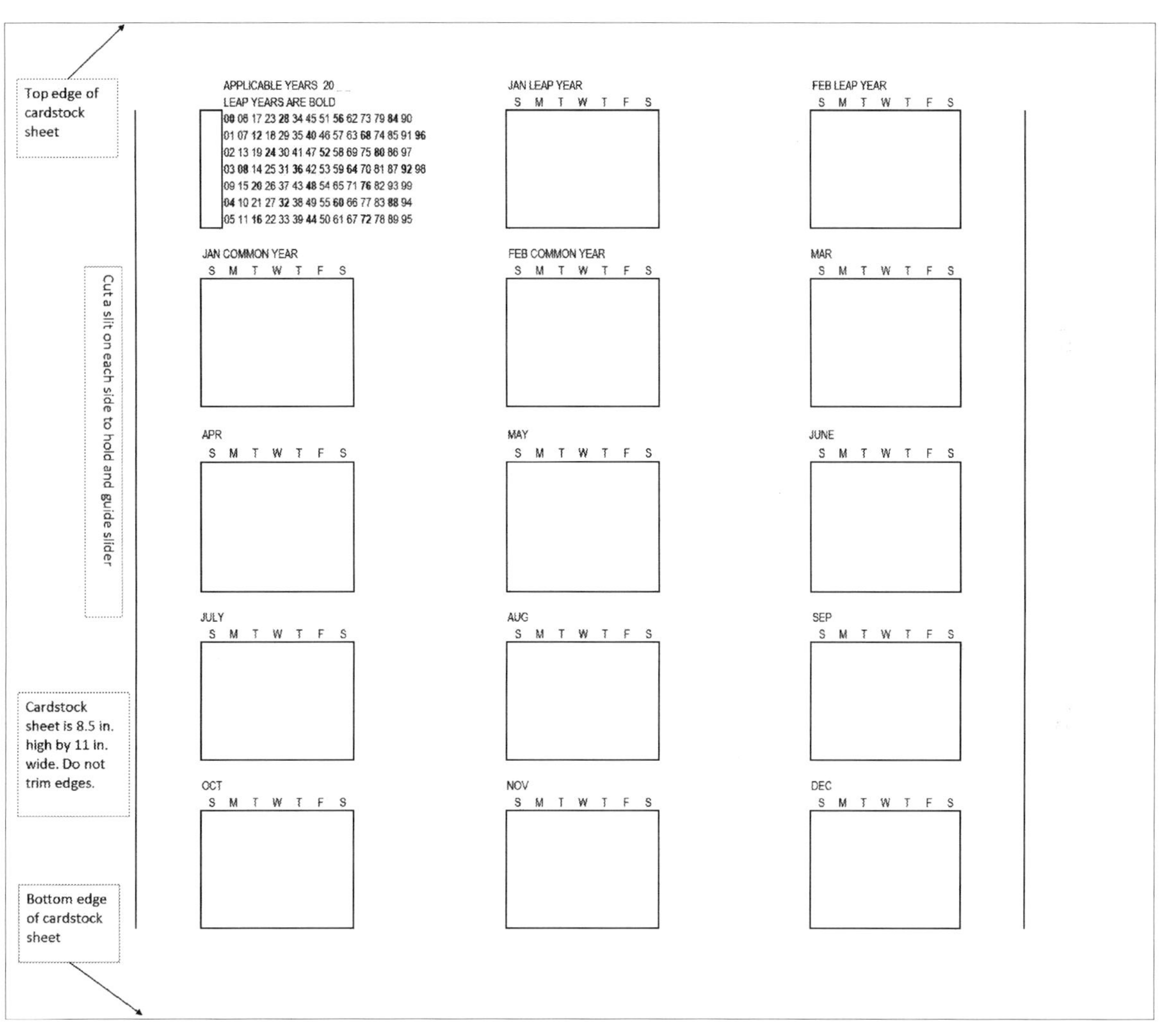
Top edge of cardstock sheet
APPLICABLE YEARS 20__
LEAP YEARS ARE BOLD
**00** 06 17 23 **28** 34 45 51 **56** 62 73 79 **84** 90
01 07 **12** 18 29 35 **40** 46 57 63 **68** 74 85 91 **96**
02 13 19 **24** 30 41 47 **52** 58 69 75 **80** 86 97
03 **08** 14 25 31 **36** 42 53 59 **64** 70 81 87 **92** 98
09 15 **20** 26 37 43 **48** 54 65 71 **76** 82 93 99
**04** 10 21 27 **32** 38 49 55 **60** 66 77 83 **88** 94
05 11 **16** 22 33 39 **44** 50 61 67 **72** 78 89 95
JAN LEAP YEAR
S M T W T F S
FEB LEAP YEAR
S M T W T F S
JAN COMMON YEAR
S M T W T F S
FEB COMMON YEAR
S M T W T F S
MAR
S M T W T F S
Cut a slit on each side to hold and guide slider
APR
S M T W T F S
MAY
S M T W T F S
JUNE
S M T W T F S
JULY
S M T W T F S
AUG
S M T W T F S
SEP
S M T W T F S
Cardstock sheet is 8.5 in. high by 11 in. wide. Do not trim edges.
OCT
S M T W T F S
NOV
S M T W T F S
DEC
S M T W T F S
Bottom edge of cardstock sheet

Figure 8-2b: Face of the full-year calendar with a single-sided slider

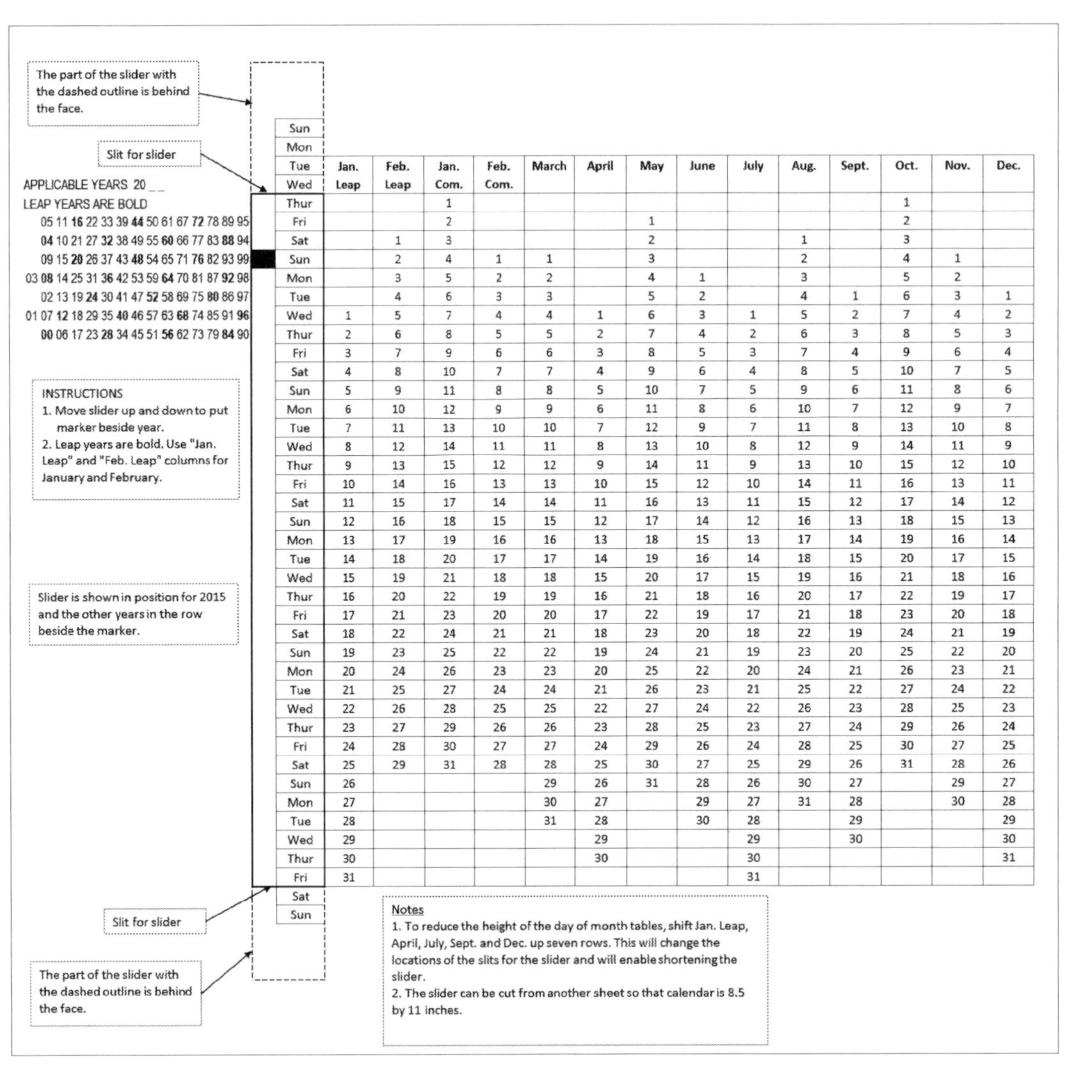
The part of the slider with the dashed outline is behind the face.
Slit for slider
APPLICABLE YEARS 20 _ _
LEAP YEARS ARE BOLD
05 11 **16** 22 33 39 **44** 50 61 67 **72** 78 89 95
**04** 10 21 27 **32** 38 49 55 **60** 66 77 83 **88** 94
09 15 **20** 26 37 43 **48** 54 65 71 **76** 82 93 99
03 **08** 14 25 31 **36** 42 53 59 **64** 70 81 87 **92** 98
02 13 19 **24** 30 41 47 **52** 58 69 75 **80** 86 97
01 07 **12** 18 29 35 **40** 46 57 63 **68** 74 85 91 **96**
**00** 06 17 23 **28** 34 45 51 **56** 62 73 79 **84** 90
INSTRUCTIONS
1. Move slider up and down to put marker beside year.
2. Leap years are bold. Use "Jan. Leap" and "Feb. Leap" columns for January and February.
Slider is shown in position for 2015 and the other years in the row beside the marker.
Sun
Mon
Slit for slider
The part of the slider with the dashed outline is behind the face.
Notes
1. To reduce the height of the day of month tables, shift Jan. Leap, April, July, Sept. and Dec. up seven rows. This will change the locations of the slits for the slider and will enable shortening the slider.
2. The slider can be cut from another sheet so that calendar is 8.5 by 11 inches.

| Tue | Jan. Leap | Feb. Leap | Jan. Com. | Feb. Com. | March | April | May | June | July | Aug. | Sept. | Oct. | Nov. | Dec. |
|---|---|---|---|---|---|---|---|---|---|---|---|---|---|---|
| Wed | | | | | | | | | | | | | | |
| Thur | | | 1 | | | | | | | | | 1 | | |
| Fri | | | 2 | | | | 1 | | | | | 2 | | |
| Sat | | 1 | 3 | | | | 2 | | | 1 | | 3 | | |
| Sun | | 2 | 4 | 1 | 1 | | 3 | | | 2 | | 4 | 1 | |
| Mon | | 3 | 5 | 2 | 2 | | 4 | 1 | | 3 | | 5 | 2 | |
| Tue | | 4 | 6 | 3 | 3 | | 5 | 2 | | 4 | 1 | 6 | 3 | 1 |
| Wed | 1 | 5 | 7 | 4 | 4 | 1 | 6 | 3 | 1 | 5 | 2 | 7 | 4 | 2 |
| Thur | 2 | 6 | 8 | 5 | 5 | 2 | 7 | 4 | 2 | 6 | 3 | 8 | 5 | 3 |
| Fri | 3 | 7 | 9 | 6 | 6 | 3 | 8 | 5 | 3 | 7 | 4 | 9 | 6 | 4 |
| Sat | 4 | 8 | 10 | 7 | 7 | 4 | 9 | 6 | 4 | 8 | 5 | 10 | 7 | 5 |
| Sun | 5 | 9 | 11 | 8 | 8 | 5 | 10 | 7 | 5 | 9 | 6 | 11 | 8 | 6 |
| Mon | 6 | 10 | 12 | 9 | 9 | 6 | 11 | 8 | 6 | 10 | 7 | 12 | 9 | 7 |
| Tue | 7 | 11 | 13 | 10 | 10 | 7 | 12 | 9 | 7 | 11 | 8 | 13 | 10 | 8 |
| Wed | 8 | 12 | 14 | 11 | 11 | 8 | 13 | 10 | 8 | 12 | 9 | 14 | 11 | 9 |
| Thur | 9 | 13 | 15 | 12 | 12 | 9 | 14 | 11 | 9 | 13 | 10 | 15 | 12 | 10 |
| Fri | 10 | 14 | 16 | 13 | 13 | 10 | 15 | 12 | 10 | 14 | 11 | 16 | 13 | 11 |
| Sat | 11 | 15 | 17 | 14 | 14 | 11 | 16 | 13 | 11 | 15 | 12 | 17 | 14 | 12 |
| Sun | 12 | 16 | 18 | 15 | 15 | 12 | 17 | 14 | 12 | 16 | 13 | 18 | 15 | 13 |
| Mon | 13 | 17 | 19 | 16 | 16 | 13 | 18 | 15 | 13 | 17 | 14 | 19 | 16 | 14 |
| Tue | 14 | 18 | 20 | 17 | 17 | 14 | 19 | 16 | 14 | 18 | 15 | 20 | 17 | 15 |
| Wed | 15 | 19 | 21 | 18 | 18 | 15 | 20 | 17 | 15 | 19 | 16 | 21 | 18 | 16 |
| Thur | 16 | 20 | 22 | 19 | 19 | 16 | 21 | 18 | 16 | 20 | 17 | 22 | 19 | 17 |
| Fri | 17 | 21 | 23 | 20 | 20 | 17 | 22 | 19 | 17 | 21 | 18 | 23 | 20 | 18 |
| Sat | 18 | 22 | 24 | 21 | 21 | 18 | 23 | 20 | 18 | 22 | 19 | 24 | 21 | 19 |
| Sun | 19 | 23 | 25 | 22 | 22 | 19 | 24 | 21 | 19 | 23 | 20 | 25 | 22 | 20 |
| Mon | 20 | 24 | 26 | 23 | 23 | 20 | 25 | 22 | 20 | 24 | 21 | 26 | 23 | 21 |
| Tue | 21 | 25 | 27 | 24 | 24 | 21 | 26 | 23 | 21 | 25 | 22 | 27 | 24 | 22 |
| Wed | 22 | 26 | 28 | 25 | 25 | 22 | 27 | 24 | 22 | 26 | 23 | 28 | 25 | 23 |
| Thur | 23 | 27 | 29 | 26 | 26 | 23 | 28 | 25 | 23 | 27 | 24 | 29 | 26 | 24 |
| Fri | 24 | 28 | 30 | 27 | 27 | 24 | 29 | 26 | 24 | 28 | 25 | 30 | 27 | 25 |
| Sat | 25 | 29 | 31 | 28 | 28 | 25 | 30 | 27 | 25 | 29 | 26 | 31 | 28 | 26 |
| Sun | 26 | | | | 29 | 26 | 31 | 28 | 26 | 30 | 27 | | 29 | 27 |
| Mon | 27 | | | | 30 | 27 | | 29 | 27 | 31 | 28 | | 30 | 28 |
| Tue | 28 | | | | 31 | 28 | | 30 | 28 | | 29 | | | 29 |
| Wed | 29 | | | | | 29 | | | 29 | | 30 | | | 30 |
| Thur | 30 | | | | | 30 | | | 30 | | | | | 31 |
| Fri | 31 | | | | | | | | 31 | | | | | |
| Sat | | | | | | | | | | | | | | |
| Sun | | | | | | | | | | | | | | |

Slider

Sun
Mon
Tue
Wed
Thur
Fri
Sat
Sun
Mon
Tue
Wed
Thur
Fri
Sat
Sun
Mon
Tue
Wed
Thur
Fri
Sat
Sun
Mon
Tue
Wed
Thur
Fri
Sat
Sun
Mon
Tue
Wed
Thur
Fri
Sat
Sun
Mon
Tue
Wed
Thur
Fri
Sat
Sun

Figure 8-3: Vertical full-year perpetual calendar

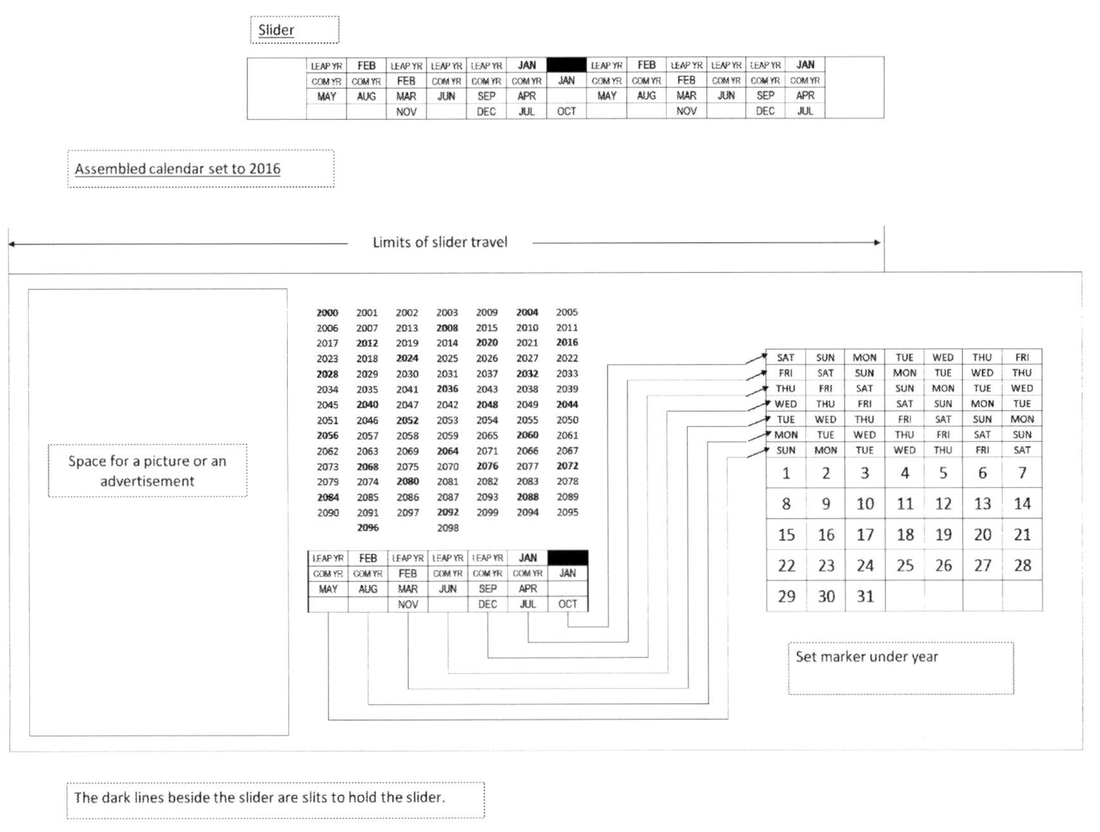
Slider
LEAP YR FEB LEAP YR LEAP YR LEAP YR JAN LEAP YR FEB LEAP YR LEAP YR LEAP YR JAN
COM YR COM YR FEB COM YR COM YR COM YR JAN COM YR COM YR FEB COM YR COM YR COM YR
MAY AUG MAR JUN SEP APR MAY AUG MAR JUN SEP APR
NOV DEC JUL OCT NOV DEC JUL
Assembled calendar set to 2016
Limits of slider travel
Space for a picture or an advertisement
2000 2001 2002 2003 2009 2004 2005
2006 2007 2013 2008 2015 2010 2011
2017 2012 2019 2014 2020 2021 2016
2023 2018 2024 2025 2026 2027 2022
2028 2029 2030 2031 2037 2032 2033
2034 2035 2041 2036 2043 2038 2039
2045 2040 2047 2042 2048 2049 2044
2051 2046 2052 2053 2054 2055 2050
2056 2057 2058 2059 2065 2060 2061
2062 2063 2069 2064 2071 2066 2067
2073 2068 2075 2070 2076 2077 2072
2079 2074 2080 2081 2082 2083 2078
2084 2085 2086 2087 2093 2088 2089
2090 2091 2097 2092 2099 2094 2095
2096 2098
LEAP YR FEB LEAP YR LEAP YR LEAP YR JAN
COM YR COM YR FEB COM YR COM YR COM YR JAN
MAY AUG MAR JUN SEP APR
NOV DEC JUL OCT
SAT SUN MON TUE WED THU FRI
FRI SAT SUN MON TUE WED THU
THU FRI SAT SUN MON TUE WED
WED THU FRI SAT SUN MON TUE
TUE WED THU FRI SAT SUN MON
MON TUE WED THU FRI SAT SUN
SUN MON TUE WED THU FRI SAT
1 2 3 4 5 6 7
8 9 10 11 12 13 14
15 16 17 18 19 20 21
22 23 24 25 26 27 28
29 30 31
Set marker under year
The dark lines beside the slider are slits to hold the slider.

Figure 8-4a: Single day-of-month table full-year calendar with a horizontal slider

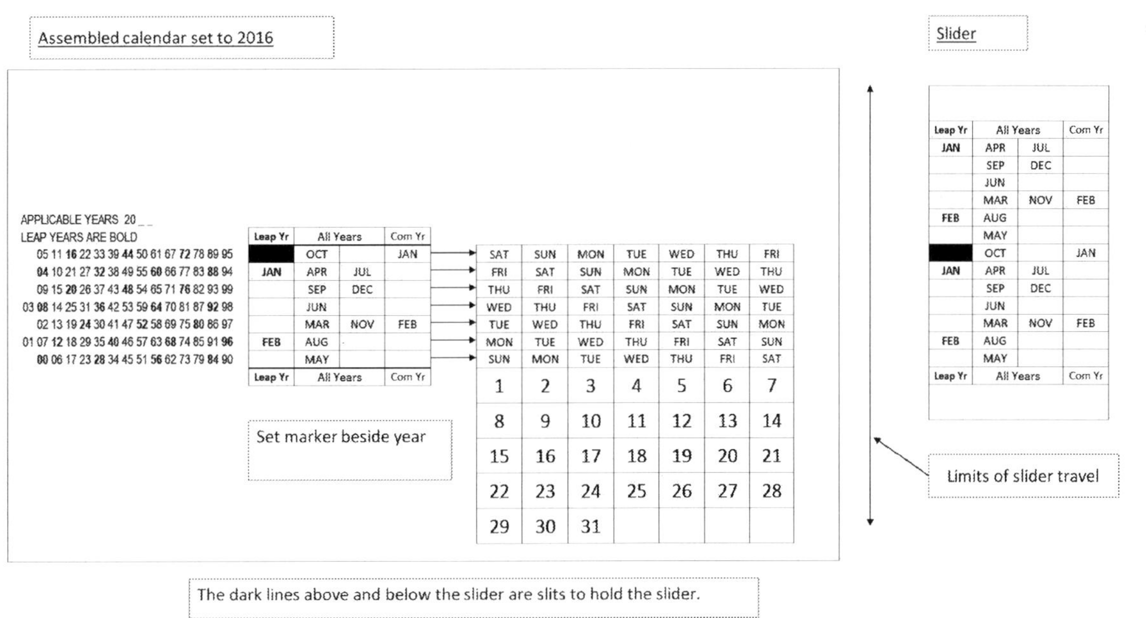
Assembled calendar set to 2016
Slider
APPLICABLE YEARS 20 _ _
LEAP YEARS ARE BOLD
05 11 16 22 33 39 44 50 61 67 72 78 89 95
04 10 21 27 32 38 49 55 60 66 77 83 88 94
09 15 20 26 37 43 48 54 65 71 76 82 93 99
03 08 14 25 31 36 42 53 59 64 70 81 87 92 98
02 13 19 24 30 41 47 52 58 69 75 80 86 97
01 07 12 18 29 35 40 46 57 63 68 74 85 91 96
00 06 17 23 28 34 45 51 56 62 73 79 84 90
Leap Yr All Years Com Yr
OCT JAN
JAN APR JUL
SEP DEC
JUN
MAR NOV FEB
FEB AUG
MAY
Leap Yr All Years Com Yr
SAT SUN MON TUE WED THU FRI
FRI SAT SUN MON TUE WED THU
THU FRI SAT SUN MON TUE WED
WED THU FRI SAT SUN MON TUE
TUE WED THU FRI SAT SUN MON
MON TUE WED THU FRI SAT SUN
SUN MON TUE WED THU FRI SAT
1 2 3 4 5 6 7
8 9 10 11 12 13 14
15 16 17 18 19 20 21
22 23 24 25 26 27 28
29 30 31
Set marker beside year
Limits of slider travel
The dark lines above and below the slider are slits to hold the slider.

Figure 8-4b: Single day-of-month table full-year calendar with a vertical slider

# CHAPTER 9

# APPLICATIONS AND PRODUCTS SUMMARY

## General

The perpetual calendars described in Chapters 5 to 8 include all types, from small pocket calendars to large wall planners. Unlike presently available perpetual calendars, which either are difficult to read or require reference to another calendar to set, these are stand-alone and look almost the same as a conventional calendar. Except in applications where a calendar is written on during the year, my calendars can replace all in use with one that is more environmentally friendly and useful. Widespread adoption of the designs and concepts in *Practical Perpetual Calendars* would eliminate the wasteful and inconvenient practice of throwing away billions of calendars every year because they are no longer of any use. The ideas herein can be adopted to make low-cost perpetual calendars from paper and cardstock that wear out in 5 to 20 years, and to make pieces of art from more durable materials that can last a century. Buying a calendar can become more like buying a durable product such as a watch and less like buying a consumable such as printer paper.

All of the calendars in *Practical Perpetual Calendars* are based on four basic types: (1) single-sheet perpetual calendars, (2) multisheet perpetual calendars with a year table on each sheet, (3) multisheet perpetual calendars with a single year table and (4) full-year perpetual calendars. These types can be made into attractive products for markets that include the following:

- advertisers
- office supply stores and large retail stores
- specialty stores and gift shops
- promotional merchandise
- fundraisers
- craft kits

The following sections identify in general terms the designs that might be attractive to diverse markets.

I believe that many of the calendar designs described in *Practical Perpetual Calendars* have tremendous potential for high sales volume. However, most of them need some refinement to make them pleasing and to make the manufacturing process easy, and they all need to be marketed in such a way to convince consumers that a practical perpetual calendar is a valuable and useful product.

## Products for Advertisers

The designs most attractive to advertisers are calendars made from cardstock that can replace the calendars they presently give away. Although a perpetual calendar may initially cost more than a conventional one, the longer life results in a considerably lower cost per year. Calendars purchased and not given away do not become obsolete and are available for distribution anytime. The type of calendar most suitable to a particular organization depends on what they are presently distributing and their budget.

Many organizations give away desk calendars. For a versatile low-cost calendar, there is nothing equal to the basic single-slider tent calendar shown in Figures 5-1a to 5-1d. The calendars shown in Figures 5-2a and 5-2b are similar. Organizations that presently give away multisheet calendars would find the multisheet calendars with a year table on each sheet attractive replacements. The flip-down-window type in Figures 6-1a and 6-1b is very similar to the common multisheet tent desk calendar bound with Wire-O. Other than the window, the construction is identical. The lift-out-pad calendar shown in Figure 6-2 is fairly similar and may be easier for some suppliers to manufacture. A lower-cost alternative is the seven-column multisheet calendar with a single year table shown in Figures 7-6a to 7-6c.

Since perpetual calendars last many years, advertisers may want to give away ones that enable their customers to add their favourite photo. The calendars shown in Figures 5-6a and 5-6b are low-cost options for this. Two other options are the multisheet calendars with a single year table in Figures 7-2 and 7-3. Calendars with provision for adding a user's photo can come with a picture that the photo can cover. Figures 5-10a, 5-11, 5-12, 7-4 and 7-5 also show calendars that can hold photos. However, the cost of these may be too high for calendars that are given away in large quantities.

A low-cost alternative to a desk calendar is a pocket calendar or a bookmark calendar, as shown in Figures 5-3a to 5-3e and 5-4, respectively. The full-year calendar in Figure 8-2 is also a reasonably low-cost alternative to a desk calendar. Since many customers may prefer a desk calendar or a pocket calendar, companies may not want to have only full-year calendars to give away.

Wall calendars are given away in as large or larger numbers as desk calendars. There will always be a high demand for wall calendars that can be written on. The only perpetual calendars in *Practical Perpetual Calendars* that can be easily built into a holder that has sheets for notes are the ones shown in Figures 5-16a and 5-16b. As they have a nonstandard format, they may not have wide appeal. Therefore, conventional calendars may be the best choice when calendars have to be written on. Figures 6-4 to 6-7 (a and b) show various concepts for making permanent wall calendars. The cost of these calendars is estimated to be about one and a half times the cost of conventional ones of the same size.

An application where a perpetual wall calendar offers considerable advantage over a conventional one is when the calendar has a large amount of timeless information printed on it. One year, I was a member of a group that made a special calendar that was given away to seniors. Considerable effort was put into listing important telephone numbers, and providing tips for each month. At the end of the year, the calendar expired, but the information was still valid. If this calendar had had a clip-on window as in Figure 6-5, or a window on each sheet as in Figures 6-7a and 6-7b, it would have had a life of at least five years.

## Products for Office Supply Stores and Large Retail Stores

Perpetual calendars are ideal items for office supply stores and large retail stores to stock year-round. Some types to always keep in stock are the following:

- a range of desk calendars, including the basic single-slider tent calendars shown in Figures 5-1a to 5-1d, 5-2a and 5-2b, the multisheet calendars shown in Figures 6-1a, 6-1b and 6-2, and the seven-column multisheet calendar with a single year table shown in Figures 7-6a to 7-6c
- undated planners that include perpetual calendars
- pocket calendars and pocket notepads with a calendar on the inside of the cover, as in Figures 5-3a to 5-3e and 5-4
- full-year calendars for three-ring binders as in Figures 8-2a and 8-2b
- full-year wall calendars based on the concepts in Figures 8-2 and 8-2b or Figure 8-3
- perpetual wall calendars as in Figures 6-4 to 6-7 (a and b)

Wall planners based on the designs in Figures 5-14b, 5-15a and 5-15b, or 5-16a, could be stocked by office supply stores. Although these planners would eliminate the inconvenience of having to write the days of the month each month, they would be considerably more expensive and may not be competitive with the simple commercial roll-out wall chart.

These stores can also stock calendars that have provision for adding a photo, although some of these designs may be more suited to a specialty store or gift shop. Some stores may want to offer special-order calendars in large quantities for the buyer to give away for advertising and in small quantities for family use. These can be desk and wall calendars with the customer's photos. The wall calendars can have fixed dates added as in Figure 6-3. Special-order items for family use would be similar to what is presently available from photo labs.

The lowest-cost calendars are ones made from cardstock. However, for a desk calendar that has space for 100 years in its year table, there likely is a fair demand for this type of calendar to be made from more durable materials—and office supply stores may want to stock this type. A person could receive one of these calendars on his or her first day of work and pass it on to his or her successor 40 years later!

## Products for Specialty Stores and Gift Shops

Perpetual calendars that would be attractive to specialty stores and gift shops vary, from low-cost single-sheet calendars that would sell for not much more than a postcard to ornate holders for photos and keys that would cost up to $50. The lift-out-pad desk calendar in Figure 6-2 can be made with scenes from areas near a gift shop. The wall calendars in Figures 6-4 to 6-7 (a and b) can also be made with local scenes. Variations of the hybrid calendar in Figure 5-17a would be attractive to gift shops that already sell similar items. The designs for key holders in Figures 5-7a, 5-7b and 7-1d could be adapted to make stands for block and similar calendars that display a number for the day of the month, along with the month and the day of the week. The clocks in Figures 5-8 and 5-9 would also be attractive products for gift shops.

## Promotional Merchandise

Desk, pocket and wall calendars given away for advertising can be considered promotional merchandise. Many people would be happy to receive one of them, rather than another pen or mug. Promotional items such as binders, water bottles, t-shirts and tote bags cost more than simple paper or cardstock calendars. Some possible substitutes for these products are as follows:

- binders and notepads that include a perpetual calendar (Figures 5-3a and 5-3b, and 8-2a and 8-2b)
- pencil holders (Figure 5-5)
- key holders mass-produced from plastic (Figures 5-7a, 5-7b and 7-1d)
- desk calendars mass-produced from plastic (Figures 5-1e, 5-2c and 6-2)
- photo holders (Figures 5-12 and 7-2 to 7-5)
- J-style wall calendars made in a small size and attached to a fridge magnet (Figure 7-2)
- clocks (Figures 5-8 and 5-9)

Receiving a perpetual calendar product that will be useful for many years will be much more satisfying than receiving something that you already have. Whether or not a product is inexpensive enough to be given away as a promotion is highly dependent on how many are produced and the materials used. A key holder made in small quantities from wood is much more expensive than one stamped out from plastic in large quantities.

Many vendors of low-cost promotional merchandise for advertising also sell more expensive products that are for special customers or for employee recognition. Many of the perpetual calendars listed in Chapters 5 to 8 can be made in more ornate versions for this market. The perpetual calendar may not be an exact replacement for a product presently on the market. One example is a hinged holder that has a photo on one side and a non-stand-alone perpetual calendar on the other. Although one of my perpetual calendars can be designed to fit almost any size photo frame, a more satisfactory replacement for this application may be a photo holder with a calendar below it, as in Figures 5-12, 7-2, 7-3, 7-4 and 7-5.

## Fundraisers

Perpetual calendars have the potential to be sold by organizations to raise funds. Over the next few years, as awareness of these unique and practical calendars increases, the market will expand and people will prefer to buy a low-cost perpetual desk calendar rather than another box of chocolate-covered almonds. The more expensive promotional items previously mentioned can also be sold for fundraising. In time, as more people acquire perpetual calendars, the market will decline and organizations may have to revert to selling consumable items.

## Craft Kits

Packaging a perpetual calendar product as a craft kit enables reducing the selling price, because the consumer will do the assembly that would have required additional labour expense at the factory. A craft kit can also provide a fun activity for the purchaser. Clocks, key holders, lamps, the hybrid calendar and some wall calendars can be made into craft kits.

## Types of Manufacturers

Perpetual calendars for different markets can be supplied by various sizes and types of manufacturers, including the following:

- large manufacturers and printers
- local print shops
- small craft shops

The following sections identify, in general terms, the markets that may be attractive to these manufacturers and the products they might supply.

## Large Manufacturers and Printers

Large manufacturers and printers can easily justify the design and setup costs to make almost any type of calendar for all of the various markets. The products that will be attractive to them depend on their capabilities (printing on cardstock, or making products from plastic and other materials), the development costs and their perception of the potential market. Large printers can supply large quantities to national companies, and smaller quantities to companies that order online. Some are also able to supply custom orders to consumers, such as calendars with family photos on them.

The markets that have the most potential for large manufacturers and printers are advertising, office supply stores and large retail stores, and promotional merchandise. Depending on their present customer base, the large manufacturer may not be interested in all of these markets.

## Local Print Shops

The market with the most potential for local print shops is advertising, especially producing calendars for present customers. Barriers for local print shops include setup costs to make special dies, machines to fold and, for some shops, something as basic as a machine to do Wire-O binding. These barriers can be overcome by selecting designs that require a minimum amount of special fabrication or by contracting out specialized work, or both. Shops that are a franchise may be able to get assistance with development from their head office, which can spread these costs among many small printers.

## Small Craft Shops

The market with the most potential for small craft shops is specialty stores and gift shops. They can also market their products themselves through farmers' markets and online venues. Some small craft shops may be interested in making calendars from cardstock, but most would make ones that have some wood or other rigid material in them. Products suitable for these shops include the following:

- pencil holders (Figure 5-5)
- table lamps (Figure 5-5; use the same calendar as for a pencil holder)
- table lamps (Figures 5-16a and 5-16b; use single-slider vertical perpetual calendar)
- key holders (Figures 5-7a, 5-7b and 7-1d)
- desk calendars (Figures 5-1e, 5-2b and 6-2)
- photo holders (Figures 5-12, 7-2, 7-3, 7-4 and 7-5)
- clocks (Figures 5-8 and 5-9)
- hybrid calendars (Figure 5-17a; make a new product or enhance a present product)
- block calendars (Figure 5-18, make a new product or enhance a present product)
- lift-out-pad desk calendars (Figure 6-2)
- lift-out-pad wall calendars (Figure 6-6)
- flip-sheet desk calendars (Figure 6-8)
- wooden frame desk calendars (Figure 7-4)
- full-year wall calendar (Figures 8-2a and 8-2b, with construction ideas from Figures 5-1e and 5-2b)
- vertical full-year wall calendar (Figure 8-3)

Shops that presently manufacture non-stand-alone perpetual calendars would find adding the perpetual feature in Figure 5-17a to an existing product attractive. Adding some of the other calendar designs to their product line should not be a particularly risky move. Shops that presently do not manufacture non-stand-alone perpetual calendars may be reluctant to try making a new product. However, the potential market is very large and they may be missing a good opportunity if they do not put a small amount of effort into developing a product that would be attractive to their existing customer base.

One characteristic of perpetual calendars that may discourage small craft shops is that there is a great deal of printing required. The year table, month table and day-of-month table (or calendar sheets) all have to be printed. Some shops may want to limit their product line to designs that require them to do a minimum amount of printing. The desk calendar in Figure 6-2 would be attractive to them. They can make the holder and have the calendar pad made by a local print shop. Alternatively, they can make the pad on their own printer. The only printing required on the holder are the abbreviations for the days of the week (SMTWTFS) above the window. This can be done by hand, with a stencil or by gluing the letters on. If the first letter is used for the days of the week, there are no letters, such as an *A*, that cannot be fully made with a stencil.

## Printing on Wood

Where there is more to print than a person would like to hand-letter, the figures in the previous chapters suggest printing on cardstock or paper and then gluing to the wood or hardboard. After the glue is dry, the cardstock or paper can be coated with clear lacquer. This is simple and should be satisfactory for many applications. For other applications, printing on wood may be preferred. This can be done by printing a reverse image on transfer paper and then following the manufacturer's instructions for transferring to wood. More information on how to transfer an image to wood can be found by doing an Internet search with the term "how to print on wood with transfer paper" or "how to print on wood." There are various methods that do not require commercial transfer paper. However, be aware that a laser printer cannot be used to print on wax paper or any heat-sensitive paper.

Word and Excel will not directly reverse an image. Some printers have this option. If your printer cannot do this, there are two ways to reverse an image before printing, as follows:

1. Use the Windows Accessories program Paint. Simply copy and paste what you want reversed into Paint. Then under "Rotate" in Paint, select "Flip horizontal." The image will then be reversed. It can be printed from Paint, saved in various formats or copied and pasted back into Excel.
2. Use "Flip horizontal" in Excel. The material to be reversed must be a picture. To make an Excel spreadsheet into a picture, copy the part desired and paste into a new spreadsheet. When pasting, paste as a picture. Then select the picture (if it is not already selected), and click "Picture Tools Format," "Rotate" and "Flip horizontal."

I have tried both methods using Excel 2016 and found they work equally well. I have also tried both methods using an older version of Excel and found that using Paint produces a clearer image.

Craft shops with the capability of laser engraving can make functional and ornate perpetual calendars by burning the tables into wood or other materials.

The discussion on how to print on wood, hardboard or other rigid materials shows that the process is not too difficult. The need to print should not discourage a small craft shop from adding perpetual calendars to its product line.

## Calendars for Home Projects

All of the calendars listed under the subheading *Small Craft Shops* can be made as home projects in single units or small quantities. The types suitable for an individual depend on that person's skill and the tools available. Local print and craft shops can produce parts of a calendar that are difficult for an individual to make. At the present time when perpetual calendars are unfamiliar to these shops, individuals will have to do detailed design themselves and adapt standard products to their needs. Batches of calendars to be sold to raise funds for organizations can be made as home projects.

## Creating a Job for Yourself

The most obvious way to create a job for yourself is to make perpetual calendars in a small craft shop. When I come across the term *small craft shop*, I imagine someone making products with his or her own tools in a small shop. Many people make a good living in this environment, but there are limitations on what can be made. Some limitations are the skill of the craftsperson, the tools available, the material options (often limited to wood) and the types of hardware, such as screws, that are available for purchase. An alternative to a small craft shop arrangement is the craftsperson as designer and assembler. In this arrangement, the craftsperson designs a product, an outside shop cuts and engraves the parts and the craftsperson assembles the product. The craftsperson needs creative and computer skills, but does not need specialized manual skills. The only special tool required is a computer, which is likely already available in the home for other purposes. With an outside shop doing specialized work, materials other than wood are an option, and parts that are difficult to make in a home shop may be available for a reasonable cost. Many of the calendar designs in *Practical Perpetual Calendars* could be made from plastic using this arrangement. One United States company that offers laser cutting and engraving to small craft shops is Ponoko (https://www.ponoko.com/). They also offer 3-D printing. Products that are assembled at home from parts made by outside shops can be listed for sale on Etsy (www.etsy.com).

A graphics designer may be able to create and then copyright designs for sale to print shops. As perpetual calendars using my concepts are not presently standard products for print shops, there may be a limited market. Another approach is to make a general design of a desk calendar or other product that would be attractive to many companies for advertising. No one company may ask for a large enough quantity to make a print shop interested in doing special setup work such as making dies. However, if you can find several companies that want calendars that differ only in the logos or pictures on them, you may find many print shops interested in doing the work. The cardstock calendars described herein are not much more difficult to make than presently available conventional calendars. For many designs, the setup costs are estimated to be $10,000, which would require a quantity of 10,000 or more to avoid having an excessive cost per calendar. As few as 10 companies might want this total quantity. Since perpetual calendars can be expected to last five years or longer, there should be a market for them at two to three times the cost of a conventional calendar. With large enough quantity, this will provide a good margin to offset setup costs and the costs of graphic design.

Someone who is skilled in both making crafts and writing could write a book for hobbyists on how to make practical perpetual calendars. The figures in Chapters 5 to 8 of *Practical Perpetual Calendars* can be expanded into detailed drawings of useful projects. To be attractive, a book would have to have both good artwork and photos of completed calendars. This may require six months to a year of work, but there may be a good market. There are many books on various crafts, which I assume have given the authors some return for their efforts, or at least personal satisfaction. Therefore, writing a book on practical perpetual calendars should be a worthwhile project. Two alternatives to writing a complete book are to write plans for individual calendars, or to prepare YouTube videos about how to make individual calendars. Presently, there are a few YouTube videos on how to make non-stand-alone block and tile calendars, so there should be some demand for practical stand-alone perpetual calendars. As I do not have any plans to write a craft book as a sequel to *Practical Perpetual Calendars*, I would be delighted if someone did so.

## Conclusion

Included within these pages is a large number of ideas and concepts for making practical perpetual calendars. I also suggest how to add these calendars to products such as key holders, clocks and photo frames. When writing *Practical Perpetual Calendars*, I tried to exclude ideas that are not technically sound, but I did not exclude ideas on the basis of other ideas being better. For example, the flip-down-window calendar in Figures 6-1a and 6-1b, the lift-out-pad calendar in Figure 6-2 and the seven-column calendar in Figures 7-6a to 7-6c are all presented as alternatives to the conventional multisheet tent desk calendar. Each of these has advantages and disadvantages. I feel that the person making a perpetual calendar is in a better position to discard an idea than I am.

I hope that all readers have enjoyed learning more about perpetual calendars and that some readers will use the concepts presented herein to make practical perpetual calendars for their own use and for the use of others.

# APPENDIX

# HISTORY, PATENTS AND MANUFACTURED PERPETUAL CALENDARS

## History

This section provides a brief history of the work that I did to develop the practical perpetual calendar concepts described herein. The purpose of this history is to help readers understand the design process, and to provide insight into why some design decisions were made. Readers who are interested in a history of calendars can consult Further Reading and Annotated References, which follow this Appendix.

As I recall, I first thought of the 13-column day-of-month table calendar concept with a window that displays 7 columns in the fall of 1989. This is the basic building block shown in Table 3-1. As stated in the Introduction, the *Oxford Dictionaries* definition of a perpetual calendar is "a calendar in which the day, the month and the date are adjusted independently to show any combination of the three." If some tags or tiles for month to indicate the year were used with this building block, the resulting combination would fit this definition.

At that time, I was aware of the following two perpetual calendars that display a full month:

1. The common type, where tiles numbered 1 to 31 are arranged each month.
2. A type that has seven columns that are snapped together in the appropriate arrangement each month. The first column piece has the numbers 1, 8, 15, 22 and 29; the second has the numbers 2, 9, 16, 23 and 30; and so forth. This is the same concept as shown in Figures 5-15 (a and b) and 5-17a. The one that I had seen was made in limited quantities from plastic and given away for advertising.

My original concept, which is used in many calendars in *Practical Perpetual Calendars*, has a fixed window in the centre of the face to display the applicable 7 columns of the 13-column day-of-month table. On each side of the window, there is a panel to hide the parts of the table that do not apply to the current setting. Up to 6 columns have to be hidden on each side of the window. Therefore, the face has to be 19 columns wide, plus borders. My 13-column concept with a fixed 7-column window has the advantage over the two calendars that I was aware of in that this type of calendar can be set by simply moving a slider. It has the disadvantage that the face is 19 columns wide plus borders, compared to 7 columns wide plus borders for the others. The wide face is an inherent characteristic of most of the calendars in this book. The width of the face can be reduced to 13 columns plus borders by having the window move instead of the day-of-month table. Many of the calendars in Chapter 6 use this construction. With the exception of the 7-column multisheet calendars in Table 4-14 and Figures 7-6a to 7-6c, all of my calendars have a face width of either 13 or 19 columns plus borders. The width of the face of all of my calendars can be reduced to seven columns plus borders by having the day-of-month table made from thin material that can be rolled up. I never pursued this concept since it has a more complicated construction.

With the basic concept in place, I looked at ways of making a product. I have forgotten what ideas I had for the month display, but I might have considered having a list of months on the face and putting a peg in a hole beside the current month. One area that I gave some thought to was how to hide 29, 30 and 31 when these numbers were not applicable. I could not think of a simple, satisfactory solution. At this point in the development, I believed that being able to hide these numbers was very important. Now, after making the calendar stand-alone, I do not give much importance to hiding single numbers, especially when I have multisheet designs for which this is not an issue.

During the 1990s, I did not spend much time on my calendar. I picked it up again in the early 2000s, and developed a full-year calendar that was similar to the double-sided slider full-year calendar in Figures 8-1a to 8-1c, but it did not have year indication. I made a 12-window prototype that would fit in a 3-ring binder. Even without year indication, this prototype had some merit. At this point, I stopped working on perpetual calendars for 5 or 10 years.

In January 2012, I decided to spend one month working on perpetual calendars again. This turned out to be a 5-year project requiring approximately 400 hours each year. Initially, I worked on lookup tables so that the calendars I had previously developed would be stand-alone. I also gave some thought to being able to hide 29, 30 and 31, which I still considered important.

Figure A-1 shows one of my early attempts at lookup tables. The face has one table for common years and another for leap years. When you know what day of the week January 1 falls on, you can look in one of the tables and find the day of the week for the first of any other month. These tables were to be accompanied by a year table, which would indicate which day of the week January 1 fell on for the entire century. The year table could possibly have been placed on the back of the calendar, with some way of indicating on the front which day of the week January 1 fell on.

Figure A-2 shows an early version of the single-sheet perpetual calendar with dual-slider configuration. The month slider was derived from the slider in the 12-window prototype of a full-year calendar. The number *1* for the first of each month is replaced with a marker, and all the other numbers were deleted. With 12 windows to display a marker for each month, the face is quite large.

Within about six weeks of developing the early version in Figure A-2, I had a dual-slider configuration similar to the one in Table 3-6b. However, it had a common year table on one side of the window and a leap year table on the other side. The concept in Table 3-8 of having March to December the same for common years and leap years did not come until later in 2012. Figure A-3 shows the state of the dual-slider design in October 2012.

By early December 2012, I had a prototype for the fold-down moving-slider pocket calendar shown in Figure 5-3d. This calendar uses the single-slider concept shown in Tables 3-11 and 3-12, which is also used in the tent desk calendar shown in Figure 5-1a and many other designs. I am uncertain whether the pocket calendar or the desk calendar came first.

At about the same time, I made the first prototype of the multisheet perpetual calendar with a single year table. The early prototypes had an end stop to line up the month sheets with the applicable year column. Six months to a year elapsed before I decided that lining up a marker on each sheet with the year column would be as good or better than an end stop, and much easier to make. Continuing refinement resulted in the concepts described in Chapter 4 and the designs in Chapter 7.

The first design of a full-year calendar with year indication had the last two digits of the year appear in a window. To set this calendar, the slider had to be moved from side to side until a column with the year of interest appeared in the window. This arrangement is not convenient, as the direction in which to move the slider is not obvious. The two final designs, as shown in Figures 8-1a to 8-1c and Figures 8-2a and 8-2b, have a year table on the face and a marker in the window.

In 2013, I began doing a small amount of marketing. The local tourist bureau expressed some interest in the J-style wall/desk calendar shown in Figure 7-2. I tried getting some quotes, but I was unable to obtain any because companies were reluctant to do an estimate for development and setup work when there was no assurance of an order. Today, four years later, the concepts have been refined, but the J-style and the other cardstock calendars in *Practical Perpetual Calendars* still require a small amount of development work before they are ready to roll off the press. Just as was needed then, what is needed now is someone who would like to purchase 10,000 calendars and is willing to spend \$0.50 to \$1.00 per unit on development and setup costs.

Many of the calendars in this book have an initial cost of \$5,000 to \$10,000 for a large production run. The single-slider tent calendar in Figure 5-1a has low setup costs for mass production. The calendars for small craft shops also have low setup costs. An advantage that small craft shops have is that they can charge a fairly high price for what consumers consider a piece of art.

Another marketing barrier is the fact that many individuals do not understand the term *perpetual calendar*. If they do, they envision a non-stand-alone perpetual calendar that is a piece of art, rather than a practical and useful office tool. Three years ago, I offered to give 100 custom-made single-slider tent calendars using the design in Figure 5-1a to a nature education society for sale in their gift shop. All I wanted in return was a charitable receipt for a gift-in-kind. The manager suggested that the calendars would not sell, saying that individuals can access a calendar on their cell phone. I did not rebut, but I noticed a multisheet tent calendar near the cash register. That calendar has now been replaced three times. Another society did agree to give me a charitable receipt in exchange for calendars. A tent calendar that uses the design in Figure 5-1a has been for sale in their gift shop for three years. It has not sold well because their gift shop experiences low traffic, and those who have seen it may not appreciate the calendar's usefulness and uniqueness. Having had one of those particular tent calendars on my desk for three years, I do not want to go back to using a single-year calendar.

In the fall of 2013, I prepared a brochure for a general business event. It described the following three calendars:

1. the J-style wall/desk calendar shown in Figure 7-2
2. the moving-window tent calendar shown in Figure A-4
3. the full-year calendar with double-sided slider shown in Figures 8-1a to 8-1c.

The moving-window tent calendar, which is a variation of the single-slider tent calendar shown in Figure 5-1a, is not included in the main body of this book because of its more complicated construction. Another disadvantage is that the year table on its face has space for only 21 entries. For years not on the face, a lookup table on the back can be referred to for setting the marker, but this is inconvenient. I do not see a great potential for this design, especially at this point when practical perpetual calendars are just getting established. However, it has larger numbers than the calendar in Figure 5-1a, and may be worth considering in the future. As suggested in Figure A-4, ideas from perpetual calendar charts could possibly be used to improve the calendar so that the lookup table on the back covers three or four centuries instead of only one century. (A chart is a lookup table.)

Figure A-5 shows a variation of a multisheet perpetual calendar with a single year table. In this design, the window moves, and the year table below the window moves with it. When I first made this design, I thought that it would be a good replacement for the conventional multisheet tent desk calendar whose sheets are turned each month. As can be seen in Figure A-5, this calendar looks quite different, but I could not think of anything else that met the criterion of being able to see the year setting at a glance. I spent quite a bit of time designing a rigid cardstock tent that had a ledge for supporting the pad. Figure A-5 does not show any details of cardstock folded at a right angle to provide rigidity. Although I found ways of making a rigid tent, the tent may have been difficult to manufacture. I also experimented with ways of attaching a moving window to the tent, but I did not find a satisfactory solution. After some work on this design, I concluded that it would be difficult to manufacture, and that it was not close enough in appearance to a conventional tent calendar to be an attractive replacement.

I decided that a perpetual calendar that had a flip-down moving window but that otherwise looked similar to a conventional tent calendar would be more attractive. My first flip-down-window calendar had a lookup table on the back, and space on the front for a sticky note to indicate the year setting. Although a bit crude, this calendar is an improvement over presently available perpetual calendars. While looking for a way to make a built-in indication for the year to replace the sticky note, I realized that a year table could be added to each sheet. This led to the flip-down moving-window calendar shown in Figures 1-2a and 6-1 (b and c), and the lift-out-pad calendar shown in Figures 1-2c and 6-2. I believe that these designs are truly innovative, convenient and green—and with good marketing, they have great potential.

The major breakthrough of having a year table on each sheet came in early 2015. Since then, I have been making refinements that have led to wall calendars (Figures 6-4, 6-5 and 6-6), the 12-sheet design (Table 4-8) and the window-on-each-sheet design (Figures 6-7a and 6-7b). Having also worked on completing the range of products, I realized that the single-sheet calendar with a single slider could be reduced in size to make a pocket calendar. During 2015, I sent e-mails to several print shops, but did not find any interest for adding any of my perpetual calendars to their product lines. I concluded that the best approach for making a wide audience aware of my calendar concepts would be to write a book. During the writing of *Practical Perpetual Calendars*, I have made numerous refinements to designs and have added the following:

- a pencil holder (Figure 5-5)
- a single-slider calendar with the year table beside the window (Figures 5-7b and 5-18)
- two clocks (Figures 5-8 and 5-9)
- a line-style monthly wall planner (Figure 5-16a)
- a vertical slider three-ring binder planner (Figure 5-16b)
- an ornate hybrid calendar (Figures 5-17a to 5-17c)
- a single day-of-month table full-year calendar (Figures 8-4a and 8-4b)
- a seven-column multisheet calendar with a single year table (Figures 1-3c, 1-3d and 7-6a to 7-6c)
- a full-year wall planner concept (Table 8-4)
- a vertical full-year wall calendar (Figure 8-3)

The refinements and new designs made during the writing of *Practical Perpetual Calendars* show the value of documenting work. Writing brings many ideas together, and through the act of writing, an author gains insights that were missed previously. Writing also requires explaining and defending ideas to others. In doing so, an author discards ideas that are not sound and finds ways of making designs simpler. When discarding an idea, I based the decision more on technical grounds and less on whether or not an idea was practical. I used this approach to make *Practical Perpetual Calendars* as complete as possible, and to avoid discarding ideas that may have some merit.

I thought of the 7-column multisheet perpetual calendar with a single year table as I was almost finished writing *Practical Perpetual Calendars*. I was describing the multisheet manufactured perpetual calendar in Figure A-9a and realized that it could be improved by adding a year table to each month's title sheet. I put the Appendix on hold to describe the concept at the end of Chapter 4. While adding to Chapter 4, I decided that a single year table with a slider would be a better improvement. I regarded this calendar significant enough to include it in Chapter 1 (Figures 1-3c and 1-3d). The vertical full-year calendar (Figure 8-3) was the last design to be added.

## Patents

The purpose of this section is to briefly describe some patents for devices to get a feel for what has been patented. Some of the patents cover features that are used in my calendar designs, but I have not found any for calendars quite like mine. Prior to disclosure in *Practical Perpetual Calendars*, some of my designs may have been patentable. Implementations of my designs, such as a novel flip-down window, may be patentable. I decided not to try to patent anything because of the expense involved and also because I had the ability to reach a wider audience by publishing a book on the subject.

There are hundreds, if not thousands, of patents for perpetual calendars. A search on the site *FreePatentsOnline.com* (http://www.freepatentsonline.com/) using the term *perpetual calendar* yielded over 3,500 results. A quick check showed that many of these results are not relevant to perpetual calendars, or else they cover watch mechanisms, electronic devices or other devices that have no similarity to my calendars. However, there could be a few hundred patents for devices similar to my calendars that have a manually positioned wheel, disk, slider or other part to determine the day of the week that a particular date falls on. There are also many patents for displays for non-stand-alone perpetual calendars. United States Patent 6,269,563, August 7, 2001, is included below as an example.

Searching patents online is very interesting, but also time-consuming. Some of the information that I have found confirms that my perpetual calendar concepts are better than the concepts in some patents, and other information has inspired new designs or refinements to designs. The following summarizes a number of patents that I found interesting, along with comments on how these patents relate to my designs.

**United States Patent 1,048,413, Calendar, December 24, 1912:** This is the earliest patent that I have seen for a calendar that has a 13-column day-of-month table. It is stand-alone and can be made from cardstock. There are some similarities between this calendar and my single-sheet, single-slider desk calendar shown in Figures 1-1a and 5-1a. A major difference is that the slider does not have a month table. The stationary table below the slider has a row for each month and a column for each day of the week. The years are put in the appropriate columns. For example, June 1, 1912, was on a Saturday, so *1912* is entered in the *Saturday* column of the *June* row. July 1, 1912, was on a Monday, so *1912* is also entered in the *Monday* column of the *July* row—and so forth. Thus, each year is entered in the applicable day-of-week column for each month. The calendar is set by lining up the *1* on the slider with the year in the applicable month row. Since each year is entered 12 times, a given-size table cannot cover as many years as my calendar, where each year is entered only once based on the day of the week that January 1 falls on.

**United States Patent 1,286,058, Perpetual Calendar, November 26, 1918:** This is a stand-alone slider-type calendar that is more complicated than mine and the one described in Patent 1,048,413. The patent shows a flat design for desktop use, and a compact round design for the tip of a pencil or other writing instrument. The basic concept of the day-of-month table for the round design is used in the rotary calendar described in United States Patent 7,140,132.

**United States Patent 1,494,792, Perpetual Calendar, May 20, 1924:** This calendar is made from cardstock and has a 13-column day-of-month table. It is not stand-alone.

**United States Patent 1,718,314, Perpetual Calendar, June 25, 1929, and United States Patent 1,784,117, Perpetual Calendar, December 9, 1930:** These two patents were filed by the same inventor. The second patent is a division of the first. These two patents inspired my single day-of-month table full-year calendars shown in Figures 8-4a and 8-4b. I use a slider to bring months into position, whereas this calendar uses a rotating disk. In addition to this change, I have a marker on the slider to point to the applicable years, rather than having a second window. This is my only design in which I have used all the parts from another calendar without independently developing the overall concept on my own. As noted under other patents and elsewhere in *Practical Perpetual Calendars* (e.g. the hybrid calendar shown in Figure 5-17a), I have been inspired by other designs and have enhanced some of them.

**United States Patent 1,949,328, Calendar, February 27, 1934:** Figure A-6 is a sketch of this calendar, which is similar to my single-sheet, single-slider calendar. It has a slider with a 13-column day-of-month table above a row of 13 letters. As in my calendars, seven columns of the slider appear in a window. Below the window, there is a table of months arranged in an order related to that in the month table on my slider. The calendar is set by finding the letter that applies to the year of interest and then lining up that letter with the month of interest. This is similar to the way my single-sheet, single-slider calendar (Figure 5-1a) is set. However, my tables are arranged differently so that I line up the month with the year without having to do a lookup. In addition to making this improvement, I have extended the basic concepts in this patent to multisheet calendars and a full-year calendar. I was not aware of this patent when I was developing my calendars.

**United States Patent 3,427,740, Perpetual Calendar, February 18, 1969:** This calendar is similar to my full-year calendar. It has seven day-of-month windows, and when two months of the year begin on the same day of the week, both are written above one window. A window for each month would have been better. The calendar is set by moving the slider until the year of interest appears in a window.

**United States Patent 3,765,111, Perpetual Calendar, October 16, 1973:** This invention is a complicated conical-shaped desk calendar that has many rotating parts. The patent claims that the calendar is easier to use and less prone to error than using a chart. According to the patent, "any selected decade and year of any century of any millennium may be found by selective rotation of the disks and cylindrical members in combination with the color code with the days of a desired month of a year exposed through the window in the outer wall."

**United States Patent 5,289,649, Perpetual Calendar, March 1, 1994:** "This invention relates to a perpetual calendar, and more particularly a pocket calendar which uses a rotating disk to get the calendar of a month and year desired for a period extending over more than 5,000 years." There appear to be more patents for calendars that use a rotating disk than for ones that use a slider. When a calendar is made from rigid materials, two disks can be simply bolted together, whereas a track must be made for a slider. This is the only advantage a disk has over a slider that I can see. Laying out tables on the arc of a circle is much more complicated than laying out tables on a rectangular grid. Circular tables are more difficult to read and do not have as pleasing an appearance as rectangular tables. With a year table of only 50 to 60 years, my pocket calendars appear weak in comparison to the calendar described by this patent. My calendars, which are designed for daily use and have a year table starting at 2000, cannot determine what day of the week July 1, 1867 (the day that Canada became a nation) fell on, or even the day of the week when I was born. However, mine are easier to build and use, and the year table can be set up to cover the years of most interest.

**United States Patent 5,313,723, Perpetual Calendar, May 24, 1994:** This invention, of a rotary calendar with two disks, is similar to the common rotary one-month calendar. Two advantages are that none of the years are hidden by the top disk and the years are in consecutive order around the circumference of the bottom disk. Overall, it is a better calendar than the common rotary one, but it also has many of the inherent disadvantages of rotary calendars.

**United States Patent 5,560,127, Perpetual Calendar, October 1, 1996:** This calendar has some similarities to the line-style monthly wall planner shown in Figure 5-16a in that it has SMTWTFS repeated many times on a moving part. However, it is not a stand-alone perpetual calendar. The moving part is a belt that wraps around the ends, not a slider.

**United States Patent 5,930,924, Perpetual Calendar, August 3, 1999:** This calendar has 12 windows to display all the months of the year. It also has a window to display the year. Thus, it performs the same function as my full-year calendars shown in Figures 8-1 (a to c) and 8-2 (a and b). The year display is a number that refers to a lookup table. My calendars have a marker in a window beside the row that has the applicable years, thereby eliminating any need to refer to a lookup table. The patent shows 7 different month charts with 13 columns like mine. One of the charts is the same as Table 4-1, and the others have January 1 under different days of the week. Why there are seven common year charts when only one is needed is not obvious after doing a quick read of the patent. My assessment of this patent is that the invention came close to capturing the simplicity of my full-year calendars, but did not achieve this. The patent cites U.S. 1,949,328 and U.S. 3,427,740.

**United States Patent 6,269,563, Perpetual Calendar, August 7, 2001:** An interesting quotation from this patent is, "Perpetual calendars have been known since antiquity and innumerable arrangements have been devised, limited only by human ingenuity and imagination and ranging from mundane utilitarian objects to inspired works of art. Creativity in this field is far from exhausted and a continuing demand exists for intriguing new designs." This invention is definitely an inspired work of art, whereas my calendars could be considered mundane utilitarian objects. However, mine are stand-alone, whereas the one in this invention requires another calendar to determine the day of the week for any date. Figure A-7a illustrates the concept. There is a straight piece of material with the numbers 1 to 31 on it, and a circular piece of material with *January* to *December* along an arc. These pieces have magnets imbedded in them to hold a small-diameter ball in position. The ball that indicates the day of the month is not attached to anything. It is placed at the applicable position along the straight piece and held in place by the magnet at that position. The ball that indicates the month is on a tether. The ball is placed near the applicable month and held in midair by the magnet at that position. This calendar is sold through the Museum of Modern Art in New York City at a cost of US$32 for the small size and US$45 for the large size. The subsection *Other Applications for the Single-Slider Vertical Calendar* in Chapter 5 describes how the concept in Figure 5-16a can be combined with that of the magnetic type calendar in Figure A-7a. The result would be a novel and artistic stand-alone perpetual calendar.

**United States Patent 6,826,857, Perpetual Calendar, December 7, 2004:** This calendar has windows on a rotating cylinder and is a bit complicated, although not as complicated as the one in U.S. Patent 3,765,111. One stated objective of the invention is "to create a perpetual calendar that displays the entire relationship between the dates, days, months and years." It does not display each month separately, but relationships between months can be determined. My full-year calendar is easier to use and more practical.

**United States Patent 7,140,132, Perpetual Calendar Wheel Chart, November 28, 2006:** This is a rotary calendar with 12 windows to display a full year. Unlike the common rotary one-month calendar, which is described in detail in the next section, this calendar always has Sunday in the leftmost column of the day-of-month display. The instructions printed on the calendar read, in part, "To use the calendar wheel, simply align the first two and last two digits of the year in the inner white area." None of these digits are ever hidden, so finding the year should be easier than it is on the common rotary one-month calendar. The calendar claims to work for the years CE 1 to CE 7500, with provision for using either the Julian or Gregorian calendar during the 1500s, 1600s and 1700s. There is a chart, along with a complicated formula, on the back for determining the date of the paschal full moon, which is used to determine the date of Easter Sunday. Overall, it appears to be superior to the common rotary one-month calendar, although the tables are more difficult to lay out. The patent states the following:

> Perpetual calendar wheel charts or perpetual calendar devices that can determine the day of the week for a particular date are known in the art. U.S. Pat. No. 5,930,924 to Beard, U.S. Pat. No. 5,313,723 [May 24, 1994] to Cregg, and U.S. Pat. No. 5,289,649 [March

> 1, 1994] to Perez are examples of devices that are capable of such a task. However, the problem with these devices is that they are relatively complex devices that are relatively difficult to manufacture, operate, and store.

The first patent mentioned is for a calendar with 12 windows. The other two patents are for rotary calendars. Although the calendar described by U.S. Patent 7,140,132 is certainly a novel device with a lot of capability, it is not as convenient for everyday use as my full-year calendars are.

**United States Patent 8,266,831, Promotional Multi-Year Rotational Calendar, September 18, 2012:** The following is according to the abstract.

> There is a felt need on the part of business people to have an affordable individualized promotional piece similar to and about the size of a standard business card that will have some inherent practical value to the recipient of the piece that induces the recipient to keep and to use the practical feature of the piece. ... The calendar uses a coded wheel and the edge of the table area to get the correct code which then acts as a key to reveal the days and dates for the entire month on the inner semi-circles.

This calendar is more complicated to build, set and read than my pocket calendars shown in Figures 5-3a and 5-3b. However, it is a more novel design.

**United States Patent Application 2014/0346765, Erasable Loop Scheduler, November 27, 2014:** This patent application is for an erasable loop scheduler with a board and a loop system. The board has a front side and a back side to view different parts of the loop. When the loop is configured as a calendar, one month's dates and appointments can be written on one side of the board, with the second month's information on the other side. In this configuration, the scheduler acts as a wall planner with a non-stand-alone calendar. After seeing this patent application, I decided to add a description of a full-year wall planner to Chapter 8. The description, which includes Table 8-4, is under the subheading *Single-Sided Slider Full-Year Wall Planner.* My planner consists of a long sheet with a roller at each end, rather than a continuous loop. The sheet is long enough to hold a full year, with one month or parts of two months displayed at a time. The window is part of a stand-alone perpetual calendar. Thus, my full-year wall planner is quite different from this erasable loop scheduler, although reading this patent application did make me think of this other way of configuring my full-year calendar.

**United States patents for rotary calendars:** I have found several patents that have elements of the common rotary one-month calendar, which has two disks. However, I have not found a patent for the design that is widely available. Some that I found are as follows:

- Patent 903,192, November 10, 1908—an early rotary calendar
- Patent 1,600,874, September 21, 1926—a calendar with four disks
- Patent 1,784,117, December 9, 1930—see earlier discussion in this Appendix

- Patent 2,919,511, January 5, 1960—a device with similarities to the calendar with four disks (U.S. Patent 1,600,874)
- Patent 5,313,723, May 24, 1994—see earlier discussion in this Appendix

## Common Rotary One-Month Calendar

Figures A-8a to A-8c illustrate what I call the common rotary one-month calendar, which is a stand-alone perpetual calendar. The figures have sketches of an assembled rotary calendar and of the two disks that are the main parts. This calendar covers 40 years (similar designs cover 100 years). Depending on the design, the rear disk has either three or four sectors with SuMTuWThFSa repeated on the inner circle and with years on the outer circle. Table A-1 indicates which years are associated with each day of the week on each sector of a three-sector calendar. This table was prepared by setting January 1 of a common year to Sunday, Monday and so forth, and recording the years on the outer circle. The numbers in Table A-1 are the actual numbers on a manufactured calendar. Figures A-8d and A-8e show the body of the single-sheet, single-slider desk calendar for reference.

### Table A-1
### Years Associated with Days of the Week on a Common Rotary One-Month Calendar that Covers 2009 to 2048

| | Years indicated when January 1 of a common year is on ... | | | | | | |
|---|---|---|---|---|---|---|---|
| *Sector* | **Su**[1] | **M** | **Tu** | **W** | **Th** | **F** | **Sa**[1] |
| 1 | 2023 | 2029 | **2024**[2] | 2025 | 2009 | 2010 | **2044** |
| | | 2018 | 2030 | **2048**[3] | 2043 | 2038 | 2039 |
| 2 | **2028** | **12–40**[4] | 2013 | 2014 | 2015 | 2027 | **2016** |
| | 2045 | 2046 | 2041 | 2042 | 2037 | **2032** | 2033 |
| 3 | 2017 | 2018 | 2019 | 2031 | **2020** | 2021 | 2022 |
| | 2034 | 2035 | 2047 | **2036** | 2026 | | 2011 |

Notes:

1. The manufactured calendar uses *S* for both Saturday and Sunday, with the *S* in red for Sunday.
2. Leap years are boldface in Table A-1, but are not marked any different from common years on the calendar.
3. **2048** is in the wrong column. It should be under "Th."
4. **12–40** indicates **2012** and **2040**.

In Table A-1, when January 1 for a common year is on a particular day of the week, the year is under that day. For example, January 1, 2009, was on a Thursday; therefore, *2009* is under *Thursday*. Leap years are entered under the day of the week *after* the day that January 1 falls on. January 1, 2016, was on a Friday; therefore, *2016* is under *Saturday*. A comparison of Table A-1 with Table 3-9b (the latter of which is the year table used in the single-sheet, single-slider desk calendar in Figure 5-1a) shows that the same years are in the same columns from left to right. Table A-2 shows the month table on the rotary calendar.

**Table A-2**
**Month Table on the Common Rotary One-Month Calendar**

| JAN<br>OCT | MAY | AUG<br>**FEB** | MAR<br>FEB<br>NOV | JUNE | DEC<br>SEP | JULY<br>APR<br>**JAN** |
|---|---|---|---|---|---|---|

Note: *JAN* and *FEB* in boldface apply to leap years. The manufactured calendar uses red rather than boldface. *JAN* and *FEB* not in boldface apply to common years. March to December are the same for leap years and common years.

A comparison of this table with the month table part of Table 3-12 (which has the tables used in the single-sheet, single-slider desk calendar in Figure 5-1a) shows that the entries are the same as in the seven leftmost columns, but in the reverse order. The correlation is, of course, not unexpected, as the basic principles of my single-slider calendar are the same as the basic principles of the rotary calendar.

The headings on the rotary calendar, which appear over the days of the month, begin with the day of the week that the first of the month falls on, instead of Sunday. Table A-3 shows the calendar for January 2009.

**Table A-3**
**January 2009 on the Common Rotary One-Month Calendar**

| Th | F | Sa | Su | M | Tu | W |
|---|---|---|---|---|---|---|
| 1 | 2 | 3 | 4 | 5 | 6 | 7 |
| 8 | 9 | 10 | 11 | 12 | 13 | 14 |
| 15 | 16 | 17 | 18 | 19 | 20 | 21 |
| 22 | 23 | 24 | 25 | 26 | 27 | 28 |
| 29 | 30 | 31 | | | | |

This type of display is a distinct disadvantage of the common rotary one-month calendar. Another disadvantage is that the years can be difficult to find. For example, to go from December 2010 to January 2011, you have to go from sector no. 1 to sector no. 3. The year 2011 is not in view, and the disk has to be rotated to find it. If you rotate clockwise, 2011 will come into view after rotating approximately 90 degrees. If you rotate counterclockwise, 2011 will come into view after rotating about 270 degrees. Overall, the common rotary one-month calendar is a novelty, unlike my single-sheet, single-slider and other designs, which are practical working calendars.

## Manufactured Perpetual Calendars

To find a variety of manufactured perpetual calendars, do a Bing or Google search for images of perpetual calendars. Another site to search is www.etsy.com. It has limited quantities of perpetual calendars that are no longer manufactured. The following list gives a brief description of some representative calendars.

1. Full-Month Tile Calendar
   Figure 5-17a illustrates this type. The one in this figure has been enhanced with the addition of the year table and month slider from my single-sheet dual-slider calendar. These features make the calendar stand-alone, but all of the manufactured full-month tile calendars that I have seen require reference to another calendar to set. Most of these calendars have 31 tiles for the days of the month, although some (as in Figure 5-17a) have column tiles so that the month is put together one column at a time, rather than one day at a time.

2. Magnetic Calendar
   This calendar is discussed under United States Patent 6,269,563, and is illustrated in Figure A-7a.

3. Slider Calendar
   Figure A-7b illustrates this calendar, and Figures 5-13a and 5-13b show how to make it stand-alone.

4. Triple-Cylinder Calendar
   This is a novel design that enables determining what day of the week a particular date fell on. It covers the period 1600 to 2999. Figure A-7c illustrates the concept. The month cylinder is turned to find the month of interest, the century cylinder is turned to find the century of interest and the year cylinder is turned to find the year of interest. Lines on the cylinders connect each row in the date list on the far left with a day of the week in the day list on the far right. To keep the illustration simple, Figure A-7c shows only the lines on the cylinders that connect 1, 8, 15, 22 and 29 with a day of the week. The settings in Figure A-7c are as follows:

   - Months: January leap year, and April and July, both common years and leap years
   - Century: 1900 to 1999
   - Year: All the years shown in the window

   For these settings, the day of the week is Wednesday.

5. Rotary Calendar
   This calendar is shown in Figures A-8a, A8b and A8c.

6. Multisheet Calendar
   Figure A-9a illustrates one with a clock that I found on www.etsy.com. This particular calendar with a clock is likely not available other than through a secondhand store. However, there are currently manufactured calendars without a clock that use this concept. One supplier is Baudville (https://www.baudville.com). The calendar has seven

day-of-month sheets, with each one beginning on a different day of the week. Figure A-9a shows the sheets for months that begin on a Friday, Saturday or Sunday. There are three double-sided name-of-month sheets. Figure A-9a shows a sheet that has January and February on one side of it. The back side, which is not shown, has March and April. The calendar is set by consulting a conventional calendar to determine the day of the week that the first of the month of interest falls on. The day-of-month sheet with that configuration is then selected, and the sheet with the name of the month is placed behind the selected day-of-month sheet.

In the configuration shown in Figure A-9a, the calendar is not stand-alone. To make it stand-alone, a year table could be added to the name-of-month sheets. The calendar would then be set by selecting the sheet that has the name of the month of interest, looking at the year table to find the day of the week that the first of the month falls on and then selecting the applicable day-of-month sheet. Some details would have to be worked out, but the resulting calendar would be similar to my multisheet calendars. It would be 7 columns wide, rather than 13. Setting it would not be as convenient, as the user would have to search for the applicable day-of-month sheet instead of just flipping the page. See Tables 4-12, 4-13 and 4-14 for tables that can be used for this concept. See Figures 1-3c and 1-3d, and 7-6a to 7-6c, for a practical design with a slider to enable using a single year table instead of a year table for each month.

7. Single-Day Tile Calendar
   Figure A-9b illustrates a single-day tile calendar that has tiles for the day of the week, the month and the day of the month. Other tile types display the day of the week and the day of the month, or just the day of the month. This type of calendar is often hung on a wall in a bank.

8. Rubik's Cube Calendar
   Figure A-9c shows the face of a Rubik's Cube–type perpetual calendar that is set to Sunday, December 25. It is non-stand-alone. This is a novel calendar, but only Rubik's Cube experts would find it easy to set.

9. Block or Cube Calendar
   This is a fairly common non-stand-alone perpetual calendar. As shown in Figure A-9d, the calendar is comprised of four blocks or cubes that are approximately 1.5 inches on each edge. The far left block is for the month, the two middle blocks are for the day of the month and the far right block is for the day of the week.

## Make Your Own Perpetual Calendar

A Google search I did using the phrase "how to make a perpetual calendar" yielded a million results. A Bing search using the same phrase yielded five million. So, there are lots of ideas for making perpetual calendars. The first few pages of the Google results are more significant than the Bing results. Some of the more interesting and typical finds from the Google search are the following:

- The link to images leads to sites that show how to make a rotary calendar. The URL of one of these sites is http://www.instructables.com/id/Improved-Perpetual-Calendar/, which has downloads that can be printed on cardstock. This calendar is similar to the common rotary one-month calendar. Two significant differences are that it has more disks and it always shows the week with the columns from Sunday to Saturday.
- The site with the URL http://ladybrayton71.blogspot.ca/2014/01/how-to-make-wooden-block-perpetual.html shows how to make a block- or cube-type perpetual calendar from wood. There are other sites that show how to make a similar calendar from a kit. An unfinished wood-block kit is available from http://www.joann.com/unfinished-wood-block-calendar-4-1%2F4-x-2-x-3-inches/12638284.html.
- The URL www.marthastewart.com/998318/how-make-perpetual-calendar-part-1 is a link to a video showing how to make a tile-type perpetual calendar.
- The site at https://www.timeanddate.com/ has calendars for any year that can be displayed on the screen or printed out. There are many similar sites with calendars in PDF or Excel format.
- The site at http://www5a.biglobe.ne.jp/%257eaccent/calendar/making.htm shows how to make a full-year calendar from cardstock.

The last item in this list was a surprise find. The calendar on this site, which I call a full-year calendar with 24 windows for the months, is similar to my double-sided slider full-year perpetual calendar in Figures 8-1a to 8-1c. The biggest difference is that the slider is single-sided, with the day-of-month tables for common years on the left end and the tables for leap years on the right end. There is a year table between the two sets of day-of-month tables. Figure A-10 is a conceptual drawing of the face. There are 12 windows on the left end for common year months, 12 windows on the right end for leap year months and a window in the middle for the year table. Having a separate set of windows for leap years eliminates having to turn the slider over, as is the case for my double-sided slider full-year calendar. However, the face is wider and not as pleasing in appearance. My single-sided slider full-year perpetual calendar in Figures 8-2a and 8-2b also eliminates the need to turn the slider over for leap years. It has 14 windows for the months and is overall a more practical and more pleasing design than the calendar in Figure A-10. As noted in Figure A-10, the year table has 7 columns for common years and 7 for leap years, so the slider can be in 14 different positions. The year table on the slider covers 1900 to 2099. I believe that an improvement to this design would be to interchange the year table and the marker, so that the year table is printed on the face and the marker is printed on the slider. Then the entire year table would always be visible. Another improvement would be to use concepts from my single-sided slider full-year calendar to reduce the number of windows for months from 24 to 14.

## Charts

In addition to the calendars above, there are various charts that do not have any moving parts. Chart-type perpetual calendars can be found by doing an Internet search for the phrase "perpetual calendar charts" or "perpetual calendars." A representative chart is produced by the Astronomical Society of South Australia. See https://www.assa.org.au/media/9855/ronscal.pdf.

This chart covers all the years from CE 1583 to CE 3899. It displays a full year on one page. Tables A-3 and A-4 illustrate the concept.

The first step in using the calendar is to line up a row and a column in Table A-3 to find the letter (or letters) that applies to the year of interest. Common years have one letter. Leap years have two, with the first letter for January and February, and the second letter for March to December. The next step is to use the letter (or letters) to find the column that applies in Table A-4. Suppose the year is a common year and the letter found in the first step is *D*. In this case, we learn from Table A-4 that January 1 is on a Wednesday and February 1 is on a Saturday.

### Table A-3
### Lookup Table for Representative Chart Perpetual Calendar

| First two digits of year | Last two digits of year |
|---|---|
| 4 rows and 6 columns | 4 rows and 29 columns |

### Table A-4
### Full-Year Calendar for a Representative Chart Perpetual Calendar

| A | B | C | D | E | F | G | January | | | | | February | | | | | |
|---|---|---|---|---|---|---|---|---|---|---|---|---|---|---|---|---|---|
| Su | M | Tu | W | Th | F | Sa | 1 | 8 | 15 | 22 | 29 | | 5 | 12 | 19 | 26 | This space is for March to June. There is a similar table below for July to December. |
| M | Tu | W | Th | F | Sa | Su | 2 | 9 | 16 | 23 | 30 | | 6 | 13 | 20 | 27 | |
| Tu | W | Th | F | Sa | Su | M | 3 | 10 | 17 | 24 | 31 | | 7 | 14 | 21 | 28 | |
| W | Th | F | Sa | Su | M | Tu | 4 | 11 | 18 | 25 | | 1 | 8 | 15 | 22 | 29 | |
| Th | F | Sa | Su | M | Tu | W | 5 | 12 | 19 | 26 | | 2 | 9 | 16 | 23 | | |
| F | Sa | Su | M | Tu | W | Th | 6 | 13 | 20 | 27 | | 3 | 10 | 17 | 24 | | |
| Sa | Su | M | Tu | W | Th | F | 7 | 14 | 21 | 28 | | 4 | 11 | 18 | 25 | | |

A comparison of this chart with my two full-year calendars in Figures 8-1a to 8-1c and Figures 8-2a and 8-2b shows the following:

- The chart is easier to make, as it is just one printed sheet and has no moving parts.
- My calendars have the days of the week as column headings as in a conventional calendar, whereas the chart has the days of the week as row headings. If my calendars had the days

of the week as row headings, the slider would move up and down instead of from side to side.

- My calendars always have the columns labeled *Sunday* to *Saturday* from left to right. In the chart, the first row is labeled *Sunday* if January 1 is on a Sunday; *Monday* if January 1 is on a Monday; and so forth. This makes the calendar difficult to read, but this characteristic cannot be eliminated without having a moving slider.
- The chart covers more than 2,000 years, whereas the year table on my calendars would become too large if it covered much more than 100 years.

Overall, a chart provides a low-cost perpetual calendar that can cover thousands of years. It is good for occasional lookup, but my calendars are easier to read and use in daily activities.

Calendar Face

| Common Year | | | | | | | |
|---|---|---|---|---|---|---|---|
| Jan | Su | M | Tu | W | Th | F | S |
| Feb | W | Th | F | S | Su | M | Tu |
| Mar | W | Th | F | S | Su | M | Tu |
| Apr | Sa | Su | M | Tu | W | Th | F |
| May | M | Tu | W | Th | F | Sa | Su |
| Jun | Th | F | Sa | Su | M | Tu | W |
| Jul | Sa | Su | M | Tu | W | Th | F |
| Aug | Tu | W | Th | F | Sa | Su | M |
| Sep | F | Sa | Su | M | Tu | W | Th |
| Oct | Su | M | Tu | W | Th | F | S |
| Nov | W | Th | F | S | Su | M | Tu |
| Dec | F | Sa | Su | M | Tu | W | Th |

| S | M | T | W | T | F | S |
|---|---|---|---|---|---|---|
| 1 | 2 | 3 | 4 | 5 | 6 | 7 |
| 8 | 9 | 10 | 11 | 12 | 13 | 14 |
| 15 | 16 | 17 | 18 | 19 | 20 | 21 |
| 22 | 23 | 24 | 25 | 26 | 27 | 28 |
| 29 | 30 | 31 | | | | |

| Leap Year | | | | | | | |
|---|---|---|---|---|---|---|---|
| Jan | Su | M | Tu | W | Th | F | S |
| Feb | W | Th | F | S | Su | M | Tu |
| Mar | Th | F | S | Su | M | Tu | W |
| Apr | Su | M | Tu | W | Th | F | Sa |
| May | Tu | W | Th | F | Sa | Su | M |
| Jun | F | Sa | Su | M | Tu | W | Th |
| Jul | Su | M | Tu | W | Th | F | Sa |
| Aug | W | Th | F | Sa | Su | M | Tu |
| Sep | Sa | Su | M | Tu | W | Th | F |
| Oct | M | Tu | W | Th | F | S | Su |
| Nov | Th | F | S | Su | M | Tu | W |
| Dec | Sa | Su | M | Tu | W | Th | F |

Day of Month Slider

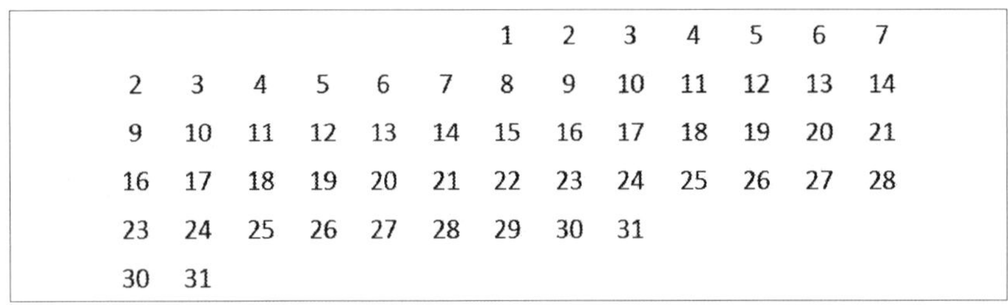

| | | | | | | | | | | | | |
|---|---|---|---|---|---|---|---|---|---|---|---|---|
| | | | | | | 1 | 2 | 3 | 4 | 5 | 6 | 7 |
| 2 | 3 | 4 | 5 | 6 | 7 | 8 | 9 | 10 | 11 | 12 | 13 | 14 |
| 9 | 10 | 11 | 12 | 13 | 14 | 15 | 16 | 17 | 18 | 19 | 20 | 21 |
| 16 | 17 | 18 | 19 | 20 | 21 | 22 | 23 | 24 | 25 | 26 | 27 | 28 |
| 23 | 24 | 25 | 26 | 27 | 28 | 29 | 30 | 31 | | | | |
| 30 | 31 | | | | | | | | | | | |

The tables on the face enable determining what day of the week the first of any month falls on when the day of the week that January 1 falls on is known. For example, from the table on the left for common years September 1 is on Tuesday when January 1 is on Thursday.

Figure A-1: An early attempt at lookup tables

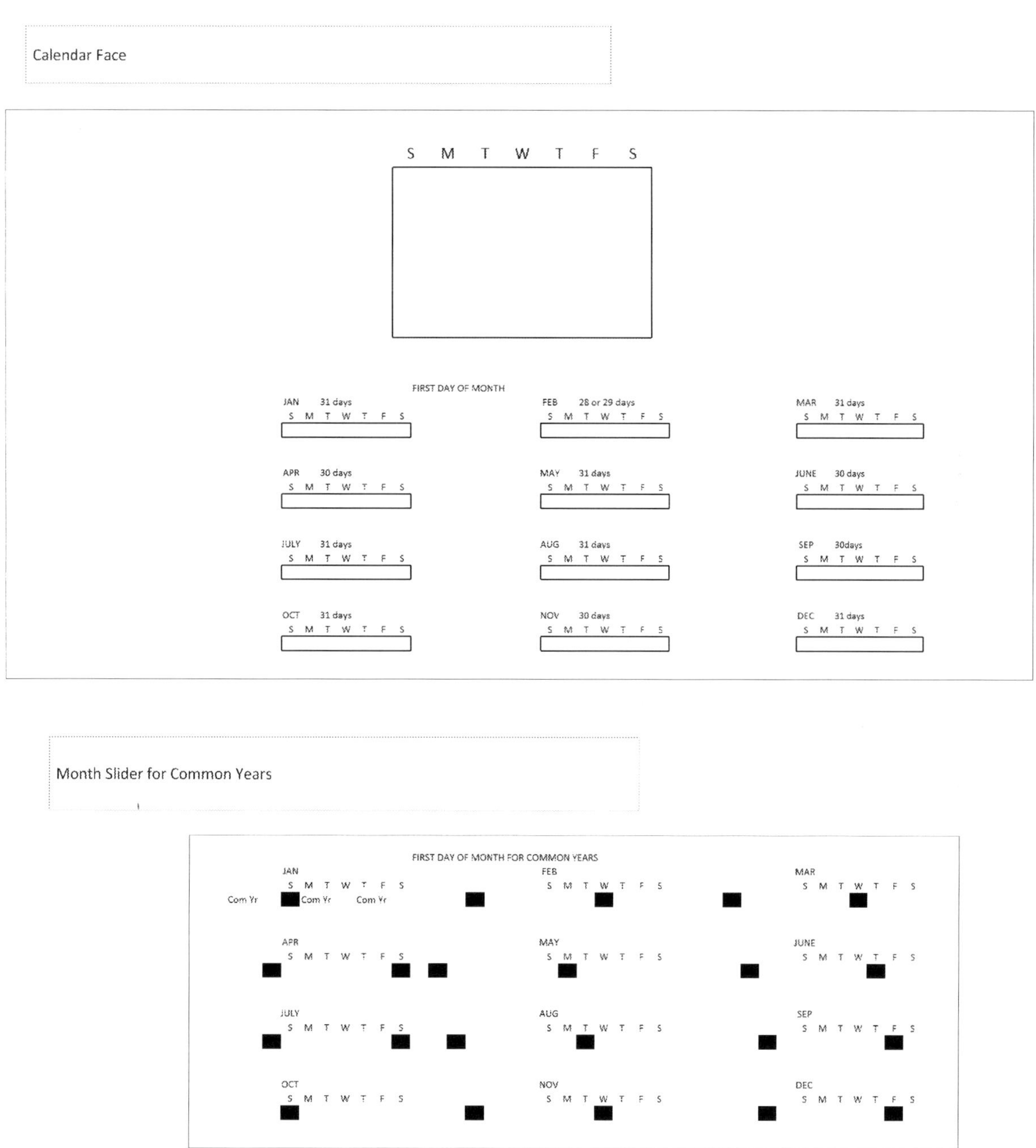
Calendar Face
S M T W T F S
FIRST DAY OF MONTH
JAN 31 days
FEB 28 or 29 days
MAR 31 days
APR 30 days
MAY 31 days
JUNE 30 days
JULY 31 days
AUG 31 days
SEP 30days
OCT 31 days
NOV 30 days
DEC 31 days
Month Slider for Common Years
FIRST DAY OF MONTH FOR COMMON YEARS
JAN
FEB
MAR
Com Yr
Com Yr
Com Yr
APR
MAY
JUNE
JULY
AUG
SEP
OCT
NOV
DEC

Figure A-2: An early version of the single-sheet perpetual calendar with dual-slider configuration

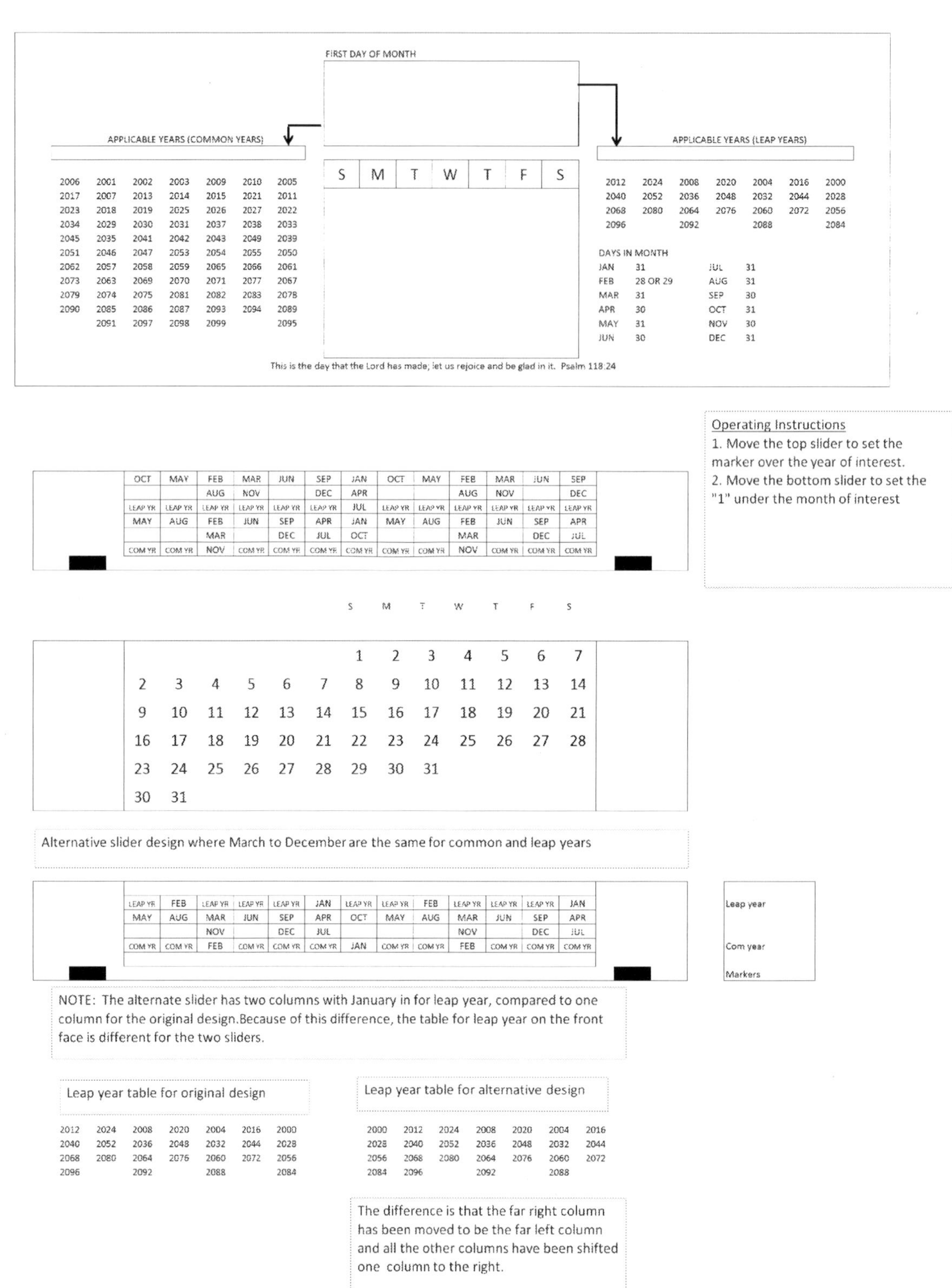
FIRST DAY OF MONTH
APPLICABLE YEARS (COMMON YEARS)
APPLICABLE YEARS (LEAP YEARS)
S M T W T F S
2006 2001 2002 2003 2009 2010 2005
2017 2007 2013 2014 2015 2021 2011
2023 2018 2019 2025 2026 2027 2022
2034 2029 2030 2031 2037 2038 2033
2045 2035 2041 2042 2043 2049 2039
2051 2046 2047 2053 2054 2055 2050
2062 2057 2058 2059 2065 2066 2061
2073 2063 2069 2070 2071 2077 2067
2079 2074 2075 2081 2082 2083 2078
2090 2085 2086 2087 2093 2094 2089
2091 2097 2098 2099 2095
2012 2024 2008 2020 2004 2016 2000
2040 2052 2036 2048 2032 2044 2028
2068 2080 2064 2076 2060 2072 2056
2096 2092 2088 2084
DAYS IN MONTH
JAN 31
FEB 28 OR 29
MAR 31
APR 30
MAY 31
JUN 30
JUL 31
AUG 31
SEP 30
OCT 31
NOV 30
DEC 31
This is the day that the Lord has made; let us rejoice and be glad in it. Psalm 118:24
Operating Instructions
1. Move the top slider to set the marker over the year of interest.
2. Move the bottom slider to set the "1" under the month of interest
OCT MAY FEB MAR JUN SEP JAN OCT MAY FEB MAR JUN SEP
AUG NOV DEC APR AUG NOV DEC
LEAP YR LEAP YR LEAP YR LEAP YR LEAP YR LEAP YR JUL LEAP YR LEAP YR LEAP YR LEAP YR LEAP YR LEAP YR
MAY AUG FEB JUN SEP APR JAN MAY AUG FEB JUN SEP APR
MAR DEC JUL OCT MAR DEC JUL
COM YR COM YR NOV COM YR COM YR COM YR COM YR COM YR COM YR NOV COM YR COM YR COM YR
S M T W T F S
1 2 3 4 5 6 7
2 3 4 5 6 7 8 9 10 11 12 13 14
9 10 11 12 13 14 15 16 17 18 19 20 21
16 17 18 19 20 21 22 23 24 25 26 27 28
23 24 25 26 27 28 29 30 31
30 31
Alternative slider design where March to December are the same for common and leap years
LEAP YR FEB LEAP YR LEAP YR LEAP YR JAN LEAP YR LEAP YR FEB LEAP YR LEAP YR LEAP YR JAN
MAY AUG MAR JUN SEP APR OCT MAY AUG MAR JUN SEP APR
NOV DEC JUL NOV DEC JUL
COM YR COM YR FEB COM YR COM YR COM YR JAN COM YR COM YR FEB COM YR COM YR COM YR
Leap year
Com year
Markers
NOTE: The alternate slider has two columns with January in for leap year, compared to one column for the original design. Because of this difference, the table for leap year on the front face is different for the two sliders.
Leap year table for original design
2012 2024 2008 2020 2004 2016 2000
2040 2052 2036 2048 2032 2044 2028
2068 2080 2064 2076 2060 2072 2056
2096 2092 2088 2084
Leap year table for alternative design
2000 2012 2024 2008 2020 2004 2016
2028 2040 2052 2036 2048 2032 2044
2056 2068 2080 2064 2076 2060 2072
2084 2096 2092 2088
The difference is that the far right column has been moved to be the far left column and all the other columns have been shifted one column to the right.

Figure A-3: State of the dual-slider design in October 2012

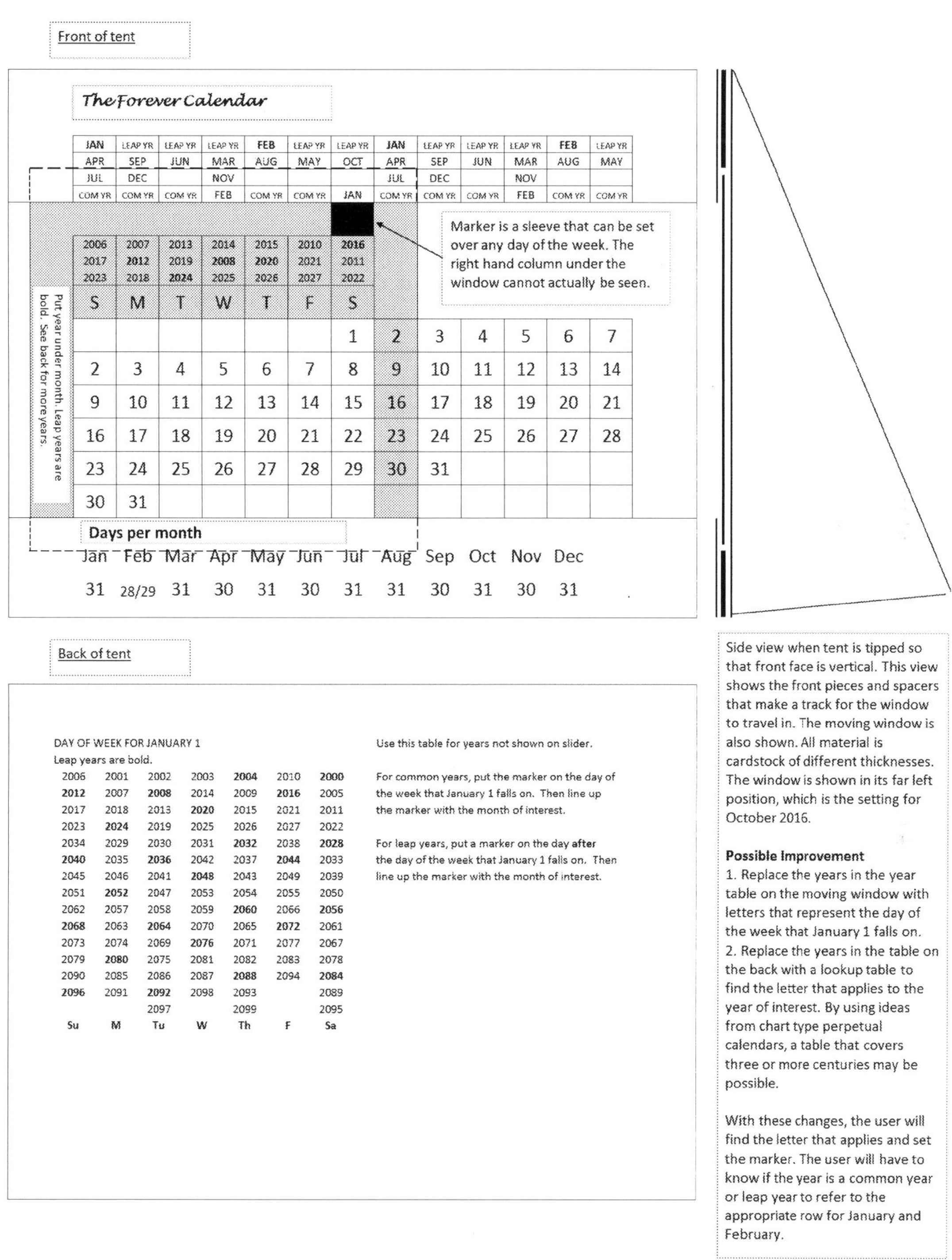
Front of tent
The Forever Calendar
JAN LEAP YR LEAP YR LEAP YR FEB LEAP YR LEAP YR JAN LEAP YR LEAP YR LEAP YR FEB LEAP YR
APR SEP JUN MAR AUG MAY OCT APR SEP JUN MAR AUG MAY
JUL DEC NOV JUL DEC NOV
COM YR COM YR COM YR FEB COM YR COM YR JAN COM YR COM YR COM YR FEB COM YR COM YR
2006 2007 2013 2014 2015 2010 2016
2017 2012 2019 2008 2020 2021 2011
2023 2018 2024 2025 2026 2027 2022
S M T W T F S
Marker is a sleeve that can be set over any day of the week. The right hand column under the window cannot actually be seen.
Put year under month. Leap years are bold. See back for more years.
Days per month
Jan Feb Mar Apr May Jun Jul Aug Sep Oct Nov Dec
31 28/29 31 30 31 30 31 31 30 31 30 31
Back of tent
DAY OF WEEK FOR JANUARY 1
Leap years are bold.
2006 2001 2002 2003 2004 2010 2000
2012 2007 2008 2014 2009 2016 2005
2017 2018 2013 2020 2015 2021 2011
2023 2024 2019 2025 2026 2027 2022
2034 2029 2030 2031 2032 2038 2028
2040 2035 2036 2042 2037 2044 2033
2045 2046 2041 2048 2043 2049 2039
2051 2052 2047 2053 2054 2055 2050
2062 2057 2058 2059 2060 2066 2056
2068 2063 2064 2070 2065 2072 2061
2073 2074 2069 2076 2071 2077 2067
2079 2080 2075 2081 2082 2083 2078
2090 2085 2086 2087 2088 2094 2084
2096 2091 2092 2098 2093 2089
2097 2099 2095
Su M Tu W Th F Sa
Use this table for years not shown on slider.
For common years, put the marker on the day of the week that January 1 falls on. Then line up the marker with the month of interest.
For leap years, put a marker on the day after the day of the week that January 1 falls on. Then line up the marker with the month of interest.
Side view when tent is tipped so that front face is vertical. This view shows the front pieces and spacers that make a track for the window to travel in. The moving window is also shown. All material is cardstock of different thicknesses. The window is shown in its far left position, which is the setting for October 2016.
Possible Improvement
1. Replace the years in the year table on the moving window with letters that represent the day of the week that January 1 falls on.
2. Replace the years in the table on the back with a lookup table to find the letter that applies to the year of interest. By using ideas from chart type perpetual calendars, a table that covers three or more centuries may be possible.
With these changes, the user will find the letter that applies and set the marker. The user will have to know if the year is a common year or leap year to refer to the appropriate row for January and February.

Figure A-4: Moving-window tent calendar

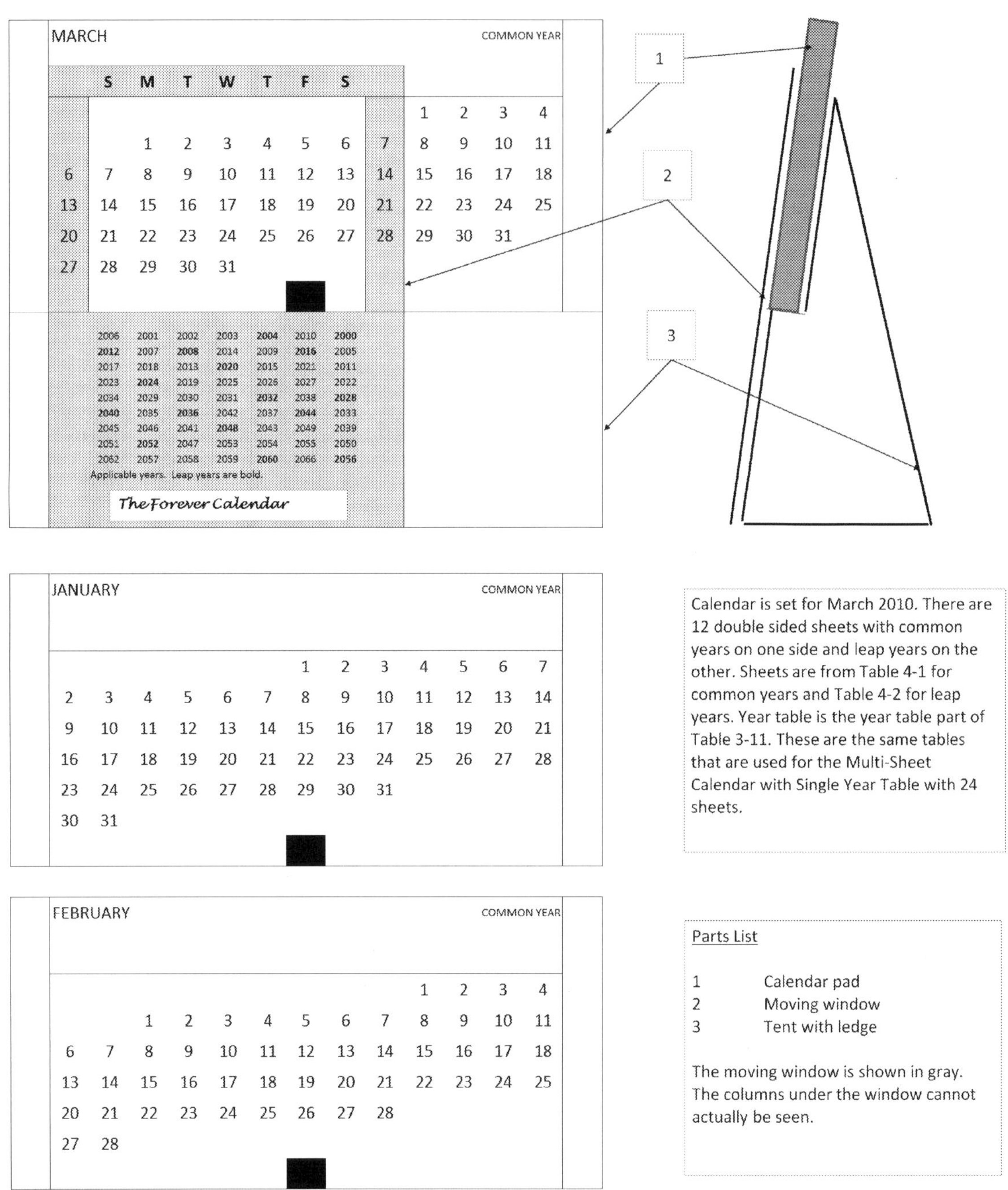
MARCH
COMMON YEAR
S M T W T F S
1 2 3 4
1 2 3 4 5 6 7 8 9 10 11
6 7 8 9 10 11 12 13 14 15 16 17 18
13 14 15 16 17 18 19 20 21 22 23 24 25
20 21 22 23 24 25 26 27 28 29 30 31
27 28 29 30 31
2006 2001 2002 2003 2004 2010 2000
2012 2007 2008 2014 2009 2016 2005
2017 2018 2013 2020 2015 2021 2011
2023 2024 2019 2025 2026 2027 2022
2034 2029 2030 2031 2032 2038 2028
2040 2035 2036 2042 2037 2044 2033
2045 2046 2041 2048 2043 2049 2039
2051 2052 2047 2053 2054 2055 2050
2062 2057 2058 2059 2060 2066 2056
Applicable years. Leap years are bold.
The Forever Calendar
1
2
3
JANUARY
COMMON YEAR
1 2 3 4 5 6 7
2 3 4 5 6 7 8 9 10 11 12 13 14
9 10 11 12 13 14 15 16 17 18 19 20 21
16 17 18 19 20 21 22 23 24 25 26 27 28
23 24 25 26 27 28 29 30 31
30 31
Calendar is set for March 2010. There are 12 double sided sheets with common years on one side and leap years on the other. Sheets are from Table 4-1 for common years and Table 4-2 for leap years. Year table is the year table part of Table 3-11. These are the same tables that are used for the Multi-Sheet Calendar with Single Year Table with 24 sheets.
FEBRUARY
COMMON YEAR
1 2 3 4
1 2 3 4 5 6 7 8 9 10 11
6 7 8 9 10 11 12 13 14 15 16 17 18
13 14 15 16 17 18 19 20 21 22 23 24 25
20 21 22 23 24 25 26 27 28
27 28
Parts List
1 Calendar pad
2 Moving window
3 Tent with ledge
The moving window is shown in gray. The columns under the window cannot actually be seen.

Figure A-5: A variation of a multisheet perpetual calendar with a single year table

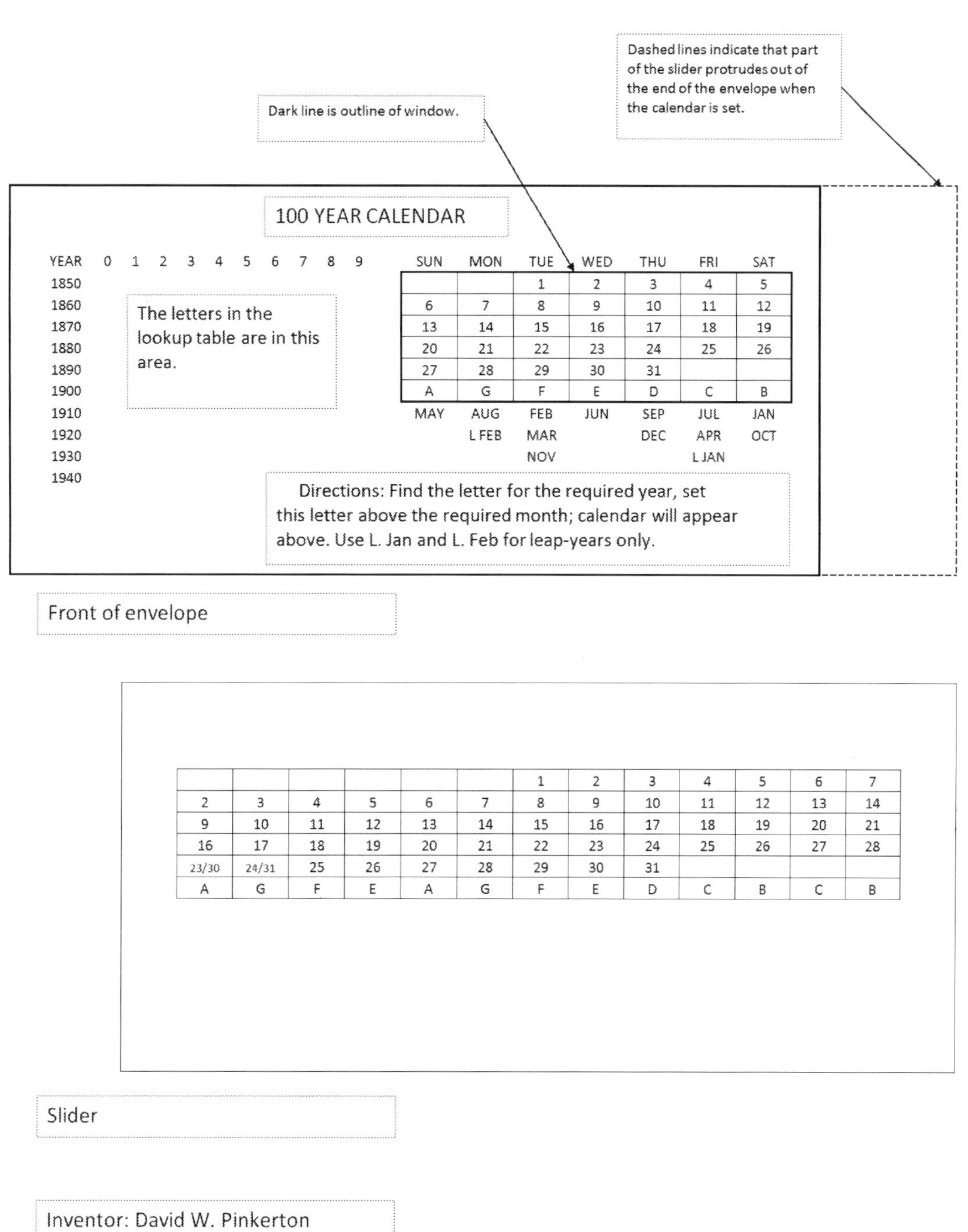

Dark line is outline of window.
Dashed lines indicate that part of the slider protrudes out of the end of the envelope when the calendar is set.
100 YEAR CALENDAR
YEAR 0 1 2 3 4 5 6 7 8 9
1850
1860
1870
1880
1890
1900
1910
1920
1930
1940
The letters in the lookup table are in this area.
SUN MON TUE WED THU FRI SAT
1 2 3 4 5
6 7 8 9 10 11 12
13 14 15 16 17 18 19
20 21 22 23 24 25 26
27 28 29 30 31
A G F E D C B
MAY AUG FEB JUN SEP JUL JAN
L FEB MAR DEC APR OCT
NOV L JAN
Directions: Find the letter for the required year, set this letter above the required month; calendar will appear above. Use L. Jan and L. Feb for leap-years only.
Front of envelope
1 2 3 4 5 6 7
2 3 4 5 6 7 8 9 10 11 12 13 14
9 10 11 12 13 14 15 16 17 18 19 20 21
16 17 18 19 20 21 22 23 24 25 26 27 28
23/30 24/31 25 26 27 28 29 30 31
A G F E A G F E D C B C B
Slider
Inventor: David W. Pinkerton


Figure A-6: Slider-type perpetual calendar, United States Patent 1,949,328, February 27, 1934

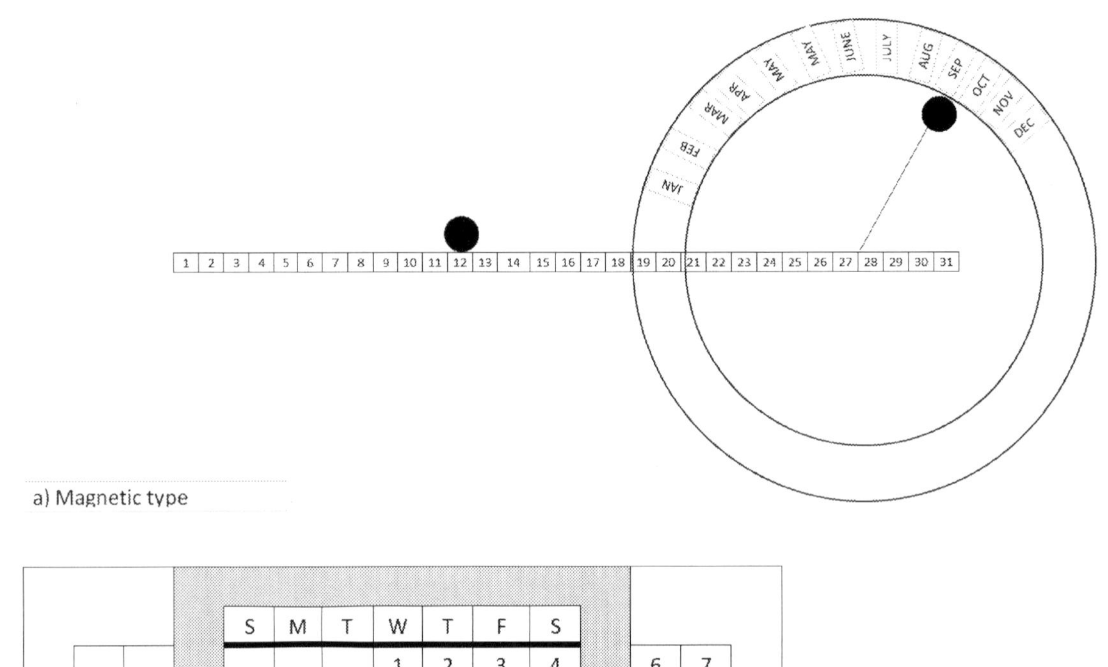
JAN FEB MAR APR MAY MAY JUNE JULY AUG SEP OCT NOV DEC
1 2 3 4 5 6 7 8 9 10 11 12 13 14 15 16 17 18 19 20 21 22 23 24 25 26 27 28 29 30 31

a) Magnetic type

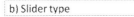

| | | S | M | T | W | T | F | S | | |
|---|---|---|---|---|---|---|---|---|---|---|
| | | | | | 1 | 2 | 3 | 4 | 6 | 7 |
| 2 | 3 | 5 | 6 | 7 | 8 | 9 | 10 | 11 | 13 | 14 |
| 9 | 10 | 12 | 13 | 14 | 15 | 16 | 17 | 18 | 20 | 21 |
| 16 | 17 | 19 | 20 | 21 | 22 | 23 | 24 | 25 | 27 | 28 |
| 23/30 | 24/31 | 26 | 27 | 28 | 29 | 30 | 31 | | | |

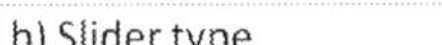

b) Slider type

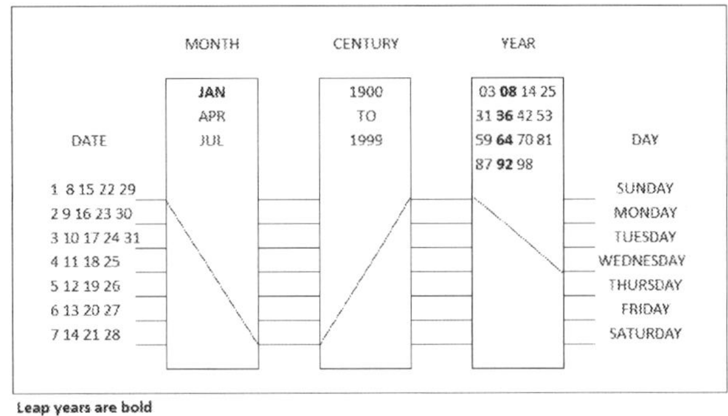
MONTH
CENTURY
YEAR
JAN
APR
JUL
1900
TO
1999
03 08 14 25
31 36 42 53
59 64 70 81
87 92 98
DATE
DAY
1 8 15 22 29
2 9 16 23 30
3 10 17 24 31
4 11 18 25
5 12 19 26
6 13 20 27
7 14 21 28
SUNDAY
MONDAY
TUESDAY
WEDNESDAY
THURSDAY
FRIDAY
SATURDAY
Leap years are bold

c) Triple-cylinder type

Figures A-7a to A-7c: Magnetic-type, slider-type and triple-cylinder-type perpetual calendars

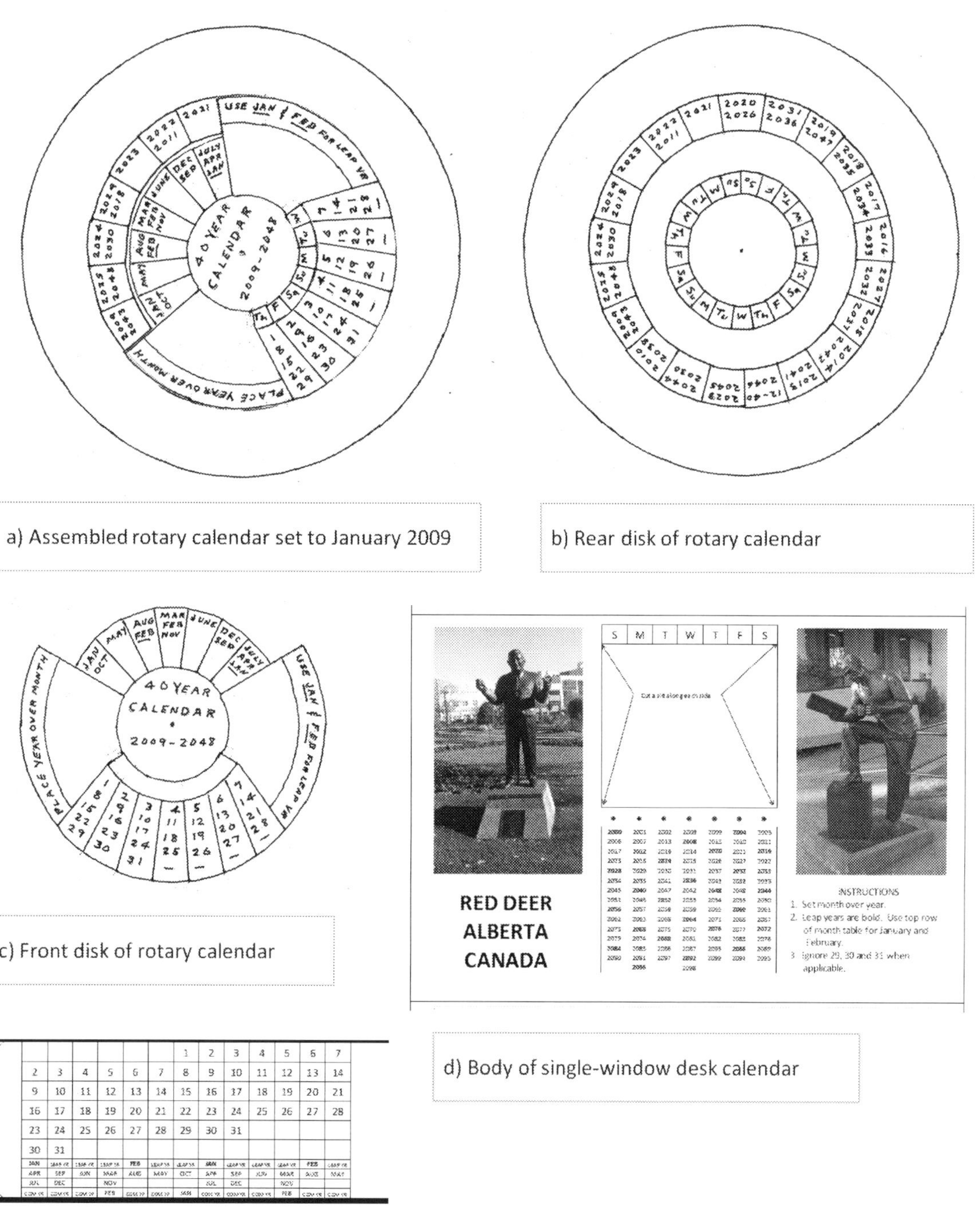
40 YEAR CALENDAR 2009-2048
USE JAN & FEB FOR LEAP YR
PLACE YEAR OVER MONTH
RED DEER
ALBERTA
CANADA
INSTRUCTIONS
1. Set month over year.
2. Leap years are bold. Use top row of month table for January and February.
3. Ignore 29, 30 and 31 when applicable.

a) Assembled rotary calendar set to January 2009

b) Rear disk of rotary calendar

c) Front disk of rotary calendar

d) Body of single-window desk calendar

e) Slider of single-window desk calendar

Figures A-8a to A-8e: Common rotary one-month calendar compared to my single-window desk calendar

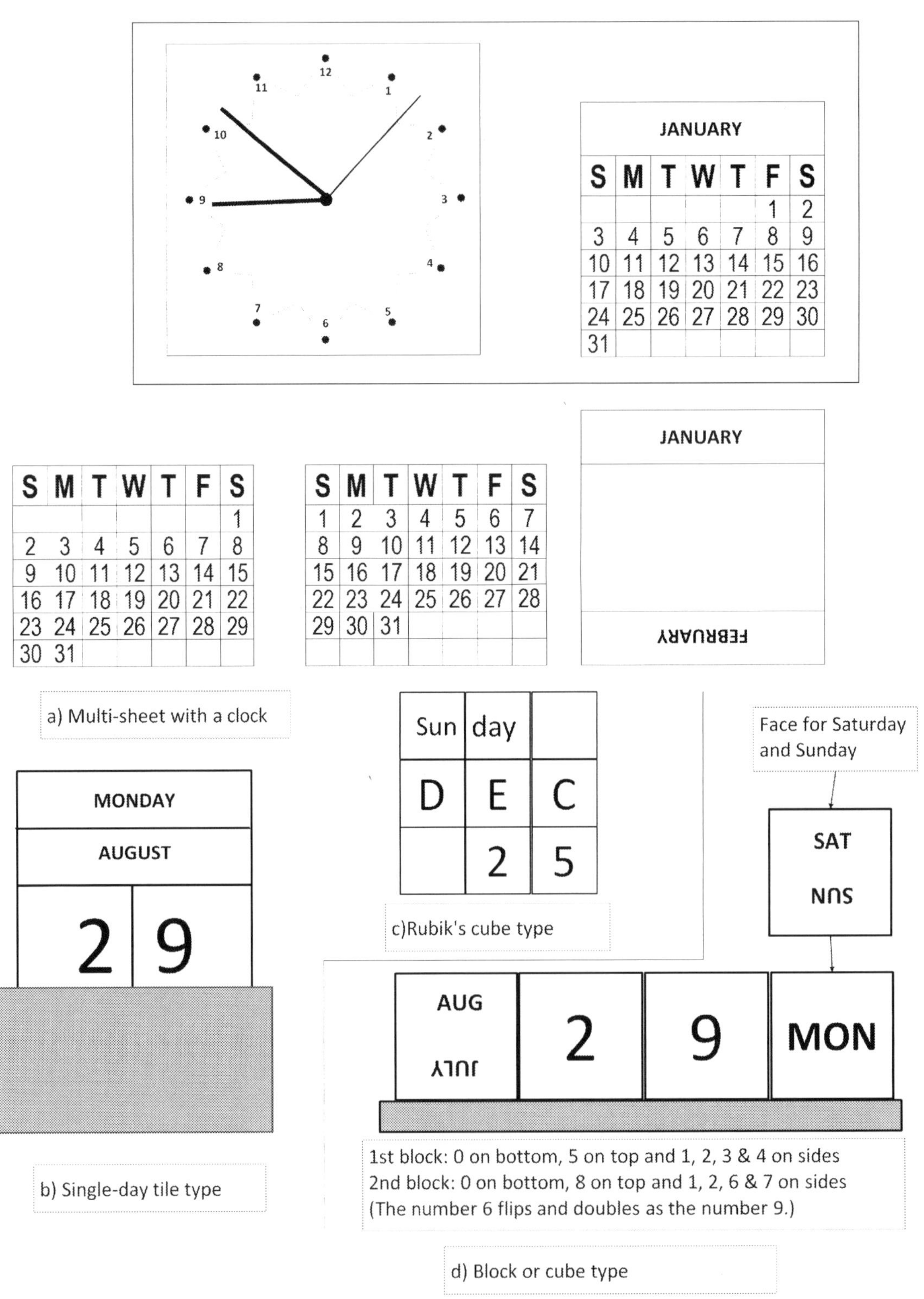

12
1
2
3
4
5
6
7
8
9
10
11
JANUARY
S M T W T F S
1 2
3 4 5 6 7 8 9
10 11 12 13 14 15 16
17 18 19 20 21 22 23
24 25 26 27 28 29 30
31
S M T W T F S
1
2 3 4 5 6 7 8
9 10 11 12 13 14 15
16 17 18 19 20 21 22
23 24 25 26 27 28 29
30 31
S M T W T F S
1 2 3 4 5 6 7
8 9 10 11 12 13 14
15 16 17 18 19 20 21
22 23 24 25 26 27 28
29 30 31
JANUARY
FEBRUARY
a) Multi-sheet with a clock
Sun day
D E C
2 5
c)Rubik's cube type
Face for Saturday and Sunday
SAT
SUN
MONDAY
AUGUST
2 9
b) Single-day tile type
AUG
JULY
2
9
MON
1st block: 0 on bottom, 5 on top and 1, 2, 3 & 4 on sides
2nd block: 0 on bottom, 8 on top and 1, 2, 6 & 7 on sides
(The number 6 flips and doubles as the number 9.)
d) Block or cube type


Figures A-9a to A-9d: Four types of commercial perpetual calendars

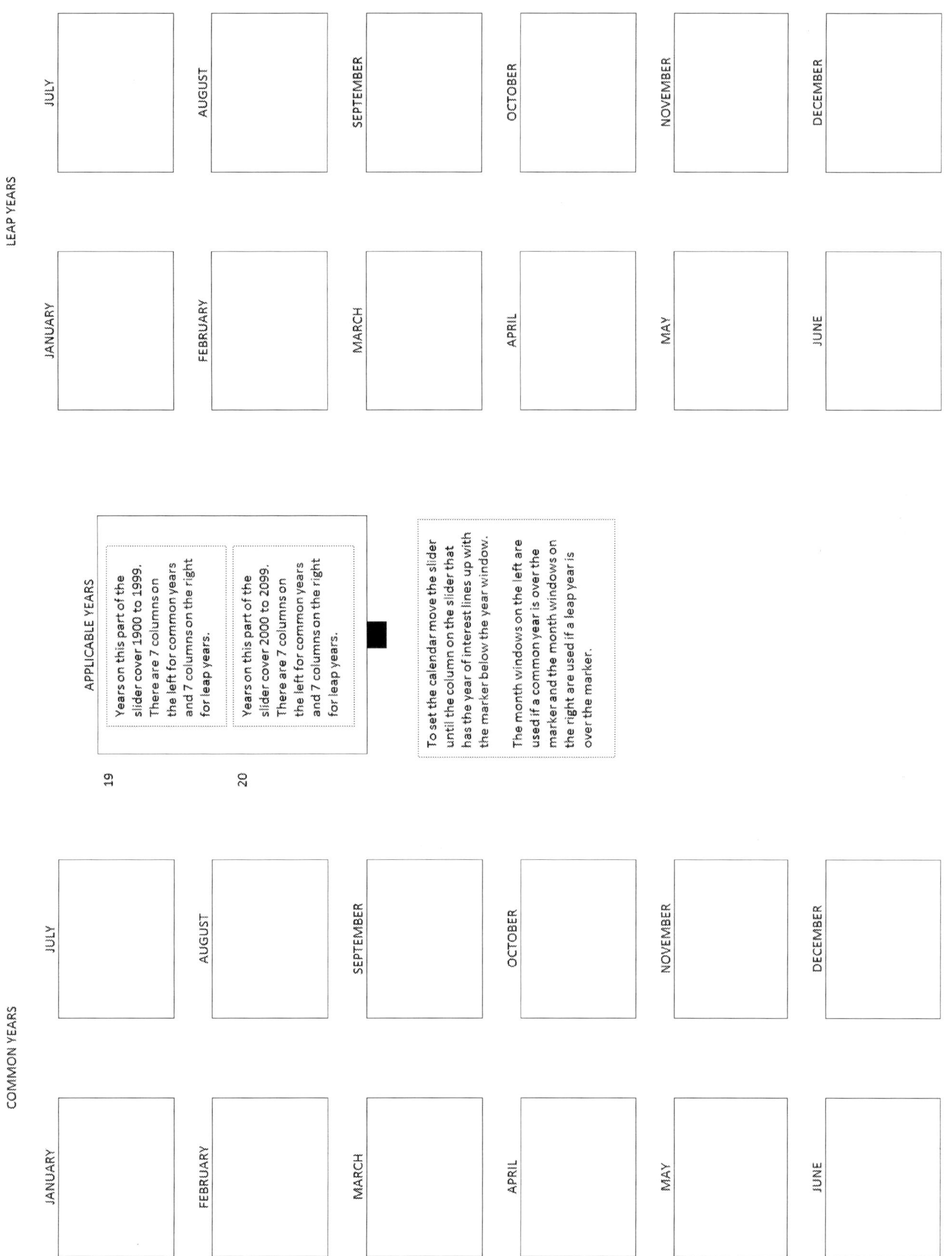
LEAP YEARS
JANUARY
FEBRUARY
MARCH
APRIL
MAY
JUNE
JULY
AUGUST
SEPTEMBER
OCTOBER
NOVEMBER
DECEMBER
APPLICABLE YEARS
19
Years on this part of the slider cover 1900 to 1999. There are 7 columns on the left for common years and 7 columns on the right for leap years.
20
Years on this part of the slider cover 2000 to 2099. There are 7 columns on the left for common years and 7 columns on the right for leap years.
To set the calendar move the slider until the column on the slider that has the year of interest lines up with the marker below the year window.
The month windows on the left are used if a common year is over the marker and the month windows on the right are used if a leap year is over the marker.
COMMON YEARS
JANUARY
FEBRUARY
MARCH
APRIL
MAY
JUNE
JULY
AUGUST
SEPTEMBER
OCTOBER
NOVEMBER
DECEMBER

Figure A-10: Conceptual drawing of the face of a full-year calendar with 24 windows for the months

# FURTHER READING

## Where to Find More Information

One place to find more information about perpetual calendars, or about calendars in general, is to search patents. I have found the following URLs to be good for this:

- http://www.google.com/patents/
- https://www.google.com/advanced_patent_search
- http://www.freepatentsonline.com/
- https://www.uspto.gov/ (United States Patent and Trademark Office)

The two Google sites give the same results for the search term "perpetual calendar." The site for advanced patent search gives more search options. For both sites, "Search tools" can be clicked to filter the results after a search has been completed. I used *Free Patents Online* for many of my searches.

Searches can be done via the following URLs to obtain images of perpetual calendars:

- https://www.google.com/imghp?gws_rd=ssl
  The easiest way to reach this site is to type "google.com/images" in the browser address bar. This will bring up the image search box. Depending on the browser used, the characters following ".com/" may be different than "imghp?gws_rd=ssl"
- http://www.bing.com/images/
- https://www.etsy.com/
- http://www.ebay.com/

The Google and Bing sites tend to give fairly consistent, but not necessarily the same, results whenever a search is done. There is a large number of images that provide a good picture of the variety of perpetual calendars that have been manufactured. The results of a search on Etsy or eBay depend on whatever happens to be for sale at the time the search is done. They are good sites for finding single or limited quantities of perpetual calendars that are no longer manufactured. There is more for sale on eBay than on Etsy.

Books about perpetual calendars can be found at the following URL:

- https://books.google.com/

Some books can be downloaded. The site has the capability of finding the nearest library that has the book.

Books and other material can be found at the following URLs:

- http://www.worldcat.org/
  The site states "WorldCat is the world's largest library catalog, helping you find library materials online." This site can also help you find the nearest library that has the book.
- https://archive.org/
  The site has the statement "Internet Archive is a non-profit library of millions of free books, movies, software, music, websites, and more." Items listed in the Annotated References that have "archive.org" in the URL were found by searching for "perpetual calendar" or "calendar history" on this site. Since many recent documents are protected by copyright, this site tends to bring up old books.

There are many websites that can create a calendar for any year. A good site that I have found is at the URL http://www.timeanddate.com/calendar/generate.html.

# ANNOTATED REFERENCES

Duncan, David Ewing. *The Calendar: The 5000-Year Struggle to Align the Clock and the Heavens—and What Happened to the Missing Ten Days* (London: Fourth Estate, 1999; paperback edition, 2011). A fact-filled book on the history of the calendar.

Franklin, Philip. "Discussions: An Arithmetical Perpetual Calendar." *The American Mathematical Monthly* 28 (June/July 1921), 262. https://ia801604.us.archive.org/32/items/jstor-2973335/2973335.pdf. Accessed November 16, 2016. This paper has a formula for calculating the day of the week that a particular date falls on. No indication is given for the range of dates that the formula applies to. This paper comments on the paper by Frank R. Morris.

Freeman, Gordon R. *Canada's Stonehenge—Astounding Archaeological Discoveries in Canada, England, and Wales* (Calgary, AB: Kingsley Publishing, 2009). This book shows how Stonehenge in England and a stone arrangement in Alberta, Canada, are related to the calendar.

Grand Illusions. "Perpetual Calendar" (2012). *Internet Archive.* https://archive.org/details/henders007-464_20120601. Accessed November 16, 2016. The website has a video of a perpetual calendar made by the French company Sculptures-Jeux in 1991. I call it a triple-cylinder calendar in the Appendix, and illustrate it in Figure A-7c. If you know the date of an event, you can use the calendar to determine which day of the week that event happened, anywhere between 1600 and 2999.

Harper, David. "A Brief History of the Calendar" (1998). *Obliquity.* http://www.obliquity.com/calendar/calendar.pdf. Accessed November 14, 2016. This is an excellent 14-page paper that describes various calendars that have been used throughout history, and the reluctance of some countries to adopt the Gregorian calendar. The website www.obliquity.com is the personal domain of David Harper and Lynne Marie Stockman. (Part of Harper's paper and another short history were accessed on November 16, 2016, on http://www.httpro.com/history/history-of-the-calendar.html.)

Hart-Davis, Adam. *The Book of Time: The Secrets of Time, How It Works and How We Measure It* (Buffalo, NY: Firefly Books, 2011). This book covers many topics, including clocks and various calendars that have been used throughout history. I found it to be of interest that week lengths different than seven days have been tried (pp. 148 and 149) and that a year with 13 months of 28 days was proposed by Moses Bruine Cotsworth in 1902 (p. 140). Cotsworth's calendar has weeks of seven days. Since 13 × 28 = 364, one week has an extra day in common years and two weeks have an extra day in leap years. These extra days do not advance the day of the week, so the day of the week for any date does not change from year to year. If this calendar were adapted, my perpetual calendars would not be needed.

Kummer, Patricia K. *Inventions That Shaped the World: The Calendar* (New York: Franklin Watts, 2005). This is a good introductory book on the various calendars that have been used throughout history. Although written for teenagers, it is interesting reading for adults as well.

McCready, George W. *A Chronological Chart of the Christian Era.* Canada Department of Agriculture, 1897. Filed in the John James Stewart Collection at Dalhousie College Library, Halifax, Nova Scotia, Canada. (The complete document was accessed on November 15, 2016, via https://ia600203.us.archive.org/12/items/cihm_25933/cihm_25933.pdf.) The title page has the following statements: "Showing a correct Calendar for every year of the first 2000 years of the Era, and explaining how the same system may be extended for an indefinite number of centuries to come" and "It is a Perpetual Time Reckoner, always reliable, and so conveniently arranged as to be eminently suited for everyday use as an Office Calendar." The document is 28 pages long and includes charts along with a few notes. It describes an early example of a chart-type perpetual calendar.

Morris, Frank R. "The Theory of Perpetual Calendars." *The American Mathematical Monthly* 28 (March 1921), 127–130. https://www.jstor.org/stable/pdf/2972392.pdf. Accessed November 16, 2016. This paper presents the mathematical theory upon which practically all perpetual calendars are based. In a footnote, Mr. Morris challenges the following statement: "All perpetual or adjustable calendars are arranged so as to present the first day of the month as the first day of the week" (Roman, Irwin. *The American Mathematical Monthly* (1915), 241). Mr. Morris's comment is, in part, "During the past 25 years more than 100 calendars have been patented and more than a score of these present the days of the week in the natural order." Unfortunately, my research shows that the rotary calendar illustrated in Figure A-8 (which does not have the days of the week in the natural order) has been manufactured in large quantities, whereas better calendars with the days of the week in the natural order are almost unknown outside of patent records. Mr. Morris is the inventor of the calendar described under United States Patent 1,286,058 in the Appendix.

Philip, Alexander. *The Calendar: Its History, Structure and Improvement* (London: Cambridge University Press, 1921). Filed in the library of the University of Michigan. (The complete book was accessed on November 15, 2016, via https://ia601202.us.archive.org/2/items/TheCalendar/TheCalendar.pdf.) The book is 104 pages, and gives a good history of various calendars, particularly the Gregorian calendar.

Richards, E. G. *Mapping Time: The Calendar and Its History* (Oxford: Oxford University Press, 1998). I found this book by searching *Google Books* for "calendar history." It is 438 pages, and covers calendars from ancient times to the present. The book has more detail than many readers may want, but it is an excellent reference nonetheless.

The World Calendar Association. "The World Calendar." http://www.theworldcalendar.org/. Accessed June 20, 2017. The World Calendar Association advocates the adoption of a calendar that does not change from year to year. In this respect, their calendar is similar to the one described in Hart-Davis' book. However, The World Calendar has 12 months rather than 13. The first month of each quarter has 31 days and the other two months have 30 days, for a total of 91 days or 13 weeks. The months are named January to December. December has 30 regular days and one *world* day at the end of the month that does not advance the day of the week. In leap years, June also has a *world* day that does not advance the day of the week.

# INDEX

*f* denotes figure; *t* denotes table


**A**

advertisers, products for, 171–172
appointment books, 70–71

**B**

basic tear-off sheet calendar, 3, 7*f*
basic tent calendar, 2, 5*f*
block calendar, 192
bookmark calendar, 64*t*, 68, 69, 70, 81, 96*f*, 171

**C**

calendar manufacturers, suggested gratuity to be paid to author by, xix–xx
cardstock, as calendar construction material, 1, 2, 9, 10, 11, 13, 75–76, 87*f*, 90*f*, 98*f*, 99*f*, 132*f*
clip-on-window wall calendar, 119*t*, 128, 129, 130, 136*f*, 172
clock, xix, 64*t*, 77–79, 80, 82, 102*f*, 103*f*, 140, 162, 173, 174, 175, 178, 183, 191
commercial 13-column calendars, 81–82, 108*f*, 109*f*
common rotary one-month calendar, 189–190, 203*f*
common years, 14
conventional full-year calendar, 4, 8*f*, 160
conventional multisheet desk calendar, 6*f*
conventional tent calendar, 5*f*, 183
craft kits, 170, 174
cube calendar, 192

**D**

date problems, solving, 85–86
day planner, 65*t*, 73–74, 84
day-of-month slider, 15, 16, 17, 19, 25–30, 78
day-of-month tables for every month, 40–45
desk calendar, 1, 3, 4, 10, 15, 39, 57, 63, 64*t*, 67–68, 71, 85, 87*t*, 88*t*, 89*t*, 90*t*, 91*t*, 117*t*, 118, 119*t*, 120–124, 125, 126, 128, 130, 131*f*, 132*f*, 133*t*, 141*t*, 142–144, 145, 146, 147, 149*f*, 150*f*, 151*f*, 171, 172, 173, 174, 175, 176, 177, 178, 181, 182, 203*f*
development costs
  for adding perpetual features, 3
  of flip-down-window wall calendar, 127
double-sided slider full-year perpetual calendar, 156–157, 163*f*, 164*f*, 165*f*, 180, 182, 193
double-window desk calendar, 64*t*, 68, 90*f*, 91*f*
dual-slider configuration/design, 2, 15–22, 23, 26, 30, 39, 61, 64*t*, 65*t*, 66*t*, 75–76, 77, 78, 79, 80, 82, 84, 85, 100*f*, 102*f*, 107*f*, 180–181, 197*f*, 198*f*

**E**

Excel, use of for graphics, 12–13

**F**

fixed window style multisheet perpetual calendar with single year table, 3, 7*f*, 143
flip-down window perpetual calendar, 6*f*, 141, 145, 146, 171, 178

flip-down-window configuration, 3, 10, 184
flip-down-window desk calendar, 118, 119*t*, 120–122, 124, 131*f*, 132*f*, 147
flip-down-window wall calendar, 119*t*, 126–127, 129, 135*f*
fonts, on calendars, 3
full-month tile calendar, 191
full-year perpetual calendars
  applications and designs, 156
  described, 1, 4
  double-sided slider full-year perpetual calendar, 156, 163*f*, 164*f*, 165*f*
  illustrations of, 8*f*
  impractical example, 56
  setting up for production of, 10–11
  single day-of-month table full-year perpetual calendar, 162, 169*f*
  single-sided slider full-year perpetual calendar, 157–159, 166*f*, 167*f*
  variations of, 56
  vertical full-year perpetual calendar, 162, 168*f*
fundraisers, 174

**G**

gift shops, products for, 173
graphics, use of Excel for, 12–13

**H**

home projects, calendars for, 177
hybrid calendar, 61, 65*t*, 84–85, 114*f*, 115*f*, 116*f*, 162, 173, 174, 175, 183

**J**

jobs, creating of for yourself, 177–178
J-style calendars, 141*t*, 143–144, 149*f*, 150*f*, 173, 181, 182

**K**

key holder, 4, 63, 64*t*, 76–77, 100*f*, 101*f*, 141*t*, 143, 173, 174, 175, 178

**L**

lamp, 64*t*, 75, 84, 97*f*
leap years, 14, 19*t*, 20*t*, 22–25, 36*t*, 43–45, 47, 165*f*
lift-out calendar, 4, 10
lift-out pad perpetual calendar, 6*f*
lift-out-pad configuration, 3
lift-out-pad desk calendar, 119*t*, 122–124, 133*f*, 141, 145, 146, 147, 171, 173, 175, 178
lift-out-pad wall calendar, 119*t*, 128–129, 137*f*

**M**

magnetic calendar, 191
manufacturing costs
  for multisheet perpetual calendars with single year table on each sheet, 4
  for multisheet perpetual calendars with year table on each sheet, 3
  for single-sheet perpetual calendars, 2
marketing
  author's efforts at, 181
  barriers, 181–182
  potential markets for multisheet desk calendar, 3
modified sliding-window commercial perpetual calendar, 65*t*
monthly planner, 83
month-table slider, 20*t*, 21, 22, 24*t*, 25–30
moving window, 3, 46, 68, 70, 81, 92*f*, 119*t*, 120, 122, 123, 124, 161, 182, 183, 199*f*
multisheet calendar with single year table
  12 sheets, 51
  14 sheets, 50–51
  24 sheets, 51
multisheet perpetual calendars with single year table
  applications, overview, 140–141, 148*f*
  described, 1, 3–4
  illustrations of, 7*f*
  selling price for, 11

setting up for production of, 10
multisheet perpetual calendars with year table on each sheet
applications, overview, 118–120, 119*t*
described, 1, 3
extension of single-sheet perpetual calendars to, 51–55, 130, 139*f*
illustrations of, 6*f*
selling price for, 11
setting up for production of, 10

**N**

notepad calendar, 64*t*, 68, 70, 71–73, 172, 173

**O**

office supply stores, products for, 172–173

**P**

patents, for perpetual calendars, 184–189
pencil holder, 64*t*, 75, 97*f*, 173, 175, 183
perpetual calendars
advantages of, 9
basic types of, 1. *see also* full-year perpetual calendars; multisheet perpetual calendars with single year table; multisheet perpetual calendars with year table on each sheet; single-sheet perpetual calendars
chart-type, 194–195
defined, xvii
disadvantages of, 9
as eliminating inconvenience of replacement, 9
as enabling looking ahead and back, 9
history of, 179–184
making your own, 192–193
manufacturers, types of, 174–176
manufacturing of, 190–192
patents for, 184–189
as saving resources, 9
selling price for, 11
stand-alone nature of, 15
photo holder, 64*t*, 98*f*, 99*f*, 144, 173, 174, 175
photos, on calendars, 2
picture frame, 4, 33, 65*t*, 79–80, 85, 104*f*, 105*f*, 106*f*, 107*f*, 140, 141*t*, 144–145, 152*f*
picture tent calendar, 6*f*
planners, 39, 64*t*, 70–71, 113*f*, 130, 172, 183. *see also* day planner; pocket planner; wall planner
pocket calendar, 64*t*, 68–70, 85, 92*f*, 94*f*, 95*f*, 170, 171, 172, 181, 183
pocket notepad, 68, 73*t*, 172
pocket planner, 71–73
pocket/tent calendar, 64*t*, 93*f*
production, setting up for, 9–11
products
for advertisers, 171–172
for gift shops, 173
for office supply stores, 172–173
for retail stores, 172–173
for specialty stores, 173
promotional merchandise, 173–174

**R**

retail stores, products for, 172–173
rotary calendars, xviii, 189–190, 191, 193
Rubik's Cube calendar, 192

**S**

seven-column/7-column, 21-sheet perpetual calendar with single year table, 147
seven-column/7-column multisheet calendar, 119*t*, 180
seven-column/7-column multisheet calendar with single year table, 7*f*
seven-column/7-column multisheet perpetual calendar, 56–57, 184
seven-column/7-column multisheet perpetual calendar with single year table, 61, 142*t*, 145–147, 153*f*, 154*f*, 155*f*

seven-column/7-column multisheet perpetual calendar with year table for each month, 57–61
sheet, use of term, 1
single day-of-month table full-year perpetual calendar, 162, 169*f*
single slider configuration/design, 2, 15, 26, 27, 28*t*, 29*t*, 30–39, 51, 52, 64*t*, 65*t*, 66*t*, 67–69, 75, 76, 77, 78, 79–80, 82, 83–84, 95*f*, 101*f*, 103*f*, 130, 140, 145, 162, 171, 172, 175, 181, 182, 183, 184, 185, 187, 189, 190
single-day tile calendar, 192
single-sheet, dual-slider calendar from cardstock, 75–76
single-sheet, single-slider calendar in picture frame, 79–80
single-sheet, single-slider desk calendars, 67–68
single-sheet, single-slider pocket calendars, 68–70
single-sheet perpetual calendars
  applications, overview, 63–66
  described, 1, 2
  with dual sliders, 5*f*
  extension of to multisheet with year table on each sheet, 51–55, 130, 139*f*
  face of, 16*t*
  selling price for, 11
  setting up for production of, 10
  with single slider, 5*f*
  variations of, 39
single-sided full-year wall calendar, 159–160
single-sided slider full-year perpetual calendar, 74, 156, 157–159, 166*f*, 167*f*, 193
single-sided slider full-year wall planner, 160–162
single-slider vertical calendar, 37–39, 65*t*, 66*t*, 82, 83–84, 162
single-window desk calendar, 89*f*
single-window tent desk calendar, 64*t*, 87*f*, 88*f*
slider calendar, 191
specialty stores, products for, 173
stand for desk calendar, 117*f*
stand with calendar, 65*t*, 85
stand-alone perpetual calendar, use of term, xviii

**T**

table lamp, 64*t*, 75, 84, 97*f*
tables
  for multisheet and full-year perpetual calendars, 40–62
  for multisheet perpetual calendar with single year table, 142
  for single-sheet perpetual calendars, 14–39
  tile calendar, xviii, 84, 191, 192
  triple-cylinder calendar, 191

**V**

vertical full-year perpetual calendar, 74, 162, 168*f*

**W**

wall calendar, 3, 4, 39, 65*t*, 83, 84, 114*f*, 115*f*, 116*f*, 119*t*, 124–130, 134*f*, 135*f*, 136*f*, 137*f*, 138*f*, 141*t*, 143, 144, 147, 149*f*, 159–160, 171–172, 173, 174, 175, 183
wall planner, 65*t*, 82–83, 110*f*, 111*f*, 112*f*, 156, 160–162, 183, 188
window-on-each-sheet wall calendar, 119*t*, 129–130, 138*f*, 183
wood, as calendar construction material, 10, 12, 13, 67, 68, 84, 89*f*, 91*f*, 142, 173, 175, 176–177, 193

**Y**

year table
  for 12-sheet design, 49–50
  for 14-sheet design, 47–48
  for 24-sheet design, 45–47

Printed in the United States
By Bookmasters